VOICES OF ISLAM

VOICES OF ISLAM

Volume 1

VOICES OF TRADITION

Vincent J. Cornell, General Editor and
Volume Editor

PRAEGER PERSPECTIVES

Westport, Connecticut
London

Library of Congress Cataloging-in-Publication Data

Voices of Islam / Vincent J. Cornell, general editor.
  p. cm.
  Includes bibliographical references and index.
  ISBN 0–275–98732–9 (set : alk. paper)—ISBN 0–275–98733–7 (vol 1 : alk. paper)—ISBN
0–275–98734–5 (vol 2 : alk. paper)—ISBN 0–275–98735–3 (vol 3 : alk. paper)—ISBN 0–
275–98736–1 (vol 4 : alk. paper)—ISBN 0–275–98737–X (vol 5 : alk. paper) 1. Islam—
Appreciation. 2. Islam—Essence, genius, nature. I. Cornell, Vincent J.
  BP163.V65 2007
  297—dc22   2006031060

British Library Cataloguing in Publication Data is available.

Library of Congress Catalog Card Number: 2006031060
ISBN: 0–275–98732–9 (set)
     0–275–98733–7 (vol. 1)
     0–275–98734–5 (vol. 2)
     0–275–98735–3 (vol. 3)
     0–275–98736–1 (vol. 4)
     0–275–98737–X (vol. 5)

First published in 2007

Praeger Publishers, 88 Post Road West, Westport, CT 06881
An imprint of Greenwood Publishing Group, Inc.
www.praeger.com

Printed in the United States of America

The paper used in this book complies with the
Permanent Paper Standard issued by the National
Information Standards Organization (Z39.48–1984).

10 9 8 7 6 5 4 3 2 1

CONTENTS

———————————— • ————————————

VOICES OF ISLAM

———————————— • ————————————

Vincent J. Cornell

It has long been a truism to say that Islam is the most misunderstood religion in the world. However, the situation expressed by this statement is more than a little ironic because Islam is also one of the most studied religions in the world, after Christianity and Judaism. In the quarter of a century since the 1978–1979 Islamic revolution in Iran, hundreds of books on Islam and the Islamic world have appeared in print, including more than a score of introductions to Islam in various European languages. How is one to understand this paradox? Why is it that most Americans and Europeans are still largely uninformed about Islam after so many books about Islam have been published? Even more, how can people still claim to know so little about Islam when Muslims now live in virtually every medium-sized and major community in America and Europe? A visit to a local library or to a national bookstore chain in any American city will reveal numerous titles on Islam and the Muslim world, ranging from journalistic potboilers to academic studies, translations of the Qur'an, and works advocating a variety of points of view from apologetics to predictions of the apocalypse.

The answer to this question is complex, and it would take a book itself to discuss it adequately. More than 28 years have passed since Edward Said wrote his classic study *Orientalism,* and it has been nearly as long since Said critiqued journalistic depictions of Islam in *Covering Islam: How the Media and the Experts Determine How We See the Rest of the World.* When these books first appeared in print, many thought that the ignorance about the Middle East and the Muslim world in the West would finally be dispelled. However, there is little evidence that the public consciousness of Islam and Muslims has been raised to a significant degree in Western countries. Scholars of Islam in American universities still feel the need to humanize Muslims in the eyes of their students. A basic objective of many introductory courses on Islam is to demonstrate that Muslims are rational human beings and that their beliefs are worthy of respect. As Carl W. Ernst observes in the preface to his recent work, *Following Muhammad: Rethinking Islam in the*

Contemporary World, "It still amazes me that intelligent people can believe that all Muslims are violent or that all Muslim women are oppressed, when they would never dream of uttering slurs stereotyping much smaller groups such as Jews or blacks. The strength of these negative images of Muslims is remarkable, even though they are not based on personal experience or actual study, but they receive daily reinforcement from the news media and popular culture."[1]

Such prejudices and misconceptions have only become worse since the terrorist attacks of September 11, 2001, and the war in Iraq. There still remains a need to portray Muslims in all of their human diversity, whether this diversity is based on culture, historical circumstances, economic class, gender, or religious doctrine. Today, Muslims represent nearly one-fourth of the world's population. Although many Americans are aware that Indonesia is the world's largest Muslim country, most are surprised to learn that half of the Muslims in the world live east of Lahore, Pakistan. In this sense, Islam is as much an "Asian" religion as is Hinduism or Buddhism. The new reality of global Islam strongly contradicts the "Middle Eastern" view of Islam held by most Americans. Politically, the United States has been preoccupied with the Middle East for more than half a century. Religiously, however, American Protestantism has been involved in the Middle East for more than 150 years. Thus, it comes as a shock for Americans to learn that only one-fourth of the world's Muslims live in the Middle East and North Africa and that only one-fifth of Muslims are Arabs. Islam is now as much a worldwide religion as Christianity, with somewhere between 4 and 6 million believers in the United States and approximately 10 million believers in Western Europe. Almost 20 million Muslims live within the borders of the Russian Federation, and nearly a million people of Muslim descent live in the Russian city of St. Petersburg, on the Gulf of Finland.

To think of Islam as monolithic under these circumstances is both wrong and dangerous. The idea that all Muslims are fundamentalists or anti-democratic religious zealots can lead to the fear that dangerous aliens are hiding within Western countries, a fifth column of a civilization that is antithetical to freedom and the liberal way of life. This attitude is often expressed in popular opinion in both the United States and Europe. For example, it can be seen in the "Letters" section of the June 7, 2004, edition of *Time* magazine, where a reader writes: "Now it is time for Muslim clerics to denounce the terrorists or admit that Islam is fighting a war with us—a religious war."[2] For the author of this letter, Muslim "clerics" are not to be trusted, not because they find it hard to believe that pious Muslims would commit outrageous acts of terrorism, but because they secretly hate the West and its values. Clearly, for this reader of *Time,* Islam and the West are at war; however the "West" may be defined and wherever "Islam" or Muslims are to be found.

Prejudice against Muslim minorities still exists in many countries. In Russia, Muslim restaurateurs from the Caucasus Mountains must call themselves "Georgian" to stay in business. In China, being Muslim by ethnicity is acceptable, but being a Muslim by conviction might get one convicted for antistate activities. In the Balkans, Muslims in Serbia, Bulgaria, and Macedonia are called "Turks" and right-wing nationalist parties deny them full ethnic legitimacy as citizens of their countries. In India, over a thousand Muslims were killed in communal riots in Gujarat as recently as 2002. As I write these words, Israel and Hizbollah, the Lebanese Shiite political movement and militia, are engaged in a bloody conflict that has left hundreds of dead and injured on both sides. Although the number of people who have been killed in Lebanon, most of whom are Shiite civilians, is far greater than the number of those killed in Israel, television news reports in the United States do not treat Lebanese and Israeli casualties the same way. While the casualties that are caused by Hizbollah rockets in Israel are depicted as personal tragedies, Lebanese casualties are seldom personalized in this way. The truth is, of course, that all casualties of war are personal tragedies, whether the victims are Lebanese civilians, Israeli civilians, or American soldiers killed or maimed by improvised explosive devices in Iraq. In addition, all civilian deaths in war pose a moral problem, whether they are caused as a consequence of aggression or of retaliation. In many ways, depersonalization can have worse effects than actual hatred. An enemy that is hated must at least be confronted; when innocent victims are reduced to pictures without stories, they are all too easily ignored.

The problem of depersonalization has deeper roots than just individual prejudice. Ironically, the global village created by international news organizations such as CNN, BBC, and Fox News may unintentionally contribute to the problem of devaluing Muslim lives. Depictions of victimhood are often studies in incomprehension: victims speak a language the viewer cannot understand, their shock or rage strips them of their rationality, and their standard of living and mode of dress may appear medieval or even primitive when compared with the dominant cultural forms of modernity. In her classic study, *The Origins of Totalitarianism,* Hannah Arendt pointed out that the ideology of human equality, which is fostered with all good intentions by the international news media, paradoxically contributes to the visibility of difference by confusing equality with sameness. In 99 out of 100 cases, says Arendt, equality "will be mistaken for an innate quality of every individual, who is 'normal' if he is like everybody else and 'abnormal' if he happens to be different. This perversion of equality from a political into a social concept is all the more dangerous when a society leaves but little space for special groups and individuals, for then their differences become all the more conspicuous."[3] According to Arendt, the widespread acceptance of the ideal of social equality after the French Revolution was a major reason why genocide, whether of Jews in Europe, Tutsis in Rwanda, or Muslims in the former Yugoslavia, has become a characteristically modern phenomenon.

The idea of equality as sameness was not as firmly established in the United States, claimed Arendt, because the "equal opportunity" ideology of American liberalism values difference—in the form of imagination, entrepreneurship, and personal initiative—as a token of success.[4] This ideology enabled Jews in America to assert their distinctiveness and eventually to prosper in the twentieth century, and it provides an opportunity for Muslim Americans to assert their distinctiveness and to prosper today. So far, the United States has not engaged in systematic persecution of Muslims and has been relatively free of anti-Muslim prejudice. However, fear and distrust of Muslims among the general public is fostered by images of insurgent attacks and suicide bombings in Iraq, of Al Qaeda atrocities around the globe, and of increasing expressions of anti-Americanism in the Arabic and Islamic media. In addition, some pundits on talk radio, certain fundamentalist religious leaders, and some members of the conservative press and academia fan the flames of prejudice by portraying Islam as inherently intolerant and by portraying Muslims as slaves to tradition and authoritarianism rather than as advocates of reason and freedom of expression. Clearly, there is still a need to demonstrate to the American public that Muslims are rational human beings and that Islam is a religion that is worthy of respect.

Changing public opinion about Islam and Muslims in the United States and Europe will not be easy. The culture critic Guillermo Gomez-Peña has written that as a result of the opening of American borders to non-Europeans in the 1960s, the American myth of the cultural melting pot "has been replaced by a model that is more germane to the times, that of the *menudo chowder*. According to this model, most of the ingredients do melt, but some stubborn chunks are condemned merely to float."[5] At the present time, Muslims constitute the most visible "stubborn chunks" in the *menudo chowder* of American and European pluralism. Muslims are often seen as the chunks of the *menudo chowder* that most stubbornly refuse to "melt in." To the non-Muslim majoritarian citizen of Western countries, Muslims seem to be the most "uncivil" members of civil society. They do not dress like the majority, they do not eat like the majority, they do not drink like the majority, they do not let their women work, they reject the music and cultural values of the majority, and sometimes they even try to opt out of majoritarian legal and economic systems. In Europe, Islam has replaced Catholicism as the religion that left-wing pundits most love to hate. Americans, however, have been more ambivalent about Islam and Muslims. On the one hand, there have been sincere attempts to include Muslims as full partners in civil society. On the other hand, the apparent resistance of some Muslims to "fit in" creates a widespread distrust that has had legal ramifications in several notable cases.

A useful way to conceive of the problem that Muslims face as members of civil society—both within Western countries and in the global civil society that is dominated by the West—is to recognize, following Homi K. Bhabha, the social fact of Muslim *unhomeliness*. To be "unhomed," says Bhabha, is not to be homeless, but rather to escape easy assimilation or accommodation.[6] The problem is not that the "unhomed" possesses no physical home but that there is no "place" to locate the unhomed in the majoritarian consciousness. Simply put, one does not know what to make of the unhomed. Bhabha derives this term from Sigmund Freud's concept of *unheimlich,* "the name for everything that ought to have remained secret and hidden but has come to light."[7] Unhomeliness is a way of expressing social discomfort. When one encounters the unhomed, one feels awkward and uncomfortable because the unhomed person appears truly alien. Indeed, if there is any single experience that virtually all Muslims in Western countries share, it is that Islam makes non-Muslims uncomfortable. In the global civil society dominated by the West, Muslims are unhomed wherever they may live, even in their own countries.

This reality of Muslim experience highlights how contemporary advocates of Muslim identity politics have often made matters worse by accentuating symbolic tokens of difference between so-called Islamic and Western norms. The problem for Islam in today's global civil society is not that it is not seen. On the contrary, Islam and Muslims are arguably all too visible because they are seen as fundamentally different from the accepted norm. Like the black man in the colonial West Indies or in Jim Crow America, the Muslim is, to borrow a phrase from Frantz Fanon, "overdetermined from without."[8] Muslims have been overdetermined by the press, overdetermined by Hollywood, overdetermined by politicians, and overdetermined by culture critics. From the president of the United States to the prime minister of the United Kingdom, and in countless editorials in print and television media, leaders of public opinion ask, "What do Muslims want?" Such a question forces the Muslim into a corner in which the only answer is apologetics or defiance. To again paraphrase Fanon, the overdetermined Muslim is constantly made aware of himself or herself not just in the third person but in *triple person.* As a symbol of the unhomely, the Muslim is made to feel personally responsible for a contradictory variety of "Islamic" moral values, "Islamic" cultural expressions, and "Islamic" religious and political doctrines.[9]

In the face of such outside pressures, what the overdetermined Muslim needs most is not to be seen, but to be heard. There is a critical need for Islam to be expressed to the world not as an image, but as a narrative, and for Muslims to bear their own witness to their own experiences. The vast majority of books on Islam written in European languages, even the best ones, have been written by non-Muslims. This is not necessarily a problem, because an objective and open-minded non-Muslim can often describe Islam for a non-

Muslim audience better than a Muslim apologist. The scholars Said and Ernst, mentioned above, are both from Christian backgrounds. The discipline of Religious Studies from which Ernst writes has been careful to maintain a nonjudgmental attitude toward non-Christian religions. As heirs to the political and philosophical values of European liberalism, scholars of Religious Studies are typically dogmatic about only one thing: they must practice *epoché* (a Greek word meaning "holding back" or restraining one's beliefs) when approaching the worldview of another religion. In the words of the late Canadian scholar of religion Wilfred Cantwell Smith, it is not enough to act like "a fly crawling on the outside of a goldfish bowl," magisterially observing another's religious practices while remaining distant from the subject. Instead, one must be more engaged in her inquiry and, through imagination and the use of *epoché*, try to find out what it feels like to be a goldfish.[10]

Through the practice of *epoché*, the field of Religious Studies has by now produced two generations of accomplished scholars of Islam in the United States and Canada. Smith himself was a fair and sympathetic Christian scholar of Islam, and his field has been more influential than any other in promoting the study of Islam in the West. However, even Smith was aware that only a goldfish truly knows what it means to be a goldfish. The most that a sympathetic non-Muslim specialist in Islamic studies can do is *describe* Islam from the perspective of a sensitive outsider. Because non-Muslims do not share a personal commitment to the Islamic faith, they are not in the best position to convey a sense of what it means to *be* a Muslim on the inside—to live a Muslim life, to share Muslim values and concerns, and to experience Islam spiritually. In the final analysis, only Muslims can fully bear witness to their own traditions from within.

The five-volume set of *Voices of Islam* is an attempt to meet this need. By bringing together the voices of nearly 50 prominent Muslims from around the world, it aims to present an accurate, comprehensive, and accessible account of Islamic doctrines, practices, and worldviews for a general reader at the senior high school and university undergraduate level. The subjects of the volumes—*Voices of Tradition; Voices of the Spirit; Voices of Life: Family, Home, and Society; Voices of Art, Beauty, and Science;* and *Voices of Change*—were selected to provide as wide a depiction as possible of Muslim experiences and ways of knowledge. Taken collectively, the chapters in these volumes provide bridges between formal religion and culture, the present and the past, tradition and change, and spiritual and outward action that can be crossed by readers, whether they are Muslims or non-Muslims, many times and in a variety of ways. What this set does *not* do is present a magisterial, authoritative vision of an "objectively real" Islam that is juxtaposed against a supposedly inauthentic diversity of individual voices. As the Egyptian-American legal scholar and culture critic Khaled Abou El Fadl has pointed out, whenever Islam is the subject of discourse, the authoritative quickly elides into the authoritarian, irrespective of whether the voice of authority is

Muslim or non-Muslim.[11] The editors of *Voices of Islam* seek to avoid the authoritarian by allowing every voice expressed in the five-volume set to be authoritative, both in terms of individual experience and in terms of the commonalities that Muslims share among themselves.

THE EDITORS

The general editor for *Voices of Islam* is Vincent J. Cornell, Asa Griggs Candler Professor of Middle East and Islamic Studies at Emory University in Atlanta, Georgia. When he was solicited by Praeger, an imprint of Greenwood Publishing, to formulate this project, he was director of the King Fahd Center for Middle East and Islamic Studies at the University of Arkansas. Dr. Cornell has been a Sunni Muslim for more than 30 years and is a noted scholar of Islamic thought and history. His most important book, *Realm of the Saint: Power and Authority in Moroccan Sufism* (1998), was described by a prepublication reviewer as "the most significant study of the Sufi tradition in Islam to have appeared in the last two decades." Besides publishing works on Sufism, Dr. Cornell has also written articles on Islamic law, Islamic theology, and moral and political philosophy. For the past five years, he has been a participant in the Archbishop of Canterbury's "Building Bridges" dialogue of Christian and Muslim theologians. In cooperation with the Jerusalem-based Elijah Interfaith Institute, he is presently co-convener of a group of Muslim scholars, of whom some are contributors to *Voices of Islam,* which is working toward a new theology of the religious other in Islam. Besides serving as general editor for *Voices of Islam,* Dr. Cornell is also the volume editor for Volume 1, *Voices of Tradition;* Volume 2, *Voices of the Spirit;* and Volume 4, *Voices of Art, Beauty, and Science.*

The associate editors for *Voices of Islam* are Omid Safi and Virginia Gray Henry-Blakemore. Omid Safi is Associate Professor of Religion at the University of North Carolina at Chapel Hill. Dr. Safi, the grandson of a noted Iranian Ayatollah, was born in the United States but raised in Iran and has been recognized as an important Muslim voice for moderation and diversity. He gained widespread praise for his edited first book, *Progressive Muslims: On Justice, Gender, and Pluralism* (2003), and was interviewed on CNN, National Public Radio, and other major media outlets. He recently published an important study of Sufi-state relations in premodern Iran, *The Politics of Knowledge in Premodern Islam* (2006). Dr. Safi is the volume editor for Volume 5, *Voices of Change,* which contains chapters by many of the authors represented in his earlier work, *Progressive Muslims.*

Virginia Gray Henry-Blakemore has been a practicing Sunni Muslim for almost 40 years. She is director of the interfaith publishing houses Fons Vitae and Quinta Essentia and cofounder and trustee of the Islamic Texts Society of Cambridge, England. Some of the most influential families in Saudi

Arabia, Egypt, and Jordan have supported her publishing projects. She is an accomplished lecturer in art history, world religions, and filmmaking and is a founding member of the Thomas Merton Center Foundation. Henry-Blakemore received her BA at Sarah Lawrence College, studied at the American University in Cairo and Al-Azhar University, earned her MA in Education at the University of Michigan, and served as a research fellow at Cambridge University from 1983 to 1990. She is the volume editor for Volume 3, *Voices of Life: Family, Home, and Society.*

THE AUTHORS

As stated earlier, *Voices of Islam* seeks to meet the need for Muslims to bear witness to their own traditions by bringing together a diverse collection of Muslim voices from different regions and from different scholarly and professional backgrounds. The voices that speak to the readers about Islam in this set come from Asia, Africa, Europe, and North America, and include men and women, academics, community and religious leaders, teachers, activists, and business leaders. Some authors were born Muslims and others embraced Islam at various points in their lives. A variety of doctrinal, legal, and cultural positions are also represented, including modernists, traditionalists, legalists, Sunnis, Shiites, Sufis, and "progressive Muslims." The editors of the set took care to represent as many Muslim points of view as possible, including those that they may disagree with. Although each chapter in the set was designed to provide basic information for the general reader on a particular topic, the authors were encouraged to express their individual voices of opinion and experience whenever possible.

In theoretical terms, *Voices of Islam* treads a fine line between what Paul Veyne has called "specificity" and "singularity." As both an introduction to Islam and as an expression of Islamic diversity, this set combines historical and commentarial approaches, as well as poetic and narrative accounts of individual experiences. Because of the wide range of subjects that are covered, individualized accounts (the "singular") make up much of the narrative of *Voices of Islam,* but the intent of the work is not to express individuality per se. Rather, the goal is to help the reader understand the varieties of Islamic experience (the "specific") more deeply by finding within their specificity a certain kind of generality.[12]

For Veyne, "specificity" is another way of expressing typicality or the ideal type, a sociological concept that has been a useful tool for investigating complex systems of social organization, thought, or belief. However, the problem with typification is that it may lead to oversimplification, and oversimplification is the handmaiden of the stereotype. Typification can lead to oversimplification because the concept of typicality belongs to a structure of general knowledge that obscures the view of the singular and the different. Thus, presenting the voices of only preselected "typical Muslims" or "representative Muslims" in a work such as *Voices of Islam* would only aggravate the tendency of many Muslims and non-Muslims to define Islam in a single, essentialized way. When done from without, this can lead to a form of stereotyping that may exacerbate, rather than alleviate, the tendency to see Muslims in ways that they do not see themselves. When done from within, it can lead to a dogmatic fundamentalism (whether liberal or conservative does not matter) that excludes the voices of difference from "real" Islam and fosters a totalitarian approach to religion. Such an emphasis on the legitimacy of representation by Muslims themselves would merely reinforce the ideal of sameness that Arendt decried and enable the overdetermination of the "typical" Muslim from without. For this reason, *Voices of Islam* seeks to strike a balance between specificity and singularity. Not only the chapters in these volumes but also the backgrounds and personal orientations of their authors express Islam as a lived diversity and as a source of multiple wellsprings of knowledge. Through the use of individual voices, this work seeks to save the "singular" from the "typical" by employing the "specific."

Dipesh Chakrabarty, a major figure in the field of Subaltern Studies, notes: "Singularity is a matter of viewing. It comes into being as that which resists our attempt to see something as a particular instance of a general idea or category."[13] For Chakrabarty, the singular is a necessary antidote to the typical because it "defies the generalizing impulse of the sociological imagination."[14] Because the tendency to overdetermine and objectify Islam is central to the continued lack of understanding of Islam by non-Muslims, it is necessary to defy the generalizing impulse by demonstrating that the unity of Islam is not a unity of sameness, but of diversity. Highlighting the singularity of individual Islamic practices and doctrines becomes a means of liberating Islam from the totalizing vision of both religious fundamentalism (Muslim and non-Muslim alike) and secular essentialism. While Islam in theory may be a unity, in both thought and practice this "unity" is in reality a galaxy whose millions of singular stars exist within a universe of multiple perspectives. This is not just a sociological fact, but a theological point as well. For centuries, Muslim theologians have asserted that the Transcendent Unity of God is a mystery that defies the normal rules of logic. To human beings, unity usually implies either singularity or sameness, but with respect to God, Unity is beyond number or comparison.

In historiographical terms, a work that seeks to describe Islam through the voices of individual Muslims is an example of "minority history." However, by allowing the voices of specificity and singularity to enter into a trialogue that includes each other as well as the reader, *Voices of Islam* is also an example of "subaltern history." For Chakrabarty, subaltern narratives "are marginalized not because of any conscious intentions but because they represent moments or points at which the archive that the historian mines develops a degree of intractability with respect to the aims of professional history."[15] Subaltern narratives do not only belong to socially subordinate or minority groups, but they also belong to underrepresented groups in Western scholarship, even if these groups comprise a billion people as Muslims do. Subaltern narratives resist typification because the realities that they represent do not correspond to the stereotypical. As such, they need to be studied on their own terms. The history of Islam in thought and practice is the product of constant dialogues between the present and the past, internal and external discourses, culture and ideology, and tradition and change. To describe Islam as anything less would be to reduce it to a limited set of descriptive and conceptual categories that can only rob Islam of its diversity and its historical and intellectual depth. The best way to retain a sense of this diversity and depth is to allow Muslim voices to relate their own narratives of Islam's past and present.

NOTES

1. Carl W. Ernst, *Following Muhammad: Rethinking Islam in the Contemporary World* (Chapel Hill and London: University of North Carolina Press, 2003), xvii.

2. *Time,* June 7, 2004, 10.

3. Hannah Arendt, *The Origins of Totalitarianism,* rev. ed. (San Diego, New York, and London: Harvest Harcourt, 1976), 54.

4. Ibid., 55.

5. Guillermo Gomez-Peña, "The New World (B)order," *Third Text* 21 (Winter 1992–1993): 74, quoted in Homi K. Bhabha, *The Location of Culture* (London and New York: Routledge Classics, 2004), 313.

6. Bhabha, *The Location of Culture,* 13.

7. Ibid., 14–15.

8. Frantz Fanon, *Black Skin, White Masks* (London, U.K.: Pluto, 1986), 116. The original French term for this condition is *surdéterminé.* See idem, *Peau noire masques blancs* (Paris: Éditions du Seuil, 1952), 128.

9. Ibid., 112.

10. Wilfred Cantwell Smith, *The Meaning and End of Religion* (Minneapolis, Minnesota: The University of Minnesota Press, 1991), 7.

11. Khaled Abou El Fadl, *Speaking in God's Name: Islamic Law, Authority, and Women* (Oxford, U.K.: Oneworld Publications, 2001), 9–85.

12. Paul Veyne, *Writing History: Essay on Epistemology,* trans. Mina Moore-Rinvolucri (Middletown, Connecticut: Wesleyan University Press, 1984), 56.

13. Dipesh Chakrabarty, *Provincializing Europe: Postcolonial Thought and Historical Difference* (Princeton and Oxford: Princeton University Press, 2000), 82.

14. Ibid., 83.

15. Ibid., 101.

INTRODUCTION: ISLAM, TRADITION, AND TRADITIONALISM

———————————————— • ————————————————

Vincent J. Cornell

"Tradition is the living faith of the dead, traditionalism is the dead faith of the living."[1] This statement by the historian of Christianity Jaroslav Pelikan sums up the challenge faced by Islam at the beginning of the twenty-first century of the Common Era. It may further be said, as Pelikan added about Christianity, "Traditionalism is what gives tradition a bad name." This has certainly been the case with some kinds of traditionalism in contemporary Islam. Most Muslims would condemn the Taliban of northwest Pakistan and Afghanistan, who reject the intellectual traditions of the Islamic past in the name of a superficial traditionalism that puts more emphasis on tribal custom and the vanities of male self-image—such as kohl-rimmed eyes, henna-dyed beards, and elegant turbans—than on the pursuit of justice or respect for women. Most Muslims would also reject the postmodern traditionalism of Al Qaeda, which combines a nearly wholesale rejection of modern political and social thought with a passionate embrace of the destructive forces of modern technology. The innovative use of technology by Usama bin Laden and his followers stands in stark contrast to their literalistic interpretation of the Qur'an, the ascetic simplicity of their personal lives, and their desire to create an idealized City of God on Earth. Such a utopia has not existed since the time of the Prophet Muhammad, if it has ever existed at all.

Outside the Muslim world, the belief that Muslims are arch-traditionalists has given Islam a bad name. Recent polls suggest that over 40 percent of Americans have a negative opinion of Islam. In Western Europe, Islam has replaced Catholicism as the religion that secular intellectuals most love to hate. According to this view, the traditionalism of Islam is the main problem. Islamic traditionalism, it is said, leads to the ghettoization of Muslim minorities in Western societies. It leads as well to the rejection of Western political values and the oppression of women. It desires theocracy rather than democracy. Muslims, it is said, are the most uncivil members of civil society. The negative attitude toward Islamic tradition in contemporary Europe is summed up in the following statement by Jacques Ellul, a right-wing Protestant thinker from France: "What a wonderfully civilized empire would have been set up if all Europe had been invaded [by Muslims]! This position, the opposite of the prevailing one in history up to about 1950, leads people to forget the horrors of Islam, the dreadful cruelty, the general use of torture, the slavery, and the absolute intolerance notwithstanding zealous apostles who underline Islam's toleration."[2] In short, for many in the West, the traditions of Islam are fanatical, intolerant, antidemocratic, oppressive of women, and a representation of all the evils of religion that the Enlightenment sought to overcome.

Of course, the aware reader hardly needs to be reminded how unfair Ellul's criticism of Islam is or how easy it would be to apply the same arguments to the history of Christianity. Furthermore, many Muslims in countries such as France, Russia, Germany, Denmark, and Israel would respond that the majority populations of these countries are not civil to them either, even when they try to act as responsible citizens. The road to toleration is a two-way street. School districts in the United States offer civics classes because responsible citizenship needs to be taught to everyone, not just to religious minorities. Being a citizen in a pluralistic society is a skill that is learned, not a characteristic that is present from birth. It is a challenge for democratic societies to maintain the principle of minority rights along with majority rule. This challenge is particularly acute when the rights claimed by minorities are sanctioned by religious beliefs not shared by the majority or when minority traditions go against majoritarian norms. The right for women to cover their hair is just as important for Orthodox Jews as it is for Muslims, and the right to have more than one wife is claimed by Mormon Fundamentalists just as it is claimed by some traditional Muslims. When the state interferes with the free practice of such traditions, issues that normally would remain in the background suddenly take center stage. The relationship between religious minorities and democratic states is characterized by negotiations that constantly pit the demands of tradition against the pluralistic values of modernity. The challenge for religious people today is to remain authentically true to the traditions of the past while recognizing that all human beings now share the "original sin" of modernity.

"Tradition demands to be served even when it is not observed."[3] This further aphorism by Jaroslav Pelikan is particularly apt for Islam and Muslims. One of the most important issues debated by Muslims today is where cultural traditions end and where religion begins. The Qur'an, Islam's Holy Scripture, states, "Verily, the religion (*din*) of God (*Allah*) is Islam" (Qur'an 3:19) and "I have chosen Islam for you as a religion (*din*)" (Qur'an 5:3). Some observers have taken these verses as a sign of Islam's unique ability to define itself doctrinally and ideologically.[4] However, these verses alone do not tell us what either "Islam" or "religion" means. *Din* is indeed the modern Arabic word for "religion." In premodern times, however, *din* meant both more and less than the Western idea of a "church" or an institutionalized religion. The root from which this word comes has four primary significations: (1) mutual obligation, (2) submission or acknowledgment, (3) judicial authority, and (4) natural inclination or tendency. Never, in its premodern connotation, did the term *din* refer to a "system" or to the idea of religion as a subject to be studied in comparison with other subjects called religions.[5] However, two of the classical significations of *din*, mutual obligation and judicial authority, have social implications. This means that religion in Islam is more than just a personal relationship with God. It also entails a relationship with a community of believers and a society, which necessitates an involvement with culture and tradition. Throughout Islamic history, the traditions of the majority of believers always had to be served, even by those who chose to reject them.

The early chapters in this volume deal with the concept of religion in Islam and its relationship to traditions of personal practice and Qur'anic scholarship. "The *Qur'an*, the Word of God" by Mustansir Mir introduces the reader to the basic scripture of Islam, the only scripture in which every sentence—indeed every word—must be accepted by Muslims as divine truth. For Muslims, the Qur'an is not only the foundation of religious teachings but also the touchstone for religion itself. In "Encountering the Qur'an: Contexts and Approaches," James Winston Morris introduces the reader to the experience of the Qur'an. He shows the non-Muslim reader the different ways by which Muslims traditionally encounter their sacred scripture, and how one can "see," "hear," and ritually enact the Word of God. He does this not only by explaining how the Qur'an can be approached by those who read and recite it, but also by providing a unique guide for non-Muslim and non-Arabic-speaking readers who approach the Qur'an in English. Finally, by demonstrating how the Qur'an has inspired the arts and intellectual life in the Muslim world, he reconnects the idea of religion in Islam to the wider traditions of Islamic expression that are often overlooked in the debate between religion and culture.

The above analysis of the premodern meanings of the word *din* reminds us that the concept of religion in Islam puts a high premium on the idea of reciprocity, which creates both personal and social obligations. The Qur'an tells believers that God "owes" the human being a fair return for her worship. "Who is the one who will lend to God a goodly loan, which God will double to his credit and multiply many times?" (Qur'an 2:245) asks the Holy Book. The Qur'an also reminds believers that a person's "loan" to God is to be paid not only in worship but also in works of charity for other human beings: "Verily, we will ease the path to salvation for the person who gives out of fear of God and testifies to the best. But we will ease the path to damnation for the greedy miser who thinks himself self-sufficient and rejects what is best" (Qur'an 92:5–10). Qur'anic teachings such as these moved the Moroccan

Sufi Abu al-'Abbas al-Sabti (d. 1205 CE) to declare, "Divine grace is stimulated by acts of generosity." For Sabti, each charitable act performed by a
human being called forth a response from God that rewarded the giver in
proportion to her gift. Sabti, the patron saint of the city of Marrakesh, used
this doctrine to encourage the elites of the city to provide charity for the
poor.[6] How should the modern reformer of Islam assess a tradition such as
this: is it "culture" or is it "religion"?

The idea of reciprocity that leads from the Qur'an to the social ethics of
Abu al-'Abbas al-Sabti is an important corollary to the Five Pillars of Islam,
which are discussed in Karima Diane Alavi's chapter, "Pillars of Religion
and Faith." Alavi's chapter comes first in this volume because for Muslims,
the Five Pillars of Islam frame the entire concept of religion, including the
divine revelation of the Qur'an. The pillars of religion and faith are also a
product of tradition, since they come from a *Hadith* account, discussed by
Alavi, in which the Angel Gabriel quizzes the Prophet Muhammad on these
subjects. An important part of the tradition of the Hadith of Gabriel is the
concept of virtue (*ihsan*). This means, in the words of the *hadith*, "to worship
God as if you see Him, for even if you do not see Him, He sees you." The
notion of reciprocal awareness that is expressed in this tradition—the human
being looks to God as God looks to the human being—is fundamental to the
concept of religious obligation in Islam. It is also a bridge to the type of social
awareness expressed by the Moroccan Sufi Sabti, for Muslims are accountable
to God both for how they fulfill their responsibilities of worship and for how
they fulfill their responsibilities toward their brothers and sisters in the family
of Adam.

In the Qur'an, accountability to God is expressed as a covenant, in which
humanity takes responsibility for the heavens and the earth. This covenant
constitutes a major criterion by which faith and actions are judged. Sometimes called "God's covenant" (Qur'an 2:27), it separates Muslim hypocrites
and those who assign spiritual or material partners to God from true
believers, who maintain their trust in the Qur'anic message (Qur'an 33:73).
The person who trusts in God and does not break the covenant in thought,
word, or deed is a trustee or vicegerent (*khalifa*) of God on earth (Qur'an
2:30–33). The society that is made up of such individuals is a normative community, one that serves as an example for the world and is a collective witness
to the truth (Qur'an 2:143). The Qur'an calls such a community the *Umma
Muslima* (Qur'an 2:128), a community of people who submit to God. The
word *umma*, which is related to *umm*, "mother," connotes a primary community, literally, a "Mother Community." It implies that all Muslims, wherever they may live, share a common bond that transcends all other ties, from
nationality to family. The tradition of being part of this community is as
much a part of Islam as are its traditions of worship.

The leading members of the universal *Umma Muslima* are the Prophets of
Islam, who are discussed in Joseph Lumbard's chapter, "Prophets and

Messengers of God." According to Lumbard, God's Prophets are the keepers of the promises and signs (*ayat*) of God. They are bearers of the divine
message and reminders to countries and peoples of humanity's obligations
to God and to each other. Because all Prophets serve the same function and
transmit the same general message, all of them are Muslims, even if they are
revered by the followers of other religions, such as Jews and Christians. Start-
ing with Adam and ending with the Prophet Muhammad, they form a single
holy community that represents the continuity of tradition in what scholars
of comparative religion call the "Abrahamic Faiths."

The collective tradition of the Prophets of Islam forms the background of
the *Sunna*, the model of religious and ethical practice established by the
Prophet Muhammad. Hamza Yusuf Hanson's chapter on the Sunna is called
"*The Sunna*: the Way of Muhammad." However, it is understood by Muslims that the values the Prophet Muhammad's way of life promoted are the
same as those of the other Prophets of Islam. Thus, the Sunna of Muhammad, the last Prophet, is also the Sunna of the previous Prophets, just as the
message of the Qur'an is the same as the message of all previous revelations.
The Sunna is also the basis for the second type of scripture in Islam, the collections of traditions of the Prophet Muhammad known as *Hadith*. The
acceptance of a particular Hadith account is not an article of faith in Islam
as is the acceptance of a verse of the Qur'an. However, taken collectively,
the Sunna has become an authoritative teaching on par with the Qur'an in
the eyes of many Muslims.

The Sunna as a model for Islamic practice was developed in the community
created around the Prophet Muhammad in Medina between the years 622
and 632 CE. The practice of this community also established the foundations
for "The *Shari'a*: Law as the Way of God," which is the title of the chapter by
Mohammad Hashim Kamali. As Kamali explains, when Muslim jurists looked
to the Hadith for sources on Islamic law and ethics, they found that some
accounts elucidated religious precepts, while others dealt with customary
behaviors such as matters of personal hygiene and etiquette. Modern scholars
of the Sunna look at these traditions to decide which are part of "religion,"
and hence obligatory, and which are part of "culture," and hence optional.
Premodern jurists asked similar questions, although without the modern
concern for the concept of culture. They developed the tradition of Islamic
jurisprudence (*fiqh*) to determine how to integrate the Qur'an and the Sunna
into the social and religious life of the Muslim community.

The final chapters in this volume trace the historical development of three
major Islamic traditions that developed out of the teachings of the Qur'an,
the Sunna, and the early history of the Islamic community. The most important development of this period was the separation of the Muslim *Umma* into
separate communities over the issue of leadership after the Prophet Muhammad and over who—the leader of the community, the community itself, or a
special class of scholars—has authority over the interpretation of the Qur'an

and the Sunna. These issues are detailed in the chapters, "What Is Sunni Islam?" by Feisal Abdul Rauf, and "What Is Shiite Islam?" by Azim Nanji and Farhad Daftary. Both these chapters take the question of tradition into political, juridical, and theological dimensions that relate to present-day concerns, such as the tension between Sunni and Shiite communities in modern Iraq. Each chapter is unique in its own way. Abdul Rauf's chapter on Sunni Islam focuses discussion on the technical term for the Sunnis, *Ahl al-Sunna wa al-Jama'a*, and details how the concept of Sunni Islam was based on the authority of the collective opinion of the community and the jurists (the meaning of *al-Jama'a*). The chapter on Shiite Islam by Nanji and Daftary is unique in that it devotes more space than usual to a discussion of Ismaili Shi'-ism. Although the Ismailis are a minority among today's Shiites, they were the majority for more than two centuries and created the only major Shiite state until the rise of Safavid Iran in the early sixteenth century. Finally, "What is Sufism?" by Ahmet T. Karamustafa recounts the development of the most important nonsectarian tradition in Islam today, *tasawwuf*, which is often described as "Islamic mysticism." Karamustafa's chapter is an important corrective to those who overemphasize the "mystical" aspect of Sufism. In particular, he traces Sufism's origins to early Muslim traditions of renunciation and the desire to explore the inner dimensions of faith and the human personality.

The chapters in this volume are called *Voices of Tradition* because they not only introduce the reader to some of the most important traditions of Islam but also provide a glimpse of how Muslims engage tradition in their life and experience. The authors of these chapters originate or live in regions that span the world of global Islam: Afghanistan, East Africa, Egypt, Malaysia, South Asia, Turkey, and the United States. They are scholars, jurists, imams, government officials, community activists, and poets. All speak from years of experience with the traditions about which they write. Abu Madyan (d. 1198), one of the greatest teachers of the Sufi tradition of Islamic Spain and North Africa, said: "The Qur'an is a divine inspiration and a revelation, both of which remain until the Day of Judgment."[7] Each of the chapters in this volume details how the Word of God is manifested across time in the foundational and historical traditions of Islam. Abu Madyan also said: "The truth is on the tongues of the scholars of every generation, according to the needs of the people of their time."[8]

Each of the chapters in this volume was written with two audiences in mind. The primary audience is the non-Muslim reader, who will use this volume as a sourcebook for the traditions of Islam and for school assignments, background information, or general knowledge. However, another important audience for this volume is the Muslim reader, especially the young Muslim, who can use the information provided in these pages by internationally recognized Muslim scholars to present an alternate voice or even a corrective to the information that may be given in mosques and Islamic centers. Finally, the voices of Islam in the present volume, as in the volumes that follow, provide answers to two questions that have been often asked since September 11, 2001: Where are the Muslim voices that speak out against extremism? Where are the Muslim voices that speak for the traditions that made Islam a world religion and gave birth to a major civilization?

NOTES

1. Jaroslav Pelikan, *The Vindication of Tradition: The 1983 Jefferson Lecture in the Humanities* (New Haven and London: Yale University Press, 1984), 65.

2. Jacques Ellul, *The Subversion of Christianity*, translated by Geoffrey W. Bromley (Grand Rapids, MI: William B. Eerdmans Publishing Company, 1986), 96, n. 3.

3. Pelikan, *The Vindication of Tradition*, 70.

4. See, for example, Wilfred Cantwell Smith, *The Meaning and End of Religion* (1962; repr., Minneapolis: Fortress Press, 1991), 80–82.

5. The idea of Islam as a system (Ar. *nizam*) appears to have come from South Asia around the time of the Second World War. In 1943, Mawlana Hamid al-Ansari Ghazi used the term to refer to Islam as a political system. In 1942, the modernist reformer Abu al-'Ala al-Mawdudi (d. 1979) used the Urdu term *Islami nizam* (Islamic system) in a speech about Islamic ideology. The concept was later popularized in the Arab world through the works of the Muslim Brotherhood activist Sayyid Qutb (d. 1966). Ibid, 274, n. 10.

6. On Sabti, see Vincent J. Cornell, *Realm of the Saint: Power and Authority in Moroccan Sufism* (Austin, TX: University of Texas Press, 1998), 79–92.

7. Vincent J. Cornell, *The Way of Abu Madyan: Doctrinal and Poetic Works of Aby Madyan Shu'ayb ibn al-Husayn al-Ansari (509/1115-16— 594/1198)* (Cambridge: Islamic Texts Society, 1996), 116.

8. Ibid., 118.

1

Miracle of Sound at the Ka'ba

Daniel Abdal-Hayy Moore

What sounds are heard around God's House?

First, utter silence, silence within silence. Then
   its echo,
more silent still.

A silence that sits deep under the Throne of God—
all other silence surrounds it and
     slowly turns.

Every other silence partakes of that silence. Silence in
eyes, silence in tongues, silence in the
   womb, the silence of death.

The Ka'ba sits in the
shaft of that silence from the height of heaven,
and generates silence.

Then, just around this great circle of silence
the sound of an ocean, not of water or salt,
but of human longing, aswirl with
   sound, slow roar, slow-motion crash of
     surf, suspended animation of all
tremendous sounds in creation, the
exhalation of giant beasts, outbreath of
earth as God created caves and
sea depths and

seismic shifts.

Then more distinctly,
articulating what shines through both
    silence and sound,
the Word of God,
that aural text that floats from the
Heart of Light into the hearts of mankind,
tongue-tripped into articulate words, formed and
    filled with breath,
flowing like the sea, but from
        sea-depths of meaning,
light to the eyes and
sweet relief to the heart.

Then out from that circle,
the sound of all human speech, words of
    admonition, snatches of
        conversation, starlight of
God's Compassion sprinkled throughout it,
Turkish bursts, Arabic stutter, a child's distant cry,
then roar again, sea-surf,
    silence,
silence above all, and the
    twelve-dimensional
        echo of that silence.
Then a phrase of Urdu, Afghani, Malay,
low rumble of
Qur'an recitation, pauses, people
    looking around, metallic
        clatter from far away, the
rhythmic supplications of a group of pilgrims
        circling God's House.

Then the click sound of a microphone in sonic superspace
        turning on.

Then words enveloped by the Word,

the Word enveloped in a roar,

the roar enveloped in silence,

the articulate silence of God, then

the silence of silence.

Then the echo of that silence.

Then the looking around.

NOTE

This poem first appeared in Daniel Abdal-Hayy Moore, *Mecca/Medina Time-warp*. Reprinted here from a Zilzal Press chapbook, by permission from the author.

2

PILLARS OF RELIGION AND FAITH

•

Karima Diane Alavi

Proclaim! (or Read!)
In the name of thy Lord and Cherisher, who created—
Created the human being out of a clot of blood.
Proclaim! And thy Lord is Most Bountiful—
He who taught by the Pen—
Taught the human being that which he knew not.

(Qur'an 96:1–5)

Like many Muslims, I am often called upon to speak about Islam at churches, synagogues, and schools. Part of my job at a New Mexico Islamic educational center is to present workshops about our religion at schools and conferences. I enjoy meeting people from across the country, and many of my encounters have been poignant, like the time a Jewish boy reached into his pocket and handed me a bunch of half-melted M&M's after my presentation on Ramadan. "I know you cannot eat these for lunch," he whispered. "But once you're done fasting today, you can have these for dessert and think of me." Though I never ate one of those mashed-up candies, I often think of him.

With the increase of immigrant and U.S.-born Muslims in American communities, I have encountered both teachers and students who can list the Five Pillars of Islam with ease. They have studied them—in terms of what Muslims *do*—but most have not taken the next step, which is asking what Muslims *believe*. In other words, what are the reasons behind the Five Pillars, and are there other foundational beliefs within Islam that go beyond the pillars? How can non-Muslims avoid reducing their impression of Islam to these Five Pillars? This chapter not only covers the Five Pillars of Islam and the Articles of Faith but also touches upon other elements of Islam that are not considered pillars but are nonetheless essential aspects of a Muslim worldview and important criteria for living one's life the way a pious Muslim should. These include things such as harboring a deep reverence for nature, reflecting on the signs of

God's mercy and power through contemplating the amazing world around us, and walking the earth in a spirit of humility and grace.

THE CONCEPTS OF ISLAM AND RELIGION

Before we can begin to explore Islam's Pillars and Articles of Faith, it is first necessary to take a deeper look at the Arabic language in order to give more meaning to some of the terms many people are already familiar with. The word *Islam* itself is the best one to begin with. Almost all Arabic words are based on a three-consonant root that is shared with other words that have a related meaning. There are a small number of words with a four- or five-letter root, but the three-letter linguistic pattern is predominant. The three-letter root for the word *Islam* is S-L-M. Other words in Arabic that share the same root have the meanings of "peace," "submission," "security," "sincerity," and "safety." The inference here is that one who submits to the will of God is at peace, but one who is in constant conflict with God's will and the world around her is destined to live a life filled with tension and agitation, as if something is missing; for Muslims, what is missing are faith and serenity.

When Muslims use the expression, "submission to the will of God," it is not a call to fatalism, but rather a reference to the fact that there are many times in a person's life when taking an easy path is tempting, and following the dictates of a religion can be demanding. A devout Muslim submits to God's injunctions without challenging or questioning them, while trying to understand their inner meanings. A good example is the fasting month of Ramadan. For a Muslim, this is a time when getting out of bed even earlier than usual, in order to eat before dawn, can be a challenge. Of course for most people, staying in bed and curling up under their blankets in the morning is far more appealing than getting up to eat and pray, and not every Muslim has the willpower to actually pull those blankets off and get moving. Yet those who do, soon discover that Ramadan is a time of joy as well as hardship. It is a time when people renew their commitment to their faith and reconnect with the Muslims in their community, perhaps some whom they have not seen for a long time. What was initially a hardship soon comes with ease, and those who succeed in their Ramadan efforts often exhibit an outer calm that reflects their inner peace at knowing that they have heeded the call of their Lord. They have submitted to His will, and it has brought them a feeling of serenity and detachment. The Qur'an describes such people thusly:

> [They] feared God, Most Gracious and unseen
> And brought a heart turned in devotion to Him.
> Enter ye therein in peace and security.
> This is a day of eternal life!

(Qur'an 50:33–34)

Religiously speaking, a *Muslim* is not simply a follower of the religion of Islam, but also a person who has reached a state of peace through submission to the will of God. This is someone who has obtained *salama,* another term that shares the S-L-M root and means "perfection," "wholeness," and "security." This is a person who is devout in her *din,* or religion. This concept, *din,* also has a linguistic root (D-Y-N) that reveals a deeper meaning of Islamic belief and practice. Meanings of other Arabic words that share this root are "indebted," "requited," "at the disposal of," "judgment," and "brought to account." As we shall see, Islam is a religion that constantly reminds its followers that they owe a debt to their creator, and the Five Pillars of Islam are just one segment of that sacred indebtedness that serves as a daily guide for the truly devout.

THE HADITH OF THE ANGEL GABRIEL

One of the most widely used teaching methods among traditional Islamic scholars is the study of *Hadith,* the recorded sayings and actions of the Prophet Muhammad. The primary hadith for teaching the Five Pillars of Islam and the Articles of Faith is referred to as the "Hadith of the Angel Gabriel." Students around the world memorize this tradition and use it as a primary guide to their understanding of Islam. Below is this hadith—which will inform this entire chapter—to demonstrate how such a time-honored teaching tool continues to be useful in the study and practice of Islam:

'Umar ibn al-Khattab said: One day when we were with God's Messenger, (Prophet Muhammad) a man with very white clothing and very black hair came up to us. No mark of travel was visible on him, and none of us recognized him. Sitting down before the Messenger of God, leaning his knees against his, and placing his hands on his thighs, he said, "Tell me, Muhammad, about Islam."

The Messenger of God replied, "Islam means that you should bear witness that there is no god but God and that Muhammad is God's Messenger, that you should perform the ritual prayer, pay the alms tax, fast during Ramadan, and make the pilgrimage to the House (the Ka'ba in Mecca) if you are able to go there."

The man said, "You have spoken the truth." We were surprised at his questioning the Prophet and then declaring that he had spoken the truth. He said, "Now tell me about faith (*iman*)."

The Messenger of God replied, "Faith means that you have faith in God, His angels, His books, His messengers, and the Last Day, and that you have faith in the measuring out, both its good and its evil."

Remarking that the Prophet had spoken the truth, the man then said, "Now tell me about virtue (*ihsan*)."

The Messenger of God replied, "Virtue means that you should worship God as if you see Him, for even if you do not see Him, He sees you."

Then the man said, "Tell me about the Hour [of Judgment]."

The Messenger of God replied, "About that, he who is questioned knows no more than the questioner."

The man said, "Then tell me about its signs."

The Messenger of God said, "The slave girl will give birth to her mistress, and you will see the barefoot, the naked, the destitute, and the shepherds vying with each other in constructing tall buildings."

Then the man went away. After I had waited for a long time, the the Messenger of God said to me, "Do you know who the questioner was, 'Umar?" I replied, "God and His Messenger know best." The Messenger of God said, "He was Gabriel. He came to teach you your religion (*din*)."[1]

In this chapter, I hope (*In sha'Allah*, God willing) to take the reader on the first step of a journey toward understanding the deeper meanings of the Five Pillars of Islam, along with the other aspects of Islam that guide Muslims along their spiritual path. So come along on a joyous *rihla*—an Arabic term that means "journey for the sake of knowledge"—and open up to the various beliefs, books, angels, and prophets that have served as guides for Muslims since the first light of dawn graced our world with its beauty. As the Holy Qur'an says: "Relate the story so that they might reflect upon it" (Qur'an 7:176).

THE FIRST PILLAR OF ISLAM: THE PROCLAMATION OF FAITH (*SHAHADA*)

There is no god but He:
That is the witness of God, His angels, and those endowed with knowledge,
Standing firm in justice. There is no god but He—
The Exalted in Power, the Wise.

(Qur'an 3:18)

La ilaha illa' llah wa Muhammadun Rasul Allah, "There is no deity but God, and Muhammad is the Messenger of God." Muslim fathers traditionally whisper the *Shahada,* the Islamic declaration of faith, into the ears of their newborn children to ensure that commitment to a strict monotheist faith is the first thing they hear. For those who were not born into Islam, stating this declaration out loud in front of witnesses is their first step in conversion to Islam. The three-letter root of the word *Shahada,* SH-H-D, means "to bear witness" or "to testify." In the noun form, it means "testimony" or "that which is witnessed." A *shahid* is one who witnesses. The Qur'an uses the word *Shahada* for one of the titles or names of God: Knower of the Unseen (*al-Ghayb*) and the Seen or Witnessed (*al-Shahada*).

For the Muslim, reciting the Shahada is a verification of what is in the heart, as well as a commitment to follow the Divine Command to worship our Creator. What is witnessed or testified when one takes this vow to become a Muslim is that this person believes in the reality of one God and agrees to submit to His divine will and that Muhammad is the Messenger of God. By pronouncing the Shahada, Muslims also imply their intention to perform the other four pillars of Islam and live their life as a Muslim, to the best of their ability. This is clearly stated in the Hadith of the Angel Gabriel in which Muhammad is asked to discuss the meaning of Islam. The reply begins with, "Islam means that you should bear witness that there is no god but God and that Muhammad is God's Messenger." Gabriel continues with, "You should perform the ritual prayer, pay the purification tax, fast during Ramadan, and make the pilgrimage to the House (the Ka'ba in Mecca) if you are able to go there." All of these five pillars are inherent in the declaration of faith called the Shahada.

When a new Muslim makes this proclamation, it is a joyous occasion that often attracts more than the required two witnesses and that sometimes takes on a partylike atmosphere with food and celebration afterward. From that point on, the new Muslim is a member of the *Umma,* the Community of Muslims. Other Muslims are expected to take the responsibility of offering guidance and advice to new converts and comforting them in times of need, just as one's mother would. This group responsibility is reflected in the fact that the Arabic term for mother, *umm,* shares the same root (U-M-M) as *Umma* or "community."

The Shahada consists of two declarations that are sometimes referred to as the First Shahada and the Second Shahada. The First Shahada, "There is no deity but God," is an expression of *Tawhid,* a concept that means "the oneness or unity of God." Islam stresses monotheism so strictly that God states in the Qur'an—which Muslims believe to be the Word of God—that the only unforgivable sin is the association of other deities with Him.

God forgiveth not that partners should be set up with Him,
But he forgiveth anything else, to whomever He pleaseth.
To set up partners with God is to devise a sin most heinous indeed.

(Qur'an 4:48)

Islam's deep commitment to monotheism is evidenced by the fact that the first part of the first Pillar of Islam is the declaration that there is only one God and that He is the only entity that is truly worthy of worship. The concept of divine unity that is inherent in the first part of the Shahada also refers to the believer's indebtedness to the Creator and one's gratitude for God's creation. The concept of unity within the word *tawhid* is a reminder to Muslims that they are part of something so much greater than themselves that it is almost impossible to fathom. When one considers everything that has been created—every human being, every animal, and every drop of water since the beginning of time—it creates a sense of awe and humility. To worship something other than the One who created everything is an act of arrogance, a sin. Likewise, to deliberately or carelessly harm any part of creation except in self-defense, to mistreat a dog, for example, is also a sin. Part of a person's commitment to living a truly Islamic life is to see the created world as a reflection of Divine Mercy and to be a gentle presence on this planet for the short time that she is here.

According to the Islamic faith, a primary element of primordial human nature is an innate, instinctive awareness of the reality of the one God and an understanding that it is the worship of God that makes one fully human. The Arabic term for this original human nature is *Fitra,* which uses the three-letter root F-T-R. Its related words are *fatara,* "to originate," and *tafattara,* "to be split open or rent asunder," which implies that something has opened up and come forth. The Qur'an states that all of humanity—all descendants of Adam and Eve, past, present, and future—has entered into a covenant with God and have agreed to worship only Him. If they stray from this belief, they have departed from what Islam calls "The Straight Path" (*al-Sirat al-Mustaqim*).

> When your Lord drew forth from the Children of Adam and
> From their loins, their descendants,
> And made them testify concerning themselves,
> Saying, "Am I not your Lord who cherishes and sustains you?"
> They said: "Yea! We do so testify!"
> Lest you should say on the Day of Judgment:
> "Of this, we were never mindful."

(Qur'an 7:172)

Muslims are reminded of their covenant with God on a daily basis: the five canonical prayers each include a recitation of the Shahada, as does the call to prayer. By proclaiming the Shahada, Muslims signify that they have joined a tradition of revelation and a spiritual journey that began even before the creation of the first human being on the face of the Earth.

The Second Shahada declares, "Muhammad is the Messenger of God." Revelation is the means by which God has offered guidance to human beings. As previously stated, Muslims revere the Qur'an as the eternal Word of God that was transmitted to all people via the Prophet Muhammad, who was illiterate and did not "write" the Qur'an as some books mistakenly claim. Instead, Gabriel, the Angel of Revelation, recited the holy writ of Islam to the Prophet. While Muslims see the First Shahada as a reflection of a universal, cosmic truth—all beings were created to worship their Lord—the Second Shahada is germane specifically to the religion of Islam. Muslims do not assume that members of the other two Abrahamic faiths, Judaism and

Christianity, will view Muhammad as one of their prophets. And yet, inherent in the Muslim declaration of faith is the very seed of the universalism that makes Islam unique. Muhammad is presented to Muslims as the final prophet in a long tradition of divine revelation that includes—but is not limited to—the messages given to former prophets of the Abrahamic tradition. According to the teachings of Islam, God has proclaimed the same basic truth to all peoples of faith: "I am your Lord: worship me and I will offer you mercy, salvation and paradise." The Qur'an clearly points out that this is the same universal message that was sent through the Hebrew and New Testament prophets as well.

> Say, We believe in God and that which was revealed unto us,
> That which was revealed unto Abraham and Ishmael and Isaac and Jacob
> And the tribes, that which Moses and Jesus received,
> And that which other Prophets received from their Lord.
> We make no distinction between any of them
> And unto Him we have surrendered.

> (Qur'an 2:136)

This verse reminds Muslims that when they proclaim the Shahada, they also attest to their acceptance not only of the prophecy of Muhammad but also of the long line of prophets that preceded the advent of Islam, as a new faith that sprung up in seventh-century Arabia.

THE SECOND PILLAR OF ISLAM: PRAYER (*SALAT*)

> Those believe in our signs, who—when they are recited to them—
> Fall down in adoration, and celebrate the praises of their Lord,
> Nor are they ever puffed up with pride.
>
>   Their limbs forsake their beds of sleep
> While they call upon their Lord in fear and hope:
> And they spend (in charity) out of the sustenance that
> We have bestowed upon them.

> (Qur'an 32:15–16)

It is prayer that continuously marks the passing of time for Muslims. Every day opens with prayer, is punctuated throughout by prayer, and ends in prayer. In countries that are predominantly Muslim, it does not take long for a non-Muslim visitor to perceive how the rhythm of daily life is marked by the *Adhan*, the call to prayer. The word for prayer in Arabic is *Salat* and is formed by the three-letter root S-L-A. Another meaning that comes from this root is "blessing."

There is no other aspect of Islamic practice that has been broadcast across the world more often than prayer. This is probably due to the beauty and grandeur that one perceives when witnessing massive numbers of people moving in graceful unison to the melodious sound of Qur'anic recitation. Other scenes, equally touching, depict the opposite: when a person quietly offers herself up to her Creator in solitary prayer, it makes it seem as though all of existence at that moment—at least in that person's heart—is contained in her prayer rug.

While the first Pillar of Islam, the Shahada or Proclamation of Faith, can be performed publicly with a minimum of two witnesses, prayer extends a Muslim's religious practice into the community. It is considered best to pray in congregation whenever possible, and according to some schools of Islamic law, it is incumbent upon males to pray together on Fridays. Women are permitted to pray in the mosque too, but they also reserve the right to pray at home if they prefer to do so.

The formal prayers of Islam are basically the same around the world. This means that a Muslim can join in prayer from Demak in Indonesia to Detroit in the United States and move right into the flow of the Salat without missing a beat. Before the prayer begins, Muslims must make sure that they, and the place where they pray, are ritually pure. Things that make a person or a place impure are any human or animal excretion, such as blood or urine. Menstruating women do not pray, and according to some schools of Islamic law, people with seeping or bleeding sores cannot perform the ritual prayers because those who are bleeding are considered impure, regardless of gender. People who are too sick to participate in the physical movements of the formal prayers are required to pray while sitting or even lying down if they are able to do so. However, one must be clear of mind while praying, so a person using strong medication that affects one's mental capacities can be excused from prayer.

Before the prayer Muslims perform *wudu'*, an ablution that consists of cleaning the hands, mouth, nose, arms, face, head, ears, and feet. To an outsider, this act of ritual cleaning may seem like nothing more than an empty physical activity, but to the Muslim there is a spiritual significance to this practice as well. Often, prayers are silently recited while seeking a state of purity, and certain inner reflections are expected to accompany the act of making ablutions. For example, I am expected to consider my speech while washing my mouth, being mindful of whether I have used the faculty of speech to do good or evil since the last prayer. The same is done with the rest of their body; did my feet take me to places that are acceptable, places where God's work is done? Did my hands participate in actions that harm or help the rest of God's creation? In this way, the physical purity of my bodily members becomes a reflection of the inner, spiritual purity toward which I must strive at all times.

After cleaning themselves, Muslims line up shoulder to shoulder following the instructions of a hadith in which the Prophet Muhammad stated that when Muslims allow gaps between themselves in lines of prayer, the one who slips between the lines is Satan. The Muslim prayer is made up of cycles of repeated movements called *raka'at*. Each *rak'a* or cycle consists of standing straight, bending at the waist with hands on the knees, standing straight again, lowering oneself into prostration, rising to a kneeling position, and then prostrating a second time. Some scholars believe that the positions of the human body while performing the Muslim prayer take on the shapes of the Arabic letters that spell the word "Allah."

Every Muslim must pray five times a day: (1) in the morning just before dawn, (2) when the sun is at the midpoint in the sky, (3) in the afternoon when the sun is halfway between the midpoint and sunset, (4) just after sunset, and (5) in the evening at least an hour and a half after sunset. The number of *raka'at* for each of the five daily prayers has been set at two in the morning prayer, four in the midday prayer, four in the afternoon prayer, three in the sunset prayer, and four in the evening prayer. This means that a Muslim has her face to the ground a minimum of 17 times a day, bringing to mind God's injunction to submit to Him in a spirit of humility and gratitude. Prayers are often performed in a mosque—*masjid* in Arabic—a term that means "place of prostration." It is this position of total prostration—with feet, knees, hands, and face on the ground—that is described by most Muslims as their favorite part of the ritual prayer, affirming the notion that their lowest, most humble physical position leads them to their highest spiritual point.

The verbal portion of the prayers, whether done out loud or in silence, shares elements that are the same across different sects and schools. Each *rak'a* begins with the recitation of *Surat al-Fatiha,* "The Opening," which is the seven-line opening chapter of the Qur'an. This is followed by recitation of other Qur'anic verses. Some segments of the prayers are done out loud, and some are done in silence. People often follow the group prayer with a silent prayer of supplication called *du'a.*

That fact that males and females are separated during the prayer sometimes draws criticism from outsiders who have failed to consider the extremely physical nature of Muslim prayer. During the prayer, our bodies rub against the people standing next to us. When in prostration, we are often in a position that may be considered immodest. Islam is a religion that recognizes human nature and deals with it in a direct manner. For this reason, the distractions that might arise by mixing genders in such close proximity that they are touching each other's bodies during prayer is avoided by separating males and females.

It is interesting to note how *harim,* the word for the women's section of a mosque or a home, has taken on a connotation in the West that is the opposite of the original meaning of the word. When non-Muslims hear the word "harem," they often conjure up Hollywood images of scantily clad women waiting to fulfill the desires of a powerful male, usually in some remote desert oasis. However, the true meaning of *harim* is "holy place," "sanctuary," or "asylum." Related forms of this word mean "to make sacred," "prohibited," "forbidden," or "holy." In other words, the women's section of a mosque or a home is considered so sacred that it is forbidden territory. To whom is it forbidden? In the home, the *harim* is forbidden to outsiders. In the mosque, the *harim* is forbidden to men. Non-Muslims usually fail to see that Muslim women often enjoy their private, sacred space. Many women do not want to lose the sense of sanctuary that offers such privacy. Some Muslim women are currently trying to integrate genders within the mosque, particularly in the United States. But interestingly, objections to this movement are often just as loud from their female co-religionists as it is from the males.

When the prayer is over, Muslims extend greetings to the right and left (or according to some schools of law, just to the right if no one is to the left). This extends greetings of peace to their coworshippers. But it is also done in recognition of the Qur'anic verse (Qur'an 50:17) that tells Muslims to behold the two Guardian Angels that accompany them at all times. The angel to the right notes one's good deeds, and the angel to the left notes one's bad deeds. By extending greetings to each of these unseen angels, Muslims are reminded to consider the sanctity of their thoughts, speech, and actions throughout their daily activities. In this way, prayer is the ultimate reminder of the interweaving of the divine and angelic worlds with earthly existence.

The Qur'an does not describe how to practice the five daily prayers. Islamic tradition states that it was the Angel Gabriel who taught the Prophet Muhammad how to do the prayers so that he could pass that knowledge on to his followers. Another popular tradition that is often depicted in Persian miniature paintings describes the event in Muhammad's life called the Ascension (*Mi'raj*). It was this sacred journey to heaven that led to the number of daily prayers being set at five.

One evening the Angel Gabriel awakened the Prophet Muhammad and mounted him on a winged creature similar to a horse named Buraq (from the Arabic word for "lightning"). Within a short time Buraq whisked the prophet from Arabia to Solomon's temple at Jerusalem, which the Qur'an refers to as "The Farthest Mosque" (*al-Masjid al-Aqsa*) to indicate its distance from Mecca. The prophet ascended through the seven heavens to the very Throne of God. As he passed through the various stages of heaven, he encountered other prophets such as Jesus, Adam, and Abraham. At the final moment before meeting God, the Angel Gabriel told Muhammad that he would have to continue alone because the power and majesty of God's light would burn Gabriel's wings. Muhammad went on alone and received instructions from God for his *Umma*, the Muslim Community.

Muhammad began his return to the earthly realm, but on the way, he encountered Moses who asked what acts of worship were required of Muhammad's followers. Muhammad replied that his people were to pray to God 50 times a day. Moses insisted that human beings would never follow through on such a difficult requirement and told Muhammad to go back and ask for the load to be lightened. He returned to God and the number of prayers was reduced to 40. According to the Prophet's story, "I went back, and when God had reduced the prayers by ten, I returned to Moses. Moses said the same as before, so I went back, and when God reduced the prayers by ten more, I returned to Moses."[2] After multiple entreaties to God, Muhammad was finally too embarrassed to return again, and thus the final number of prayers was set at five. For the most pious Muslims, these five prayers are seen as a minimum. Muslims often follow the required prayers with extra *raka'at,* as the Prophet Muhammad and his companions did.

There are numerous Qur'anic verses that refer to God's command that believers remember Him through prayer, but perhaps the best known are the following:

Establish regular prayers at the sun's decline
Till the darkness of the night,
And the Morning Prayer and recitation; for the prayer and recitation in the
morning
Carry their testimony.

   And pray in the small hours of the morning.
It would be an additional prayer (or spiritual profit) for thee;
Soon will thy Lord raise thee to a Station of Praise and Glory!

(Qur'an 17:78–79)

The Morning Prayer is singled out as special because of the belief in Islam that early morning is a particularly spiritual time, when dawn has arrived and the soul of the believer is awakening from the evening's rest. The above Qur'anic comment about the extra prayers in "the small hours of the morning" is assumed to be a reference to prayers that the Prophet Muhammad performed after midnight and into the morning hours.

God makes it clear in the Qur'an that humans are not the only aspect of His creation that glorify Him through prayer. The Qur'an also states that all beings praise their Creator simply by doing what comes naturally to them:

Do you not see that it is God whose praises all beings
In the heavens and on earth celebrate,
And the birds (of the air) with wings outspread?
Each one knows its own mode of prayer and praise
And God knows well all that they do.

(Qur'an 24:41)

If one reflects upon all of the prayers taking place—with millions of Muslims praying at least five times a day—it soon becomes clear that there are concentric rings of prayers circling our world at all times. As the sun moves slowly across the surface of the Earth, someone at each moment is doing her morning prayers, just as someone else is following the evening shadow that just covered her world, by offering up her nighttime prayers. Though most people are not consciously aware of it, these consecutive rings of prayers toward Mecca never stop.

Each mosque around the world has some sort of indicator for the direction of prayers. This may be something as elaborate as a tall niche covered with turquoise tiles and Qur'anic verses, or it can be the word "Allah" scratched into the wall of a simple adobe structure to indicate the *Qibla*, the direction of prayer. Most people are aware that Muslims around the world face toward Mecca as they perform their five daily prayers. However, it is not the city itself that draws the prayers; it is the *Ka'ba* or sanctuary at the center of the Sacred Mosque of Islam that is the focus of these prayers.

Muslims originally faced toward Jerusalem when they prayed, reflecting Islam's close kinship with the earlier revelations of Judaism and Christianity. The Qur'an refers to the Great Mosque in Mecca as "The Sacred Mosque" (*al-Masjid al-Haram*) and to the Great Mosque in Jerusalem as "The Far-thest Mosque" (*al-Masjid al-Aqsa*)—the place from where Muhammad ascended to heaven and prayed with the other Abrahamic prophets. The Prophet's Night Journey from Mecca to Jerusalem and his ascension through the seven stages of heaven also reflect the universalistic nature of Islam, with its strong ties to the Jewish and Christian revelations. For this reason, Jerusalem continues to be an important city in the hearts and minds of Muslims.

In the earliest days of Islam, there were no "instructions" or revelations from God informing Muhammad about the direction of the prayers, but 16 months after Muhammad and his early followers had fled Mecca for Medina, a revelatory verse came forth, finally determining that the Muslims should pray toward the Ka'ba that sits at the center of the Sacred Mosque of Mecca. The *Qibla*, the direction of prayer toward the Ka'ba, reminds Muslims that Islam is not a "new" religion. It is a return to the earliest roots of human piety. Islamic tradition credits Adam as the first person to have built a shrine at this site. The structure is empty and serves as a symbolic link between monotheism and the recognition of God's omnipresence in all of creation. During a time when shrines were filled with pagan idols, the Prophet Abraham and his son Ishmael rebuilt the Ka'ba to serve as the house of worship dedicated to the One God. Since that ancient time, it has continued to be the focal point of millions of Muslims as a reminder of God's covenant with Abraham and his descendents:

> Remember that We made the House a place of assembly for people
> And a place of safety. So take the Station of Abraham
> As a place of prayer; and We covenanted with Abraham and Ishmael,

That they should sanctify my House for those who compass it round,
Or use it as a retreat, or bow, or prostrate (therein in prayer).

(Qur'an 2:125)

THE THIRD PILLAR OF ISLAM: THE PURIFICATION TAX AND CHARITY (*ZAKAT*)

Those who believe, who do deeds of righteousness,
And establish regular prayers and regular charity,
Will have their reward with their Lord.
On them shall be no fear, nor shall they grieve.

(Qur'an 2:277)

Zakat, the requirement of charity in Islam, is often translated as "Alms Tax," but there are several important nuances to the meaning of this word. The three-letter root of *Zakat* is Z-K-A. To give *Zakat* means, "to give charity," but more importantly, it also means, "to purify." This deeper meaning of the word refers to the Qur'anic injunctions against arrogance and the hoarding of wealth, and to remember that all things we own come from God and will return to God, including our souls. By sharing our worldly possessions with others, we purify ourselves of the arrogance of thinking that these blessings are simply the result of our efforts rather than the grace of God.

The rules for calculating Zakat are complex and depend upon the nature of one's wealth and the way in which it was acquired; a person's mandatory Zakat can range from 2.5 to 10 percent. The Qur'an lists the eight categories of people who have the right to receive Zakat: (1) the needy, (2) the poor, (3) those who collect the Zakat, (4) those whose hearts are to be reconciled to Islam, (5) captives who need to be ransomed, (6) those who are in debt, (7) those who fight in God's path, and (8) travelers. Today there are many Muslim charitable organizations that collect Zakat and dispense it to needy people around the world.

Giving alms is really a way of giving thanks to God for the benefits received, both by sharing them and by using them to perform good deeds that will benefit others. Even good health is considered a benefit received from God. Using the body to do good works is also considered Zakat, so that speaking sympathetic words or using one's body to perform acts of kindness are considered to be acts of charity. In this respect, health is a blessing for which every limb "pays alms." Thus, giving charity does not always assume the passing on of money or material goods. Even poor people can be charitable to others, as the Prophet Muhammad made clear:

The Prophet said: "Charity is a necessity for every Muslim." He was asked: "What if a person has nothing?" The Prophet replied: "He should work with his own hands for his benefit and then give something out of such earnings in charity." The Companions asked: "What if he is not able to work?" The Prophet said: "He should help poor and needy people." The Companions further asked, "What if he cannot do even that?" The Prophet said: "He should urge others to do good." The Companions said: "What if he lacks that also?" The Prophet said: "He should prevent himself from doing evil. That is also charity."[3]

The Prophet Muhammad once listed those people who will be comforted by the "Shade of God" on Judgment Day. Among them, he mentioned "the person who practices charity so secretly that his left hand does not know what his right hand has given."[4] This comment refers to the fact that Muslims are supposed to give charity in the subtlest manner possible and not draw undue attention to their good works by making them known to others; in fact, drawing attention to one's acts of charity is worse than not doing any charity at all. This is stated clearly in the Qur'an: "Oh ye who believe! Cancel not your charity by reminders of your generosity" (Qur'an 2:264). A Qur'anic parable follows this admonition, likening the person who brags about her charitable deeds to a barren rock that cannot bring forth anything live and green, even after a heavy rain. On the other hand, those who are quietly generous and spend their earnings in the Way of God are said to have souls like a fertile garden that springs forth with life, even after the slightest rain (Qur'an 2:265).

While Zakat is a mandatory Purification Tax included in the Five Pillars of Islam, Muslims often go beyond this minimum requirement and give additional voluntary charity that is called *Sadaqa*. The three-letter root of this word, S-D-Q, also means, "to speak the truth," "to be sincere," and "to fulfill one's promise." All of these aspects of honorable behavior indicate the links between generosity and a healthy society. Hence, there is an emphasis in Islam on weaving together the concept of charity and the sincerity of one's faith. This interconnectedness is expressed in the Qur'anic verse that defines true piety as spending one's substance on such things as the support of orphans, the ransom of those in bondage, and the fulfillment of contracts (Qur'an 2:177).

The issue of whether it is better to give than to receive has woven its way through many religious traditions. In Acts 20:35 Jesus is quoted as saying, "It is more blessed to give than to receive." There are several Hadith that quote the Prophet Muhammad affirming the same religious truth. Perhaps the most familiar story is that of Hakim ibn Hazm, a wealthy man who became a Muslim and a close companion of the Prophet. The story of ibn Hazm's love for worldly goods and the gentle lesson the Prophet taught this new Muslim is still used as a teaching tool to encourage discussion on the issue of charity.

Although Hakim was generous in his spending for the sake of God, he still liked to have much. After the battle of Hunayn, he asked the Prophet for some of the booty that the Prophet was distributing among the believers. He then asked for more and the Prophet gave him more. Hakim was still a newcomer to Islam and the Prophet was more generous to newcomers so as to reconcile their hearts to Islam. Hakim ended up with a large share of the booty. Then the Prophet, peace be upon him, said to him: "O Hakim! This wealth is indeed sweet and attractive. Whoever takes it and is satisfied will be blessed by it but whoever takes it out of greed will not be blessed. He would be like someone who eats and is not satisfied. The upper hand is better than the lower hand" (that is, it is better to give than to receive). These kind words of advice had a deep and immediate effect on Hakim. He was mortified and said to the Prophet, "O Messenger of God! By Him who has sent you with the truth, I shall not ask anyone after you for anything."[5]

If one imagines two people, one giving a coin and the other receiving it, one is most likely to picture the hand of the giver in a higher position, dropping the coin into the other person's open palm. This imagery has inspired reflection among Islamic scholars on the issue of who has the "upper hand" in a charitable situation. In such situations, feelings of power and superiority often affect us at the subconscious level when we donate money to someone else. Some scholars even went so far as to support the idea that the receiver of *Sadaqa* is actually doing the giver a favor by enabling that individual to perform one of the requirements of his faith. A classic example of such a commentary can be found in the eleventh-century book *Kashf al-Mahjub* (Unveiling the Veiled), by the Persian Sufi 'Ali al-Hujwiri:

> Those in poverty are under a divine compulsion to accept alms, not for their own wants, but for the purpose of relieving a brother Muslim of his obligation. In this case, the receiver of alms, not the giver, has the upper hand; otherwise the words of God, "And He accepts the alms"[6] are meaningless, such that the giver of alms must be superior to the receiver, a belief that is utterly false.[7]

How can this notion manifest itself in daily life? Once I was in Chiang-Mai Thailand during a year when I had not given much Sadaqa. I was thinking about this subject as I joined some tourists in the back of a Tuk-Tuk, a small taxi made out of a motorcycle attached to an open frame with seats and a canopy. After several minutes of weaving in and out of traffic, the engine of the Tuk-Tuk began to sputter and overheat. The driver, in a desperate attempt to get his foreign passengers to their destinations, continued driving until the Tuk-Tuk broke down. He pulled to the side of the busy road just as the engine died. The other passengers of the Tuk-Tuk berated the driver for dropping them off on a crowded sidewalk. They hailed another Tuk-Tuk without paying the confused driver one Baht.

I saw this as a golden opportunity to fulfill one of my religious duties by giving *Sadaqa*. I told my son, who is fluent in Thai, to explain to the driver that I was a Muslim and that I was supposed to give charity as part of my religious practice. We explained to the Tuk-Tuk driver that he would be doing me a favor if he accepted my gift of 30 U.S. dollars, which I hoped he could use to fix his vehicle. By now a crowd had surrounded us out of concern that two foreigners might be giving the man a hard time. Soon people were shaking their heads in disbelief as I thanked the driver for allowing me to perform my religious duty by giving him more than the normal 50-cent fee for his services. In a flush of embarrassment because of all the attention I was drawing, I quickly disappeared into the busy street to hail another Tuk-Tuk.

Wealth is seen in Islam not only as a blessing but also as a test. Those who hoard their wealth and fail to recognize the rights of the needy to a portion of their goods are told that their greed will lead to their own demise and will serve as a cause for their punishment in the afterlife:

> By the Night as it conceals; By the Day as it appears in glory;
> By the mystery of the creation of male and female;
> Verily the ends you strive for are diverse!
> So those who give (in charity) and fear (God),
> And (in all sincerity) testify to that which is moral and just,
> We will indeed make smooth for them the path to bliss.
> But those who are greedy misers and think themselves self-sufficient
> And give lie to the best— We will indeed make smooth for them
> The path to misery!

(Qur'an 92:1–10)

THE FOURTH PILLAR OF ISLAM: THE RAMADAN FAST (*SAWM*)

> Ramadan is the month in which was sent down
> The Qur'an, as a guide for humanity,
> And clear signs for guidance and judgment.
> So every one of you who is present (at his home) during that month
> Should spend it in fasting. But if anyone is ill, or on a journey,
> The prescribed period should be made up by days later.
> God intends every facility for you: He does not want to cause you difficulties.
> He wants you to complete the prescribed period and to glorify Him.
> In that He has guided you; so perchance you shall be grateful.

(Qur'an 2:185)

The Arabic word for fasting is *Sawm*, with the three-letter root S-W-M. The meaning of this root is "to abstain," whether it be from food or even from speaking. Although there are times throughout the year when believers perform fasts that are not required for all Muslims, the obligatory fast takes place during *Ramadan,* the ninth month of the Islamic calendar. The Islamic calendar is a lunar calendar, one that follows the phases of the moon. The Qur'an states that the new moons of each lunar month are "signs to mark fixed periods of time" (Qur'an 2:189). This refers to the fact that each lunar month lasts either 29 or 30 days. The lunar year is 11–12 days shorter than a solar year. Thus, when compared to our solar Gregorian calendar, Ramadan moves forward about 11 days each year. If one were to place a solar calendar next to a lunar one, one would see that the dates of the fast move backward; for example, in 2004, most Muslims in the United States began fasting on October 16, but in 2005 the Ramadan fast began on October 5.

According to Islamic tradition, every month begins when the new moon is sighted with the naked eye. This makes determining the first day of Ramadan difficult if the night sky is cloudy. If the clouds are too thick for a moon sighting, then the new month begins after the thirtieth day of the previous month. The motion of the moon around the Earth and the turning of the Earth itself further complicate the determination of the new month. Thus, the new Ramadan moon may be sighted in Saudi Arabia the day before it is sighted in California. Fasting begins at dawn on the morning after the new moon is sighted, but special Ramadan evening prayers start on the evening when the crescent moon is first sighted.

Once the sighting has been officially announced either in the neighborhood, or via radio, television, or Internet, a sense of excitement permeates the Muslim community. People quickly phone friends and relatives to wish them success and blessings during this special month of heightened piety. It is often difficult to sleep that night because of the anticipation of the first day of fasting, yet this is when people need their sleep the most: they will be getting up earlier than usual the next morning to give themselves time to eat a hearty breakfast to sustain them through the day. According to the Qur'an, they must finish their breakfast before the "white thread of dawn" can be distinguished from "its black thread" (Qur'an 2:187). This is about an hour and a half before sunrise. The fast ends for the day at the time of the sunset prayers.

Where I live in New Mexico, the winter sunset can be as early as 5:30 PM, but in the summer it can be as late as 8:30 PM. In a place like Reykjavik, Iceland, however, there can be as little as three hours of darkness in the summer. In mid-June the sun rises at 3:00 AM and does not set until midnight, which means that Icelandic Muslims would have to fast for 21 hours. In the winter, the nights are longer than the days, which would make the fasting period very short. Thus, the Ramadan fast can be easier or more difficult depending upon time and location. Scholars differ about what Muslims should do if they live in an area where the length of darkness or light is extreme. Some suggest that Muslims in far northern climes should follow the times of the day in Mecca, while others say that they should follow the timing of a city in their region that has a reasonably normal amount of day and night. A few scholars suggest that Muslims should try to complete the fast, no matter how difficult the circumstances, and hope for the greater reward they will receive for their efforts. However, when discussing the fast, the Qur'an states that the purpose of the fast is not hardship: "God intends every facility for you: He does not want to cause you difficulties. Complete the prescribed period, and glorify Him. In that He has guided you; perchance you shall be grateful" (Qur'an 2:185).

During Ramadan, those who are fasting must refrain from eating, drinking, smoking, and sexual activity. Those who are sick, elderly, or traveling are exempt from fasting until a time when they are able to make up the missed days, if they are physically able to do so. Fasting is forbidden for women who are pregnant or menstruating, again with the expectation that they will make up the days later. Those who are physically unable to make up these days should feed a needy person for each day that was missed.

Those who are fasting are expected to carry on with their daily activities rather than spend daylight hours sleeping or relaxing. This makes them more aware of their hunger and fatigue and enables them to reap the benefit of becoming more sympathetic toward those who are hungry the year round because of poverty. For this reason, fasting during Ramadan has a strong social component that links it with the third Pillar of Islam, *Zakat,* or Purification Tax, in that both are meant to develop compassion toward those who are in need of assistance.

Fasting is primarily an exercise in the affirmation of faith and the denial of desires. It is a tradition that has a long history within many faiths, including Hinduism, Buddhism, Judaism, and Christianity. In Islam fasting is used to increase and confirm *taqwa* among believers. *Taqwa* can be defined as "piety," "righteousness," or "God-consciousness." A person who has *taqwa* does good deeds for the sake of God, rather than for the sake of her own enjoyment or aggrandizement. For this reason, the patience and perseverance required during the month of Ramadan serves to increase one's *taqwa* and bring the believer to a state of humility, especially when one contemplates how easy it is to fall into the snares of temptation and greed. According to a hadith stated by the Prophet Muhammad:

> God said, "All the deeds of Adam's descendants are for themselves, except fasting which is for me, and I will give the reward for it."... There are two pleasures for the fasting person, one at the time of breaking his fast, and the other at the time when he will meet his Lord; then he will be pleased because of his fasting.[8]

The Qur'an speaks of *al-Nafs al-Ammara,* the rebellious Ego or the Lower Soul (Qur'an 12:53). This is the carnal self, which is the lowest of the three stages of development of the human soul. The second stage of the soul's development is *al-Nafs al-Lawwama,* the Self-Blaming Soul

(Qur'an 75:2). At this stage, the person feels conscious of evil, asks forgiveness of her sins, and tries to avoid sin in the future. The highest stage of the soul is *al-Nafs al-Mutma'inna*, the Soul at Peace (Qur'an 89:27). At this stage, one achieves peace and serenity through submission of the desires of the Ego to the will of God. The goal of fasting in Islam, as well as in other religious traditions, is to defeat the lower desires of the Ego and attain movement toward the higher Self. Victory over the part of our being that wishes to fulfill our basest desires can lead to inner freedom—a refreshing freedom from desire itself.

This ability to say, "No" to desire is the ultimate goal of the Ramadan fast, but it is also something that should indicate the behavior of the devout Muslim in others areas besides food and drink. We are also supposed to avoid temptations toward things such as unkind speech or selfish acts. One can say that in Ramadan the whole body fasts: the hands "fast" against stealing, the feet "fast" against going where prohibited actions take place, the tongue "fasts" from backbiting, and the eyes "fast" from looking at things in a manner that is displeasing to God. In this way, the person who fasts aspires to bring forth the Godly qualities that are innately present within all human beings.

Ramadan is a month not only of fasting but also of increased prayer, worship, and religious reflection. It is considered a time of self-purification for the believer and a time of cutting oneself off from worldly desires so that the difference between "need" and "greed" can become clear. Because Ramadan is the month during which the revelation of the Holy Qur'an to the Prophet Muhammad began, it is also considered an especially blessed time. Often evenings are spent in the mosque where one-thirtieth of the Qur'an is recited each night, enabling those in attendance to hear the entire sacred text from beginning to end every Ramadan.

Special prayers called *Tarawih* are recited after the evening prayers, because it was the practice, or *Sunna,* of the Prophet Muhammad. The *Tarawih* prayers are optional and can be performed either at home or in a mosque. The Prophet preferred to recite these prayers at home. However, after Prophet's death, 'Umar, the Second Caliph of Islam, initiated the practice of performing the *Tarawih* prayers in the mosque, when he noticed that there were several small groups doing the prayers separately rather than praying behind a single *imam* or Prayer Leader.[9] The nightly atmosphere within the mosque during Ramadan offers an interesting mix of animated rejoicing and pensive quietude as the pious reflect upon their faith and their lives. The feeling that these nights are very special is supported by a hadith of the Prophet Muhammad: "If one establishes prayers during the nights of Ramadan out of sincere faith and hopes to attain God's reward, then all his past sins will be forgiven."[10]

The precise marking of time is crucial in Ramadan and weaves its way through the daily and the monthly activities of those who are fasting.

The final 10 days of Ramadan are considered to have special significance because it is believed that the highly spiritual *Laylat al-Qadr,* or "Night of Power," falls somewhere within this period. The Qur'an states that it was on this blessed night that the Prophet Muhammad received his first revelation from God (Qur'an 97:1).[11] During the last part of Ramadan, the Prophet Muhammad used to devote special effort to his worship in the hope of drawing himself nearer to his Creator. For this reason, Muslims often use this time to seek forgiveness for their sins, mend arguments, give extra charity, offer additional prayers—especially for deceased loved ones—and generally aim toward the highest spiritual level they can achieve. Those who are able, sometimes go into a spiritual retreat at this time in the hope of leaving all worldly concerns behind while they focus on things of a religious nature.

Toward the end of each day, as sunset approaches, Muslims prepare for *Iftar,* the breaking of the fast. This is usually a time of gathering with family and friends, so it often takes on an atmosphere of gaiety and anticipation. This is not only because people can eat after sunset but also because of the approach of special evening prayers and Qur'anic recitation. Many years ago, when I lived in Iran, each evening of Ramadan was a celebratory event, and communities used to put up large white lights—similar to Christmas lights—to illuminate the village alleyways that led to the local mosque.

Muslims break the Ramadan fast immediately after sunset, which is defined as when the sun sinks below the horizon. It is not unusual for a large gathering of people to be seated at home or in a café, patiently waiting for the sun to set. After fasting for several days, waiting for sunset becomes a surprisingly easy task, and some people will wait a few moments after the sun has set just to be sure it is permissible to eat and drink. Muslims usually follow the practice of the Prophet Muhammad by drinking water and eating an odd-number of dates when they break their fast. The sunset prayer and then a full meal follow the initial breaking of the fast.

'Id al-Fitr, the "Feast of Fast-Breaking," is the holiday that marks the end of Ramadan. This is a truly joyous occasion that can range from family gatherings to events that draw hundreds or even thousands of people to public celebrations. Children often receive gifts on this day—especially if they have succeeded in their first Ramadan fast, or at least made a sincere attempt to do so—and often street fairs are set up in cities to accommodate large crowds. During the *'Id* celebration in Cairo, amusement parks offer discounts and small mobile rides, such as swings, or small Ferris wheels are scattered throughout the city. Storytellers, puppeteers, and magicians create a carnival atmosphere. Colorful banners sparkle in the sunlight and children ride decorated bicycles through their neighborhoods while ringing their bike bells to announce the end of Ramadan. Smaller towns have a more subdued holiday, with shared meals and special prayers. But whether the gathering is large and noisy or small and tranquil, Muslims around the world share this special

celebration and hope that the piety they gained during Ramadan will remain with them for the rest of the year. As the Prophet Muhammad said: "Make your bellies hungry and your livers thirsty and leave the world alone, so that perchance you may see God with your hearts."[12]

THE FIFTH PILLAR OF ISLAM: THE PILGRIMAGE TO MECCA (*HAJJ*)

> And complete the *Hajj* or *'Umra* in the service of God.
> But if you are prevented [from completing it],
> Send an offering for sacrifice such as you may find.

(Qur'an 2:196)

The final Pillar of Islam is the religious pilgrimage to Mecca, the *Hajj*. The three-letter root of this word H-J-J simply means, "to go on a pilgrimage." This journey is incumbent upon all who are physically and financially able to perform it. In a sense, it is the culmination of years of longing and preparation in both religious and economic terms. While there are millions of Muslims around the world who have succeeded in making the pilgrimage, there are millions of others who will go to their graves with the unfulfilled longing to complete the Hajj in their hearts.

The focus of the Hajj is not the city of Mecca, but the Ka'ba, the "House of God" at the center of the Sacred Mosque in Mecca. Muslims believe that Adam built a sanctuary on this spot and dedicated it to the worship of the One God; later on, Abraham and his son Ishmael rebuilt it. There is one stone in the contemporary building that is thought to be the only remaining piece of Abraham's original structure. This is the famous Black Stone that worshippers try to touch as they circumambulate the Ka'ba.

For Muslims, the significance of the Ka'ba as a sacred site goes back literally to the beginning of human existence. For this reason, when Muslims perform the rites of the Hajj, there is a sense of joining a long thread of existence that twists through time and space to connect them with ancient rituals and Old Testament prophets. It is a return to the primal source of divine mercy here on earth. Muslims pray five times a day toward Mecca for this very reason. It serves to reinforce their links to God through a long line of prophets and reminds them of the covenant between all of humanity and their creator, in which the descendents of Adam and Eve reaffirm their commitment to dedicate themselves to the worship of God:

> When thy Lord drew forth from the Children of Adam and
> From their loins, their descendants,
> And made them testify concerning themselves,
> Saying, "Am I not your Lord who cherishes and sustains you?"

They said: "Yes! We do so testify!"
Lest you should say on the Day of Judgment:
"Of this, we were never mindful."

(Qur'an 7:172)

Because of their primordial nature, the rites of the Hajj are meant to draw pilgrims out of the present world and into a more sacred space where they can become a link in the cosmic chain that takes them back to the beginning of human existence. The unity of all peoples becomes abundantly evident to pilgrims as they realize that they are surrounded by virtually every language and skin color on earth.[13] This experience is so moving that pilgrims often claim that they feel as though they have participated in a rehearsal for Judgment Day. They become like a drop in the ocean of humanity that is swirling around the Ka'ba at the center of Mecca's Sacred Mosque. It is while circling the Ka'ba that I first became aware of the existence of the rings of Islamic prayer—directed toward this sacred site—that circle our world without stop as they follow the rising and setting of the sun across the planet Earth.

People made pilgrimages to Mecca long before the birth of the Prophet Muhammad and the coming of Islam. The city rose out of the desert as an early oasis and a stopping place for merchants and other travelers, where they could buy and sell goods in the active markets that surrounded the Ka'ba. Upon arrival and before departing, they prayed to the clay tribal idols that filled the sanctuary, even though Adam and Abraham had built the structure to be a symbolic "House" for the One God. The Prophet Muhammad entered the sanctuary and destroyed the idols in the year 630 CE.

The Prophet Muhammad was born in Mecca in the year 570 CE. He was a member of an influential Meccan clan from the Quraysh tribe that controlled Mecca and took in the profits from trade and pilgrimage to the Ka'ba. When the revelation of Islam came to Muhammad, the Quraysh were afraid that these profits would be threatened by a monotheistic faith that forbids idol worship: at that time, there were 360 tribal idols in the Ka'ba and the pilgrims that worshipped them served as Mecca's primary source of wealth. Because they threatened the source of livelihood for the Quraysh, the early Muslims were persecuted, tortured, and even killed. Despite this, the small group of the Prophet's followers grew in size. Eventually, they had to flee Mecca to the desert town of Yathrib, the birthplace of Muhammad's mother. This town was given the name *Madinat al-Nabi*, "The City of the Prophet," after Muhammad's arrival. This city is now referred to as Medina, and it is the place where the Prophet Muhammad is buried.

It was in Medina that Muhammad was able to form a community of Muslims that transcended tribal ties. The conflict with the Quraysh continued, as did the Qur'anic revelations that eventually led Muhammad to take back the city of Mecca—this time, with virtually no opposition. The first thing Muhammad did after taking back Mecca was to promise its people that his army would not attack them or seek revenge. Next he cleared the Ka'ba of all idols—an act that many feared would bring upon him the wrath of the Arabian gods. When they saw how helpless their clay idols were, even the powerful Quraysh submitted to the call to Islam. The city has been a center of Islamic pilgrimage since then, now drawing approximately two-and-a-half million *Hajjis* (pilgrims) per year, as well as millions of other Muslims who perform the lesser pilgrimage known as the *'Umra*.

The *'Umra* is a series of rites that can take place any time of the year, other than the days of the official Hajj, which occurs in the twelfth month of the Islamic calendar. The 'Umra contains some, but not all, of the rites of the Hajj. The 'Umra is not one of the Pillars of Islam. One who makes the 'Umra is still required to make the Hajj pilgrimage. However, millions of Muslims perform the 'Umra each year, some because they are too old or frail to deal with the huge crowds during the Hajj and some because they want to become familiar with the rites of the pilgrimage before making the more difficult Hajj.

Books on Islam often claim that the Hajj serves to commemorate the Prophet Muhammad. However, it would be more accurate to state that the Hajj reconfirms the believer's commitment to the practice of one's faith and the worship of God. The rites that pilgrims perform actually have as much connection with the Prophet Abraham—to whom Muslims trace their religious roots along with Jews and Christians—as they do with the Prophet Muhammad. Abraham's connection with Mecca begins with a prayer for a son. God told Abraham that, despite his advanced age, he would be blessed with a son. Soon afterward, Abraham fathered his first son, Ishmael (Arabic *Isma'il*), with the Egyptian slave Hagar. According to Islamic tradition it was this son, Ishmael, whom Abraham was commanded to sacrifice. As both the Qur'an and the Bible state, Abraham passed this supreme test of faith and was rewarded with a lamb to be sacrificed in the place of his son. According to Islamic tradition, it was Abraham and Ishmael who later constructed (or re-constructed) the Ka'ba in Mecca and dedicated it with a prayer, as is related in the Qur'an:

> And remember that Abraham and Ishmael raised the foundations
> Of The House with this prayer: "Our Lord! Accept this from us;
> Thou art the All-Hearing, the All-Knowing.
>
> Our Lord! Make of us Muslims, bowing to Thy will, and of our progeny
> Make a Muslim people, bowing to Thy will. Show us our places
> For the celebration of rites, and turn unto us in Mercy;
> For Thou art the Oft-Returning, the Most Merciful."

(Qur'an 2:127–128)

When they had finished rebuilding the Ka'ba, God told Abraham to summon people to make pilgrimage to this holy site:

> And Lo! We made the Temple a goal to which people might repair
> Again and again, as a sanctuary. Take, then,
> The place where Abraham once stood as your place of prayer.
> Thus did We command Abraham and Ishmael: "Purify My Temple for those
> who will walk around it, and those who will abide near it in meditation, and
> those who will bow down and prostrate themselves in prayer."

(Qur'an 2:125)

The use of the word "purify" is worthy of note here because Abraham was raised in a time and culture of pagan religions when people worshipped the moon, the stars, and even clay idols. Abraham, the patriarch of Monotheism, built the Ka'ba to be empty, and there is a significant symbolism to this emptiness. This symbolizes the transition that some early humans made from the worship of tangible objects, such as clay statues, to the more sophisticated idea of worshipping a transcendent God who is not seen, but whose presence is manifested in all of creation. In a sense, Abraham's reconstruction of the Ka'ba marks a return to the spiritual purity of the beginning of time, such as that found in Adam and Eve before the Fall.

Abraham was eventually blessed with two sons, first Ishmael by Hagar and later Isaac by Sarah. It was through these two sons that he was destined to become the father of two great streams of humanity. But things did not continue peacefully for Abraham. According to Islamic tradition, when Hagar's son Ishmael was still an infant, God instructed Abraham to take the two of them to the desert and return home alone. It was in the barren valley of Bacca (the ancient name for Mecca) that Abraham dutifully left them and walked away, leaving Hagar and Ishmael in God's care. It is here that the element of submission now appears in the story of Hagar and creates her connection with the rites of Hajj. Stunned by Abraham's behavior, she asks if her abandonment in the desert is "something from God." When Abraham answered her in the affirmative, she submitted to this trial.

When her water and food ran out, it became obvious to Hagar that without help she and her son would die. In a frantic search for the assistance that she believed God would send, Hagar ran seven times to the top of two hills called Safa and Marwa, looking for water or for a trade caravan that could provide something to eat or drink. After seeing nothing each time, Hagar prayed to God for help. God sent the Angel Gabriel, who struck the ground with his foot and caused water to flow from the well in Mecca called Zam Zam. It is believed that this water has healing powers and can relieve both thirst and hunger. For centuries pilgrims have enjoyed the water from this well, and it still shows no sign of going dry. The experiences of Hagar, Abraham, and Ishmael, including their fears, sorrows, and blessings, have been woven into the rites of the Hajj for centuries. These rites are described and sanctified in the Qur'an and have remained unchanged since the seventh century when the sacred text of Islam was revealed to Muhammad.

The first rite of the Hajj is the donning of simple, white seamless cloths. This act puts the Muslim into the state of *Ihram*, which means "ritual purity." Men wear two cloths—one wrapped around the lower part of the body, and the other wrapped around the upper part. Women have more options, but they must dress modestly. While many women choose to wear white, others wear clothing that is of some other subdued color. For this reason, one can see women pilgrims dressed in a wide variety of clothing, with their decision often influenced by traditions within their home country. The main point is to avoid drawing attention to oneself during a time when one's efforts are supposed to be focused on the sacred rites rather than the aesthetics of the face, body, or clothing.

The word *Ihram* refers both to the clothing one wears and to the state of purity one enters after performing ablutions and donning the simple clothes. When people are dressed in *Ihram*, it creates a sense of humility. When we perform the Hajj we have no idea if the person praying next to us is a member of a royal family or a farmer. This reminds the *Hajjis* (people making the Hajj) that all people are equal in the eyes of God. The clothing also serves as a visual connection between modern pilgrims and their religious ancestors such as Abraham, who would have circled the Ka'ba dressed in a similar manner. After making the pilgrimage, Hajjis are expected to dedicate themselves to pious activities and deny the vanities that create a sense of separation or superiority among people.

As people make ablutions and dress in our *Ihram*, they recite a prayer that states our intention to make the pilgrimage. From that point on, certain behaviors are forbidden until the Hajjis are out of the state of *Ihram*. These include sexual intercourse, cutting the hair or nails, killing game, arranging or performing marriages, and using perfume—a prohibition that includes the use of perfumed soap or shampoo. However, it is permissible to have used perfume before donning *Ihram*, even if the scent remains for a while. Women are also not supposed wear a face veil during the Hajj. In addition to these restrictions, unkind behavior—although always forbidden in Islam—is considered even more sinful during the Hajj and actually makes the pilgrimage invalid. The prohibitions of the Hajj are listed clearly in the Qur'an:

> For Hajj the months are well known.
> If any one undertakes that duty,
> Let there be no obscenity, nor wickedness, nor wrangling in the Hajj,
> For whatever good you do, (be sure) God knows it.
> And take provisions for the journey,

But the best provision is right conduct.
So fear me, O you who are wise."

(Qur'an 2:197)

Because of television, many non-Muslims are familiar with the sight of thousands of pilgrims circling the Ka'ba during the Hajj. This act of circling, also called a circumambulation, is known as *Tawaf* in Arabic. It is important to remember that Muslims do not believe that God is "in" the Ka'ba. This empty structure has many symbolic meanings for Muslims, including the omnipotent presence of God everywhere. The Ka'ba also serves to remind pilgrims that God is the source of all creation. The spot where the Ka'ba is situated is literally seen as the center of creation. Often the most emotional moment for the Hajji is the instant that she first lays eyes on this awesome scene. When I first entered the Great Mosque of Mecca my attention was drawn to the marble floors, the enormous chandeliers, and all the people praying to my side as I walked past pillar after pillar toward the center. It was from a distance that I first laid eyes upon the Ka'ba, and I knew that this was the most magnificent sight I would ever see. There was a virtual sea of people continuously swirling around the solid black structure, and I wondered how I would ever manage to find a place in that crowd of tens of thousands of worshipers. With astonishing ease, I became like a drop of water in that ocean of people and joined the waves of worshippers who were praying, walking in silence, or crying as they became overwhelmed with emotion.

Pilgrims circumambulate the Ka'ba seven times in obedience to the Qur'anic verse in which God told Abraham to purify His House for those who walk around it, meditate near it, and bow and prostrate themselves in prayer (Qur'an 2:125). It is crowded and hot during the *Tawaf:* some people are lost in prayer and some are simply trying to make it through the rites of the Hajj without getting crushed. Because of the large number and fervor of the pilgrims, this happens fairly often during the pilgrimage. On the other hand, during the few days that I was in Mecca, I saw three one-legged Hajjis making their way around the Ka'ba on crutches. People with such determination will perform the Hajj against all odds.

There are specific prayers to be offered during each part of the Hajj. However, there is one that people pray during the *Tawaf* and then continue to chant throughout the pilgrimage, creating a rhythmic echo like a heartbeat that reverberates throughout Mecca 24 hours a day:

Here I am at your service, oh Lord, here I am–here I am.
No partner do you have. Here I am.
Truly all praise and favor are yours, and dominion.
No partner do you have.

After making the *Tawaf,* the pilgrims, if possible, pray at the station of Abraham near the Ka'ba, although this is not mandatory. They do not pray to Abraham: instead, they pray to God at the place where Muslims believe Abraham once stood with his son Ishmael and dedicated the rebuilt sanctuary to God.

The next rite of the Hajj, which is also physically demanding, is the act of running seven times between the two hills of Safa and Marwa. This running, known in Arabic as *Sa'i,* is also mentioned in the Qur'an: "Behold! Safa and Marwa are among the symbols of Allah. So those who visit the House in the [Hajj] season or at other times should compass them round" (Qur'an 2:158). These hills, Safa and Marwa, are the same to which Hagar ran in her search for water for her infant son Ishmael. This re-enactment of a mother's desperate attempt to save her child commemorates both Hagar's faith in God and her spiritual strength at a time when many would have doubted God's mercy. The appearance of the Angel Gabriel, who revealed the well of Zam Zam to Hagar, serves as a symbol of God's reward for those who remain firm in their trust. "O ye who believe!" calls the Qur'an. "Seek help with patient perseverance and prayer: for God is with those who patiently persevere" (Qur'an 2:153).

After the Running, the pilgrims reward their spiritual efforts by refreshing themselves with water from the well of Zam Zam—a cooling water that is known to have healing powers. Recent studies of this water, which has flowed continuously since before the coming of Islam, has shown high levels of calcium, magnesium and germicidal fluorides, which may explain why the Prophet Muhammad called it the best water on earth.

The pilgrims then travel by foot or bus to the tent city of Mina to prepare for the next rite of the Hajj, which is standing on the Plain of Arafat. In Mina the accommodations are more rustic than those in Mecca, where the luckiest pilgrims can stay in hotel rooms. Thousands of poorer Hajjis simply set up camp on the streets or sidewalks of Mecca. Pilgrims spend the evening in Mina in tents that house up to 75 people each. It is here that all class distinctions really fade, and modern conveniences that are usually taken for granted, such as a clean shower, become treasured luxuries.

On the ninth day of the Month of Hajj, all pilgrims depart Mina for the plain of Arafat. The word *'Arafat* is related to the Arabic word *ma'rifa,* which means "knowledge"; in this case, the knowledge of God. Pilgrims stand in prayer and religious contemplation at Arafat for the entire day. This is one of the most emotional Hajj rites and people often reclaim their religion here, having drifted away from it over the years. Arafat is thus a place of spiritual reunion, and prayers offered here are said to have special *baraka,* or blessings. The devotional rites of this gathering recall the actions of the Prophet Muhammad, shortly before his death. Fourteen centuries ago, the Prophet climbed atop Mount Arafat and presented his last public speech and the following revelation, in which God said: "This day have I perfected your Religion for you, completed my favors upon you, and have chosen for you Islam as your religion" (Qur'an 5:3).

After sunset the Hajjis leave Arafat and move *en masse* again, this time to the plain of Muzdalifa. Here they spend the entire evening outdoors praying, sitting in contemplation, eating, and sleeping on thin "Hajji mats" or sharing a blanket that someone has placed on the ground. They also gather stones to be thrown at the *Jamarat* (Pillars) on their return to Mina. When I was making the Hajj, I decided to walk the five miles back to the American section of the tent city in Mina rather than sit in the cramped bus. My efforts paid off when I arrived and realized that my friend and I had the entire women's area of the American section to ourselves—an area that was normally crammed with hundreds of Hajjis. A long, hot shower and a quiet cup of tea reinvigorated us for the next step, the Stoning.

This part of the Hajj has often been deadly because people are liable to be trampled by crowds.[14] There is only a short window of time during which more than two million people must throw seven stones at each of three pillars. These pillars represent the three times that Satan tried to persuade Abraham not to sacrifice his son, Ishmael, to God. The ritual of Stoning is performed three times over two days. It encourages pilgrims to consider temptation and to think about how they will turn away from temptation when they return to their homes and their daily activities. It also serves to remind the Hajjis of Abraham's willingness to submit to God's will when he was asked to sacrifice his eldest son, who was most dear to him.

The state of *Ihram* ends in Mina after the Stoning and a mood of gaiety arises out of the exhausted pilgrims. Women cut off a lock of their hair, in a symbolic gesture to commemorate the end of the state of *Ihram*. Men get a haircut or have their head completely shaved, according to their preference. Colorful clothing reappears on the Hajjis as they celebrate '*Id al-Adha,* the Feast of Sacrifice that celebrates the completion of the Hajj. This holiday is celebrated around the world so that Muslims who are unable to make the Hajj can nonetheless partake in the celebration of yet another annual pilgrimage. This holiday serves to unite Muslims from diverse regions in the Muslim world and reinforces the sense of the *Umma,* the Community that binds Muslims together across time and space.

The Feast of Sacrifice is a three-day celebration. During this time, Muslims sacrifice a sheep or another animal to commemorate God's mercy when a ram was offered to Abraham to sacrifice in place of his son. Every Hajji must sacrifice a lamb or a portion of a larger animal such as a camel or a cow. Booths can be found throughout Mecca and Mina, where Hajjis can make their payment for this sacrifice and have it done by professionals. Those who have the money to do so can sacrifice a larger animal such as a camel or a cow, but that is not a requirement of the pilgrimage. There are so many people on the Hajj that in 2005 the butchers of Mecca slaughtered 505,000 sheep, as well as 4,619 camels and cattle.[15] After the sacrifice, the meat is stored in massive freezers and sent to various parts of the world as donations, particularly to areas that have suffered from natural disasters. All of the meat must be distributed before the next pilgrimage, so that people around the world—both Muslims and non-Muslims—can benefit from this final sacrifice of the Hajj.

The last thing the Hajjis do before departing for home is to make a final *Tawaf,* a circumambulation of the Ka'ba, in Mecca. Once again the pilgrims circle the Ka'ba seven times and then depart to their homes around the world to share their memories with friends and family. Although it is not an official requirement of the Hajj, many pilgrims also visit the mosque and tomb of the Prophet Muhammad in Medina. This offers a respite from the crushing crowds of Mecca and gives people a chance to feel the blessings of the Prophet's presence. The comparative quiet that one finds in the City of the Prophet encourages the pilgrim to reflect upon the peace one finds in protective love, as Muhammad discovered at the hands of his mother's tribe and from God.

PILLARS OF FAITH

In the Hadith of the Angel Gabriel reproduced at the beginning of this chapter, the Five Pillars of Islam are followed by another set of principles called the Pillars of Faith. While the Five Pillars of Islam rest in the realm of what Muslims do, the six Pillars of Faith lie in the realm of what Muslims believe. One can also look at the Pillars of Islam as visible, external behaviors, while the Pillars of Faith are more internalized: you can see Muslims praying, but that does not tell you what beliefs are supported by their religious tradition.

The Arabic word for faith is *iman.* Other words that share the same three-letter root, A-M-N, have the meanings of "security," "trust," and "deposit." These shared linguistic roots indicate the links in Islamic theology between having faith in God and finding a sense of security through that faith. The Qur'an makes this link clear: "Truly, it is in the remembrance of God that the heart finds rest" (Qur'an 13:28).

At the time of her conversion the person who embraces Islam affirms the Pillars of Faith and the Pillars of Islam. When considering the first Pillar of Faith, belief in one God, it is important to note that the fundamental message of all prophets within the Abrahamic tradition has been the same: there is only one God, and God's creation should worship Him and give thanks to Him. In addition, the Qur'an teaches that all elements of creation—not just humans—partake in praising God simply by doing what comes naturally to them. Many Qur'anic verses weave the manifestations of the created world into a tapestry of continuous worship, in which, for instance, birds praise their Lord by flying and clouds celebrate God's mercy by drifting across the sky. The following is an excellent example of such a verse:

Seest thou not that it is God whose praises all beings
In the heavens and on earth do celebrate,
And the birds of the air with wings outspread?
Each one knows its own mode of prayer and praise.
God knows well all that they do.

(Qur'an 2:41)

For Muslims the primary source of understanding the nature of God is the
Qur'an, which they believe to be the literal word of God. Whereas Christians
see Jesus as the *Logos,* or the "Word," Muslims see the Qur'an as the Holy
Writ, or the "Word." In this respect, the Qur'an holds the same place within
Islam as Jesus does within Christianity. In the Qur'an, God reveals His nature
to the believer. He is, among other things, "The Cherisher," "The Helper,"
and "The Ruler of Judgment Day." There are 99 names for God in the
Qur'an. These "Most Beautiful Names" as they are called, reflect the duality
of God's nature. Some names, such as "The Merciful" and "The Protector,"
reflect a gentle, forgiving God. Others, such as "The Avenger" and "The
Reckoner," serve to remind believers of God's overwhelming power. However, when one looks at all of the 99 names together, the names of compassion
and mercy prevail. This does not mean that God does not bring about
judgment and punishment, but it does indicate that one can turn to God for
mercy and forgiveness.

The duality of God's nature is further expressed through the dichotomy of
two words that are often used by Muslims in theological discussions. "Transcendence" (*tanzih*) refers to God's infinitely powerful nature, indicating that
He is beyond all that we can imagine or compare. "Immanence" (*tashbih*)
reflects God's familiarity with His creation. According to the Qur'an, God is
so intimately involved with us that He is nearer to us than our jugular vein
(Qur'an 50:16).

Finally, there is a strong element of *taqwa* within Islam, a term best translated as "God-consciousness." In the Hadith of the Angel Gabriel, the
Prophet Muhammad is asked to describe virtue (*ihsan*). He answered: "Virtue means that you should worship God as if you see Him, for even if you
do not see Him, He sees you." To the Muslim who is completely enveloped
in *taqwa*, even a shadow can serve as a reminder to worship the Creator in a
spirit of humility:

Do they not look at Gods' creation, even among inanimate things?
How their very shadows turn around, from the right and the left,
Prostrating themselves to God, in the humblest manner?

And to God doth obeisance, all that is in the heavens and on earth,
Whether moving creatures or angels,
For none are arrogant before their Lord.

(Qur'an 16:48–49)

The second Pillar of Faith is the belief in God's angels. Muslims believe that angels bring messages and carry out God's commands. As messengers, they serve as intermediaries between the sacred and the earthly realms. The Qur'an tells us that God is the Light of the Heavens and the Earth (Qur'an 24:35). In the Islamic tradition angels are genderless beings made of light. For this reason, they are closest to God. Angels enlighten us by illuminating that which is unseen. Angels also "reveal" things to humans, particularly the Angel Gabriel who is the Angel of Revelation in both the Christian and the Muslim traditions. A good example of this shared tradition is the story of the Annunciation. In both the Christian and the Muslim stories, it is Gabriel who tells the Virgin Mary of the pending birth of her son, Jesus.

The Qur'an states that everyone has two Guardian Angels who record their deeds, both good and bad (Qur'an 82:11). The angel on the right records our good deeds, and the angel on the left records our bad deeds. This personal record of one's thoughts and deeds will be opened on Judgment Day. For this reason, at the end of each prayer Muslims turn their heads to each side and offer greetings to these unseen angels. In this way, they are reminded at least five times a day of the angels' presence.

Several angels are mentioned by name in the Islamic tradition. These include Michael, Gabriel, and Harut and Marut, two angels that gave knowledge to the people of Babylon. Two other angels, Nakir and Munkar, question the dead in their graves. Other unnamed angels perform such duties as bringing God news of His creatures, or travel across the earth in search of places where people have gathered for the sake of remembering God. As noble and pure beings, angels are a reflection of God's merciful nature. For this reason, they pray for the forgiveness of all creatures on earth:

> The heavens are almost rent asunder from above them (by His glory),
> And the angels celebrate the praise of their Lord and pray for forgiveness
> For all beings on earth. Behold! Verily God is He,
> The Oft-forgiving, the Most Merciful.

(Qur'an 42:5)

The Prophet Muhammad had a special connection with the Angel Gabriel that went all the way back to his ancestors, Abraham, Hagar, and Ishmael. When Abraham was instructed by God to leave Hagar and Ishmael in the desert, the Angel Gabriel struck the Earth and brought forth water for them. This water was sent by God as a mercy to Hagar and the small child, who was dying of thirst in her arms. This child, Ishmael, survived the desert heat to become the ancestor of the Prophet Muhammad, who would one day hear the voice of Gabriel announcing the revelation of Islam. This is the same angel that sits with Muhammad and questions him about faith in the Hadith of Gabriel.

The third Pillar of Faith is belief in God's revealed books. In Islamic theology, it is noted that humans sometimes become weak in their faith. For this reason, God sends both "signs" and "reminders" to them. Humans are constantly surrounded by Signs of God's mercy and majesty. One simply needs to take the time to contemplate such elements of creation as a leaf, a breeze, or a newborn infant to understand that God is all around us, as well as within us. A "Reminder," however, can take the form of a messenger, a Prophet, or a sacred text.

The sacred texts that Muslims believe to be inspired by God are the Torah (*al-Tawrat*), the Psalms of David (*al-Zabur*), the Gospel of Jesus (*al-Injil,* "The Evangel"), and the Qur'an. Muslims believe that God sent a series of sacred texts to humanity. This series culminated with the Qur'an, which God identifies as the final holy writ: a "Criterion" (*Furqan*) through which He makes clear to believers the difference between truth and falsehood:

> Thus, (O Prophet) He has revealed to you this book with the Truth— confirming the prophecies that preceded it— and (for the same purpose) He had revealed the Torah and the Evangel before it, as guidance for humankind. He has (now) revealed this Criterion.

(Qur'an 3:3)

Within the Islamic tradition, the Old and New Testaments are not accepted in their entirety. The Arabic word *Tawrat* (Torah), refers to the "Five Books" of the Pentateuch: Genesis, Exodus, Leviticus, Numbers, and Deuteronomy. The Arabic word *Injil* (Evangel) refers to the gospel that was revealed to Jesus. This word comes from the Greek *Evangelion,* which can be translated as "Good Tidings." Because of the special reverence given to these sacred texts, the Qur'an refers to Jews and Christians as *Ahl al-Kitab,* "People of the Book," and accords them special respect.

The fourth Pillar of Faith is belief in God's Messengers. These messengers include many of the Hebrew prophets of the Torah, as well as Jesus, John the Baptist, and prophets who are specific to the Arab people, such as Hud and Salih. Perhaps the best-known Qur'anic verse in reference to this long line of prophets is the following:

> Say: We believe in God and what was revealed unto us,
> And what was revealed unto Abraham and Ishmael and Isaac and Jacob
> And the tribes, and what Moses and Jesus received,
> And what other Prophets received from their Lord.
> We make no distinction between any of them. Unto Him (alone) we have surrendered.

(Qur'an 2:136)

Although Muhammad is the most important Prophet for Muslims, he is only mentioned twice by name in the Qur'an. The Prophet who is named most often is Moses, whose primary role is that of a lawgiver. Abraham also holds a central place in Muslim theology as the first monotheist. Abraham's central place within Islam is also reflected in the fact that many rites of the Hajj pilgrimage to Mecca commemorate him.

One difference between the Judeo-Christian and Islamic traditions is the concept of sinlessness when dealing with all the Prophets. According to Muslim belief, the Prophets were selected by God himself to deliver His message to humanity in its pure form. They are incapable of lying, acting immorally, or making a mistake about the revelations that are entrusted to them. This is not only due to their sinless nature but also because the Qur'an makes it clear that if a Prophet were to lie about a revelation, God's punishment would be so severe that nothing could protect him from God's wrath (Qur'an 69:44–47). Prophets also serve as models for believers to emulate. This does not mean that a Prophet cannot make a minor mistake and then be corrected by God. For example, God admonished the Prophet Muhammad for turning away a blind man who sought religious guidance while the Prophet was busy talking to someone else (Qur'an 80:1–16). However, Prophets do not sin because that would be a willful disobedience of their Lord and an act of arrogance toward God.

Because of Islam's strict adherence to the principle of *Tawhid,* the absolute oneness of God, Muslims are forbidden to worship anything other than God. For this reason, the nature of Jesus within Islamic theology is that of a Prophet of God, a Sign of God, and a Mercy sent to the believers. The words of Jesus himself, as quoted in the Qur'an, best summarizes the Islamic concept of his nature:

> He said: "Behold, I am a servant of God. He has vouchsafed unto me revelation and made me a Prophet,
> And made me blessed wherever I may be; and He has enjoined upon me prayer and charity as long as I live,
> And has endowed me with dutifulness toward my mother; and He has not made me haughty or bereft of grace.
> Peace was upon me the day I was born, and on the day of my death, and on the day when I shall be raised to life again.
>
> (Qur'an 19:30–33)

Muslims likewise are forbidden to worship Muhammad. Although he was selected by God to receive and pass on revelation, they are reminded of his humanity in the Qur'an (Qur'an 3:144). He is referred to as the "Seal of the Prophets," indicating that he is the last in a long line of prophets through whom God has sent a universal message to His creation. "Muhammad is not the father of any of your men; he is the Messenger of God and the Seal of the

Prophets and God has knowledge of all things" (Qur'an 33:40). Muhammad was a humble and unlettered man who never learned to read or to write. He was pious from an early age and devoted much of his time to contemplation and prayer. He lived in poverty without complaint, always trusting in God's provision. He also had a reputation for being very kind to children, to the point where they enjoyed playing with him. The Qur'an presents Muhammad as a role model whose conduct serves as an inspiration for Muslims, both male and female: "You indeed have in the Messenger of God a beautiful pattern of conduct for any one whose hope is in God and the Final Day, and for those who engage much in the praise of God" (Qur'an 33:22).

The fifth Pillar of Faith is belief in the Last Day (*al-Yawm al-Akhir,* also known in Arabic as *Yawm al-Qiyama,* the Day of Judgment). Islamic traditions about the Day of Judgment are very close to those of Christianity and even include a role for Jesus as an intercessor before God. Many Muslims also believe in a quasi-prophetic figure called the *Mahdi,* "The Guided One," who will come after Jesus and bring a period of peace and justice that will last until the Day of Judgment. This figure does not appear in the Qur'an, but is a later addition from the Hadith.

Like the Christians, Muslims believe that people will be taken to account for their actions, both good and evil. They will either be rewarded with a place in the gardens of Paradise or be punished by the tribulations of hell. The primary moral question that one needs to ask oneself is really about time: Did I use my time here on earth to sow peace and kindness, or did I use my time to sow disharmony and grief? The duality of God's nature—He is a God of mercy and forgiveness and at the same time He is a God of power and revenge—plays an important role in the Islamic concept of Judgment Day. Islam is a strict religion, in that it lacks the idea of vicarious atonement such as one finds in Christianity. In Islamic theology, believers are held completely responsible for their thoughts and actions. Since no human being is perfect, one can only pray for God's mercy when she needs it the most. In the Qur'an, God tells the Prophet Muhammad to remind believers of His merciful nature: "When those come to you who believe in Our Signs, say: 'Peace be upon you. Your Lord has inscribed for Himself the rule of Mercy. If any of you does evil out of ignorance, and afterward repents and amends his conduct, [God] is oft-forgiving, Most Merciful'" (Qur'an 6:54).

We are clearly told in the Qur'an that we are the ones who wrong our own souls through the actions and deeds that we commit. Therefore, if we feel a sense of doom on Judgment Day, there is only one person to blame for it— ourselves. This is made clear in a very well-known hadith in which the Prophet Muhammad commented that the greatest *jihad,* or Struggle, that a believer must confront is the struggle against oneself.

Qur'anic descriptions of the Last Day paint a picture of the utter destruction of the world as we know it. A great trumpet will be blown and mountains will crumble to dust. The sky will be like molten brass, and the Earth will be thrown into convulsions. At that time, all people both living and dead will be raised and questioned about what they did, and nothing will be hidden. The Qur'an presents a graphic description of what will happen to those of us who have devoted our lives to the violent pursuit of power and wealth:

By the steeds that run, with panting breath, and strike sparks of fire,
And press home the charge in the morning, and raise the dust in clouds,
And penetrate into the midst of the foe en masse,
Truly, man is ungrateful to his Lord,
And to that fact he bears witness by his deeds, for violent is his love of wealth!
Does he not know— When what is in the graves is scattered abroad,
And what is locked in human breasts is made clear,
That their Lord has been well acquainted with them, even to that day?

(Qur'an 100:1–11)

On that day, the two angels that have recorded all the deeds of the Muslims will testify either for or against them. The angels Nakir and Munkar will question everyone in their grave, and a Time of Reckoning will come when the veil of denial is removed and people will see before them a scroll with a summary of their life. "Then shall each soul know what it has sent forward and what it has kept back" (Qur'an 82:5). Unique to Islam is the belief that when the souls are sorted out on the Day of Judgment, the tongues, hands, and feet of human beings will give testimony to the good that they have done. They will bear witness against human beings if they used their limbs and their faculty of speech for the pursuit of evil.

Qur'anic descriptions of hell bring forth images of utter agony in both the physical and the spiritual realms, for it is believed that the worst punishment one can experience is to be far from God. Those who submit to God's will and live a life of piety and grace are promised the garden of Paradise filled with flowing rivers, thrones of dignity, and an abundance of water and food. However, the finest reward of all is nearness to the Lord:

Thus then, if he be of those nearest to God,
There is for him rest and satisfaction, and a Garden of Delights.
And if he be of the Companions of the Right Hand, (those who did good)
For him is a salutation: Peace unto thee.

Celebrate with praises the name of your Lord, the Supreme.

(Qur'an 56:88–91, 96)

The sixth Pillar of Faith is the belief in God's determination of affairs, whether it involves fortune or misfortune. This Pillar of Faith affirms the concept of God's determination of the affairs of all creatures, which is a basic principle of Islamic theology. The Arabic word for this concept is *qadar*. This word is sometimes translated as "predestination," but it is better understood when it is considered along with the idea of God's Oneness (*Tawhid*) as manifested in His omniscient presence and power. According to Islamic belief, nothing happens without God's knowledge and permission:

> With Him are the keys of the Unseen, the treasures that no one knows but He.
> He knows whatever there is on the earth and in the sea.
> Not a leaf falls, but with His knowledge.
> There is not a grain in the darkness of the earth,
> Nor anything green or withered,
> But that it is inscribed in a Record Clear.

(Qur'an 6:59)

Related to the concept of God's omniscient power is the belief that He measures out our destinies, whether good or evil, joyous or sad. This applies to us both on a personal scale and on a grander, cosmic scale. For example, it was not my choice to decide when or where I would be born, what color my skin would be, or whom my parents would be. This was determined for me. On a larger scale, God has already determined whether I will wake up tomorrow to a sunny day or die in an earthquake. A true believer must recognize the impossibility for each one of us to determine what will happen in the grand scheme of things. Part of a Muslim's submission to the will of God is to accept the fact that our next breath may be our last. *Allahu a'lam,* as we say: God alone knows. We can only live each moment as if it is our last, and pray that it is not.

Another aspect of submission to God's will is to accept the fact that some people have more material wealth or may seem to have more blessings than others. This does not mean that people are not encouraged to better their lot. On the contrary: God measures out intelligence, sight, hearing, and the ability to reason. We show our gratitude for these faculties by using them, but only if we use them to do works of goodness, to do God's work. Using them to gain power over others or to accumulate an excess of material goods is a misuse of God's gifts, and will be dealt with on the Day of Judgment. God measures out our destinies, and we do the best we can with whatever we are given. In this sense, one who complains because other people receive more than he has, shows ingratitude. On the other hand, because money and other forms of wealth are literally gifts from God and are looked upon as something "on loan" to us, a Muslim who has been blessed with abundance is required to share his wealth. Taking on an air of superiority because of material wealth would imply that the wealthy individual assumes that his blessings are to be credited only to his efforts. This is also an example of ingratitude and arrogance toward one's Lord. In this way, God's reward or bounty can be a test. As the Qur'an reminds us, the person who fails this test creates her own misery:

Let not those who covetously withheld of the gifts
That God has given them with His grace, think that it is good for them.
Nay, it will be the worse for them.
Soon shall the things that the covetous withheld be tied to their necks,
Like a twisted collar on the Day of Judgment! To God belongs the inheritance
Of the Heavens and the Earth. And God is well acquainted with all that you do.

(Qur'an 3:180)

Just as the Qur'an reminds us that all events are known to God before they occur, it also affirms that humans have the ability to make a choice between good and evil. If this were not so, what would be the purpose of Judgment Day? What God knows ahead of time is that each person will be offered temptations in her life and that each will be forced to make a decision as to which path she will follow—the straight or the crooked. Before we are born, God knows what our challenges will be and how we will cope with them. In this sense, the Prophet Muhammad's comment that a person's final destination, whether it be heaven or hell, is already predetermined before birth is correct. The statement makes sense because God alone is all knowing. In His mercy, God has measured out His guidance along with the human capacity to discern good from evil, providing believers with a combination of predestination and free will. For this reason, "Satan has no authority over those who have faith and put their trust in the Lord" (Qur'an 16:99).

NOTES

1.   Sachiko Murata and William C. Chittick, *The Vision of Islam* (New York: Paragon House, 1994), xxv.

2.   Ibid., 167.

3.   See http://www.islamicity.com/mosque/pillars.shtml (*Sahih al-Bukhari*, 2.524).

4.   Alim CD-ROM (*Sahih al-Bukhari*, 2.504).

5.   See http://www.muslimaccess.com/sunnah/sahabah/HAKIM_IBN_ HAZM.htm (*Sahih al-Bukhari*, 2.551).

6.   In the Qur'anic verse to which this statement refers (9:104), Muslims are told that even God accepts gifts of charity in the form of repentance and righteous works from believers. However, it is not correct to insinuate that the believer is superior to God because of this. This is what Hujwiri means by an "utterly false" notion.

7.   'Ali B. 'Uthman al-Jullabi al-Hujwiri, *The Kashf al-Mahjub: The Oldest Persian Treatise on Sufism*, trans. Reynold A. Nicholson (1911; repr., London: Luzac & Co., 1976), 316.

8.   Alim CD-ROM (*Sahih al-Bukhari*, 3.128)

9.   It is thought that the Prophet Muhammad decided not to perform his *Tarawih* prayers in the mosque because of the crowd that gathered to follow his example. He was afraid that Muslims would assume that these prayers were obligatory, so he prayed

at home. See http://www.geocities.com/abusamad/tarawih.html. See also, Alim CD-ROM (*Sahih al-Bukhari*, 9.393).

10.   See http://www.islamonline.net/english/index.shtml (*Sahih al-Bukhari*, 3.227).

11.   There is a debate about exactly when in Ramadan this event took place, so it is not a spiritual necessity to pinpoint the exact date of *Laylat al-Qadr*. According to the Prophet's wife Aisha, it was on an odd-numbered evening that fell within the final ten nights of the month.

12.   Hujwiri, *Kashf al-Mahjub*, 329

13.   One of the most racially and culturally diverse groups at the Hajj is the North Americans. In 2005, there were 12,750 pilgrims (who call themselves *Hajjis*) from the United States. See, for example, http://www.saudiembassy.net/2005News/News/HajDetail.asp?cIndex=5017.

14.   One of the most tragic years at the *Jamarat* (Stoning area) was 2004, when 244 people were trampled to death, including one child. After that the government of Saudi Arabia made major changes to the traffic pattern and tried to eliminate the danger of a stampede. However, in 2006 more pilgrims were trampled at the Stoning Area. In 1990, a stampede at Safa and Marwa, the site of the Running, killed 1426 people, prompting the organization to make changes in that part of the Hajj as well.

15.   On the number of animals slaughtered at Mecca and Mina during the Hajj in 2005, see http://www.saudiembassy.net/2005News/News/HajDetail.asp?cIndex=5000.

3

RAMADAN HOUSE GUEST

•

Daniel Abdal-Hayy Moore

Fasting is Mine.

—Hadith Qudsi

Ramadan has come to live with us.
It is God's private apartments
   moved into our house
     and taking over.
Where the doors were
   are now entranceways into His Garden.
Where windows were are
   continuous waterfalls. Abundance in the

dryness. Hidden in the dust:
   clusters of roses. Sprung from our
     footsteps: *ascents.* Climbs past the
usual dimensions: *the usual
ticking clock in the antechamber.* The ancient
mahogany piano has become
   rock crystal, playing only
     God's music on
       silent keys. There is a

haunting rise and fall of
   distant melody come
     close to the inner ear, come
closer than our
   own physicality, a
sound more essential than the
     marrow of our bones or the

enormous sailing surface of the
   corpuscles of our blood, that is

His interconnecting rooms leading always past the
closed door of His Presence, the

open hallways of approach, the
retreating audience halls where
   attendants move with
      melodious precision, and speak in an
undertone of avalanche, words of
rainforests keeping earth's atmosphere filled with
   breathable air, deeps of the
nearest ocean where various
     killer whales congregate in
        affable groups.

The earth is an outdoor amphitheater of
   affable groups, and time a

   shudder of water across fans of spray at the
   source of the cascade of all
     creaturely manifestation.

When the rooms are filled with the yearly fast
the most geographical distances are drawn near,
Watusi warriors in tiger pelts arrive in silent droves,
desert men in blazing white burnooses slide
     down off their donkeys and
       come in, Siamese ladies in
   straight batik skirts stand in
    angular poses to the
click of passing birds, and a

   white wind sweeps across everything that
inhales or intakes, exhales or
   digests. The very
     air becomes a

stomach turned inside-out in which
the sun and all her
   planets turn in
    wide swinging arcs in the

tonal soup of darkness.

God says, "Fasting is Mine."

Because He alone knows its
      dimensions. It
   contains each ant and
      microbe in the

   drama of being a creature.

Ramadan has moved
   into the earth
like a different sky
      settling down on the
         same dunes.

For a month the feast takes place in a
   heavenly dimension. Trays are

brought in from

   other atmospheres.

Our house is His. Its guests
   belong to Him. The
      repast is His, the

   withholding and giving is

He alone.

                                                5 Ramadan

NOTE

   This poem first appeared in Daniel Abdal-Hayy Moore, *The Ramadan Sonnets*
(San Francisco and Bethesda, Maryland: Jusoor/City Lights Books, 1996).
Reprinted from Jusoor/City Lights Books and republished in the Ecstatic Exchange
Series. This poem is reproduced here by permission of the author.

4

THE QUR'AN, THE WORD OF GOD

Mustansir Mir

Like the scriptures of Judaism and Christianity, the Qur'an, the scripture of Islam, is considered sacred by those who believe in it as the Word of God. According to Muslim belief, God revealed the Qur'an to Muhammad (570–632 CE), the Arabian Prophet of Islam, in small and large portions over a period of about 22 years. About the size of the New Testament, the Qur'an has been preserved in Arabic, the language in which it was originally revealed. And while the Qur'an calls the variety of languages spoken by humankind as "one of the signs" of God (Qur'an 30:22), there is no doubt that Arabic, being the vehicle of the Word of God, has always enjoyed special importance in both the Islamic religion and the Islamic civilization.[1]

THE MEANING OF THE TERM, *QUR'AN*

The word *Qur'an* means both "recitation" and "reading": it is read from a text as well as recited from memory. These twin meanings carry a significance that may not be readily apparent. Today, the word *Qur'an* brings to mind a printed copy of the Qur'an. At its inception, however, the Qur'an was essentially an oral communication. But soon it was proclaimed a book. In the history of Arabia, in fact, the Qur'an was the first discourse self-consciously to call itself a book. It was only after the revelation of the Qur'an as a book that the arts of reading and writing were seriously cultivated in Arabia, this cultivation leading, relatively quickly, to a transformation of a largely oral culture into a literate one. Since the Qur'an was the Word of God, everything about it was viewed as significant—its vocabulary, its grammar, its law, its theology, and its ethics—and had to be studied with the utmost reverence and diligence. Study of the Qur'an led to the production of commentaries on the Qur'an. In this way, the science of *tafsir*, or Qur'anic exegesis, was born. But this only was one of the many sciences, or disciplines of knowledge, to which the study of the Qur'an gave rise.

A close review of Islamic intellectual history would show that practically all of the Islamic sciences are, in one way or another, grounded in the Qur'an.

In Arabic, the name *Qur'an* has the definite article prefixed to it: *al-Qur'an*. This prefix implies that the Qur'an is essential reading, that it provides crucial guidance for life, and that its message may be ignored or neglected only at one's own peril.

It is important to note a few of the many names the Qur'an uses for self-designation. To begin with, the phrase *Kalam Allah* (Qur'an 9:6; 48:15), meaning "the Word or Speech of God," sets the Qur'an apart from all other speech, even from the speech of prophets, including that of Muhammad, the bearer of the Qur'an. The name *Tanzil* (Qur'an 26:192), "sending down," simultaneously connotes (1) descent of something exalted and (2) gradual dispensation. In other words, the Qur'an is exalted Divine speech that was dispensed in portions over many years, such that it may be easy for people to understand, digest, and put it into practice. The name *Furqan* (Qur'an 25:1) means, "that which sifts, divides, differentiates." That is, the Qur'an clearly distinguishes between truth and falsehood, between right and wrong, so that it can be relied on as a safe guide. The name *Dhikr* (Qur'an 43:44) means "reminder." The Qur'an is a scripture that reminds human beings, on the one hand, of the verities that they are instinctively aware of but may have forgotten through worldly involvements and, on the other hand, of the truths presented by the previous messengers—truths forgotten or consigned to neglect in the course of time. Among the other names used for the Qur'an are *Huda* (Qur'an 27:77), "guidance," that which points out and leads to the right destination; *Nur* (Qur'an 4:174), "light," that which dispels the darkness of misguidance, causing the truth to shine forth brightly; *Hikma* (Qur'an 17:39), "wisdom;" and *Rahma* (Qur'an 27:77), "mercy." These and other names of the Qur'an not only represent the Qur'an's self-understanding but may also serve as clues and suggestions for reading the Qur'an in certain ways.

THE ORGANIZATION OF THE QUR'AN

The Qur'an has 114 chapters and over 6,000 verses. The word for "chapter" is *sura*, which literally means "an enclosing wall," like a wall that encloses a city. As such, the name signifies that each chapter of the Qur'an is like an enclosure in which reside the inhabitants—namely, the verses—that belong in it. Already one can see that the word *Sura* suggests that some kind of kinship or close relationship exists among the verses of a given chapter of the Qur'an, a suggestion that we will examine further a little later. The word for "verse" is *Aya*, which literally means "sign." It is translated as "verse" when it refers to a statement, or a portion of a statement, in the Qur'an.

Thus, the verses of the Qur'an are signs that point to certain truths and realities, God Himself being the greatest truth and the greatest reality.

The chapters of the Qur'an vary greatly in length. The shortest *suras* (103, 108, and 110) consist of three verses, the longest *sura* (2) runs to 286 verses, and many are medium sized. The length of verses also varies considerably.

In printed copies of the Qur'an, each chapter is identified as having been revealed either in the city of Mecca or in the city of Medina and is, accordingly, known as Meccan or Medinan. These designations carry more than just geographical significance. For the first 13 years of his prophetic ministry, Muhammad was in Mecca. It was here that he gained his first converts. But in Mecca, Muhammad and his followers were a minority—often a persecuted minority. The Meccan revelations deal with matters of faith, such as the fundamentals of Islamic dogma and the principles of ethics. In the last 10 years of his prophetic ministry, Muhammad was in Medina, to which he and his followers had emigrated in 622 CE. In Medina, the Muslims acquired a position of power and founded the first Islamic state. Reflecting the changed situation, the Medinan revelations deal with the political, social, and economic aspects of Muslim life. Thus, the designation "Meccan" informs the reader that a *sura* is principally concerned with subjects like faith and ethics, whereas the designation "Medinan" indicates that a *sura* is likely to focus on matters of social organization. However, in the larger scheme of Qur'anic thought, the Meccan versus Medinan distinction often breaks down. Medinan *suras* frequently take up the themes of faith and ethics, using them as a base for presenting legislative verses, and the Meccan *suras* often point ahead in the direction of Medina. Partly because of such a relationship between the two types of *suras*, Meccan *suras* sometimes contain verses revealed in the Medinan period and vice versa.

THE QUR'AN AS REVELATION

The Muslim understanding of the Qur'an as the Word of God is the basis of the Islamic view of revelation. The Arabic word for revelation is *wahy*. As a revelation from God, *wahy* carries the sense of otherness—that is, it is an objective phenomenon. In other words, *wahy* is not the product of a Prophet's mind but is transmitted by a prophet from God without any alteration of form or meaning. On this view, the Qur'an is the Word of God, not the Word of Muhammad. Revelation (*wahy*) is to be distinguished from inspiration (*ilham*). In Islamic dogma, prophets are believed to be in a general state of inspiration. Thus, when they speak in their "official"—that is to say, prophetic—capacity, their utterances have an authoritative character. Still, such utterances are to be distinguished from the Divine Word, which a prophet himself would clearly identify as divine and not his own and whose conduit he would declare himself to be.

The notion of revelation has had some ramifications in Islamic religious history; we will note two of them. First, since the Qur'an is the Word of God in respect of form no less than of meaning, the language of the Qur'an, being the language of God, is considered matchless. Islamic theology develops this idea into the doctrine of the inimitability of the Qur'an (*I'jaz al-Qur'an*). A number of Qur'anic verses challenge the Qur'an's opponents to produce something like the Qur'an if they deny its divine origin (Qur'an 2:23; 11:13; 17:88; 52:33–34). Muslim theologians take this challenge—which, they claim, has never been met in history—as proof of the Qur'an's divine origin. Second, since the language of the Qur'an is divine, a translation of the Qur'an by human beings is not the Qur'an. Accordingly, only the Arabic Qur'an may be recited in formal prayers, and only one who memorizes part or all of the Arabic Qur'an can be said to have memorized the Qur'an. This view of the Arabic Qur'an also explains why, historically, Muslims have been reluctant to translate their scripture and why a vibrant tradition of Qur'an translation—comparable to that of Bible translation, for example—has only developed recently in Islam. Even today, many Muslims have a certain distrust of the translated Qur'an.

THE COMPILATION OF THE QUR'AN

The traditional account of the compilation of the Qur'an has been criticized in some quarters of Western scholarship. But so far, this criticism has neither dislodged the Muslim account from its position nor led to the construction of a satisfactory alternative view. Under the circumstances, it would be reasonable to speak of the traditional account as being broadly valid.

According to this account, the compilation of the Qur'an occurred in three stages. The First Compilation was made during the Prophet Muhammad's lifetime. When a revelation came to Muhammad, it was, on the one hand, avidly memorized by Muslims and, on the other hand, written down in a certain sequence by designated scribes under the Prophet's instructions. Since the writing materials then available were rudimentary—parchment, thin flat stones, or animal shoulder bones—not all written records could be maintained in the new and continually evolving order of compilation. Muslims who had some or all of these records possessed them in different arrangements, although they often knew the order in which the Prophet intended those records to be arranged.

The First Compilation of the Qur'an aimed at no more than bringing into existence a written record of the Qur'an. This was because the main way for preserving the Qur'an was still memorization. There is evidence that Muslims knew the proper order of the Qur'anic revelations, but it was physically not possible to induce that order among the numerous media on which the scripture had been inscribed. Circumstances soon necessitated the making of another compilation. The Second Compilation of the Qur'an was made in 633 CE, after the death of Muhammad and under the first caliph of Islam, Abu Bakr. During Abu Bakr's caliphate, several tribes revolted against Islam, and they had to be subdued by force of arms. In the wars that resulted, a large number of people who had memorized the Qur'an—and were known as Qur'an-readers—were killed. Some people became apprehensive that the First Compilation, given the variety of the media on which it was preserved, would not be adequate. Abu Bakr accepted the suggestion of some to prepare a compilation that differed from the first one only in respect of being more accessible by being written on more standardized media.

During the rule of the third caliph, 'Uthman (644–656 CE), this compilation was used to make the Third Compilation of the Qur'an. This Third Compilation produced the definitive copy of the Qur'an that is read by all Muslims today. The Caliph 'Uthman appointed a committee of noted companions of the Prophet Muhammad and memorizers of the Qur'an to resolve disputes about a handful of verses that some thought should belong to the Qur'an and others thought should be considered Hadith, statements of the Prophet Muhammad that did not come from God. After the Third Compilation was approved, copies of this so-called 'Uthman Scripture were sent to major cities of the Islamic world so that they might serve as master copies for people to use as standard reference texts. Today, most Muslim scholars hold that the arrangement of verses and *suras* in the Qur'an follow the arrangement that Muhammad himself approved under the guidance of the Angel Gabriel. Thus, both the text of the Qur'an and the present arrangement of its verses are considered to be sacrosanct.

THE GENRE OF THE QUR'AN

What type of a book is the Qur'an, and to what genre does it belong? Is it a book of history? The Qur'an does contain history, but it does not offer a detailed historical account, neither of the world nor of any nation or country. The Qur'an is selective in its use of history. For example, it talks about previous nations and prophets, but only in reference to the message it seeks to present. So, while it contains history, it cannot be called a book of history.

Is it a book of ethics? The Qur'an states and explains principles of ethical behavior and identifies the virtues it seeks to inculcate and the vices it wants people to shun, but it cannot be compared to a research work on ethics. One will not find in the Qur'an a statement and analysis of various theories of ethics. So, while the Qur'an has a definite ethical perspective, it cannot be called a book of ethics.

Is it a book of law? The Qur'an has many legal injunctions, and these bear upon criminal law, civil law, and even international law. But again, the Qur'an does not deal with the law in a systematic and comprehensive way. Hence, it cannot be called a book of law. We can similarly ask whether the Qur'an is a book of theology, metaphysics, and so on, reaching, in each case, the same conclusion. So, how do we classify the Qur'an?

The easiest way to describe the Qur'an is to call it what it calls itself—a Book of Guidance. The Qur'an purports to furnish human beings with the fundamental guidance they need to organize their lives in order to live successfully in this world and achieve salvation in the next. This is not to say that the Qur'an has no faith in human beings' ability to find their own guidance. Quite the contrary is true. Specific prescriptive material forms only a small part of the Qur'an, though general principles and guidelines abound in it. This is an important fact that suggests that, to a large extent, the Qur'an leaves human beings free to envision and plan their lives. The imposing body of medieval Islamic law actually proves this thesis, since this body of law represents but one possible instance of the construction of a legal–cultural system undertaken by distinguished Muslim minds in light of the guidance found in the Qur'an and in the Prophet's exemplary practice, called *Sunna*. This particular historical construction does not foreclose the possibility of Muslims engaging—with proper qualifications and preparation, of course—in a similar exercise today with a view to arriving at a new construction more responsive to present-day needs. This explains why, from time to time in Islamic history, one hears the call to return to pristine Islam, such a call representing dissatisfaction with the legal and other structures that are presumed to have lost some or much of their utility after having served Muslim societies well for a long time.

THEMES OF THE QUR'AN

The Qur'an deals with a limited number of themes, but it foregrounds them again and again, in a variety of situations and from different angles. The major themes of the Qur'an can be summed up under three headings: faith, ritual, and conduct.

Faith

The most fundamental element of the Islamic faith is monotheism, the belief that there is but one God. *Sura* 102, which is called The *Sura* of Sincerity, is probably the Qur'an's most important statement of monotheism: "Say: He—God—is Uniquely One. God is the Refuge. He did not beget and He was not begotten. And He has no peers."

The so-called Throne Verse (Qur'an 2:255) is also an important statement of Islamic monotheism:

> God—there is no god but He, the Living, the Great Sustainer. He is overtaken neither by drowsiness nor by sleep. To Him belongs all that is in the heavens and the earth. Who can intercede with Him except by His leave? He knows what is in front of them and what is behind them. And they cannot encompass any part of His knowledge—except what He should wish. His Throne extends over the heavens and the earth, and guarding them does not fatigue Him. He is the Exalted, the Great.

The God of the Qur'an has many attributes. He is the creator of the universe, which He administers. He is omnipotent, omniscient, omnipresent, forgiving, just, and merciful. The most important of all of God's attributes is His mercifulness: He is quick to forgive and slow to anger. Those who repent sincerely are not only forgiven but their bad deeds are also converted into good deeds (Qur'an 25:70).

The very frequent references to God in the Qur'an might suggest that the Qur'an does nothing but talk about God—that it is theocentric. But a deeper look will reveal that the Qur'an is equally concerned with human beings and their destiny. The commandments, ethical injunctions, legal stipulations, historical accounts—in brief, nearly everything in the Qur'an makes a direct or indirect, but in every case definite, reference to the human situation, with the avowed ultimate goal of improving that situation.

Another important element of the Islamic faith is prophecy. God provides guidance to humankind through chosen individuals, called prophets, who not only convey that guidance but also exemplify it in their lives, so that both the theoretical and the practical aspects of that guidance are presented before the nations to whom those prophets have been sent. According to the Qur'an, the prophets of all ages present the same essential message. This unity of message furnishes a conceptual basis for regarding, first, the prophets as members of a single brotherhood and, second, their nations as segments of a worldwide human community. The Qur'an thus uses the notion of the unity of the prophets' message to reinforce the idea of a common humanity. This idea is further reinforced by the Qur'anic assertion that God has sent messengers among all the nations of the world (Qur'an 35:24). There is therefore no reason to regard the Middle East as the exclusive venue of prophecy. In Islam, Adam is the first prophet and Muhammad is the last.

The Qur'an presents the afterlife as a necessary complement to earthly life. According to the Qur'an, this world is not a place where complete recompense for good or evil actions is meted out. There is, thus, a need for another place where full, unbiased, and swift recompense for all actions can be given, and this need is satisfied by the Hereafter.

Ritual

The Qur'an speaks of all the four main Islamic rituals—prayer (*Salat*), mandatory almsgiving (*Zakat*), fasting (*Sawm*), and pilgrimage (*Hajj*). It gives some details about each, but the full elaboration of the rituals, as of many other matters, is left to the *Sunna,* the Way of the Prophet Muhammad. By requiring believers to devote time, energy, and money to the performance of these rituals, the Qur'an seeks to strengthen their commitment and keep them rightly oriented. The rituals of Islam have a strong social dimension; that is, they are intended to create and reinforce the bonds that ought to exist among members of a believing community. For example, the *Zakat* Alms Tax, which is one of several steps the Qur'an takes to ensure a wider distribution of wealth in society, helps alleviate economic deprivation. The annual pilgrimage to the Ka'ba and the Sacred Mosque of Mecca, which is performed together by hundreds of thousands of people from all over the world, brings home the point that race, color, language, and other such social markers are irrelevant for the purpose of defining the essential humanity of human beings.

Conduct

The Qur'an contains injunctions about legal, political, and social matters. It seeks to organize family life by laying down rules for marriage and divorce (Qur'an 2:221, 229–237, 240–241; 4:3, 19–25, 35, 128–129; 5:5; 24:3, 32), for dividing a deceased person's property (Qur'an 2:180, 4:7–9, 11–12, 176), and for making loan transactions (Qur'an 2:282). It distinguishes between lawful food and unlawful food (Qur'an 2:168, 172–173; 5:3–5; 6:118–119, 121, 145–146; 16:114–116), decrees punishments for certain offenses (Qur'an 5:38; 17:32; 24:2–9), and provides basic guidelines for running the Muslim body politic (Qur'an 4:59; 42:38). It advises kind treatment of parents (Qur'an 17:23; 29:8; 31:14; 46:15), promotes virtues like forbearance and repaying good for evil (Qur'an 23:96; 28:54; 41:34; 42:37, 40; 7:199), and forbids backbiting and calumny (Qur'an 24:4, 6–9). The ultimate goal of all such injunctions is to create ethically centered individuals, on the one hand, and to bring into existence an integrated and harmonious society, on the other. The following verses contain a few of the Qur'anic injunctions concerning conduct:

> God commands us to deliver up trusts to those to whom they belong. And when you adjudicate between people, adjudicate with justice. It is a fine piece of advice that God gives us! Indeed, God is Keen of Hearing, Very Watchful.

(Qur'an 4:58)

You will never attain piety until you spend of what you love. And anything you spend of—God has full knowledge of it.

(Qur'an 3:92)

Say: Come, I shall recite what God has made unlawful for you: That you shall not associate anything with Him and be good to your parents. Do not kill your children from considerations of poverty. We give sustenance to you and to them. Do not approach immoral acts, the obvious one among them and the hidden ones. Do not kill a soul whom God has declared unlawful to kill—except with justification. This is what He has advised you of, that you may have understanding. Do not approach the orphan's property—except in a way that is best—until he should reach full maturity. Give full measure and weight, with fairness. We do not obligate a person except to the extent of his capacity. When you speak, be just—even if [the person] should be a relative. And fulfill the commitment with God. This is what He has advised you of, that you may take remembrance.

(Qur'an 6:151–152)

The believers are brothers, so make peace between your two brothers. And have fear of God, that you may be shown mercy. O you who believe, let not one group of people make fun of another—it is possible that they are better than them—or women, of women—it is possible that they are better than them. And do not make cutting remarks about yourselves[2] or call one another names. How bad is the very word "transgression" after belief! And those who do not repent, they, and they alone, are the unjust. O you, who believe, shun most conjecture. Indeed, some conjecture is sin. And do not pry. Do not backbite one another: Would any of you like to eat the flesh of his dead brother?[3] You would detest it! And have fear of God. Indeed, God is Most Forgiving, Very Merciful.

(Qur'an 49:10–12)

THE STRUCTURE OF THE QUR'AN

Modern readers generally find the Qur'an to be a difficult book to navigate. Perhaps what troubles them most is the seeming lack of structure in the Qur'an. One sometimes gets the impression that the Qur'an moves haphazardly from one subject to another, hardly offering a sustained treatment of a given subject and without explaining why the frequent change of subjects takes place. That the Qur'an is unlike most books is soon noticed by readers, who remain puzzled as to why the Qur'an is—to borrow a word that Western scholars often use to describe it—"disjointed."

A few classical scholars in fact discussed the structure of the Qur'an, but its extensive treatment belongs in the modern period. While a detailed examination of the subject is not possible here, the following observations will suggest that there is a method, both to the sequence of the verses in a given *sura* and to the sequence of the *suras* in the Qur'an, as it has come down to us.

First, many of the Qur'anic *suras*, especially the short *suras* toward the end of the Qur'an, obviously are unities. For example, the last 35 *suras* (*Suras* 80–114) of the Qur'an, ranging from 3 to 46 verses, each seem to offer a coherent treatment of one or more themes. In many medium-sized *suras* too, the general drift of the discourse is easily noticed, even if the relationship between some of the verses or passages is not fully clear.

Second, certain themes are often grouped together in the Qur'an. For example, the same Qur'anic passage may discuss the need to protect human life and the need to protect property. *Sura* 4:29 of the Qur'an reads: "O you who believe, do not devour one another's wealth unjustly—except that it take the form of commerce, with your mutual consent. And do not kill yourselves (that is, one another). Indeed, God is very kind to you." *Sura* 2:178–182 lays down the law of retaliation for murder and, at the same time, urges that the bequest of a deceased person be executed without any wrongful alteration of the terms of the bequest.

Third, a brief statement in one *sura* sometimes finds elaboration in the following *sura*. For example, *Sura* 25 of the Qur'an (*al-Furqan*, "The Criterion") makes a general reference to previous nations' rejection of the prophets who were sent to them and cites the names of a few such prophets. Verses 35–44 open with a reference to Moses, who, according to the Qur'an, was sent to prophesy to Pharaoh and his people. The following *sura*, *Sura* 26 (*al-Shu'ara'*, "The Poets"), provides details of the rejection of prophets mentioned in *Sura* 25, citing incidents from the lives of the prophets mentioned in the previous *sura* and also from the lives of a few other prophets not mentioned in that *sura*.

Fourth, in many cases, one *sura* picks up the theme on which the preceding *sura* ends. For example, the concluding verses of *Sura* 22 (*al-Hajj*, "The Pilgrimage") enjoin Muslims to bear witness to the peoples of the world and, to that end, to discipline themselves by carrying out such religious obligations as performance of the daily prayers and payment of the *Zakat* Tax. The opening verses of *Sura* 23 (*al-Mu'minun*, "The Believers") speak of the obligations that believers must perform; these obligations include the daily prayers and the *Zakat* tax, mentioned in *Sura* 22. Similarly, *Sura* 105 (*al-Fil*, "The Elephant") speaks of God's protection of the sanctuary of the Ka'ba in Mecca against the invading army of the Yemenite ruler Abraha. *Sura* 106 (*Quraysh*, "The Tribe of Quraysh") says that the Quraysh, the tribe of Mecca's idolatrous rulers, ought to worship Allah, the only true deity. This is because they owe their affluence and prestige to their custodianship of the Ka'ba, which, as the preceding *sura* says, God protected against a major attack.

The foregoing discussion underscores the need to revisit the charge of disconnectedness that is often made against the Qur'an. Two more points need to be made. First, a main thing to consider in studying the structure of the

Qur'an is the living context of the Qur'an. The Qur'an was not revealed in a vacuum, but in a live setting composed of a wide variety of elements. The Qur'an, delivered by the Prophet Muhammad in an oral situation, addressed supporters, opponents, and doubters at the same time; it consoled the Prophet, replied to his critics, and counseled the believers; it recounted past history, commented on recent events, and charted a course for the future. Thus, for example, while addressing the believers, the Qur'an may suddenly and without giving any warning start addressing the disbelievers, for they too form part of the Qur'an's audience. Such sudden shifts of address may be perplexing to readers unfamiliar with the presumption one has to make of a live and diverse audience of the Qur'an. Second, the Qur'an, following the style of Classical Arabic, does not usually employ the transitional expressions on which modern readers rely so heavily for establishing links between the parts of a discourse. Words and phrases such as "therefore," "consequently," "however," "in view of the above," and "on a different note," which are important external aids for connecting parts of a talk or a piece of writing, are often skipped in Classical Arabic, the listener or reader being supposed to supply them mentally.

THE STYLE OF THE QUR'AN

The language and style of the Qur'an are, in many respects, akin to the language and style of pre-Islamic Arabic literature—or, more specifically, of Arabic poetry. The vocabulary and style of the Qur'an, however, are much simpler than those of pre-Islamic poetry, and, as such, are more accessible to a larger audience. In the Qur'an, as in pre-Islamic poetry, there is abundant use of imagery, and so similes, metaphors, and parables are frequently employed. Strictly speaking, the language of the Qur'an is neither prose nor poetry, although it has elements of both. The term "rhymed prose" (saj' in Arabic) is often used to describe the Qur'an's language, which, as a rule, is also quite terse.

Along with the distinction they make with regard to subject matter, scholars often make a stylistic distinction between the Meccan *suras,* which are more poetic, and the Medinan *suras,* which are more discursive and matter-of-fact. The following passage from the Meccan *Surat al-Naba'* ("The Tidings," 78:1–17) provides an example of this. Arguing from the principle that privilege entails responsibility, this *sura* says that nature is a source of blessings for human beings, who will be asked, on Judgment Day, whether they showed gratitude to God for such blessings:

What are they querying one another about?
About the Momentous News (of the Final Hour)
In regard to which they are of different opinions.
Certainly not! They will soon find out.

Again, certainly not! They will soon find out.
Have We not made the earth a cradle
And the mountains stakes?
And We created you in pairs,
And We made your sleep a comfort,
And We made the night a garment,
And We made the day a time for earning a livelihood,
And We made, above you, seven Firm Ones (that is, the seven heavens),
And We installed a blazing lamp,
And We sent down, from the wringing wet ones (the clouds), streaming water,
That We may cause to grow, by means of it, grains and vegetables
And dense gardens.
Indeed, the Day of Decision is an appointed time.

Now let us look at a passage from the Medinan *Surat al-Ma'ida* ("The Table Spread," 5:1–3). These verses, which refer to certain rituals of the Hajj pilgrimage, urge the believers to fulfill their obligations:

O you who believe, fulfill your contracts. Made lawful for you are animals of the type of cattle—except that which is being recited to you—without making hunted game lawful while you are in a state of sanctity. O you who believe, do not desecrate any of the symbols of God: the sacred months, the sacrificial offerings, the collared animals, or those intending to go to the Sacred House, seeking as they do bounty from their Lord and His pleasure. And when you leave the state of sanctity, then you may hunt. Let not the enmity of a group of people induce you—on account of their having kept you from the Sacred Mosque—to commit aggression. Cooperate in piety and Godfearingness, but do not cooperate in sin and aggression. And have fear of God. Indeed, God is swift in punishment. Made unlawful for you are carrion, blood, the flesh of the pig, that over which is taken the name of someone other than God, that which is strangled to death, that which receives a fatal blow, that which has fallen to its death, that which is butted to death, and that which predators have eaten of—except that which you have properly slaughtered—and that which is immolated at altars; and that you should take portions by means of casting arrows. This is a sinful transgression. Today, those who have disbelieved have despaired of your religion, so do not fear them, but fear Me. Today, I have perfected your religion for you, I have completed my blessing upon you, and I have approved of Islam as your religion. So, toward the one who is compelled in extreme hunger—but without having any inclination toward sin—God is Very Forgiving, Very Merciful.

The language of the Qur'an has a notable ring of Divine authority. *Allah,* the Arabic word for God, occurs about 2,700 times in the Qur'an, often several times on every page. This means that God has, literally, a ubiquitous presence in the pages of the Qur'an—a linguistic counterpart, one might say, of the theological doctrine of Divine omnipresence. Furthermore, even though the Qur'an quotes many speakers—including both good figures like Abraham, Moses, and Jesus and evil figures like Satan and Pharaoh—the

entire Qur'an is believed by Muslims to be the Speech of God, and, therefore, technically, God is the only speaker in the Qur'an. The God of the
Qur'an sometimes speaks in the first person—in the singular or in the plural
(in the latter case, it is the plural of majesty rather than the numerical plural)—and sometimes in the third person. But always it is in an authoritative
voice that is unmistakable, whether that voice describes, explicates, analyzes,
comments, praises, chides, promises, threatens, foretells, or reminds. This
voice contributes in no small way to creating solemnity, which is a major
characteristic of the Islamic scripture.

The best guide to the meaning of the Qur'an is the Qur'an itself. As has
been noted above, the Qur'an returns to its main themes again and again.
In doing so, however, it usually makes variations on the themes, approaching
them from somewhat different angles, furnishing more details where only a
little was supplied before, responding to certain issues that might have arisen
from an earlier account, or citing a parable to illustrate or reinforce a point
already made. Very often, the Qur'an breaks up a story—that of a prophet
or a previous nation, for example—into several portions and presents one
portion of it in one *sura*, another in a second *sura*, and so on. Only that portion of a story that is relevant to a theme under discussion in a *sura* will be
presented in that *sura*. Consequently, a full understanding of the story would
require that the various parts of the story be put together in a logical
sequence. Studying one part of the Qur'an, therefore, necessarily involves
studying other parts of it.

The importance of studying Classical Arabic for understanding and interpreting the Qur'an has already been hinted at. The prime source of the Arabic of the Qur'an is pre-Islamic Arabic poetry, a deep study of which yields
insights into the vocabulary, idioms, images, and structures that form the
background to the language of the Qur'an. Also important for Qur'anic
interpretation is knowledge of the sayings and conduct of Muhammad, such
knowledge being gained through the body of Prophetic reports known as
Hadith (literally, "event," "news," or "report"), which, for the sake of con-
venience, we may call the Word of Muhammad. *Hadith* is especially useful for
the explication of the legal and ethical content of the Qur'an. As one would
expect, a vast amount of exegetical and other types of material on the Qur'an
exists in Islamic tradition and is continuously being augmented. It goes without saying that a sound knowledge of this scholarly tradition is key to understanding the Qur'an at more than a superficial level.

The foregoing discussion should not be taken to imply that the Qur'an is a
closed book, in the sense that only a select few have the right to interpret it.
Since there is no priesthood in Islam, the door of Qur'anic interpretation is,
theoretically, open to anyone who brings the necessary qualifications to the
task. Today, most Muslims would agree on the need for a fresh and creative
interpretation of the Qur'an, but such interpretation will have credibility only
if it is authentic and responsible.

The Qur'an occupies an important place in the lives of Muslims. It has given rise to certain artistic disciplines, notably calligraphy and Qur'an chanting. The walls and arches of many mosques in the Muslim world are adorned by beautifully inscribed Qur'anic verses, and, even in this age of computers and printers, calligraphic copies of the Qur'an are readily available in Muslim countries. Qur'an chanting, or *tajwid*, is an art that may take a few years to perfect. Regularly held international *tajwid* competitions for men and women have enabled the public across the Muslim world to appreciate this art. In many Muslim countries, children learn to read the Qur'an at an early age. Reading the Qur'an at this stage means learning to read the Arabic script. Since the scripts of some Islamic languages are Arabic based, the ability to read the Arabic script of the Qur'an gives children, in certain cases, facility to read their own language. At any rate, early exposure to the Qur'an creates in children an attachment to the Holy Scripture and to the Isamic religion.

In the West, the field of Qur'anic studies has registered notable growth in the last two decades. In English and other languages, several new translations of the Qur'an have appeared, many scholarly works have been published, and popular expositions have not lagged behind. Still, one feels that this foundational text of Islam has not received the same attention that the political and social history of Islam has. Much exegetical material from the classical period is still in manuscript form, only a relatively small number of scholars are engaged in study of the Qur'an, and despite the production of several edited volumes—especially the *Encyclopaedia of the Qur'an*,[4] to which scholars from all over the world have contributed—close collaborative work between Muslim and Western scholars has yet to occur. However, the study of the Qur'an is likely to receive a boost from the continuing growth of the larger discipline of Islamic studies, and one can hope that the coming years will bring greater recognition of the importance of the Qur'an not only as a subject of interest in itself but also as a lived reality in Muslim life, thus necessitating study of that lived reality in all its variety.

NOTES

1. A short bibliography of works on the Qur'an may be provided here. For general introductory accounts, see Richard Bell, *Introduction to the Qur'an,* revised and enlarged by W. Montgomery Watt (Edinburgh: Edinburgh University Press, 1970), and Farid Esack, *The Qur'an: A Short Introduction* (Oxford: Oneworld Publications, 2002). On the textual history of the Qur'an, see M. M. Al-Azami, *The History of the Qur'anic Text from Revelation to Compilation: A Comparative Study with the Old and New Testaments* (Leicester: UK Islamic Academy, 2003). Two useful thematic studies of the Qur'an are Fazlur Rahman, *Major Themes of the Qur'an* (Minneapolis and Chicago: Bibliotheca Islamica, 1980), and Muhammad Abdel Haleem, *Understanding the Qur'an: Themes and Style* (London and New York: IB Tauris, 2001). See also Helmut Gätje, ed., *The Qur'an and Its Exegesis: Selected Texts with Classical*

and Modern Muslim Interpretations, translated by Alford T. Welch (Oxford: One-world, 1996; repr. 1976 Routledge edition). For the stylistic and literary aspects of the Qur'an, see, besides Abdel Haleem's above-quoted work, Issa J. Boullata, *Literary Structures of Religious Meaning in the Qur'an* (Richmond, Surrey, U.K.: Curzon Press, 2000). See also Mustansir Mir, "The Language of the Qur'an," in *The Black-well Companion to the Qur'an,* ed. Andrew Rippin (Oxford: Blackwell Books, forth-coming). Two relatively advanced studies of exegetical, historical, and other aspects of the Qur'an are *Approaches to the History of the Interpretation of the Qur'an,* ed. Andrew Rippin (Oxford: Clarendon Press, 1988), and G.R. Hawting and Abdul Kader A. Shareef, eds. *Approaches to the Qur'an* (London: Routledge, 1993). *The Encyclopaedia of the Qur'an,* ed. Jane Dammen McAuliffe (Leiden: E.J. Brill, 2001–2005) is an indispensable work for a wide variety of Qur'anic subjects. In the text above, I have given my own translations of the Qur'anic material cited.

2.   Since the Muslims are members of a well-knit brotherhood, those who make cutting remarks about other Muslims in effect make such remarks about themselves.

3.   The Arabs compared backbiting to eating the flesh of the victim, who was likened to a carcass that was being picked at by the predatory backbiter.

4.   See note 1 above.

5

Drunkenness of the Word

Daniel Abdal-Hayy Moore

Drunkenness of the Word, you ignite the nations
   as nothing else can, a flame of
     sculpted stars carried from
       arena to arena, whisper

made by a solitary singer in a vacant lot in the
spotlight of the full moon in his

uprise, rung by rung, from trashy mortality,
head dazed by successive different colors of halo
to the most celestial dimensions until,

eyes just at the level of vaporizing clouds,
he catches sight of his goal and is
transformed into a fixed aerial body

that comes back singing, and walks through the
marketplace buying a pound of figs, a dried fish,
   a trowelful of almonds, bunches of bananas and
   a pot-scraper made of wood-shavings
     somehow held together.

In the most windless place, in the shadow of the
   dunes of doom,
O Word made alive by our
   pronunciation of you
     unawares, you flower all of a sudden into

forests inhabited by prismatic birds whose
flight breaks light into the

primary colors and
   spreads their sheen on the
      broad leaves of our
   private pleas!

Word of Love, cry out of desperation,
   word half-spoken, the other half
      caught in the heart,
word like a groundhog checking the
   length of its shadow before fully
      emerging, song,
solitude's antique chorus
that, each time the lips form it,
is polished anew and
   emerges bronze and perfectly ticking
      with open face and
solid footing.

We are reversed in our lives
until the Word speaks us
and faces us forward
into the spray of the cascade of its
   meaning always coming toward us

from above sea-level where the Source of all
words and The Word itself

high atop a tower of Light
sends it down fully
propelled for the
   journey.

                                    8 Ramadan

NOTE

   This poem first appeared in Daniel Abdal-Hayy Moore, *The Ramadan Sonnets* (San Francisco and Bethesda, Maryland: Jusoor/City Lights Books, 1996). Reprinted from Jusoor/City Lights Books and republished in the Ecstatic Exchange Series. This poem is reproduced here by permission of the author.

6

ENCOUNTERING THE QUR'AN: CONTEXTS AND APPROACHES

James Winston Morris

Virtually nothing that one may encounter in the great high-cultural achievements of Islamic civilization, or within the hundreds of distinctive localized Muslim cultures, can be fully understood without a profound knowledge of the Qur'an and the multitude of ways it has been understood and interpreted. Indeed most of the Islamic humanities, in all their end-lessly creative and evolving manifestations, can be understood as efforts to communicate effectively and to translate into realized human form, the teachings and unique forms of the Arabic Qur'an. Against this vast historical panorama, the purpose of this chapter is more modest: to prepare interested lay readers, with access only to a single reliable English version of the Qur'an and to a few essential reference works, to begin to explore and appreciate those dimensions of the Arabic Qur'an that have so constantly shaped and colored the manifold forms of Islamic cultures and civilization.

The contexts, cautions, and practical guidelines that are briefly outlined in this chapter are based on several decades of accumulated experience in introducing the Qur'an to English-speaking audiences, primarily young uni-versity students interested in Religious Studies and different world-religious traditions. What this experience has repeatedly taught me is that the greatest obstacles to any serious appreciation of the Qur'an on its own terms and in traditional Islamic cultural contexts usually come from a shared body of unconscious, normally taken-for-granted cultural assumptions about the nature, language, and assumed uses of the translated English Bible (and hence of "scripture" in general). The unconscious assumptions that guide novice readers—and too often English translators of the Qur'an as well—are rooted in a set of very specific formative historical experiences and implicit concep-tions of religion that is shared by Anglo-Saxon (and mostly Protestant) cultures in North America and elsewhere. For the same reason, Muslim translators of the Qur'an into English have so far, almost without exception, continued to pay little attention to the "receiving" role of the relevant mentalities and to the assumptions of their non-Muslim audiences in the process of communication.[1]

The Arabic Qur'an is different in a number of fundamental ways from everything that non-Muslim English readers normally associate with reading "a book." Equally important, the Arabic Qur'an continues to be present and to function in the lives of the vast majority of Muslims—just as it has throughout the past millennium or more—in specific ways that are often strikingly different compared with English-speaking readers, who tend to associate with the normal approaches to the English Bible. For these reasons, I begin by briefly outlining some of the most important contexts in which the Arabic Qur'an remains present in the lives and experiences of Muslims everywhere. These contexts are normally private and familial (hence socially invisible) for Muslims in Western cultures, but they are often more public wherever Muslims are historically a majority or significant minority of the population. I then suggest ways in which students can begin to move from a reliable English translation of the Qur'an toward a deeper appreciation of the complex meanings actually conveyed by the original Arabic.

THE PRESENCE OF THE QUR'AN

The root meaning of the word *Qur'an*, as it has historically been understood, is "recitation," and the weight of historical evidence likewise suggests that the oral recitation of the revelations of the Qur'an, from the very beginning, formed an essential part of the liturgical acts of personal and communal prayers in Islam. This was certainly the primary context of use and transmission of the Qur'an prior to the subsequent efforts of recording, collection, codification, and the even longer evolution of the current forms of Arabic orthography. Hence the recited and *aural* presence of the Qur'an—whether in the ritual prayer or in a host of other contexts—has remained the primary way in which Muslims have initially encountered the Holy Book, whether or not they can actually understand and interpret the Arabic vocabulary of the Qur'an. This is true above all for non-Arabic-speaking Muslims, who have formed the great majority of Muslims throughout the world since at least the twelfth century of the Common Era.[2] Because this aural, quasi-musical dimension of the Qur'an as recitation is so fundamental, and since recordings of excellent Qur'an reciters are now readily available in all digital media and over the Internet, no one who can access good-quality recitations should begin to read an English translation of the Qur'an without first listening at length to a range of different reciters and forms of recitation.[3] I have repeatedly witnessed among students of many ages and cultural backgrounds that the immediate power and effectiveness of the properly recited Qur'an is palpable to anyone, often to the point of spontaneous tears, as the Qur'an itself notes (Qur'an 5:83).[4] For the beginning student otherwise limited to an English translation of the Qur'an, the awakened awareness of this immediately accessible, hauntingly memorable dimension of the Qur'an is a potent antidote to the repeated obstacles and misunderstandings faced by anyone who then goes on to explore those versions of the Qur'an that are so far available in English.

Hearing the Qur'an

Traditionally, a small but symbolically key portion of the Qur'an (either the *Basmalla* or *Surat al-Fatiha*)[5] is the first thing spoken into the ear of a newborn Muslim baby and the last thing heard by someone dying. This audible presence of the spoken or recited Qur'an carries on through the whole life cycle of ritual and liturgical occasions outlined below. However, the highly public nature of many of these liturgical occasions in predominantly Muslim cultures means that the recited Qur'an tends to become a virtually omnipresent public background even for everyday, nonliturgical life. This fact is true to an almost equal extent even in most non-Arabic Muslim areas of the world, from West Africa to Indonesia or the Hui Muslim neighborhoods of China's cities. Indeed, the recent mass availability of electronic and digital media has meant that recorded forms of the recited Qur'an are now almost universally accessible and audible anywhere one goes in the Islamic world: from public markets, a taxi driver's cassette or CD player, various portable media players, and dedicated television channels (now on local cable outlets in the West) to the selections of Qur'an recitation normally available on the airlines of every Muslim country. Thus, in recent years, the audible presence of the Arabic Qur'an has expanded far beyond its traditional liturgical contexts.

In addition, the centrality of the actual sounds and rhythms of the Qur'an is mirrored in diverse local forms of music, poetry, and rhythmic recitation that are often included under the central Qur'anic rubric of *dhikr*, the infinitely varied prayerful "recollection, remembrance and repetition" of the divine Reality. Forms of *dhikr* are included almost everywhere among the preeminent forms of the local Islamic humanities, both in popular and in more learned, elite contexts.[6] Whether in Arabic or in other Islamic languages such as Persian or Urdu, the richly innovative forms of spiritual music and poetry are inseparable from the constant archetypal inspirations—both symbolic and more concretely poetic and rhythmic—of the aural Qur'an, often in ways that are so self-evident that they remain virtually unconscious among the cultures concerned.

Seeing the Qur'an: The Sacred Presence of the Arabic Script

Throughout history, the assimilation of Islam within a new cultural or linguistic context has been marked by the practice of writing the local language in the sacred Arabic script of the Qur'an. This process has provided a kind of consonantal shorthand that has been adapted for more than 30 different languages. One of the bases of this phenomenon was the insistence of Muslim parents on creating locally adapted primary Qur'an schools (*maktab*) or tutoring facilities for very young children (primary age or even younger). These schools provided an initiation into the recitation of at least the minimal number of Qur'anic verses needed to perform the ritual prayers, along with some basic skills in writing and recognizing the sacred Arabic text. This initiation normally occurred at an age before what were, until very recently, the demanding and expensive processes of formal instruction and full literacy in Qur'anic Arabic or the written forms of the local vernacular languages.[7] Thus, in many areas outside of the Arab world, the recent introduction of alternative (Romanized or Cyrillic) alphabets by colonial or modern reformist powers, or even the outright suppression of formal Islamic education under Communist regimes, has gone hand-in-hand with the elimination of this once widespread proto-literacy in the basic elements of Qur'anic Arabic.

Despite these negative developments, the visual presence of the Arabic sacred alphabet of the Qur'an has remained important everywhere Muslims live. Some of the most familiar public manifestations of Qur'anic Arabic are in architectural settings, since most public buildings were funded by religious foundations until very recent times. Mosques, schools, tombs, shrines, hospitals, kitchens for the poor, and places of pilgrimage are filled with calligraphy and tiled versions of the divine names, invocations, and passages of the Qur'an. The same visual and symbolic imagery is also reflected, in tribal and domestic contexts, in prayer rugs and other carpets and textile arts. At a deeper and often more religiously significant level, the visual and symbolic (including literary) iconography of the traditional Islamic humanities is thoroughly pervaded by calligraphy and other types of Qur'anic symbolism.

Of course, Western artistic and literary traditions have also been shaped by equally wide-ranging Biblical influences. However, the Qur'anic equivalents of these manifestations, and their complex historical pathways of creativity and transformation, are usually invisible to non-Muslim (and unfortunately, even to many Western-educated Muslim) viewers. To take only one example: the colors of the four Qur'anic elements, which are inseparable from their symbolic eschatological and metaphysical associations in the Qur'an, have often implicitly determined the color schemes of religious structures, paintings, calligraphy, and other visual arts throughout the Islamic world. Hence, one encounters the relative rarity of red (symbolizing the infernal Fire), and the corresponding insistence on the blue of the spiritual heavens, or the even more pervasive presence of green, associated with the Water of Life/Spirit/

Prophethood and the complex spiritual symbolism of vegetation and the eschatological Gardens and streams repeatedly mentioned in the Qur'an. Likewise, no Muslim familiar with the Qur'an can encounter a prayer-niche or the lamps of any mosque without experiencing an immediate resonance with the elaborate metaphysical imagery of the famous Light Verses of the Qur'an (Qur'an 24:35–38).

Another quasi-liturgical motif is the importance of Arabic calligraphy across all Muslim cultures. This constitutes the most revered form of the visual arts, so that the practice of calligraphy may become a demanding spiritual discipline that begins in childhood and unfolds throughout life. The sacred role of Arabic calligraphy also includes, by extension, the similarly central role (both artistically and economically) of the "arts of the book" in Islam, from gilding, paper-making, marbling, and leather-working to the actual masterpieces of Islamicate poetry and miniature painting that such arts help communicate and illuminate. Much the same is true, on an even wider scale, of the role of Arabic script in the textile arts, which have often been economically central to premodern cultures and economies, or in the related arts of jewelry, metalworking, and glass.

In addition to the centrality of the Arabic script wherever it is still used as the script for official national languages, the script of the Qur'an is a personal marker of religious identity in private and familial contexts. This begins with the prominent display in most Muslim homes of framed calligraphy of the Qur'an, as well as divine names, prayers, or other distinctive religious images (the Ka'ba in Mecca, and so on), along with the special reverence accorded to familial copies of the Qur'an. On an even more private and intimate level, Muslims in many parts of the world wear amulets engraved with short lines or verses of the Qur'an—especially the *Basmalla*, the *Fatiha*, or the Throne Verse (Qur'an 2:255)—or seal rings engraved with the shorter Qur'anic phrases or the names of key sacred figures, or they carry prayer beads often embossed with divine names or similar Qur'anic expressions. Yet again, none of these omnipresent visual reflections of the Arabic Qur'an, in either their spiritual–aesthetic, symbolic, or social dimensions, are tied to or dependent upon prior literary knowledge of the Qur'an and its meanings.

Experiencing the Qur'an: Ritual and Liturgical Contexts

The liturgical presence of the Qur'an, which combines its near-universal aural and visual presence with active recitation in various forms of prayer and divine remembrance, is central to the three basic ritual cycles shared by virtually all forms of Islam, as well as to many other aspects of everyday life. These ritual cycles include the life cycle from birth to death, the daily individual cycle of the various forms of prayer (necessarily involving Qur'anic Arabic), and the annual public cycle of holy days and months, which has significant local and sectarian variations. In each of these situations, prior to the recent availability of printed Qur'anic texts[8] and the even more recent invention of sound recording, there was a virtually universal need—already emphasized in the earliest Hadith and historical accounts—for highly trained, spiritually effective local reciters of the Qur'an, as well as for widespread memorization of the text, given the rarity of handwritten texts in premodern times. Thus, one finds throughout the Muslim world elaborate traditional systems for training in memorization, as well as even more complex training institutions and rules governing the formal recitation of the Qur'an.[9]

In traditional and long-standing Muslim cultures, however, the presence of the Arabic Qur'an is most immediately visible not in what we usually think of as formally religious rituals but in a host of smaller customary activities that are so omnipresent as to be virtually automatic and unconscious. These include the everyday usage of the cautionary phrase "if God wills" (*In sha' Allah,* based on a Qur'anic injunction) after any reference to future actions or eventualities, the even more widespread recitation of the *Basmalla* (the formula "In the Name of God, the All-Loving, the All-Compassionate" which opens all but one of the chapters of the Qur'an) or of the opening *Surat al-Fatiha* (Qur'an 1:1–7) before eating or initiating virtually any action, the recitation of the *Fatiha* or another prayer formula when passing by places of burial, the automatic recitation of standard Qur'anically based blessings after any mention of Muhammad or other prophets and holy figures, or the widespread use of prayer beads for recitation of Qur'anic formulae of the divine names and other invocations. One could also include in this category rules for the specially reverential treatment accorded to the written Arabic text (*mushaf*) of the Qur'an, both in public places and within the home. The text of the Qur'an is normally accorded a place of high dignity, often with a distinctive reading-stand, and should never be touched or opened without special ablutions, intentions, and purification, as in the standard preparations for the ritual prayer itself.

In terms of the major rituals shared across most Muslim cultures and sects, the recitation of the Qur'an—either in elaborate public, communal forms in more traditional cultures or in more private or familial forms in Western settings—is central to many rituals associated with the Muslim life cycle. Rituals involving recitation of the Qur'an lead from birth through name giving, circumcision, the daily practice of ritual prayer, betrothal and marriage, and grave illness and death, with special prayers associated with funeral rituals. The performance of the daily cycle of five ritual prayers presupposes the memorization and faultless recitation of at least several shorter Suras of the Qur'an, as well as related ritual formulae of blessings, thanks, and petitionary prayer also in Qur'anic Arabic. Thus, a child is considered sufficiently responsible to begin performing the daily prayers only when she can correctly memorize a sufficient number of Qur'anic passages.

Although the individual recitation of this Qur'anic repertoire might take on a somewhat routine character within the daily performance of the ritual prayers, the communal performance of the prayer, whether at the Friday noon prayer or in other group settings, provides occasions when the prayer leader (*imam*) will expose the worshipper to other, less familiar sections of the Qur'an. In addition, the rules of the ritual prayer itself allow each individual to expand and include passages of the Qur'an almost indefinitely. One result of this constantly expanding, lifelong process of familiarization and recollection of the Qur'an is that the Muslim is gradually led and prepared to discover—often in the very process of praying itself—the spiritual connections between the experiences of one's own life and the corresponding lessons and insights conveyed by verses of the Qur'an. Significantly, both the individual verses of the Qur'an and the nearly infinite phenomena of creation, including all human experience, are described in the Qur'an by the same Arabic term: *ayat,* or "divine Signs." As one can see when visiting mosques almost anywhere in the world, the completion of the ritual prayer is often the prelude to individual or group recitation of traditional Arabic litanies (drawn from the Qur'an and the Prophetic sayings) of prayer and recollection, known as *dhikr.*

While Muslim societies all have important holy days and related ritual events in which Qur'anic recitation and prayer play an important role, the importance of the Qur'an is particularly heightened during the fasting month of Ramadan, which is closely associated in many Prophetic traditions with the revelation of the Qur'an itself. Thus, during the evenings of Ramadan, special *Tarawih* prayers and the public recitation of portions of the Qur'an are part of emotionally moving rituals. At the same time, Muslims are enjoined to make a special effort to read the entire text of the Qur'an—traditionally in the original Arabic, although very recently in translated versions—during the month of Ramadan. This period is typically devoted to heightened contemplation and withdrawal from the routines and distractions of normal daily life.

Cultural and Intellectual Dimensions: The Qur'an in the Religious Sciences and the Islamic Humanities

For more than a millennium, whenever Muslims have sought to understand the meaning and teachings of the Qur'an, they have not turned to translations, but to the study of the Arabic Qur'an itself. The demanding intellectual study of the Qur'an, whatever its original guiding motivations—whether legal, theological, spiritual, or political—has always been mediated. That is to say, such study has normally been embedded within a complex web of traditional interpretive perspectives and assumptions that are profoundly interrelated, even when particular traditions may articulate very different conclusions and notions of scriptural authority. Two essential, and necessarily complementary, dimensions have been associated with this ongoing mediating process: the inherited complex of the traditional Arabic religious sciences and the omnipresent, constantly evolving influence of locally adapted popular forms of the Islamic humanities. However, neither of these dimensions is readily accessible to nonspecialist Western students who approach the Qur'an through translations. Even more important, as intimated above, the parameters of these Islamic contextual and hermeneutic traditions rarely correspond to the assumptions today's Western-educated students normally have about the nature and expected uses of the Bible, or indeed of books and scriptures more generally.

To begin with, the serious intellectual study of the actual meanings of the Qur'an—in contrast to the different ritual contexts summarized above—presupposes, even for native Arabic speakers, years of dedicated study of the uniquely complex language and symbolic vocabulary of the Qur'an. This is a demanding process of familiarization with the text of the Qur'an that is quite different from rote memorization. As a result, scholarly preparation for actually understanding the Qur'an has for centuries been the preserve of a relatively small—usually urban and male—learned elite.[10] Even more important, this basic initiation into the intellectual study of the meanings and depths of the Qur'an has required, since the earliest Islamic centuries, the equally demanding mastery of a number of related preparatory and interpretive religious sciences requiring years of preparation. These essential contextual disciplines include the following: Qur'anic grammar and syntax, Arabic lexicography and philology, Qur'anic rhetoric (*balagha*), Prophetic Hadith, Islamic sacred and Prophetic history (*sira, ta'rikh,* and *qisas al-anbiya'*), specialized literatures illuminating the historical contexts of Qur'anic revelations (*asbab al-nuzul* and *tafsir*), dialectical theology (*kalam*), and the principles of jurisprudence (*usul al-fiqh*). Even today, reliable scholarly writing about the Qur'an and its interpretation necessarily presupposes an informed awareness of the structures, procedures, and sources of this historically accumulated body of related Arabic intellectual disciplines.

Because of these historical and intellectual factors, traditional Muslim cultures and their scholastic representatives, even today, have rarely admitted a religiously significant role for independent vernacular translations of the Arabic Qur'an. Just as important, one does not find any significant movement arguing for the sort of independent, highly individualized scriptural interpretation, based uniquely on such vernacular translations, that modern readers tend to take for granted when they think about religion. As any student of Islam quickly discovers, the locally operative forms of each Muslim's religious beliefs and practices have almost unimaginably complex and diverse historical roots and sources, and those actual religious realities can rarely be understood as somehow "dictated" by a particular verse or passage in a translated Qur'an.

Instead, the locally prevalent forms of Islam in a traditional Muslim setting normally reflect those Islamic humanities that have illuminated and elaborated, in a locally meaningful way, the central ethical and spiritual teachings of the Qur'an.[11] When we look more closely at the historical origins of the Islamic humanities, their most influential exponents were often highly learned scholars and poets who sought to communicate the essential teachings of the Qur'an and Hadith (as mediated by the traditional religious disciplines) to wider Muslim audiences living in extremely diverse linguistic and cultural settings. This recurrent creative sociocultural process of interpretive communication of the Qur'an is already well illustrated by the relationship between the Qur'an and the thousands of Prophetic teachings recorded in the collections of Hadith. Many of these sayings take the form of the Prophet's particular interpretation or concrete application of abstract, symbolic Qur'anic concepts in more accessible language or through memorable stories and imagery more directly meaningful for different questioners and audiences.

In short, although the traditional complex of Arabic religious sciences that earlier scholars developed to study and interpret the Qur'an necessarily remain the domain of a handful of intellectual specialists, the manifold expressions of the Islamic humanities have continued to provide other, often strikingly effective tools for conveying the meanings of the Qur'an to much wider popular audiences. Indeed, their spiritual, moral, and cultural effectiveness have been demonstrated over many centuries, especially through the complex creative passages from one Islamicate language or culture into new cultural and linguistic settings. So Western students who wish to grasp the ethical and spiritual dimensions of the Qur'an are often well advised to begin their study with such proven masterpieces of cross-cultural translation and communication as the readily available English translations of Jalal al-Din Rumi's *Masnavi,* Farid al-Din 'Attar's *Conference of the Birds,* and a rapidly expanding body of other forms of the Islamic humanities, including spiritual music and traditional visual arts. Such historically effective creative means of expressing and communicating the meanings of the Qur'an have been intimately shaped by many of the unique qualities of the language and symbolism of the Qur'an that are introduced below.

STUDYING THE QUR'AN IN ENGLISH

Students approaching the Qur'an in English have literally dozens of translations available now, with several new versions and related introductory studies appearing each year.[12] Such efforts of translation usually reflect a contrasting set of motives. Some seek to render more adequately the undeniably powerful beauty of the original Arabic Qur'an, with its unique magic of sound, imagery, and poetic rhythms.[13] Others seek to communicate what their translators consider the Qur'an's theological dimensions of meaning or right belief, whether through an emphasis on particular types of interpretation (sectarian, scientistic, or apologetic) or by incorporation of, for first-time readers, more of the complex dimensions of traditional historical and contextual scholarship discussed above.[14] Still others, like many contemporary Bible translators, strive to communicate something of the Qur'an in more popularly accessible, "easy-reading" narrative prose.

However, the suggestions, cautions, and interpretive guidelines suggested here relate to another, quite different and specifically pedagogical motive: How can students limited to the English language begin to discover the underlying meanings of the Arabic Qur'an? This kind of informed contextual understanding is indispensable for grasping the underlying connections between the unique structures of the Qur'an, on the one hand, and their subsequent interpretive unfolding throughout the two key dimensions of Islamic civilization we have just discussed, on the other hand: that is, the learned disciplines of the traditional Arabic religious sciences, and their endless creative manifestations in the Islamic humanities. This educational motive likewise reflects the pedagogically obstinate reality that the Arabic Qur'an itself is anything but easy reading, without even considering the further problems introduced by translation. At least as much as any other classical text a student is likely to encounter, the Qur'an is very challenging to understand—although the effort required to appreciate it is also revealing and rewarding, so long as its intrinsic difficulties and resulting interpretive potentials are openly recognized from the outset.

For this pedagogical purpose, there is so far no substitute for A. J. Arberry's *The Qur'an Interpreted,* despite the misunderstandings that are frequently generated by Arberry's recourse to quasi-Biblical (King James) English vocabulary. For study purposes, Hanna Kassis's *A Concordance of the Qur'an,* [15] provides an indispensable tool for opening up the distinctive semantic possibilities of the Arabic Qur'an, since it relates every word of Arberry's English translation to its underlying triliteral Arabic roots and thematic interconnections. The careful use of this concordance enables students using the Arberry translation to quickly locate all the scattered passages involving a particular Arabic root (or wider semantic field) that express and develop a common symbolic theme. Just as with music, this underlying thematic–symbolic structure, which is initially invisible or only dimly discernible in English translation, is the most basic key to discovering the multifaceted meanings and intentions of the Qur'an. Finally, the new multivolume *Encyclopaedia of the Qur'an* (supplemented by the second edition of the *Encyclopaedia of Islam*) provides helpful explanations of the Qur'an's many unfamiliar references, contexts, and literary forms in short entries that are readily understandable by nonspecialists.[16]

Since the problems encountered when students first approach the Qur'an in English differ according to each individual and the particular passages and problems the student may encounter, it is difficult to propose a single logical order of exposition that would integrate all of the cautions and suggestions that may be helpful to different readers. For this reason, the following observations have been divided into three sections, beginning with a series of fundamental considerations that apply to almost every reader of the translated Qur'an. These are followed by some helpful basic interpretive principles drawn from the Qur'an itself, as well as from a wide range of classical Muslim interpreters. The final section concludes with immediately accessible unifying themes that are central to interpreting the Qur'an. It should be kept in mind that some of the following suggestions are intended for students who are trying to understand the Qur'an as a whole, which requires demanding study and much time for beginning readers. But most of these points deal with fundamental themes and literary features that can be grasped through study and meditation on a few carefully chosen Suras, something that many students are already trained to do in the analysis of poetry, for example. This kind of close, repeated reading and empathetic, comparative study of shorter passages is most effective and rewarding for those readers who can devote only limited time to the study of the Qur'an.[17]

Initial Cautions and Considerations

Historical Contexts

Perhaps the most basic consideration that any beginning reader of the translated Qur'an must keep in mind is the radically different situations of the Prophet Muhammad and his followers during the earlier (Meccan) and later (Medinan) periods of the revelation of the Qur'an. The original audiences and aims of different Suras intricately reflect this fundamental contrast between the Prophet's spiritual guidance of a handful of often persecuted devotees during the initial Meccan period of his teaching, on the one hand, and the complexly evolving, much more publicly social and political situation throughout his leadership of the nascent Muslim community in the oasis city of Yathrib, later known as *al-Madina* (The City [of the Prophet]), on the other hand.[18] While the scholarship of traditional Muslims and modern philologists differs in many ways about where to situate chronologically particular Suras and verses in this chronology, what is most important for anyone approaching the Qur'an for the first time is to begin by focusing on those Suras—primarily located in the second half of English translations—that are normally accepted to be Meccan. This is because these earlier Suras do not pose the complex issues of relevant historical interpretive contexts and often highly problematic assumptions that are unavoidably raised by the recurrent theological, social, legal, and political issues that readers must be aware of throughout the later, Medinan Suras.

Muhammad's role, as reflected in the Meccan Suras, is that of a preacher, guide, and warner leading a threatened and initially quite small group of highly devoted monotheists in a hostile pagan city. In that early context, the revealed teachings of the Qur'an focus vividly on a recurrent set of metaphysical and spiritual concerns. These include the awareness of the reality and manifold attributes of the One God, the Creator and Sustainer of the universe; the teaching of humankind's spiritual origin and ultimate destiny and Judgment; and the appropriate ethical and spiritual responsibilities within that metaphysical context. These same metaphysical and spiritual concerns continue to pervade and inform the later, Medinan sections of the Qur'an. However in this later period, many verses of the Qur'an also refer to the Prophet's increasing role in leading and shaping a much larger and increasingly distinct socioreligious community that was constantly engaged in a military and political struggle for survival. The Medinan Suras therefore reflect the challenging circumstances and motivations of markedly different groups of supporters (and enemies) during a period in which the nascent Muslim community gradually became differentiated from surrounding religious group in both its prescribed practices and its ethical and spiritual norms.

A significant problem for readers approaching the Qur'an is that there are no contemporary historical sources that independently describe the complex local events that are constantly alluded to in these later, Medinan Suras. Instead, the traditional contextual materials that were elaborated by the scholarly Arabic disciplines in subsequent generations frequently reflect later theological, sectarian, and political concerns and assumptions. Such visibly later historical concerns include, for example, the bloody intra-Muslim civil wars and sectarian divisions that marked the century following the Prophet's death; the elaboration of different theological, juridical, and political schools of interpretation; and the complex challenges involved in relating the Qur'an to the vast body of Hadith portraying the Prophet's teaching and example that accumulated in the following centuries.

The unavoidable pedagogical problem posed by the later, Medinan verses for all readers of the Qur'an (even in the original Arabic) is therefore twofold. First, there is no way to reliably summarize all of the problematic historical contexts and corresponding interpretive assumptions in a simple and value-neutral way. Even a brief glance at the relevant scholarly literature makes clear how much each traditional interpretive approach remains essentially hypothetical and dependent on selective readings of historically later evidence. Second, Qur'an translations or commentaries that supply simplified, highly selective versions of the events in question almost inevitably lead English-speaking readers to approach the Medinan Suras as they would the more familiar "historical" or "legal" books of the Hebrew Bible. Unfortunately, such an approach tends to prevent students from grasping what in fact remains central to most later strands of Muslim Qur'an interpretation.

Rather than focusing on Medinan events simply as remote "sacred history," traditional Muslim exegetes have often highlighted the ways in which these exemplary tensions and conflicts, and the challenging ethical and spiritual issues they raise, provide archetypal situations illustrating the Qur'an's perennial ethical, practical, and metaphysical teachings. To take but one key example: the many Medinan verses referring to the "hypocrites" in the Meccan period are often understood as reflecting recurrent spiritual dilemmas that in fact all human beings necessarily encounter in the course of discovering and deepening their faith. For reasons such as these, beginning students of the Qur'an are well advised to first develop their familiarity and understanding of the Meccan Suras. Engaging the problematic historical contexts of the Medinan Suras requires a degree of well-informed, appropriately balanced tutorial guidance that is not yet fully available in English sources.

Order and Structure

Moving on to the even more fundamental issue of overall form and structure, any beginning reader of a translated Qur'an needs to take account of the manifold ways in which the Arabic Qur'an is different from what we ordinarily think of as a "book." To begin with, as already highlighted above, according to traditional accounts the initial revelations were first *recited* and then recorded, in accordance with the initially intermittent form in which they were revealed. Thus, the current written arrangement and order of Suras and their constitutive verses is generally acknowledged, even by most Muslim authorities, to have been codified at a historically later stage. This later codification process is reflected in the traditional names (included in most Arabic printed texts and many translated versions) of Suras, in the standard division of particular verses within Suras, and in the traditional designation of certain Suras as being either Meccan or Medinan.

The traditional order of the codified Suras—with the exception of *al-Fatiha*, the short "opening" Sura whose central liturgical role in Islam has already been discussed—is primarily based on their relative length. Hence traditional study and memorization of the Qur'an normally begins with the shortest Suras and then moves toward the longest ones.[19] While there is no pretense of a strictly chronological organization, the longest Suras tend to be from the later, Medinan period. Thus readers in English can safely begin at the "back" of the translated Qur'an, as already suggested, with the many shorter Suras that are almost entirely from the earlier, Meccan period.

Readers of the Qur'an in translation need to keep in mind that neither the Sura numbers nor the apparent "titles" of Suras provided in translations (these are simple mnemonic words that were used at a very early stage to identify a particular group of verses) should be considered part of the originally revealed Qur'anic text. Likewise, the original Arabic of the Qur'an is devoid of the familiar markers of punctuation, paragraphs, and capitalization that translators so helpfully—and often misleadingly—supply in English. Nor do the traditional verse designations necessarily reflect actual divisions of meaning or subject, since they often derive instead from recurring end rhymes in the original recited Arabic. This characteristic lack of punctuation in the original Arabic can lead to significant issues of interpretation. For example, in a number of cases involving important theological and juridical matters, the Qur'anic text can be read and understood in quite different ways, depending on where the reader chooses to make a stop when reading a verse or sentence. Equally important, the Arabic of the Qur'an includes, as a distinctive and constantly recurring structural feature, highly ambiguous pronoun references, with each alternative reading yielding different, yet often remarkably revealing sets of meanings. This striking feature is almost never reflected in English translations of the Qur'an, apart from the standard use of capitalization to indicate apparently "divine" references. This is particularly unfortunate, since this characteristic indeterminacy of pronouns—and the multiple alternative meanings to which it gives rise—is one of the many highly distinctive features of Qur'anic rhetoric and literary structure that was later carried over into the mystical poetic traditions of the Islamic humanities in Persian and other languages.

For the beginning reader, the importance of these characteristic Qur'anic features of indeterminacy, ambiguity, and multiple meanings is that translations ignoring such points deprive the student of the challenge of discerning multiple perspectives of meaning in the sacred text, which is so central to the experience of discovering the Arabic Qur'an. To put this more plainly, the result of such neglect, for readers relying on a translation of the Qur'an, is roughly comparable to the difference between reading Plato's *Republic* or Joyce's *Finnegan's Wake* in the original and in a condensed *Cliff Notes* study guide version.

The "Literal" is Intrinsically Symbolic

Virtually nothing in the Arabic Qur'an has a straightforward and prosaic meaning. The problematic and explicitly symbolic nature of the key expressions of the Qur'an is constantly highlighted and developed in Suras from all periods, perhaps most dramatically in the mystifying language of the earliest short eschatological Suras, which are normally found at the end of English translations. In Arabic, the uniquely mysterious, open-ended quality of Qur'anic language is particularly apparent when one compares the unique Arabic idiom of the Qur'an with the simpler and more understandable language of the Prophet's sayings (Hadith), which indeed are often responses to his followers' requests to clarify the unfamiliar symbols and vocabulary of the Qur'an. The texts of the Hadith, originally transmitted orally, are in a far more accessible, often prosaic, form of Arabic, whose rhetorical and structural qualities are quite different from the unique rhetoric of the Qur'an.

Thus the reader of the Qur'an needs to pay close attention to those passages that repeatedly refer to its central assumption of the existence of multiple, often sharply contrasted, degrees of spiritual understanding. This basic human reality is reflected throughout the Qur'an in the corresponding usage of appropriate rhetoric and symbols designed to communicate very differently to readers with varying spiritual, intellectual, and practical interests, with their distinctive receptivities and stages of discernment. The Qur'an repeatedly suggests to its readers, often in dramatically highlighted terms (as at Qur'an 3:7), how it is meant to be understood on different levels and how much of its language will defy the understanding of all but the most inspired readers.

What this means is that in the Qur'an, it is often precisely the "literal" Arabic reading that is overtly and quite intentionally symbolic, in ways that can often not be captured at all (at least without lengthy commentaries) in translations into English or other non-Semitic languages. This constant reiteration of the profoundly symbolic nature of the Qur'an—as indeed of every dimension of creation—means that readers of the Qur'an, whether in the Arabic or in the translated language, are repeatedly summoned to acknowledge their own existential ignorance with regard to at least some of the Qur'an's most central expressions and symbols. At the same time, however, such characteristic reminders of one's initial ignorance (or "heedlessness") are clearly meant to provoke a potentially revealing recognition of the essential spiritual mysteries evoked by so many challenging Qur'anic passages, because these repeated reminders of the Qur'an's own intrinsic interpretive ambiguity force each serious reader to search for the appropriate practical, intellectual, and spiritual keys that might help to open up those mysteries. This inherent Qur'anic problem of existential ignorance and mystery has nothing to do with being a "beginner" or somehow lacking appropriate sources of information. Instead, as has been attested by centuries of Qur'anic exegesis from the most diverse perspectives and traditions, this eventually illuminating experience of perplexity and mystery only increases in proportion to one's learning and familiarity with the Arabic Qur'an. This is a point where the faithful literalness of Arberry's translation of the Qur'an particularly well serves his English readers.[20]

Awareness and Experience

Some of the most influential traditional commentators on the Qur'an have focused on its insistence on the ongoing existential interplay between inner "knowing" (*'ilm*, a term perhaps better translated here as "spiritual awareness") and spiritually appropriate action (*'amal*).[21] In other words, the central metaphysical teachings of the Qur'an are expressed in such a way that the engaged reader can never withdraw into an abstract, purely intellectual and theoretical attitude toward the text. Instead, readers are obliged to make the essential existential connection between the symbolic teachings of the Qur'an and those dimensions of action and experience that reveal both the depths and the limitations of our awareness, as they gradually open up a deeper, uniquely individual appreciation of the realities underlying the Qur'anic symbols. This ascending spiral of realization is inseparable from the decisive role of imagination—or what we could more broadly call "spiritual intuition"—in perceiving and penetrating the meanings of the Qur'an.

This basic principle of interpretation through active participation—at once intellectual, imaginative, and spiritual—is equally applicable to any translation of the Qur'an. In practice, it means that each reader is obliged to imaginatively "perform" the Qur'an by discovering the actual experiences to which each key symbolic expression refers, just as one must imaginatively read a theatrical work or decipher a great poem.[22] Otherwise, a less active or engaged reading will tend to render the Qur'an flat and meaningless, or to turn it into a purely intellectual enterprise. The potential to appreciate and apply this principle of active participation has nothing at all to do with the particular reader's cultural or even religious background. Indeed many of the suggestions for readers of translations outlined in the next section may be easier for non-Muslim students to put into action, since their active questioning and inquiry may be less restricted by the range of pious cultural preconceptions normally surrounding any sacred text.

The Musical Unity of the Qur'an

One of the most distinctive features of the Arabic Qur'an—often only feebly suggested in translation—is its distinctive unity of meaning and expression, which is manifested in the "ideographic," semantically unifying function of its triliteral Arabic consonantal roots. Like classical Chinese characters, each of these linguistic roots expresses a rich range of broadly related meanings. These different inherent meanings, like harmonic correspondences in a musical composition, all resonate with the occurrence of each word derived from a particular root. Equally important, many of the meanings and grammatical functions that are normally expressed in English by very different words, which we immediately recognize as quite distinct "parts of speech," are instead expressed in the Qur'an by slightly differing grammatical forms of the *same* underlying Arabic root. Thus each appearance of the same verbal root, whatever its grammatical or other context may be, immediately brings to mind all of the other contexts of this same root, which together form a sort of conceptual hologram or semantic whole. At another level, the Arabic roots of the Qur'an form intimately related, "cross-referential" families of meaning, which likewise intersect and resonate in the same way. This is why Kassis's *A Concordance of the Qur'an* is such an indispensable tool for discovering these unifying Arabic roots and semantic complexes beneath the far greater number of disparate words that must inevitably be used in any English translation.

There is simply no way that Indo-European languages can express (except in rare forms of poetry) this fundamental feature of Qur'anic language. Those of us who speak Western languages can best imagine the linguistic and semantic resonances of the Qur'an by analogy with the procedures and effects of musical composition. Hence the powerful effects of simply *listening* to the Qur'an, even without the added complexities of trying to understand its language, are already impossible to reduce to any satisfactory form of simple prosaic expression. Perhaps most important, this holographic quality of Qur'anic Arabic means that each passage is immediately related, by a rich web of associated meanings and resonances, to virtually every other passage in the text. In addition, there are a host of distinctive rhythmic, rhyming, and stylistic features that further accentuate and intensify this musical and semantic unity. One of the most striking and pervasive of these features, as in the Hebrew Bible, is the fact that each Arabic letter of the Qur'an directly corresponds to a specific number.[23] This added mathematical dimension of textual resonance allowed traditional Muslim interpreters to call forth nearly infinite possibilities of semantic correspondences that further accentuate both the interconnections and the depths of meaning that arise within the Qur'an.

The "Verbal" Universe of the Creative Divine Act

Another fundamental feature of the Arabic Qur'an, which is also invisible in English prose translations, is the active, intrinsically "verbal" nature of Qur'anic language. Each triliteral Arabic root normally reflects an underlying active verbal meaning. More particularly, in the metaphysical contexts assumed throughout the Qur'an, God is normally understood as the ultimate creative "Actor." A sense of this inherently active quality is retained in the many derived forms ("verbal nouns", participles, and so on) of those triliteral Arabic roots that are usually translated in English as more abstract concepts, such as nouns, adjectives, gerunds, adverbs, and so forth. In radical contrast to this verbal, active immediacy of the Arabic Qur'an, the underlying structure of English and other Indo-European languages reflects a stable, *object-based* world of subject-agents, their acts, and the objects of those actions, which are implicitly situated on the same extended "horizontal" plane of spatial and temporal relations. Within this linguistic and metaphysical framework, we naturally assume that it is these subjects and objects (the "nouns") that are real and thus are part of an objective spatiotemporal continuum of past, present, and future. In the language of the Qur'an, however, what is real is not these "things," but the *divine presence*—the actual, unique, immediately creative divine Act, including all of its outwardly unfolding manifestations.

This fundamental metaphysical perception, which is constantly articulated in the Qur'an as an immediate presence and reality (not as some argument or theory), means that within the Qur'an all possible voices, perspectives, and relations—that is, all the discrete entities and spatiotemporal extensions we normally take to comprise our everyday experience—are *simultaneously* expressed and perceived as a single divine Voice and Act. This omnipresent divine reality is concretely expressed in the verbal, inherently active, and instantaneous expressions that are built into the distinctive rhetoric of the Qur'an, and it is dramatically reenacted in the daily use of the Qur'an in prayer and recitation, which itself becomes a kind of individual "reascending creation."

Another aspect of this intrinsically unifying dimension of Qur'anic Arabic is the fact that Arabic verbs have (in their most common forms) only two possible "tenses": either a *present and continuing* time or a "past" form. In the Qur'an, even the grammatically "past" form commonly expresses the timeless presence of those divine creative Acts—what we call "the world" and all creation—that by their transcendent origin are always simultaneously determined, yet constantly repeated, in the divine Present and God's "ever-renewed Creation" (Qur'an 10:4, and others). Thus, nothing could more invisibly betray those decisive individual spiritual states and experiences so powerfully evoked by the pervasive eschatological passages of the Qur'an than the way that English translators typically place these intensely present metaphysical realities into a vague, indeterminate "future."[24]

While these grammatical explanations of fundamental Qur'anic structures are mystifying to readers only accustomed to English, we are all familiar with the cinema as another contemporary artistic medium that works with a similar "presential" quality that vividly expresses our inner experience of constantly shifting and coexisting perspectives and time. The standard cinematic cues and conventions for expressing internal and external shifts of time and perspective, changing instantly (and without the slightest confusion on the part of the audience) between different "points" within a single all-encompassing reality, are recognizable even to small children. The characteristically cinematic structure and sudden perspective shifts of Qur'anic language and metaphysics, though unfortunately neglected in most English translations, has been unforgettably translated into many of the creative poetic and musical masterpieces of the later Islamic humanities.

The "Three Books": The Qur'an as Logos

What is most important about the unique formal features of the Arabic Qur'an is not their linguistic or literary dimensions as such. What matters most is that each of these distinctive rhetorical elements helps the reader grasp immediately the constant Qur'anic insistence that its actual Reality is the Logos, the creative divine "Word." Among the many symbolic expressions used by the Qur'an for this Reality are "The Book," "Wisdom," "The Mother of the Book" (*Umm al-Kitab*), and "The Criterion" (*al-Furqan*). In other words, as traditional interpreters have so frequently pointed out, the Qur'an presents itself as a spiritual mirror whose verses reflect and reveal the divine "Signs on the horizons and in their own souls" (Qur'an 41:53). The comprehensive interrelatedness between the Qur'an's verses and the Signs constituting all creation is the metaphysical counterpart of the holographic "rhetoric of allusion" referred to above, which discloses new meanings in every new circumstance and situation. As later interpreters put it, this earthly revealed book is meant to reveal the correspondence between the two cosmic "Books"—of the Spirit and of all creation—which the Spirit both mirrors and informs.

However, such grand correspondences are never presented in the Qur'an as concepts to be intellectualized or mentally "believed." This is because *iman*, or true faith, is a spiritual reality and essential connection of a different order. Instead, each reader/reciter of the Qur'an very gradually discovers its essential Reality by coming to recognize the revelatory correspondences that connect each of the Qur'an's stories, parables, "likenesses," scriptural episodes, reminders, and symbols with their existential manifestations. In the Qur'anic perspective, it is above all spiritual practice and right action (*'amal*) that opens the way to true understanding (*'ilm*). In this respect, for most beginning readers, the Qur'an can more fruitfully be compared, in its pervasive ontological focus and uniquely allusive mythic and symbolic structure, to such Asian religious classics as the Vedas, Upanishads, *I Ching*, or *Tao Te Ching*, rather than the familiar King James Bible.[25]

Interpretive Principles

Trusting One's Intuitions

The language of the Qur'an makes exquisite sense as a comprehensive and revealing "phenomenology of the Spirit"—a characterization that is illustrated, not by theological claims, but by its revelatory re-creations in the masterpieces of the Islamic humanities, whether literary, visual, or musical. However, the very uniqueness and specificity of the Qur'an's spiritual vocabulary means that the English equivalents adopted in most translations of the Qur'an simply do not make much sense in many places. This is due in part to the lack of English equivalent terms, concepts, and symbols, along with the distinctive Arabic rhetorical and grammatical dimensions alluded to above. But perhaps equally important, the opacity of translations often reflects the peculiar cultural associations surrounding English Biblical language. One quickly discovers as a teacher, for example, that most American undergraduates, whatever their family and personal religious background, cannot encounter the word "sin" without immediately associating it with a peculiar set of historical–cultural assumptions concerning doctrines of "original sin" and related Biblical associations. However, the complex Qur'anic vocabulary that uniquely expresses the various degrees and consequences of right actions and intentions (and their contraries) refers to spiritual and psychological states that are intimately familiar to each human being, without requiring any further reference to particular cultural contexts or beliefs.

The practical upshot of this observation is very simple: wherever one finds that something in a translated version of the Qur'an does not make sense, and especially when it appears to blatantly contradict one's most basic spiritual and ethical common sense (what the Qur'an calls our universal human *fitra*), the underlying difficulty is almost certainly due to an inadequacy of translation. In most cases, such misunderstandings can be cleared up by using the Kassis's *Concordance of the Qur'an,* referring back to the underlying Arabic root of the pertinent Qur'anic term and the other contexts in which it is used (along with the English synonyms and other translator's usages also cited by Kassis for each root).

Discovering the Spiritual Virtues

One particularly important aspect of the Qur'an defying adequate translation is the spiritual virtues, especially since these virtues constitute the practical core of the Qur'an in human terms. It is revealing in this respect to note that Muslims have repeatedly adopted into their own vernacular languages many of the key Qur'anic terms for the spiritual virtues. The problem here is not just one of translation, but also of the basic fact that human beings (and the cultures they constitute) tend to reduce the unique reality and inspired spiritual realization underlying each Qur'anic virtue to more familiar social, ethical, and political norms.[26]

For example, it makes relatively little difference whether one employs English words like "patience" or "perseverance" for the Qur'anic term *sabr*. Such words alone simply cannot convey the key dimension of the suffering soul's struggle to discover the unique divine purpose that underlies its particular situation of suffering. This is an individually unique illumination that each person is forced to rediscover whenever this spiritual virtue is brought into play. So *sabr* is not about suffering or grudging patience as such, but rather about the active inner search and eventual discovery of the transformative spiritual lesson underlying each test we undergo. But translators, understandably, cannot use such lengthy paraphrases for each key technical term in their Qur'an.

The same is true for each of the spiritual virtues in the Qur'an, as well as for the culturally specific images of those Prophetic exemplars (Job, for example, in the case of *sabr*) who are subject to the familiar historical processes of routinization and misunderstanding. Here again, the Islamic humanities have often come to the rescue, precisely because of the recurrent necessity of finding appropriate and spiritually effective means for communicating the realities expressed by such archetypal Qur'anic images and symbols.

The "Voices" of the Qur'an

Another important interpretive principle that is present throughout the Qur'an—while being normally invisible in most Western translations—is the understanding that God (or the truly ultimate Reality, *al-Haqq*) is the Speaker and Subject behind the mysterious play of constantly shifting voices (whether I, "We," the unnamed Narrator, Muhammad, or other prophets and individual actors) and audiences in the Qur'anic text. This constant and often mysterious shift of perspectives is one of the most distinctive rhetorical and structural features of the Qur'an. In the final analysis, all possible perspectives and persons are included within the One Real. In the later Islamic humanities, this interplay of shifting but ultimately Unitary perspectives and points of view is beautifully illustrated in many of the most extraordinary masterpieces of Islamic art, such as the incomparable lyrics of the Persian poet Hafez or the paintings of Behzad. So far, however, translators have not only failed to highlight this extraordinary semantic dimension of the Qur'an but have also often attempted to "polish" and gloss over these repeated, intentionally mysterious shifts among the different divine/human/Prophetic voices and perspectives.

Any translation of the Qur'an that adequately reflects such shifts in perspective and their accompanying pronoun indeterminacies (that is, who is it that is really speaking, and to whom?) confronts the English reader with what at first appear to be bizarre and even paradoxical ambiguities, unexplained jumps, and undefined subjects, audiences, and references. Certain Qur'anic verses and phrases (such as Qur'an 17:1 or 2:285–286), when translated literally, read like a kind of literary "Moebius strip," in which the initial Voice and its apparent addressee are supplanted, replaced, or even apparently reversed by the time one reaches the end of a single short passage. In such situations, the English reader must pay particularly close attention, just as when deciphering an unusually challenging poem (for example, Pound's *Cantos*), to note and then reflect upon the cinematic yet meaningful fluidity of this unique Qur'anic discourse.

Who Is Addressed by the Qur'anic Speech?

This interpretive principle has already been suggested by the points just discussed concerning the shifting voices and perspectives of the Qur'an. However, in existential and spiritual terms it is even more decisive. Although the Prophet Muhammad is often apparently the initial intended "receiver" of Qur'anic verses, a crucial mystery for all other readers of the Qur'an is their own individual relationship to the recurrent *singular* "you" that marks

God's address to the Prophet in the Qur'anic text. This constant dramatic interplay between the singular "you" directly addressed to the Prophet and the publicly plural "you" (in the sense of "you people in general"), which runs throughout the Qur'an, can be seen as a kind of Qur'anic representation of the mystery of transubstantiation.

In other words, the mystery of the singular "you" initially addressed to the Prophet is the repeated invitation to each reader/reciter/listener to rediscover—indeed quite literally to "remember" (the central Qur'anic theme of *dhikr*)—our shared human nature as Spirit. Each momentary glimpse of this reality of our being—of what it means to *be* Spirit—is itself a renewed revelation. The recurrent challenge and summons to actualize oneself in Spirit is lost in most English translations of the Qur'an, even those that attempt to more clearly distinguish these two radically different forms of "you."

Similar problems with metaphysical and spiritual implications are raised by the other distinctive voices in the Qur'an, such as the "We" that stands in dramatic contrast to the otherwise nameless Narrator, the rare divine "I" that stands for the most intimate Subject of the Qur'anic discourse, or the constant references to the unnameable Essence (*Huwa*) of the ultimately Real. From the earliest eras of Islamic history, cautious theological interpreters have attempted to gloss over such potentially troubling dilemmas, explaining the recurrent "We," for example, as the collective plural voice of all the divine names and attributes. But such facile verbal formulations are by no means universally accepted. Paradoxically, in such cases, the non-Muslim reader's encounter with a bare English translation of such central Qur'anic ambiguities may actually provoke more serious and open-ended spiritual and metaphysical reflections than are normally found in more traditional hermeneutical contexts.

Scattering, Singularity, and Repetition

Another important interpretive principle of the Qur'an involves the interplay between the scattering and the dispersal of its teachings (especially those that are metaphysical and eschatological) throughout the text, and the striking contrast between certain *repeated* injunctions and other uniquely *singular* symbols and expressions. Fortunately, these hermeneutical challenges are normally as apparent in translations as in the original Arabic. The Qur'an as a whole is marked by an elaborately detailed symbolic coherence, particularly in the details of its eschatological teachings, which integrate literally hundreds of scattered verses. This coherence is also reflected in the similar correspondences between the Qur'an's depiction of the ontological stages of manifestation of the divine Spirit and the corresponding stages of the human soul's spiritual purification and return to its Source. In general, the Suras of the Qur'an from all periods tend to cite repeatedly certain themes and images, especially with regard to practical ethical teachings that are understandable and applicable to everyone: for example, warnings of the Judgment, reminders of the rewards for the righteous, and so on.

However, careful readers of the Qur'an will soon begin to pick out a variety of rarer, often strange, and initially puzzling images and symbols—such as the different cosmic "Trees" mentioned in the Qur'an, or the seven parallel names assigned to different Gardens and Fires—which initially might appear opaque and mystifying. To a great extent, the attempt to piece together and make sense of such scattered symbolic expressions is necessarily driven by each reader's individual sense of "cognitive dissonance." Simply put, this means that attentive readers will find it particularly revealing to focus on apparent contradictions, inconsistencies (whether ethical, metaphysical, spiritual, or simply logical), or apparent mysteries in the Qur'an. When one reads the Qur'an seriously, this task amounts to resolving an immense symbolic and metaphysical puzzle.

Many of these initially puzzling metaphysical and eschatological "contradictions" are not always resolved, but are instead simply taken for granted in later systems of Islamic thought. And in any case, prepackaged theological "resolutions" of such problematic passages are quite distinct from the far more demanding—and rewarding—spiritual tasks that arise when those Qur'anic mysteries interact with the personal challenges that are raised for each reader by his or her own spiritual situation. Such central existential issues include the recurrent Qur'anic themes of theodicy, divine Justice, undeserved suffering, and the mystery of outwardly arbitrary destinies and earthly conditions. Serious study of the Qur'an is profoundly "interactive" in just this sense, and as such, it is intrinsically a lifelong process. The effects of actively exploring and working through the Qur'anic perspectives on such unavoidable spiritual questions are radically different from simply agreeing conceptually with this or that interpretive "resolution" drawn from later hermeneutical traditions.

Qur'anic Imagery and the Hierarchy of the Senses

One revealing interpretive perspective, dramatically expressed in the distinctive imagery of the later Islamic arts and poetry, has to do with the hierarchy of the senses—that is, of their spiritual and symbolic correlates—that is so richly developed throughout the Qur'an. In this regard, even students working with translations quickly notice the memorable imagery of taste, touch, and smell that unfolds, often in precise parallelism, throughout Qur'anic descriptions of the seven eschatological "Gardens" and "Fires."

However, readers also soon discover that the deeper and more pervasive symbolic structures of the Qur'an—especially those suggesting the spiritual dimensions of the Divine— revolve around the imagery of Light and Sound or abstract spatial metaphors of "proximity" and distance from God. What is in question here is not just peculiar literary features and rhetorical unities of the Qur'an, but rather the deeper question of the way in which different types of audiences and readers are encouraged to approach, practice, and integrate the realities of the Qur'an in ways that correspond to their own distinctive spiritual sensibilities, aptitudes, and receptivities. As always in the Qur'an, the loftiest of such symbols are also the most outwardly invisible.

The Primacy of the "Invisible"

Perhaps the most pervasive interpretive principle that one encounters in the Qur'an, even in English translation, is its constant insistence on the primacy of the "invisible" and on the corresponding depiction of the visible world as *theophany*, as an educational shadow-theater for our uniquely human task of enacting and realizing the divine names. This principle is the spiritual key to all the Islamic humanities—where the dominant later forms (music and poetry) come closest to mirroring the rhythms and translucent immateriality of the recited Qur'an itself—and to the traditional forms of *adab*, the unique spiritual expression and realization of individuality in similarly powerful but self-effacing forms of right behavior and social interaction. Nothing in the Qur'an is more obvious and omnipresent than the centrality of the spiritual world, and the actors—jinn, prophets, angels, messengers, Friends of God, and even the spiritual "birds" and other symbolic animals—that animate and direct its cosmic stage.

The Challenge of Contextualization

Readers of Arberry's translation of the Qur'an who attempt to read the Medinan Suras without any of the later tools of contextualization discussed earlier will eventually note the relative rarity of specific sociolegal "prescriptions." This observation is somewhat surprising, given the multitude of later interpretive uses made of such passages and given the widespread assumption that the Medinan sections of the Qur'an should somehow constitute a "book of laws" comparable to familiar Biblical texts. Before turning to traditional Muslim sources of contextualization and interpretation of these Medinan passages, readers should first take note of the importance of their proper contextualization and specification, both in terms of their (supposed) original historical context and of the possible wider intentions or principles underlying each situation. Behind such basic interpretive questions, of course, one also encounters the recurrent problems of authority, power, and legitimacy. This essential and far-reaching caution applies to virtually *all* of the apparently prescriptive passages from the Medinan period. One has only to think of the heated contemporary controversies surrounding the many Qur'anic passages relating to *jihad* (effort in the way of God) to recognize the perennially problematic nature of what may be at stake in such problematic Medinan contexts.

Unifying Themes

One of the most satisfying and effective approaches to appreciating the depth and unity of the Qur'an in English translation, especially for readers who are not otherwise accustomed to the metaphysical, theological, and rhetorical dimensions elaborated in the preceding sections, is to begin by noting certain unifying themes and symbols that are found in both the Meccan and the Medinan Suras. Once one has noted the recurrence of these distinctive sets of images and symbols, it is only a short step to ask the obvious follow-up question about what these recurrent themes are meant to signify.

Images of Nature

One of the most striking and obvious features of the Qur'an, even in translation, is its powerful appeal to symbolism drawn directly from the soul's experience of the natural world. The pervasive and unambiguously central role of Nature in the Qur'an—virtually neglected in many intellectualized forms of theological and philosophical interpretation—suggests a host of interpretive perspectives that are more richly developed in the later masterpieces of the Islamic humanities. In particular, readers focusing on this dimension of the Qur'an should keep in mind the sensory impact of all types of nature-imagery in the Qur'an as they were perceived in the challenging desert world of the Qur'an's original listeners. Today one can best approach these conditions and the spiritual receptivities they still engender while camping or hiking in the wilderness, or otherwise encountering relatively distant and pristine areas of the natural world. Such natural symbols, in the Qur'an as elsewhere, are most effective when they cannot be mistaken for mere abstractions.

"The Origin and the Return": The Cosmic Map

From the earliest days, students of the Qur'an have noticed that it develops an elaborate spiritual "map" or guidebook to the soul's purification and realization of its spiritual Source. The books of later Muslim interpreters approach this dimension of the Qur'an in terms of "The Origin and the Return" (al-mabda' wa-l-ma'ad) of the human soul. As already noted, careful study of the Qur'an reveals an elaborate symbolic ontology and cosmology, which closely parallels an even more complex symbolic account of eschatology and spiritual psychology. While readers may find deciphering this Qur'anic worldview an initially daunting task, it is nonetheless indispensable for understanding the scriptural origins and allusive depth of many of the later classics of the Islamic humanities, especially in Sufi, Shiite, and other the philosophico-theological traditions.

The Divine Names

For beginning readers, much of the Qur'an appears to be a catalogue of different divine names, which they simply tend to ignore. Yet these manifold names, reflecting their centrality in the Qur'an, became a central topic and inspiration in all subsequent traditions of Islamic theology and spirituality. Indeed, the very goal of human existence is portrayed in the Qur'an, in repeated accounts of Adam's creation and his inspired "knowledge of the Names," as the gradual discovery and manifestation of the full range of attributes expressed in the divine names. This school of earthly existence, with its constant presentation of spiritual and ethical choices, culminates in the active realization of what the Qur'an terms "the Most Beautiful Names" (Qur'an 7:180).

In later theological terms, this unifying Qur'anic insight was expressed in the conception of the created world and the soul as theophanic manifestations of the divine attributes. From this perspective, these recurrent Qur'anic lists of particular names can be read as more than just general reminders of the aims and parameters of the school of life. They also convey more specific allusions—a sort of ongoing "spiritual commentary," like the words of the chorus in Greek tragedy—to the lessons and insights highlighted in the specific Qur'anic contexts where those lists of names occur.

Light, Speech, and Writing

Two closely related families of imagery in the Qur'an have to do with the symbolism of all creation as a theophany of "Light" (Qur'an 24:35–40), including complex allusions to the heavenly luminaries and the alternations of "Day" and "Night," and with the symbolism of creation as a manifestation of divine speech or writing (including the divine "Words," "Book," "Pen," "Tablet," and so on). Although these symbolic images are elaborately developed in many forms of later Islamic thought, it is often illuminating to encounter them directly in their original Qur'anic contexts, where their metaphysical dimensions are not always immediately apparent. In particular, it is important to note that in these Qur'anic contexts the imagery of "Night," far from being negative or opposed to the Light, typically refers directly to the divine depths of the invisible spiritual dimensions of creation and cosmogony.

Stories, Parables, and Allusions

Traditional interpreters of the Qur'an have often tended to separate out such different literary forms in the Qur'an as "stories" (including the Sura of Joseph, described as "the most beautiful of stories" [Qur'an 12:3]), allusions to earlier sacred figures and events, or parables and "symbols" (*amthal*). Each of these Qur'anic motifs has inspired significant examples of spiritual writing and teaching in later Islamic tradition. It is particularly revealing, given the frequent parallels that are drawn with Biblical and other spiritual literatures, to examine more closely each of the explicitly divine parables detailed in the Qur'an, together with the Qur'an's own interpretive comments. These comments pointedly emphasize the contrast between such divine, spiritually valid parables and the unconscious—and ultimately illusory—"likenesses" made up by human beings. Such passages are a particularly illuminating example of the ways the Qur'an itself suggests useful ways to interpret and more fully understand its teachings.

Spiritual Virtues and Prophetic Exemplars

One of the central interpretive challenges in the Qur'an, as in the Bible, is to discover the essential connections between the spiritual virtues and their dramatization in the stories presented in the scriptures. Such stories often allude to various spiritual exemplars and intermediaries, such as the prophets of earlier eras. However, these Qur'anic allusions also extend to both exemplary and "hypocritical" Muslims (and outright enemies) from Muhammad's own surroundings, as well as other legendary figures from indigenous Arabic and Biblical traditions.[27] These exemplars and the virtues they represent are subjects that are richly amplified in later Hadith accounts, *Sira* literature (involving the life of the Prophet, his Companions, and the history of the early Muslim community), and "tales of the prophets" (*Qisas al-Anbiya'*), which often include apocryphal materials from before the advent of Islam. Here it is useful for students to begin with the typically very brief Qur'anic accounts themselves, without relying on interpretive materials from external sources, since reliance on later forms of ready-made interpretation tends to foreclose the demands of actively imaginative interpretation that are otherwise demanded by the unadorned English translation.

CONCLUSION: THE QUR'AN AS MIRROR AND PRISM

> O Beloved, through Love we are conjoined with You:
> Wherever You put Your foot, we're the ground for You!
> In this school/path of Loving, how can it be
> That we see the world through You— and yet, we don't see You?
>
> (Quatrain of Jalal al-Din Rumi)[28]

One of the key teachings of the Qur'an, indeed of the Islamic tradition more generally, is the primacy of intention. All the pointers and observations mentioned above may help to reveal unsuspected dimensions of the Qur'an, or to remove certain obstacles that stand in the way of more fully appreciating the Qur'an in translation. However, these suggestions are no substitute for the intention and receptivity that each reader alone can provide. Some of the greatest spiritual teachers in Islam have summed up their advice for anyone encountering the Qur'an in a single phrase: "You should seek to understand each verse as though it were being revealed directly to you."

As others have even more simply put it, the Qur'an is a mirror for the soul. We discover in it what we bring to it, in proportion to the effort we actually devote to penetrating its mysteries. We hear its revelations to the degree that we truly listen. Yet as the Qur'an so often reminds us, the true mirror through which we perceive the Qur'an—and all the divine "signs" —is the illumined Heart, which is itself (in the words of a famous hadith) "the Throne of the All-Merciful." For the Qur'an is like a prism, a refracting lens, that is set between the divine creative Light and its endless momentary reflections in every shifting facet of creation.

The ordinary vision of the human being, as Rumi's poem reminds us, remains entranced and beguiled by this world's shimmering shadow play of veils and colors. The Qur'an, which more than 20 times pointedly describes itself as "*the* Reminder," offers a potent response to the dilemma highlighted by the great Sufi poet. Through the revealing lens of the Qur'an, we can gradually come to discern the One luminous, invisible Source of those endlessly shifting reflections, first discovering—and then mirroring back in our own illumined responses—those "Most-beautiful Names" that are so uniquely manifested in each theophanic event. We shall show them Our Signs on the horizons and in their own souls, until it shines forth to them that He is the truly Real (Qur'an 41:53).

NOTES

1.   See the detailed discussion of these problems, particularly in connection to the recurrent misunderstandings arising from English translators' common use of familiar "Biblical" terms, in James Winston Morris, "Qur'an Translation and the Challenge of Communication: Toward a 'Literal' (Study) Version of the Qur'an," *Journal of Qur'anic Studies,* 2 (February 2000): 53–68. This article, which will be included in my forthcoming book *Openings: From the Qur'an to the Islamic Humanities,* forms a helpful supplement to the cautions outlined below.

2.   However, the unique language of the Arabic Qur'an is also different from the common dialects of spoken Arabic as well. Indeed, some of its unusual words and expressions were apparently mysterious even for its original audiences.

3.   Some helpful current Web sites, most including a range of translations and translated shorter commentaries as well as audio and video material, include http://www.quranonline.net, http://www.reciter.org, http://www.altafsir.com, and http://www.islamicity.com.

4.   In this chapter we will follow the standard abridged scholarly citation system of giving first the number of the Sura, then the number of the verse or *aya*: thus (1:3) =

Surat al-Fatiha, verse 3. Muslim sources usually give instead the standard Arabic names traditionally associated with the Suras.

5.   The *Basmalla* refers to the Arabic phrase, "In the Name of God the All-Loving, the All-Compassionate" (*Bismillah al-Rahman al-Rahim*), that opens virtually all of the Suras of the Qur'an.

6.   See Morris, "Remembrance and Repetition: The Spiritual Foundations of Islamic Aesthetics," *Sufi Magazine*, 47 (2000).

7.   For centuries, a similarly wide-ranging cultural role was played by the teaching of Latin prayers and rituals in Catholic schools, coupled with the wider use of Latin at higher levels of education, across many cultural and linguistic divides. Until recent times, the learned written forms of many of the vernacular Islamic languages (Persian, Turkish, Urdu, Malay, and so on) likewise presupposed significant knowledge of the classical Arabic of the Qur'an.

8.   Partly because of the traditional reverence for the calligraphed Qur'anic text, as well as related technical challenges involving Arabic calligraphy, printed or lithographed books only became widely available in most regions of the Islamic world during the nineteenth century, and in some areas even more recently.

9.   See Kristina Nelson, *The Art of Reciting the Qur'an* (Austin: University of Texas Press, 1985), and William A. Graham, *Beyond the Written Word: Oral Aspects of Scripture in the History of Religion* (Cambridge: Cambridge University Press, 1987).

10.   Of course much the same could be said of the fully literate scriptural specialists and authorities in most religious traditions, prior to the radically new historical developments connected with the Reformation, mass literacy, and the spread of printing and affordable vernacular books, including Bible translations. Those revolutionary developments only superficially touched much of the Islamic world until very recently. The contemporary popularization in many Muslim countries of the Internet and mass digital media is already bringing about dramatic unforeseen transformations in the traditional structures of religious education and interpretive authority.

11.   See the outlines of this process in Morris, "Situating Islamic 'Mysticism': Between Written Traditions and Popular Spirituality," In *Mystics of the Book: Themes, Topics and Typologies*, ed. R. Herrera (New York and Berlin: Peter Lang, 1993), 293–334. A wider discussion of this issue is also included in the forthcoming *Openings: From the Qur'an to the Islamic Humanities*.

12.   Two of the most comprehensive introductions to the study of the Qur'an in translation, which are accessible for university-level students, are Neal Robinson, *Discovering the Qur'an: A Contemporary Approach to a Veiled Text* (London: SCM Press, 1996), and Muhammad Abdel Haleem, *Understanding the Qur'an: Themes and Style* (London: IB Tauris, 1999).

13.   Michael Sells, *Approaching the Qur'an: The Early Revelations* (Ashland, Oregon: White Cloud Press, 1999) provides a particularly effective and accessible example of what can be accomplished in this regard. The volume includes annotated and carefully crafted translations of many of the shorter Meccan Suras, as well as a useful CD of examples of Qur'anic recitation.

14.   Perhaps the most helpful Qur'an translation of this type (providing very extensive notes dealing with related historical contexts, Hadith, and other traditional contextual material) is that of Muhammad Asad, *The Message of the Qur'an* (London:

The Book Foundation, 2003). The recently established *Journal of Qur'anic Studies* also provides an important venue for keeping track of the many new translations and scholarly publications in this field.

15.   Hanna Kassis, *A Concordance of the Qur'an* (Berkeley: University of California Press, 1984). Under each Arabic root, Kassis also mentions the different English equivalents used by several other popular English Qur'an translations, in addition to Arberry.

16.   *The Encyclopaedia of the Qur'an*, ed. Jane Dammen McAuliffe (Leiden: E. J. Brill, 2001–2005).

17.   Camille Helminski's *The Light of Dawn: Daily Readings From the Holy Qur'an* (Boston: Shambhala Books, 1998) provides a beautiful, poetically rendered illustration of the usefulness of this particular approach, which more closely reflects the actual contemplative use of the Qur'an in Islamic prayer and spiritual life.

18.   The most accessible introduction to the life of the Prophet and the early Muslim community is Martin Lings, *Muhammad: His Life Based on the Earliest Sources* (London: Inner Traditions, 1987). This work is particularly helpful in suggesting the relevant images of the Prophet in later Islamic traditions of piety and spirituality. Robinson's *Discovering the Qur'an* (see n. 12 above) provides an extensive bibliography of the wider scholarly literature on the Prophet's life, along with a balanced discussion of more recent historical and philological approaches. A wide spectrum of traditional Muslim commentary literature (*tafsir*) is summarized for Suras 1–3 in Mahmoud Ayyoub, *The Qur'an and Its Interpreters*, in 2 Vols. (Albany, New York: State University of New York Press, 1984 and 1992).

19.   Books written in Arabic (and other Islamic languages using the Arabic alphabet) normally begin from the right-hand side of the opened book, which English readers naturally assume to be the book's end.

20.   See the experimental development of a variety of intentionally literal and visually revealing translation devices in James W. Morris, "Dramatizing the Sura of Joseph: An Introduction to the Islamic Humanities," Annemarie Schimmel Festschrift issue of *Journal of Turkish Studies* 18 (1994): 201–224. An expanded version of this translation and commentary will be included in the forthcoming *Openings: From the Qur'an to the Islamic Humanities*.

21.   See the translation by M. Abul Quasem of al-Ghazali's still remarkably useful *Jawahir al-Qur'an*, which is built around this distinction, in *The Jewels of the Qur'an: Al-Ghazali's Theory* (London: Kegan Paul, 1983).

22.   See the introduction to our study, "Dramatising the Sura of Joseph," cited in n. 20 above.

23.   Our "Arabic" decimal number system originally came to the Arab world from India, and its figures are designated in Arabic as "Indian" numbers. Over the course of Islamic history, the complex system of Arabic letters and their numerical equivalents gave rise to the esoteric discipline of the "science of letters" (*'ilm al-huruf*), rooted in the sacred Qur'anic alphabet.

24.   Qur'anic Arabic uses a very specific, highly visible particle (*sawfa* or *sa-*) to indicate those cases where a verb refers specifically to a future event or contingency. Such definitely future verb forms (as in 102:3–4) are almost never highlighted as such in English translations.

25.   For an excellent and wide-ranging introduction (with very helpful bibliography) to the historically complex questions surrounding "Biblical" figures and stories in the Qur'an, see Brannon M. Wheeler, *Prophets in the Qur'an: An Introduction to the Qur'an and Muslim Exegesis* (London: Continuum, 2002). Wheeler Thackston's translation of al-Kisa'i's *Tales of the Prophets* (Chicago: Kazi Publications, 1997) provides a representative illustration of the types of popular stories and legends that often inform traditional Muslim interpretations of the Qur'an.

26.   Toshihiko Izutsu's *Ethico-Religious Concepts in the Qur'an* (Montreal: McGill University Press, 1966) still remains the best introduction to the problem of the spiritual virtues in the Qur'an, focusing on the complex Qur'anic (and early Islamic) transformation of earlier Arab ethical norms and values. See also our chapter, "The Mysteries of *Ihsan*: Natural Contemplation and the Spiritual Virtues in the Qur'an," in the forthcoming *Openings*.

27.   See n. 25 above for references to the prophetic stories in question.

28.   Jalal al-Din Rumi, *Kulliyat Shams-i Tabriz*, ed. B. Furuzanfar (Tehran, 1341/1922-3), p. 64 (no. 11 of the *Ruba'iyyat*).

7

MOSES AND THE SAINT

Daniel Abdal-Hayy Moore

A story goes that
Moses, peace be upon him, went
   to find a saint in the desert
     said to be one of the
greatest masters alive.

He went into the arid wastes,
made a camp, went further, made
   another camp, went further perhaps than
anyone dared go, being Moses, and

found, out where the world ends, in a
blazing nothingness of sand and
sky, lying face down with his
chin on the
ground, his saint,
saying with each breath, in a
barely audible voice, only:

Allah—Allah—Allah

The sound of his tongue and the
heartbeat of his body boomed all the
dunes around him to ring in
harmony with that Name.

Moses was struck dumb.

Here, without food, without water,
lay the Master of the Age, dry as
bone, nearly naked, more like
the sand itself than
a man.

He sat respectfully, the
saint not seeing him, but keeping his
invocation throbbing on dry lips with
a dry tongue:

Allah—Allah—Allah

At last the saint opened his eyes and saw
Moses, who bowed, and, as good
servant to master, asked if there was
anything the saint needed.

The saint said, in a small voice
Moses had to bend close to hear:
"Yes. If you could only bring me
a blanket against the
cold nights, I would be
   grateful."

Moses got up
and set out across the
dunes again to his
last camp, grabbed his
blanket and
brought it to the man, who was now

dead.

Shocked, Moses sat in
wonder at the sight. Then he got
up and went
off across the desert to his
camp again to bring a
shovel to bury him.

When he arrived, the body was already
dust.

Only
bones remained.

Amazed, Moses set
off again into the
glare to get a
receptacle for the
bones, to bring them back to
bury them in the town of the
saint's birth.

When he arrived back at the place where
the saint had died, Moses found
only a swirling whirlpool of dust where the
bones had been, and
nothing left but
spiraling drifts of white powder

twisting in the wind.

Moses sat down, his
eyes on the ground.

Then he put his
face on the ground in the
ache and questioning of his
heart, and asked:
O Allah! What is the
     meaning of this.? Your
     saint gone like a
     breath in the desert wind?

And God's voice in the
heart of Moses replied:

     So long as My friend needed nothing but Me
     I gave him all he required.

     As soon as he needed something from
     other than Me, I

     took him.

                                        4 Ramadan

NOTE

This poem first appeared in Daniel Abdal-Hayy Moore, *The Ramadan Sonnets* (San Francisco and Bethesda, Maryland: Jusoor/City Lights Books, 1996). Reprinted from Jusoor/City Lights Books and republished in the Ecstatic Exchange Series. This poem is reproduced here by permission of the author.

8

PROPHETS AND MESSENGERS OF GOD

———————————•———————————

Joseph Lumbard

THE SIGNS OF GOD

In the Qur'an, all of creation is presented as a sign (*aya*) of God. Nothing exists but that it is a means whereby the divine reveals a part of its glory. A bird, a tree, the stars, and the change from night to day—God is directly present in each of these. In this way, every part of creation, no matter how big or small, is like a word or a letter in an ongoing revelation. The Qur'an continuously recalls the wonders of creation as a means of reminding the reader or listener of God:

> Truly in the heavens and the earth are signs for the believers. And in your creation and in that which He spreads [over the earth] from among the beasts are signs for a people who are pious. And [in] the alteration of the night and day, and the nourishment that God sends down from the sky, then by which He revives the earth after its death, and [in] the dispensation of the winds are signs for people who discern. These are the signs of God. We recite them to you with truth. So in what account after God and His signs will they believe?

> (Qur'an 45:3–6)[1]

Reminders like this permeate the Qur'an such that the signs of the first revelation, the revelation of God's creation, are made to speak through the verses of the Qur'an, the final revelation. *Aya*, the word used for a sign from God, is the same word as that used for a verse in God's revealed books. Just as with the revelations made known to the Prophets in the form of books—the Torah, the Psalms, the Gospels, and others—every aspect of creation is conveyed through God's angels.[2] In this way, all that is around us is seen as a message and is sustained through Messengers. The great Messengers of religious history—the Prophets of God—have not been sent with anything new but with a renewal of the first message, so that human beings may reflect and return to a proper understanding of God, the cosmos, and their relation to both.

PROPHECY

The means by which the Prophets bring this message is revelation (*wahy*). Revelation is not seen as a product of reason or reflection, or as mere inspiration. Muslims maintain that revelation is cast directly into the heart of God's Prophets through the Angel Gabriel, the Faithful Spirit (*al-Ruh al-Amin*): "Truly it is a revelation of the Lord of the Worlds that the Faithful Spirit has brought down upon your heart [Muhammad]" (Qur'an 26:192–194). The message of revelation is true and beyond doubt: "Truly it is naught but a revelation revealed, taught by the One of Intense Power.... He revealed unto His servant what He revealed. The heart lied not of what it saw" (Qur'an 53:4–5, 10–11). The reception of an unerring message is not particular to the Prophet Muhammad. All Prophets are preserved from erring in the reception and deliverance of the messages revealed to them by God (Qur'an 72:26–28). One of the signs of God's infinite mercy is that there is no time in history when humankind has not had access to truth through revelation.

When human beings forget and alter the content of a previous revelation, it is time to send a new Prophet to remind them of God's message. However, the message of a new Prophet is not different in its essential content from what came before. Muslims maintain that the Qur'an has been protected from alteration. As God says in the Qur'an: "Truly, We have revealed the Remembrance [i.e., the Qur'an] and are its preservers" (Qur'an 15:9); "Falsehood does not approach it from before or after" (Qur'an 41:42). This is not taken to mean that human beings will not err in their interpretation of the message, but only that access to the true meaning of revelation will remain until the end of time. Muslims thus acknowledge and revere a panorama of Prophets to whom God has sent a message of truth. This cycle of prophecy began with Adam and ended with Muhammad, who is the "Seal of Prophets" (*Khatam al-Nabiyyin*) (Qur'an 33:40) and who said in his famous farewell address, "O people, no Prophet or Messenger will come after me and no new faith will be born after me."[3]

The station of prophecy is not attained through human aspiration. It is bestowed by God before the beginning of time. This pretemporal origination of prophecy is referred to by the Prophet Muhammad in a famous saying: "I was a Prophet when Adam was between water and clay."[4] The Prophets are sent at different points in human history to reestablish the relationship between the Divine and the human. According to the Qur'an, God's Messengers have been sent to all human communities: "We have sent to every people a Messenger, that they may worship God" (Qur'an 16:32); "For every people there is a Messenger" (Qur'an 10:48). Each Messenger is sent to teach Divine Oneness (*tawhid*) and submission to God (*Islam*): "We never sent a Messenger before you save that We revealed to him, saying, 'There is no god but I, so worship Me'" (Qur'an 21:25). God specifically says to Moses: "I am God! There is no god but Me. So worship Me" (Qur'an 20:14). The Prophets Noah, Hud, Salih, and Shu'ayb (Jethro) are presented as saying to their communities: "O my people! Worship God! You have no other god but Him" (Qur'an 7:59; 7:65; 7:73; 7:85). For this reason Muslims are commanded to believe not only in the Prophet Muhammad but in all of God's Prophets as well:

> Say: We believe in God and that which is revealed unto us and that which is revealed unto Abraham and Ishmael, and Isaac, and Jacob, and the Patriarchs, and that which Moses and Jesus received, and that which the Prophets received from their Lord. We do not distinguish between any of them, and we are unto him submitters.
>
> (Qur'an 2:136; 3:84)

SUBMISSION (*ISLAM*) AND PROPHECY

Every revelation to every Prophet of God is seen as a form of *Islam* or submission to God. The Qur'an thus presents previous Prophets and their followers as Muslims—those who submit to God. The first Prophet to refer to himself as a submitter is Noah, who said to his people, "My recompense is but with God, and I was commanded to be among those who submit to God (*muslimin*)" (Qur'an 10:72). The Qur'an says of Abraham: "Abraham was not a Jew or a Christian, rather he was a true devotee (*hanif*),[5] a submitter to God (*muslim*)" (Qur'an 3:67). According to the Qur'an, "[Abraham's] Lord said to him, 'Submit!' He said, 'I submit to the Lord of the Worlds'" (Qur'an 2:131). After Abraham and Ishmael erected the Ka'ba, they prayed, "Our Lord, make us submitters unto You, and make our offspring a nation submitting unto You. Show us our rites and turn, relenting, unto us" (Qur'an 2:128). From this prayer began the spread of "submission" among all the Children of Abraham: "And Abraham counseled his sons, as did Jacob, 'O my sons, God has chosen the religion (*din*) for you, so do not die but as submitters to God'" (Qur'an 2:132). In obedience to the wish of Jacob, the Prophet Joseph said to God, "Let me die as a submitter and bind me to the righteous" (Qur'an 12:101). Indeed, all of Jacob's sons promised their father to worship God and to be submitters to His will:

> Were you witnesses when death came upon Jacob, when he said to his sons, "What will you worship after me?" They said, "We worship your God, the

God of your fathers, Abraham, Ishmael, and Isaac, a single God, and we are submitters unto Him."

(Qur'an 2:133)

These passages demonstrate how former Prophets are presented in the Qur'an as Muslims, submitters to God. Although they are less numerous, there are other passages that refer to the followers of the Prophets as submitters as well. The first of these in order of revelation refers to Moses, who tells his followers, "O my people, if you believe in God then trust [in Him] if you are submitters" (Qur'an 10:84). Pharaoh's magicians believe in Moses after witnessing his miracles and respond to Pharaoh's threats, saying, "You only take vengeance on us because we believed in the signs of our Lord when they came to us. Our Lord, pour patience upon us and let us die as submitters" (Qur'an 7:126).

The next account in order of revelation is the story of Bilqis, Queen of Sheba, who was called with her people to follow Solomon. First, Solomon sent a bird with his message, saying: "O you people, a Noble Book has been presented to me. It is from Solomon, in the name of God the Merciful, the Compassionate, that you not resist [God] and come to [God] as submitters" (Qur'an 27:29–31). Solomon then confirms that he and his people are submitters to God, saying, "We were given knowledge before this and we were submitters" (Qur'an 27:42). After meeting Solomon, Bilqis agrees to follow his religion, saying, "My Lord, truly I have wronged myself. I have submitted with Solomon to God, the Lord of the Worlds" (Qur'an 27:44). This story gives a fresh account of one of the many Hebrew Prophets who are mentioned in both the Bible and the Qur'an. In other passages, the Apostles of Jesus also refer to themselves as submitters, saying to Jesus, "We are helpers of God! We believe! Bear witness that we are submitters" (Qur'an 3:52). This is confirmed in the following verse, where God states: "Then I revealed to the Apostles to believe in Me and My Messenger [Jesus]. They responded, 'We believe and bear witness that we are submitters'" (Qur'an 5:111).

Through passages such as these, the whole of religious history is presented as different modes of Islam—as different ways in which human beings have submitted to God. Thus, the Qur'an says of Jews and Christians: "When [the Qur'an] is recited to them, they say, 'We believe in it. Truly, it is the truth from our Lord. Indeed, before it [was revealed] we were submitters" (Qur'an 28:53). The forms of submission to God—the rites, rituals, and laws incumbent upon God's message—may differ, but the Message of submission and divine oneness never changes: "We never sent a Messenger before thee save that We revealed to him, saying, 'There is no god but Me, so worship Me'" (Qur'an 21:25).

According to Ayatollah Ja'far Sobhani, "Each of the religious dispensations brought by the Prophets was the most complete form of religion for the time and the people concerned."[6] Because of this difference in religious forms, some Prophets are favored over others, although all Prophets are equally revered as Messengers of God:

> And those Messengers— some We have favored above others. Among them was [Moses] to whom God spoke, and [God] raised some in degrees. We gave Jesus son of Mary the clear explications, and We confirmed him with the Holy Spirit.

> (Qur'an 2:253)

Yet God also says, "We do not differentiate between any of His Messengers" (Qur'an 2:285) and commands Muslims to have faith in all of them. Therefore, the degree to which one religion can be seen as superior to another depends not on the Messenger or Prophet through whom it was revealed but rather on the degree to which its adherents remain true to the teachings of God and the Messenger or Prophet through whom God revealed them.

The words Messenger (*rasul*) and Prophet (*nabi*) are often used interchangeably, but they have specific meanings in an Islamic context. According to some scholars, Messengers differ from Prophets in that Messengers bring an entirely new religion, a new *din*, whereas the Prophets reaffirm a previously revealed religion and reestablish its proper observance. A Messenger is also enjoined by God to call people to follow His message, whereas this is not incumbent upon all Prophets. A Messenger thus fulfills all of the functions of a Prophet, but a Prophet does not perform the same functions as a Messenger. The Prophets are far more numerous than Messengers, totaling 124,000 according to one tradition. Among the Messengers, Muslim scholars identify an elite group known as *Uluw al-Azm*, "Those who Possess Steadfastness" (Qur'an 46:35). This term refers to five key Prophets of the Judeo-Christian-Islamic tradition: Noah, Abraham, Moses, Jesus, and Muhammad.

All Prophets and Messengers teach divine oneness (*tawhid*) and submission (*Islam*), such that all people can follow them and implement their teachings. However, the Prophets and the Messengers are also believed to possess qualities that cannot be imitated. The most evident of these are the miracles (*mu'jizat*) they perform. Well-known examples of Prophetic miracles include Jesus' ability to raise the dead and the miracles of Moses to which both the Torah and the Qur'an attest. These include the staff that turned into a serpent (Qur'an 7:117; 27:10; 28:31, *et passim*), the hand that turned white (Qur'an 7:108; 20:22; *et passim*), the parting of the Red Sea (26:63), and Moses's bringing forth water by striking a boulder with his staff (Qur'an 2:60; 7:160).

The Messengers and the Prophets are also inimitable in their inerrancy and impeccability (*'isma*), meaning that they cannot make errors in conveying the revelation that is entrusted to them and that they cannot be disobedient toward God. The following passage is generally understood as alluding to the all-encompassing protection under which God places His Prophets:

> [He is] Knower of the Unseen; He reveals His secret unto no one, save whom He pleases as a Messenger. Then He makes a guard to go before and behind [His Messengers], that He may know if they have indeed conveyed the messages of their Lord. He surrounds all their actions, and He takes account of all things.
>
> (Qur'an 72:26–28)

Inerrancy is believed to be essential for the Prophets so that they can be fully trusted by their followers and that the ultimate purpose of prophecy, divine guidance, can be realized. As such, God says regarding the Prophets: "We chose them and guided them unto a straight path" (Qur'an 6:87). Muslims also believe that God's protection of the Prophets from sin and error must remain with a Prophet his entire life, even before the Prophetic mission begins. For if one were to have led a life without probity and then claim to be a Prophet, his former acts would cause many to doubt the veracity of the message.

Although the Judeo-Christian-Islamic Prophets are the majority of those mentioned in the Qur'an, prophecy is not necessarily limited to the Abrahamic tradition alone. As the Qur'an says:

> Truly, We have revealed to you [Muhammad] as We revealed to Noah and the Prophets after him. And We revealed to Abraham, Ishmael, Isaac, and the Patriarchs, and Jesus, Job, Jonah, Aaron, and Solomon, and We gave David the Psalms; and Messengers of whom We have told you and Messengers of whom We have not told you.
>
> (Qur'an 4:163–164)

Only 24 Prophets are mentioned by name in the Qur'an, but a *hadith*, or saying of the Prophet Muhammad, tells us that there have been either 313 or 315 Messengers throughout human history. Thus, there are far more Messengers than those who are mentioned in the Qur'an. Though most Muslim scholars maintain a narrow and exclusivist view of revelation, others have read this Hadith account as a possible reference to the Messengers of non-Abrahamic traditions, such as Buddha. The vast majority of Islamic scholars maintain that only men can be Prophets, and for this they cite the following verse of the Qur'an: "We sent no one before you but men to whom We revealed [Our message], so ask the people of remembrance if you know not" (Qur'an 21:7). A small minority of scholars, mostly in Islamic Spain, maintained that this verse should not be read as a limitation and that the Virgin Mary and Eve before her were both Prophets as well.

THE UNITY AND DIVERSITY OF PROPHECY

Because human collectivities speak different languages and face different trials, Messengers of God and their corresponding messages differ in language and in the laws they ordain. Regarding the issue of language the Qur'an says: "We have sent no Messenger save with the tongue of his people" (Qur'an 14:4). Regarding the difference in revealed laws, the Qur'an states:

> For each [people] We have made a law and a way (*minhaj*). If God willed, He would have made you a single people, but [He made you as you are] in order to try you regarding what has come to you. So compete in good deeds. To God is your return, all of you. Then He will inform you of that wherein you differed.

> (Qur'an 5:48)

There are thus different ways of understanding God and the relationship with God for different human collectivities. God has sent many laws through various Messengers. To each law corresponds a particular way—a spiritual path—and this path entails the performance of particular rites. Other passages of the Qur'an confirm that God has revealed not only different laws but also different ways of worship:

> For every people (*umma*) We have made a rite that they practice with devotion. So let them not contend with you in this matter. And call unto your Lord; truly you follow straight guidance. If they dispute with you then say, "God knows best what you do. God will judge between you on the Day of Resurrection regarding that wherein you differed."

> (Qur'an 22:67–69)

Every religion entails prayer, fasting, and almsgiving, among other obligations, although the exact forms differ. One of the reasons for such differences in creed and practice is revealed in the following verse:

> O Mankind! We have created you of a male and a female, and have made you peoples and tribes that you may know one another; surely the most honorable of you with God is the most pious; surely God is Knowing, Aware.

> (Qur'an 49:13)

Despite the different forms of human communities and beliefs, the fundamental core of each message is the same. Thus, Jesus reports in the Qur'an
that he was sent "to confirm the truth of the Torah that was before me, and
to make lawful to you certain things that were forbidden to you before"
(Qur'an 3:50). So too, the Qur'an proclaims the validity of all the Prophets
and scriptures that have preceded it: "What We have revealed to you
[Muhammad] from the Book is the Truth, confirming what was before
you" (Qur'an 35:31). Another verse states: "[God] has sent down upon
you [Muhammad] the Book with the Truth, confirming what was before it,
and He sent down the Torah and the Gospel aforetime as guidance to the
people" (Qur'an 3:3). The Qur'an thus portrays an underlying continuity
between all revelations and hence all Messengers and Prophets. As God says
to the Prophet Muhammad, "Nothing has been said to you save what was
said to the Messengers before you" (Qur'an 10:48). Regarding the Qur'an,
God states: "Truly it is a revelation from the Lord of the worlds in a clear
Arabic tongue, brought down by the Faithful Spirit (Gabriel) upon your
heart that you may be among the warners. Truly, it is in the scriptures
(*zubur*) of the ancients" (Qur'an 26:192–196).[7] And in another verse:
"Truly, this [message] is in the pages (*suhuf*) of the ancients, the pages of
Abraham and Moses" (Qur'an 87:18–19). Reaffirming the continuous line
of Prophecy, the Prophet Muhammad said, "The Prophets are half-
brothers; their mothers differ but their religion (*din*) is one."[8] In this chapter, I can only touch upon the most prominent figures in this noble lineage.

ADAM: THE FIRST MESSENGER

In the Qur'an, the first of these "half-brothers" is Adam. Whereas the
Christian tradition sees Adam as a fallen being in need of salvation through
Jesus, in the Qur'an he is presented as the first of all Prophets and the first
with whom God made a covenant: "We made a covenant with Adam before,
but he forgot; We did not find in him any determination" (Qur'an 20:115).
In Islam, the cyclical drama of receiving, forgetting, breaking, and renewing
the covenant with God, which is a central theme of the Hebrew Scriptures,
begins not with Abraham but with Adam, the first of all human beings. As
such, the Qur'an gives a different version of Adam's fall than does the Bible.
In the Qur'an, Adam is not tempted by Eve. Satan tempts both Adam and
Eve, and both are responsible for their fall from the Garden. Because of their
transgression, all of humankind was banished: "God expelled them from that
in which they were. We said, 'Descend all of you, as foes to one another'"
(Qur'an 2:36). This "descent" from the Garden as "foes to one another"
represents the consequences of forgetting and breaking God's covenant. In
the Qur'an, after the fall, Adam and Eve repent for their sins: "They said,
'Our Lord, We have wronged ourselves. If You do not forgive us and do

not have mercy upon us, we will be among those who are lost'" (Qur'an 7:23). Then God relents unto Adam and reveals His guidance:

> Then Adam received words [of revelation] from his Lord, so He relented to him; Truly, He is the Oft-Relenting, the Merciful. We said, "Descend from [the Garden] all of you, and when a guidance comes to you from Me, then for whomever follows My guidance there is no fear, nor shall they grieve."
>
> (Qur'an 2:37–38)

From one perspective, the words received by Adam from God mark the beginning of the cycle of revelation. Before falling from grace, Adam and Eve were in no need of words to remind them of the oneness of God and submission to His will. However, now that they have forgotten these truths, human beings must receive periodic reminders to bring them back to their realization. They are in need of Messengers and Prophets to remind them of the Truth.

ABRAHAM: A FATHER OF MONOTHEISM

The name Abraham is mentioned as frequently in the Qur'an as in the Hebrew Scriptures and the New Testament. Many verses are dedicated to the story of Abraham and his struggle against polytheism. These verses repeat some of the accounts from the Bible. However, as with all of the Prophets, the Qur'an provides additional information and new perspectives that are not available in the Bible.[9] These do not contradict the Biblical accounts; rather, they complement them.

One of the most important additions to the Biblical story of Abraham concerns his first turn to monotheism and his denunciation of his father and tribe. In the Bible, Abraham's father is named Terah (Genesis 11:24–32), but in the Qur'an, he is called Azar. The story begins with Abraham's opposition to his father's idol worshipping: "Abraham said to his father Azar, 'Do you take idols for gods? Truly I see you and your people in manifest error'" (Qur'an 6:74). The Bible recognizes the polytheism of Abraham's father in the book of Joshua but says little about it. In the Qur'an, however, the conflict between Abraham and the polytheism of his people is of central importance. It is presented as a foreshadowing of the conflict that the Prophet Muhammad would later experience with the idol worshippers of pre-Islamic Arabia. The Qur'an provides a direct reference to the situation in Mecca during the life of the Prophet by switching seamlessly from the story of Abraham and his tribe to that of Muhammad and the Arabs:

> When Abraham said to his father and his people, "Surely I am innocent of what you worship, save Him who originated me, for truly He will guide me." He made

it an enduring word among his posterity, so that they would return [to God].
Nay, but I gave these and their fathers enjoyment until the Truth and a clear
Messenger came to them. And when the Truth came to them, they said, "This
is sorcery; truly we do not believe in it." They say, "Why was this Qur'an not
made to descend upon a great man from one of the two cities [Mecca and Ta'if]?

(Qur'an 43:26–33)

Positioned between the two accounts, it is not clear whether the sentence
beginning with, "Nay, but I gave these and their fathers enjoyment" applies
to Abraham's people or to Muhammad's people, or to both. Indeed,
Muhammad's rebuke of his people is portrayed in the same way as Abraham's
rebuke of his father:

O my father, why do you worship that which cannot hear or see, and avails you
not? O my father, Truly there has come to me knowledge which has not come
unto you. So follow me, and I will lead you on a right path.

(Qur'an 19:41–43)

Like the idol worshippers of Mecca, Abraham's father and his people were
obstinate and unyielding. For they too were more devoted to the ways of
their ancestors than to the ways of God. The conflict between these opposing
ways is illustrated in the following passage:

Truly, We gave Abraham his guidance beforehand, and We were knowledgeable
of him, when he said to his father and his people, "What are these images to
which you pay devotion?" They said, "We found our fathers worshipping
them." He replied, "Truly you and your fathers were in manifest error!" They
said, "Have you come to us with the truth, or are you among those who jest?"
He replied, "No, rather your Lord is the Lord of the heavens and the earth,
who created [these images]; and I am among those who testify to that."

(Qur'an 21:51–56)

Having thus challenged his people, Abraham then smashes all of their idols
except the largest. When asked what had happened, he responds that the
largest idol had destroyed the others and invited his people to question the
idols regarding this. They respond, "You know well that they do not speak"
(Qur'an 21:65). To which Abraham replies, "So instead of God do you
worship what can neither benefit nor harm you? Fie, upon you and all that
you worship instead of God! Do you not understand?" (Qur'an 21:66–67)
For many Muslims Abraham represents the archetype of the sincere monotheist, who will stop at nothing to eradicate the iniquities that surround him.
They thus hearken to Abraham as a father of pure monotheism and see the
Qur'an and the *Sunna,* or custom, of the Prophet Muhammad as a renewal

of Abraham's mission. Several verses of the Qur'an imply that for his sincere belief and indefatigable opposition to polytheism, Abraham was rewarded with offspring who would maintain the line of prophecy: "And when he had withdrawn from them and what they worshipped instead of God, We granted him Isaac and Jacob and each of them we made a Prophet" (Qur'an 19:49). The line of Prophets that have come forth from Abraham's loins is thus seen as a means by which God keeps His covenant by continuing to guide all of humankind. Whereas Judaism only recognizes the line of Prophets who emerged from Abraham's son Isaac and grandson Jacob, Islam maintains that Abraham's eldest son Ishmael was also party to the covenant and that the legacy of prophecy would be continued in his progeny as well. Indeed, it is from the line of Ishmael that the Prophet Muhammad descended.

ISHMAEL AND ISAAC

Ishmael is seldom mentioned in the Hebrew Scriptures and is never mentioned in the New Testament. From this perspective, the Qur'an can be seen as the great restorer of Ishmael to his place in salvation history, for it claims that he too was party to all that was promised to the family of Abraham in the Torah.[10] Thus, the Qur'an repeatedly mentions both Isaac and Ishmael among the Prophets of God (Qur'an 2:136; 3:84; 4:163).[11]

Like the Hebrew Scriptures, the Qur'an provides extensive accounts of the descendants of Isaac, from Jacob to Jesus. However, the Qur'an focuses more upon the life of Ishmael and his relationship with Abraham than upon the life of Isaac. Even the famous sacrifice of Isaac is retold in a manner that makes it appear that the elder son Ishmael may have been the subject of the sacrifice instead of his brother. Some scholars, however, argue that the Qur'anic account supports the Biblical account in which Isaac is the one who was to be sacrificed:[12]

> Abraham said, "As for me I am going to my Lord who will guide me. My Lord, grant to me [progeny] among the righteous." Therefore, We informed him of a noble son. When he reached the age of maturity, Abraham said, "O my son, I see in my dream that I am to sacrifice you. So what is your opinion?" He said, "O my father, do what you are commanded! You will find me— God willing— one of the forbearing. When both had submitted and [Abraham] laid [his son] down upon his forehead, We called to him, "O Abraham, you have verified the vision." Thusly do We reward those who do what is beautiful. Truly, this is the clear trial. So We redeemed him with a great sacrifice, and left it for future generations. May peace be upon Abraham. Likewise do We recompense those who do what is beautiful. Truly, he is among Our righteous servants. Then We informed him of Isaac, a Prophet from among the righteous, and We blessed him and Isaac.

(Qur'an 37:100–112)

In accordance with Abraham's act of complete submission, Muslims continue to celebrate this event every year at the end of the annual Hajj pilgrimage to Mecca. This day of commemoration is the highest Holy Day of the Muslim calendar and is called the Feast of Sacrifice (*'Id al-Adha*) or the Great Feast (*al-'Id al-Kabir*). Muslims throughout the world gather for a morning prayer, pay alms to the poor, and then sacrifice a ram, designating a portion of the sacrifice for those who are less fortunate.

According to Muslim belief, the Hajj and its rites, including the sacrifice, were not originated by Muhammad; they were first consecrated by Abraham and Ishmael. In one of Abraham's visits to the desert where Hagar and Ishmael had settled, he was instructed to build the sanctuary of the Ka'ba in the valley of Mecca, also known as "Baca," and establish the annual pilgrimage:

> We established for Abraham the place of the House, [saying], "Do not associate anything with Me, and purify My House for those who circumambulate it, those who stand, and those who bow down. And announce the pilgrimage to the people, that they may come to you by foot and by every lean mount, coming from every deep ravine; that they may bear witness to the blessings they have and remember the name of God on specific days."

> (Qur'an 22:26–28)

In another verse, the command, "Purify My house," is addressed to both Ishmael and Abraham (Qur'an 2:125). According to Muslim historians, Abraham and Ishmael built the Ka'ba together on the site where Adam had built a sanctuary 20 generations before. The final piece of the Ka'ba was the Black Stone, which was brought to Abraham by an angel. Of this stone, the Prophet Muhammad said: "It descended from Paradise whiter than milk, but the sins of the sons of Adam made it black."[13] Having established a line of his progeny in the deserts of Arabia and worked with Ishmael to establish a house of worship in accordance with the command of God, Abraham prayed and thanked God:

> Our Lord, I have settled a line of my offspring in a barren valley at Your Holy House— our Lord— that they may perform prayer. So make the hearts of the people incline to them and nourish them with fruits that they may be grateful... Praise be to God who has granted me Ishmael and Isaac in spite of my old age. Truly, my Lord hears supplications.

> (Qur'an 14:37–39)

Abraham's prayer was granted, and the Ka'ba became a site of worship visited by pilgrims from Arabia and beyond. According to Muslim historians, the Arabs kept the covenant of Abraham through circumcision and pure monotheism. In recognition of this bond, the Ka'ba was honored by the descendants of both Ishmael and Isaac. The pilgrimage to Mecca or "Baca" is thus consecrated in a Psalm of David:

> Blessed are those whose strength is in You,
> And who have set their hearts on a pilgrimage.
> As they pass through the Valley of Baca,
> They make it a place of springs;
> The autumn rains also cover it with pools.
> They go from strength to strength
> Until each appears before God in Zion.

(Psalms 84:5–7*)*

In later generations, the Ka'ba came to be contaminated by the polytheism of the surrounding Arab tribes. Through the course of time, the rites of worship that had been revealed to Abraham and Ishmael were forgotten. Nonetheless, there remained in Arabia a few lone worshippers, who continued to follow the religion of Abraham and Ishmael. These were known as the *hunafa'* (sing. *hanif*), or "True Devotees." However, by the time of the Prophet Muhammad in the seventh century CE, few remained who practiced the traditions of Abraham.[14] Thus, when the Prophet Muhammad reestablished the proper observance of the pilgrimage toward the end of his life, the term "the legacy of Abraham" was constantly upon his lips.

MOSES IN THE QUR'AN

Although the Prophet Muhammad is seen in Islam as a renewer of the primordial religion of Abraham and the Qur'an alludes to correlations between Abraham and Muhammad in their confrontations with idolaters, the most prominent Messenger in the whole of the Qur'an is Moses. The basic outline of the story of Moses and the Israelites in the Qur'an is the same as that in the Bible. His mother entrusts him to the waters of the Nile, and he is found and raised in the house of Pharaoh. However, in the Qur'an it is the wife of Pharaoh, not Pharaoh's daughter, who finds Moses. When he comes of age, Moses kills an Egyptian who was abusive toward a Jew. He then flees to the land of Midian, where he marries a daughter of Jethro (the Prophet Shu'ayb in the Qur'an) and serves him for 8–10 years as part of his marriage pact. As he returns to Egypt, Moses begins his prophetic mission with his encounter with the burning bush.

> Go to Pharaoh. He has been insolent, but speak gently to him, that he may be mindful, or perchance fear. "Our Lord," said Moses and Aaron, "truly we fear that he may transgress against us, or be insolent." "Fear not," said He, "Surely I shall be with you, hearing and seeing. So go you both to Pharaoh and say, 'We

are the Messengers of your Lord, so send forth with us the Children of Israel and chastise them not.'"

(Qur'an 20:43–47)

This confrontation with Pharaoh is the most frequently referenced aspect of Moses's story in the Qur'an. It is directly mentioned in 10 separate passages and alluded to in several others.[15] It is often seen by Muslims as foreshadowing the Prophet Muhammad's confrontation with the leaders of Mecca. The penultimate condemnation of Pharaoh's unbelief in the Qur'an comes not from Moses but from "a believing man from the people of Pharaoh who concealed his belief" (Qur'an 40:28). He rebukes Pharaoh for rejecting Moses's message and for demanding that Moses be slain:

What, will you slay a man because he says, "My Lord is God," even though he has brought you clear signs from your Lord? If he is a liar, his lying is upon his own head; but if he is truthful, some of what he promises you will surely beset you. Truly, God does not guide the one who is prodigal and a liar. O my people, today the kingdom is yours, as masters in the land. But who will help us against the might of God if it comes upon us?

(Qur'an 40:28–29)

The man compares the disbelief of Pharaoh and his people to that of those who had previously disbelieved the Prophets Noah and Joseph and concludes with a warning: "As for those who dispute about the signs of God, without any authority having come to them, hateful is this in the sight of God and the believers; so God puts a seal on every proud and arrogant heart" (Qur'an 40:34–35).

As in the Bible, Moses's initial warnings are followed by many afflictions from God until Pharaoh relents and releases the Israelites. Pharaoh then follows the Israelites with his army, only to be swallowed alive by the Red Sea. However, here the Qur'an provides another new twist when Pharaoh confesses his belief in Moses immediately before he perishes, saying, "I believe that there is no god except He in whom the children of Israel believe; and I am among the submitters" (Qur'an 10:90).

As the Israelites march toward the Promised Land, the Qur'anic account continues to follow that of the Bible. Although they are acknowledged as the chosen people whom God has favored over others (Qur'an 2:47; 2:122; 45:16), the Israelites are also portrayed as an ungrateful and contentious community that continually questions the authority of Moses. As in the Bible, Moses is called to Mount Sinai, where he stays for 40 days and returns to find that the people have forsaken all that had been ordained by worshiping the golden calf. In the Qur'an, however, it is not Aaron who is blamed for this transgression. Instead, it is a man referred to as "the Samaritan" (*al-Samiri*) who tells the people, "This is your God and the God of Moses; he has

forgotten" (Qur'an 20:88). As in the Biblical account, Moses becomes infuri-
ated and destroys the tablets given to him by God (Qur'an 7:150). He then
returns to the mountain and receives a new set of tablets. Unlike the Bible,
the Qur'an does not list the commandments given to Moses, although each
of them can be found in various places and forms throughout the text.

Upon reaching the Promised Land, the Israelites again disobey Moses,
fearing its inhabitants:

> "O my people" [said Moses], "enter the Holy Land that God has ordained for
> you, and turn not back in your traces, for you will then revert to [being] losers."
> They said, "Moses, there are tyrannical people in it. Surely, we will not enter it
> until they depart from it. If they depart from it, then surely we will enter." ...
> They said, "Moses, we will not enter it so long as they remain in it. So go forth,
> you and your Lord and do battle; we will be sitting here."
>
> (Qur'an 5:21–24)

For their intransigence the Israelites are banished from entering the Holy
Land for 40 years: "Said [God], 'Then it shall be forbidden to them for forty
years, while they wander throughout the Earth'" (Qur'an 5:26).

As with the story of Abraham and his people, the Qur'anic story of
Moses is recounted in a way that bears many similarities to the struggles that
the Prophet Muhammad faced with his community. Both Moses and
Muhammad began receiving revelations at the age of 40. Both were called
to confront recalcitrant and impious rulers, over whom they achieved victory.
Each was forced to flee his home in order to found a new religion. Most
important, each brought a complete revealed law that governs both the
religious and the communal lives of their peoples. In this vein, many Muslims
have read the following account of a future Moses-like Prophet in the Torah
as an allusion to the Prophet Muhammad:

> The Lord said unto me, "They have well spoken that which they have spoken.
> Therefore, I will raise for them *a Prophet from among their brethren, like unto
> you [Moses]*, and will put My words in his mouth. And he shall speak unto them
> all that I shall command him.
>
> (Deuteronomy 18:17–18, emphasis added)

The Qur'an itself refers to such biblical allusions to the Prophet Muhammad in the following passage:

> My mercy encompasses all things. Therefore, I shall ordain for those who
> are God-fearing and pay the alms tax, and those who believe in Our signs, who
> follow the Messenger, the Unlettered Prophet (Muhammad), whom they find
> written down for them in the Torah and the Gospel, commanding them to do
> good and forbidding them from evil, making good things lawful for them and

making unseemly things unlawful, and relieving them of their loads and the fetters that were upon them. Those who believe in him, succor him, aid him, and follow the light that has been sent down with him—they are the ones that will prosper.

(Qur'an 7:155–156)

JESUS AS A MESSENGER

Perhaps the most controversial aspects of the Islamic understanding of Prophets and Messengers are the teachings regarding Jesus. Jesus is accepted as one of the five Messengers who possess steadfastness (*uluw al-azm*) and is referred to in the Qur'an as the Word of God (Qur'an 3:45; 4:171). He is aided by the Holy Spirit (Qur'an 2:87; 2:253; 5:110) and is regarded as the Messiah (*al-Masih*), but he is not accepted as the Son of God or as God incarnate.[16] The belief in the incarnation of Jesus is in fact repudiated in several verses: "They disbelieve who say, 'God is the Messiah, son of Mary'" (Qur'an 5:17; 5:72). Other verses of the Qur'an explicitly deny that God has a son:

They say that God has a son. Glory be to [God]! Rather, to [God] belong all that is in the heavens and the earth; everything is obedient to Him.

(Qur'an 2:116)

The Christians say the Messiah is the "son of God." That is what they say with their mouths; they imitate the words of those who disbelieved before. May God fight them; how deceived are they!

(Qur'an 9:30)

It is not for God to take a son. Glory be to Him! When He decrees a matter, He simply says to it "Be!" and it is.

(Qur'an 19:35)

Following upon these arguments, the Qur'an emphasizes that Jesus was not God, but a servant and Messenger of God: "The Messiah does not disdain to be a servant to God" (Qur'an 4:172); "The Messiah, the son of Mary is but a Messenger; Messengers before him have passed away. His mother was truthful and both of them ate food [like normal human beings]" (Qur'an 5:75).[17] Despite his humanity, Jesus still has a special place among the Prophets of Islam. Regarding the place of Jesus in relation to the other Prophets and Messengers, the Qur'an says:

These are the Messengers. We have preferred some of them to others. Among them is the one to whom God spoke [Moses]. We raised some of them by degrees; and We gave Jesus the son of Mary the clear proofs and supported him with the Holy Spirit.

(Qur'an 2:253)

The best example of Jesus being preferred over other Prophets is the miracle of the virgin birth, to which the Qur'an attests:

And mention in the Book Mary, when she withdrew from her people to an eastern place, secluding herself from them. Then We sent to her Our spirit, which appeared to her as a man. She said, "Truly I seek refuge in the All-Merciful from you, if you be God-fearing." He said, "I am but a Messenger from your Lord, to give you a sinless son." She said, "How shall there be a son to me when no man has touched me, nor have I been unchaste?" He said, "Thus says your Lord, 'That is easy for Me, and We will make him a sign for the people and a mercy from Us. It is a thing decreed.'"

(Qur'an 19:16–21; see also 3:45–47)[18]

The chapter of Mary in the Qur'an also tells of the virgin birth, providing details not found in any of the Gospel accounts:

She carried [Jesus in her womb] and then withdrew with him to a far-off place. When the labor pains drove her to the trunk of a palm tree, she said: "Would that I had died before this and had been utterly forgotten!" Then he (an angel?) called to her from under the tree: "Do not grieve, for your Lord has placed a stream beneath you. Shake the trunk of the palm tree and ripe dates will fall upon you. Eat and drink and be of good cheer. And if you see any person, say: 'I have consecrated a fast to the All-Merciful, so I will not speak to anyone today.'"[19] Then she came with [Jesus] to her people. They said, "O Mary! You have brought a grave thing! O sister of Aaron,[20] your father was not a bad man, nor was your mother unchaste." She pointed to him. They said, "How can we speak to one who is an infant in the cradle?" [Jesus] said, "Indeed, I am the servant of God. He has given me the Book and made me a Prophet. He has made me a blessing wherever I am and has ordained for me prayer and almsgiving so long as I live; and He has made me devoted to my mother and did not make me a wretched tyrant. Peace upon me the day I was born, the day I die, and the day I am raised up alive."

(Qur'an 19:22–33)

The Prophet Muhammad is said to have confirmed that of all human beings only Jesus and the Virgin Mary were born without the stain of sin: "There is none born among the offspring of Adam, but that Satan touches it. A child, therefore, cries loudly at the time of its birth because of the touch of Satan, except for Mary and her child."[21]

Not only was the birth of Jesus a miracle but other passages also bear witness to a creative life-giving power possessed by Jesus that was not granted to any other Prophet:

> Truly, I have come to you with a sign from your Lord. Truly, I will create for you the figure of a bird from clay, and I will breathe into it so that it becomes a real bird by the will of God. And I heal the blind and the leper, and I will give life to the dead by the will of God. And I will inform you of what you eat and of what you store in your houses. Surely in that is a sign for you if you are believers.

> (Qur'an 3:49)

> Then God said, "O Jesus son of Mary, remember My blessing upon you and upon your mother, when I supported you through the Holy Spirit. You speak to the people in the cradle and in maturity. And I taught you the Book and the Wisdom, and the Torah and the Gospel. And when you create the figure of a bird from clay and you breathe into it, then it is a real bird, by My will. You heal the blind and the lepers by My will; and you raise the dead by My will."

> (Qur'an 5:110)

Like Christians, Muslims believe that Jesus will return at the end of time to make justice reign on earth. As the Prophet Muhammad says, "By Him in whose hand is my soul, the son of Mary will soon descend among you as a just judge."[22] This is another way in which Jesus has a nature that is different not only from other human beings but also from other Messengers and Prophets. Nonetheless, Muslims do not accept the crucifixion of Jesus. As for the Resurrection, he was not raised from the dead but was raised up to the divine presence, as the following passage of the Qur'an attests:

> [The Jews] said, "Truly, we have killed the Messiah, Jesus, son of Mary, the Messenger of God." They did not kill him, nor did they crucify him, but it was made to appear so to them. Those who differ regarding this are in doubt about it. They have no knowledge regarding it, save to follow conjecture, and they certainly did not kill him. Rather, God raised him unto Himself. God is the Mighty, the Wise.

> (Qur'an 4:157–158)

Most Muslims, scholars, and laypersons alike view these verses as a straightforward denial of the crucifixion. They maintain that Jesus was assumed directly into heaven and that another was crucified in his place. However, while most Muslim scholars maintain this position, they also aver that God raised Jesus into heaven from life and that he did not suffer a mortal death. As the Qur'an states:

Then God said, "O Jesus, I am taking you, and raising you unto Me and will purify you of those who disbelieve and will place those who follow you above those who disbelieve until the Day of Resurrection."

(Qur'an 3:55)

Just as the Prophet Muhammad has a close connection with both Abraham and Moses before him, so too, Muhammad said of himself and Jesus: "I am the most worthy of Jesus the son of Mary in this life and the hereafter."[23] In addition, the Qur'an maintains that Jesus had foreseen that he would be followed by the Prophet Muhammad:

Then Jesus the son of Mary said, "O Children of Israel, truly I am a Messenger of God unto you, confirming what was before me in the Torah and bringing you good tidings of a Messenger coming after me whose name is Ahmad."

(Qur'an 61:6)[24]

The name Ahmad means, "most praised." It comes from the same root as the name Muhammad (H-M-D), and Muslims have long recognized it as one of the honorific names given to the Prophet by God Himself. This belief is based on a saying of the Prophet Muhammad: "I have several names: I am Muhammad; I am Ahmad; I am *al-Mahy* (literally, "The Eraser"), by means of which God eliminates unbelief."[25]

MUHAMMAD AS THE COMPLETION OF PROPHECY

Although according to Muslim belief, Muhammad came 62 generations after Abraham,[26] the message he brought continually emphasizes the way of Abraham. The pilgrimage to the Ka'ba had continued before the time of Muhammad, but many of its components had been corrupted or forgotten. This is why Muhammad called his followers to "the legacy of Abraham" when he was first able to make the pilgrimage to Mecca with the Muslims. In this vein, the Qur'an states: "Abraham was not a Jew or a Christian; rather he was a true devotee, a submitter (Muslim)" (Qur'an 3:67). This verse should not be understood as a condemnation of previous revelations, for even Jewish and Christian scholars acknowledge that Abraham did not have the same form of religious practice as do they. Rather, this verse is a call to the universality of "submission," which is believed to be at the heart of all religions and is the essence of the Qur'anic view of Islam. From an Islamic perspective, all of the Prophets, from Adam to Muhammad, were submitters who came to help other human beings learn how to fully submit to God. Though they came at different times to different peoples and spoke different languages, their mission was one. Expounding upon this, the Prophet Muhammad said:

The likeness of me among the Prophets before me is as a man who builds a house and then refines it and beautifies it, except for the place of one brick in a corner [of the house]. Then the people come and walk around it, marveling at it, and saying, "If only this brick were in place." I am the brick and I am the Seal of the Prophets.[27]

This does not indicate the superiority of one Prophet over others. Just as the last brick used in building a house is not thereby superior to the previous bricks, it does bring greater cohesion to the other bricks. This is why the Qur'an is filled with stories of the previous Prophets and why the Prophet Muhammad reprimanded his followers, "Do not make preferences among the Prophets."[28]

Fulfilling its self-proclaimed function as the completion of the cycle of revelation, the Qur'an renews the primordial covenant of Abraham that had been inherited by the Arabs through Ishmael. So too, it reaffirms the covenants of Judaism and Christianity. The final "brick" in the House of Prophecy is thus seen to represent the renewal of the one eternal and everlasting covenant between God and human beings, which continues to be observed in different yet complementary forms. When the history of the Abrahamic religions is considered in the way the Qur'an suggests—as a continuous line of prophecy and revelation from Adam through Abraham and Moses to Muhammad—the supposedly irreconcilable differences between different Messengers and different religions can be seen as different perspectives, rather than as contradictions. In the final analysis, all Messengers and all Prophets affirm the eternal call of the Old and New Testaments: "Whoever calls on the name of the Lord shall be saved" (Joel 2:32; Romans 10:13). As the Qur'an says:

Truly, those who believe and those who are Jews, and the Christians and the Sabeans— whoever believes in God and the Last Day and acts virtuously— they will have their reward from their Lord. No fear shall be upon them, nor shall they grieve.

(Qur'an 2:62; 5:69)

NOTES

1. See also the following verses of the Qur'an: "Truly in the creation of the heavens and the earth and the alteration of night and day are signs for those who discern" (Qur'an 3:190); "Look to His fruits, how He makes them bear fruit and causes them to ripen, truly in that are signs for people who believe" (Qur'an 6:99); "Truly in the alteration night and day and what God has created in the heavens and the earth are signs for people who revere" (Qur'an 10:6). See also, Qur'an 16:12; 16:79; *et passim*.

2. Unlike the situation in Judaism and Christianity, not all angels are messengers in Islam. Some are said to carry God's throne while others abide in heaven praising

God continuously with no knowledge of the created order below. Those who do . function as messengers serve multiple functions. The only angel who is directly referred to as a messenger in the Qur'an is the Angel Gabriel. In some Muslim traditions 'Azra'il, the Angel of Death, also called the King of Death (*Malik al-Mawt*), functions as a messenger who conducts souls to the afterlife.

3. Muhammad ibn Hisham, *al-Sira al-Nabawiyya,* ed. Muhammad al-Saqqa et al. (Cairo: Maktabat Muhammad Subayh, 1963), 969.

4. See *Sahih al-Bukhari,* Kitab al-Adab (Book of Etiquette), 119 and *Sahih Muslim,* Kitab Fada'il al-Sahaba (Book of the Virtues of the Prophet's Companions).

5. The translation of the term *hanif* as "true devotee" or "truly devout" is adopted from Muhammad Asad, who also translates the term as "devout." Asad explains: "The expression *hanif* is derived from the verb *hanafa,* which literally means 'he inclined towards [a right state or tendency].' Already in pre-Islamic times, this term had a definitely monotheistic connotation, and was used to describe a man who turned away from sin and worldliness and from all dubious beliefs, especially idol-worship; *tahannuf* denoted the ardent devotions, mainly consisting of long vigils and prayers, of the unitarian God-seekers of pre-Islamic times." Muhammad Asad, *The Message of the Qur'an: Translated and Explained* (Gibraltar: Dar al-Andalus Limited, 1984), 28, n. 110 on verse 2:135.

6. Ayatollah Ja'far Sobhani, *Doctrines of Shi'i Islam: A Compendium of Imami Beliefs and Practices,* trans. and ed. Reza Shah-Kazemi (London: IB Tauris, 2001), 61.

7. The word *zubur* is here translated as "scriptures." The singular name *al-Zabur* identifies the revelation given to the Prophet David (Qur'an 4:163; 17:55). *Zubur* could thus be translated as "Psalms" or "scriptures."

8. *Sahih al-Bukhari,* Kitab al-Anbiya' (Book of the Prophets), 48.

9. For a discussion of the presentation of Biblical prophets in the Qur'an, see Roberto Tottoli, *Biblical Prophets in the Qur'an and Muslim Literature* (Richmond, Surrey, U.K.: Curzon Press, 2002).

10. For Torah passages about God's promise to Abraham, see the following: "And in you all the families of the Earth shall be blessed" (Genesis 12:3); "To your offspring I give this land, from the river of Egypt to the great river, the river Euphrates" (Genesis 15:18); "As for Me, behold, My covenant is with you, and you shall be a father of many nations" (Genesis 17:4).

11. See also Qur'an 6:86; 37:113; 38:46.

12. For a comprehensive account of the different interpretations of the sacrifice of Abraham in the Islamic scholarly tradition, see Reuven Firestone, *Journeys into Holy Lands: The Evolution of the Abraham-Ishmael Legends in Islamic Exegesis,* (Albany, New York: State University of New York Press, 1990).

13. *Sunan al-Tirmidhi,* Kitab al-Hajj (Book of the Pilgrimage), 49.

14. For a brief account of the history of the Ka'ba in the generations preceding Islam, see Martin Lings, *Mecca: From Before Genesis Until Now* (Cambridge: Archetype Books, 2004).

15. Qur'an 2:49–50; 7:103–138; 10:75–92; 11:96–99; 14:5–6; 17:101–104; 20:46–79; 23:45–49; 25:35–36; 26:10–68; 28:3–6, 36–42; 40:23–47; 43:46–56; 44:17–33; 51:38–40; 54:41–42; 73:15–16; 79:20–26.

16.   Qur'an 3:45; 4:157; 4:171–172; 5:17 twice; 5:72 twice; 5:75; 9:30–31, *et passim.*

17.   From one perspective, such verses can be seen as a reference to Jesus' human nature and are an extension of the verses in the Gospel of John where Jesus states that he was sent by the Father. See John 5:23; 5:30; 5:36–37; 6:39; 6:44; 6:57; 8:16; 8:18; 8:29; 8:42; 10:36; 12:49; 14:24; 17:21; 17:25; 20:21; *et passim.*

18.   This is similar to the account of the Annunciation in the Gospel of Luke, according to which Mary shows fear and asks the Angel Gabriel: "How will this be since I am a virgin?" (Luke 1:34) To this Gabriel responds, "There is no deed that is impossible for God" (Luke 1:37).

19.   The reference to a voice calling to Mary from under the palm tree has been understood by some exegetes as a reference to Jesus. Others see it as a reference to an angelic Messenger. Taken in light of the Muslim belief that the Qur'an clarifies and affirms previous scriptures but does not necessarily contradict them, the latter interpretation seems more viable.

20.   The epithet "Sister of Aaron" is used here in reference to Mary's line of descent through her mother Anne from the Essenes, who were descendants of Aaron. For this lineage, see *The Life of Jesus Christ and Biblical Revelations, from the Visions of the Venerable Anne Catherine Emmerich,* Vol. 1 (Rockford, Illinois: TAN Books and Publishers Inc., 2004) 117–120.

21.   See *Sahih al-Bukhari*, Kitab Ahadith al-anbiya' (Book of Accounts of the Prophets), 51; Kitab al-tafsir (Book of Qur'an Exegesis), 33. Another account of this saying reads: "No child is born but that he is pricked by Satan and begins to weep because of the pricking of Satan, except for the son of Mary and his mother." See *Sahih Muslim*, Kitab al-Fada'il (Book of Virtues), 40. A third version states: "Satan touches every son of Adam on the day when his mother gives birth to him, except for Mary and her son" (Ibid.).

22.   *Sahih al-Bukhari*, Kitab Ahadith al-anbiya,' 50.

23.   Ibid., 48.

24.   Some Muslims have argued that references to the Paraclete in the Gospel of John (John 14:15–16; 16:7–14) refer in fact to the Prophet Muhammad. However, it is difficult, if not impossible, to substantiate such claims objectively.

25.   See *Sahih Muslim,* Kitab al-Fada'il, 34.

26.   The lineage from Abraham to Muhammad is as follows: Abraham, Ishmael, Kedar, 'Adnan (40th descendant from Kedar) Ma'ad, Nizar, Mudar, Ilyas, Mudrika, Khuzaima, Kinana, al-Nadr, Malik, Quraysh (Fihr), Ghalib, Lu'ayy, Ka'b, Murra, Kilab, Qusayy, 'Abd al-Manaf, Hashim, 'Abd al-Muttalib, 'Abdallah, and Muhammad.

27.   *Sahih al-Bukhari*, Kitab al-Manaqib (Book of Excellences), 18.

28.   *Sahih al-Bukhari*, Kitab Ahadith al-anbiya', 36.

9

The Loom and the Bridge

Barry C. McDonald

The Loom

A unity within a Unity;
Each bird and flower forms a single strand.
The universe reflects a tapestry
Where every thread is woven by God's Hand.

The carpet spreads as far as we can see—
Its weft is Peace, its warp Reality.
To know things deeply and to understand
The loom of God weaves wisdom into man.

The Bridge

Because there cannot be two Absolutes
The Truth is that there is no god but God.
All beauty blossoms from a sacred root
And everything we love flows from the Good.

This knowledge is a bridge to Paradise.
These words, forever new, can set us free.
Each day we rise and walk into the light,
The heart knows more than what the eye can see.

10

THE *SUNNA:* THE WAY OF THE PROPHET MUHAMMAD

Hamza Yusuf Hanson

From the time of the Prophet Muhammad to the present day, the *Sunna,* the Way of the Prophet, has had a profound influence on the daily life of Muslims, providing guidance in both the celestial and the mundane aspects of their existence. From the way Muslims raise their open palms in prayer to the way they enter and exit their homes, their source of guidance is the Sunna of the Prophet as handed down through generations from fathers to sons, mothers to daughters, teachers to pupils, and friends to one another. The centrality of the Sunna in their lives is such that when the name of the Prophet Muhammad is mentioned, both speaker and listener follow it with a prayer of peace and blessings upon him.

Calligraphic inscriptions of *Hadith,* the Prophet Muhammad's sayings, are found in almost every Muslim's house. And although it might be the death of a loved one that causes a person to pull a book of prophetic wisdom off the shelf, Muslims will at some time or another read his words as recorded by the great Hadith scholars of the past and derive sustenance from them. When a child is born into a Muslim family, the rituals surrounding its birth—whether it be the chewed date given to the newborn as its first taste, the shaving of its hair on the seventh day, or its circumcision—are all derived from the Sunna. When Muslims marry, they often recite the Prophet's marriage sermon at the wedding, and when they die, it is in accordance with the Sunna that the body is washed, wrapped, prayed over, and lowered into its final earthly abode. From cradle to grave, Muslims are influenced, in greater or lesser degrees, by the Sunna of the Prophet Muhammad.

The Sunna is the second most important source of authority and legislation in Islam after the Qur'an. Scholars of Islamic jurisprudence base the foundation of Islamic Law, the *Shari'a,* on four primary sources: the Qur'an, the Sunna, the consensus of legal scholars (*ijma'*), and analogical reasoning (*qiyas*). This chapter explores the differences of opinion among authoritative

Muslim scholars as to the precise meaning and application of the word
Sunna. It also examines a number of important issues related to the Sunna,
including the basis of its authority, its relation to the major Hadith collections, its role in the development of Islamic jurisprudence, the contribution
of women in collecting and authenticating the Hadith and the Sunna, and
the significance of the Sunna in the Sufi tradition. Finally, this chapter examines some of the modern and postmodern critiques of the Sunna, the
responses of Muslim scholars to these critiques, and the weighty problems
modern Muslims face because of the divergent views on the Sunna.

THE QUR'ANIC BASIS FOR THE AUTHORITY OF THE SUNNA

Islam connotes "submission" or "surrender." According to the Qur'an, it
is the true religion of God (Qur'an 3:19). An adult moral agent who enters
into this covenant of surrender is a *Muslim,* one who submits to the will of
God. Muslims believe that God communicates His will through divine
revelation. Like Judaism, which has both a written and an oral tradition in
the Pentateuch and the Talmud, respectively, the central traditions of Islam
are twofold: the Qur'an, which Muslims accept in its entirety as the revealed
Word of God, and the Sunna, which includes the inspired sayings, acts, and
tacit approvals of the Prophet Muhammad. Both the Qur'an and the Sunna
were taught by the Prophet Muhammad. The Qur'an, however, was written
down in its entirety during the Prophet's lifetime and was gathered into a single collected work (known as the *mushaf*) after his death. The Sunna was
transmitted orally and was written down haphazardly by the first two generations of Muslims. After approximately 70 years, the process of systematically
collecting the sayings, acts, and approvals of the Prophet began and continued well into the third century of Islamic history.

According to the majority of Muslim scholars, the basis of the authority of
the Sunna is found in the Qur'an. One verse that establishes the authority of
the Sunna states: "Take whatever the Messenger has brought you, and avoid
whatever he has prohibited" (Qur'an 59:7). Early scholars understood this
verse to refer to the Sunna of the Prophet Muhammad. The jurist Muhammad ibn Idris al-Shafi'i (d. 820) was the formulator of the principles of
Islamic jurisprudence (*usul al-fiqh*). In his famous work, *al-Risala* (The
Epistle), he notes that in the Qur'an, the word "Book" (meaning the
Qur'an) is paired seven times with the word "wisdom" (*hikma*). For Shafi'i,
the Book and the Wisdom are the Qur'an and the Sunna. One verse of the
Qur'an that proves this states: "[God] is the one who sent among the unlet-
tered peoples (*al-ummiyyin*) a Messenger who recited His signs to them and
purified them and who taught them the Book (that is, the Qur'an) and the
Wisdom (that is, the Sunna)" (Qur'an 62:2).

According to the scholars, the obligation of referring to the Sunna as a source of legislation is derived from the verses in the Qur'an that command believers to "obey God and obey the Messenger" (Qur'an 5:92; 24:54). The Qur'an states: "By your Lord, they do not truly believe until they make you [Muhammad] the arbiter in controversies among them, and until they find in their souls no objection to what you decide, but accept approvingly" (Qur'an 4:65). In another verse, the Qur'an warns: "Let those who oppose [the Messenger's] command beware lest a trial befall them, or a painful punishment strike them" (Qur'an 24:63). The Qur'an also states: "Obey God, and obey the Messenger, and those with authority among you. If you dispute over anything, refer it to God and to the Messenger, if you believe in God and the Last Day. That is best and most excellent as a determination" (Qur'an 4:59). Perhaps the most explicit verse in this regard is the following: "Whoever obeys the Messenger is obedient to God" (Qur'an 4:80).

Many Hadith accounts also refer to the importance of the Sunna. Ahmad ibn Hanbal (d. 855 CE) related a hadith in which the Prophet said: "I counsel you to conscious awareness of God, and to hearing and obeying. Those among you who will live shall see much tribulation and bickering, so follow my way (that is, the Sunna) and the way (Sunna) of the rightly-guided leaders who follow me."[1] In the *Muwatta'* (The Trodden Path), the earliest extant collection of legislation by the Prophet and his Companions, the jurist Malik ibn Anas (d. 795 CE) relates the following admonition of the Prophet to the Muslim community: "I have left two things by which, as long as you do not abandon them, you will never go astray: the Book of God and my Sunna."[2]

The Qur'an also states that the role of the Prophet vis-à-vis the Qur'an is to clarify its meanings and provide explanations for its verses: "And We revealed to you the Reminder, that you might clarify to people what had been revealed to them, and that they might reflect" (Qur'an 16:44). This clarification is part of the Prophet's Sunna. Without the Sunna, people would not know how to perform ablution (*wudu'*), perform the five daily prayers (*Salat*), perform the Friday congregational prayer (*jumu'a*), make the call to prayer (*adhan*), and perform many other actions required of Muslims that are not explained in the Qur'an.

There are numerous statements from the Companions of the Prophet (*al-Sahaba*) confirming that one of the purposes of the Sunna is to clarify the meaning of the Qur'an. For example, 'Ali ibn Abu Talib (d. 661 CE), the fourth Caliph of Islam, sent the Prophet's cousin Ibn 'Abbas (d. 687 CE) to debate with a group of Muslims called the Khawarij (The Seceders). Because of their misunderstanding of several verses in the Qur'an, the Khawarij considered grave sinners to be unbelievers. Before sending Ibn 'Abbas to talk to the Khawarij, 'Ali advised him: "Do not use the Qur'an to argue with them, for it can be interpreted in many ways. Rather, debate with them using the Sunna, for they cannot escape its clarity."[3]

Although the exact content of the Sunna was widely debated in the first centuries of Islam, by the fourth century (ninth century CE), scholars had agreed upon certain methodologies for determining the content of the Sunna. Imam Shafi'i, after whom the Shafi'i school of jurisprudence was named, codified this methodology in his *Risala*. One of his primary objectives in writing this book was to establish the authority of the Sunna alongside that of the Qur'an. In it, he states:

> God said: "The believers are only those who have faith in God and His Messenger without wavering, and strive for the sake of God by means of their property and their persons. They are the ones who are sincere" (49:15). Thus, God prescribed that the perfect beginning of the faith, to which all other things are subordinate, is the belief in Him and then in His Messenger. For if a person believes only in [God] and not in His Messenger, he cannot be described as one who has "perfect faith"; he must have faith in His Messenger together with Him .... God has imposed the duty upon men to obey His divine communications as well as the Sunna of His Messenger.[4]

DEFINITIONS AND QUALIFICATIONS OF THE SUNNA

In classical Islamic scholarship, definitions are divided into three categories: linguistic (*lughawi*), customary (*'urfi*), and legal (*shar'i*). Each of these categories may include more than one meaning for any given term. Thus, a single word may have several linguistic, customary, and legal meanings. In the case of *Sunna*, its linguistic meaning is "path" or "custom" because it connotes the "norms or practices of a people." Its customary meaning refers to "acts of worship that are not obligatory but encouraged in Islam," such as the performance of extra prayers before or after the obligatory prayers. Its legal meaning may differ depending on the legal school of thought.

The three main groups of scholars that have used the term *Sunna* are Hadith scholars (sing. *muhaddith*), who collect and authenticate the sayings of the Prophet; jurists (sing. *qadi*), who apply the rules of the Shari'a in daily life; and juridical theorists (sing. *faqih* or *mufti*), who derive legal opinions (sing. *fatwa*) from the systematic analysis of Qur'an and Hadith. Hadith scholars use the term *Sunna* to refer to anything attributed to the Prophet, including his words, deeds, and tacit approvals, as well as descriptions of his appearance and character—including, even, how he sat, slept, and ate. Some also include in this definition the actions of the Prophet's Companions and their students. Jurists use the term *Sunna* to refer to behaviors that are recommended as praiseworthy but are not mandated by law. Juridical theorists, who use the Sunna in formulating legal opinions, consider it as "anything attributed to the Prophet, either in explicit word, deed, or tacit approval."[5] Certain scholars among this latter group added to the definition of Sunna personal qualities that the Prophet embodied. However, the most authoritative definition of the Sunna remained the actual words of the Prophet, his actions, and matters that he sanctioned.

The first category of the Sunna comprises the *statements* of the Prophet as recorded by his Companions in Hadith literature, such as, "Let there be no harm and no reciprocating harm,"[6] or "The water of the ocean is pure, and its carrion is permissible"[7] (unlike land animals, which must be slaughtered properly). The second category of the Sunna consists of the *actions* of the Prophet as recorded by his Companions. For example, the Prophet stated, "Pray as you see me pray." Thus, the *Salat* prayer that Muslims perform five times a day is based on the Companions' descriptions of the Prophet's actions when he prayed.

Prophetic actions fall under three subcategories. The first subcategory consists of the Prophet Muhammad's personal preferences and activities, such as his likes and dislikes. Sufis tend to emphasize these aspects of the Prophet's behavior, but most juridical scholars argue that such matters are not part of the Sunna. Instead, they are regarded as mere cultural habits of the Arabian Peninsula or are seen to reflect personal preferences that have no legal value. The West African authority on the Sunna, 'Abd Allah Ould Hajj Ibrahim (d. 1814 CE) commented on this subject as follows: "The Prophet sometimes performed acts that he himself discouraged in order to clarify their permissibility. Also, any of his actions that resulted from his particular nature, such as what and how he ate or drank, or how he sat or stood up, do not fall under the rubric of Sunna."[8] Despite such qualifications, many Muslims follow the Prophet's personal practices out of love and devotion. Hence, some Muslims wear a ring on either the ring finger or small finger, sit on the floor when eating, or eat with their hands because the Prophet did so. Some Muslims even avoid foods that the Prophet avoided and prefer foods that he preferred.

The second subcategory involves actions of the Prophet that were legislated by God specifically for him. For instance, God commanded the Prophet in the Qur'an to stand in prayer for at least a third of the night and obliged him to pray extra prayers every morning. Pious actions such as these are encouraged for ordinary believers but are not obligatory for anyone but the Prophet himself. Similarly, the Prophet was allowed to fast for days without food or water, but he prohibited such extreme fasts for his followers. The license to marry more than four women at one time also falls under this category. While this practice was permissible for the Prophet, it is prohibited for others. The Prophet exercised this dispensation by marrying older women, divorcées, widowed single mothers, and women whose tribal ties strengthened the unity of the Muslim community. Although Islam allows Muslim men to marry up to four women at a time, no jurist considers this practice part of the Sunna. Rather, it is merely a permissible act and sometimes it is even prohibited. Many jurists discourage this practice because of the near impossibility of treating wives equally, as the Qur'an demands. According to the Maliki school of law, a woman entering into a marriage has the right to stipulate that the man will not take another wife without divorcing her.

The third subcategory of the Prophet's acts consists of actions that are neither part of his particular nature nor from his special obligations and dispensations. These consist of cultural habits that the Prophet picked up by virtue of his participation as a member of seventh-century Arab society.

The third category of the Sunna includes acts that are *sanctioned* by the Prophet. For the most part, the Prophet's Companions performed these acts in his presence. Such acts were either approved by the Prophet directly or approved by his silence. According to Islamic tradition, the Prophet was not permitted by God to remain silent in the presence of a prohibited act. For instance, the Prophet once inquired about the condition of a young boy's bird that he kept as a caged pet in his house. Because the Prophet did not prohibit the boy from keeping the bird in a cage, it is understood that keeping birds as pets is permissible. Thus, the Prophet's Sunna is seen as sanctioning the keeping of pets. According to some scholars, over 300 rulings were derived from this one hadith, including the Sunna of inquiring about people's pets and the permissibility of keeping a bird in a cage.

Some scholars consider *Sunna* a synonym for *Hadith*, while others consider *Hadith* to be a reference to the words of the Prophet and therefore more specific than the Sunna. In spite of this scholarly distinction, the words "Sunna" and "Hadith" are largely synonymous in the minds of most Muslims. The term *Sunna,* which is mentioned 16 times in the Qur'an to refer to "precedent" or "custom," is used specifically in collections of Hadith to refer to the normative practice of the Prophet. In early Islam, "Sunna" connoted the normative practice of the Muslim community that was either legislated or sanctioned by the Prophet. Under the influence of Imam Shafi'i, the term *Sunna* came to refer specifically to the Prophet's practice as embodied in sound Hadith. Today, Sunna refers to what Muslims consider the practice and behavior of the Prophet as recorded by his Companions and collected by the great Hadith scholars of Islamic history. Even the Maliki school of jurisprudence (followed mostly in North and West Africa), which in earlier times had favored a broader application of the term, has largely capitulated to the current usage of the term. The efforts of the Hadith scholars in collecting and systematizing Prophetic traditions enabled the jurists to glean from them the normative practice of the Prophet, based on the respective schools' methodologies.[9] One useful way to distinguish Hadith from Sunna is described as follows:

> Hadith differs from Sunna in the sense that Hadith is a narration of the conduct of the Prophet whereas Sunna is the example or the law that is deduced from it. Hadith in this sense is the vehicle or the carrier of the Sunna, although Sunna is a wider concept and used to be so especially before its literal meaning gave way to its juristic usage.[10]

According to Imam Shafi'i, most scholars agreed that the concept of Sunna comprised the following three categories: (1) Qur'anic legislations that the Prophet specified or elucidated, (2) the Prophet's clarifications of ambiguities in the Qur'an, and (3) actions the Prophet performed that are not mentioned in the Qur'an. According to Shafi'i, scholars unanimously accepted the first two categories but disagreed about the third, since it lacked a supportive text from the Qur'an itself. In the *Risala,* Shafi'i provides many examples of the first two categories and establishes the soundness of the third. He concludes: "As for the Sunna, which [the Prophet] laid down on matters for which a text is not found in the Book of God, the obligation to accept them rests upon us by virtue of the duty imposed by God to obey the [Prophet's] command."[11]

Today, all of the major schools of Islamic jurisprudence accept all three categories of the Sunna. For example, the times for prayer and how they are performed fall under the third category of the Sunna. Neither the prayer times nor how to pray is clearly elucidated in the Qur'an. An example of the Sunna allowing exceptions to Qur'anic injunctions is found in the requirement to make an ablution before praying: while the Qur'an requires washing the feet, the Sunna provides the dispensation of wiping over a covered foot with wet hands.

DEVELOPMENT OF THE SUNNA

Ahmad Zarruq (d. 1493 CE), a prominent Maliki jurist and Sufi from North Africa, identified three stages in the formation of Islamic theology and law. The first was the *prophetic stage,* during which the Prophet's Companions and those who learned from them absorbed what the Prophet taught. The second was the *compilation stage,* the period in which the Qur'an and the Hadith were compiled into the form we have today. Last was the *codification stage,* in which the texts of the Qur'an and the Sunna were examined and codified into devotional practice and Sacred Law. The scholars who codified the sayings and actions of the Prophet fell under two categories: biographers (*'ulama' al-Sira*) and Hadith scholars (*muhaddithun*). The biographers of the Prophet were liberal in their narrations and did not authenticate the stories and sayings they related with great rigor. This caused the jurists to reject their narrations as a source of legislation. *Sira,* biographical literature about the Prophet Muhammad, does not have legislative authority. It is primarily read as devotional literature, since knowing the Prophet's biography draws one nearer to him. In a more systematic sense, it is also read as sacred history and serves to contextualize verses of the Qur'an that refer to events that occurred during the Prophet's lifetime.

Unlike the biographers, Hadith scholars developed a rigorous science that enabled them to determine, with a high degree of accuracy, the veracity of the many traditions that circulated among common people and scholars alike. The most important element in the assessment of Hadith is the reliability of the chain of transmission (*sanad* or *isnad*). In order to be accepted, a hadith must be transmitted by a chain of reliable narrators who relate it as closely to the original as possible. Scholars allow hadith accounts to be transmitted in different words, as long as the same meaning is retained.

In addition, scholars classified hadith accounts into three broad categories: sound (*sahih*), good (*hasan*), and weak (*da'if*). Sound hadith are subcategorized into narratives that are supported by multiple chains of transmission at every stage (*mutawatir*), narratives that are supported by multiple chains of transmission at most stages (*mashhur*), and solitary (*ahad*) narratives that are not supported by multiple chains of transmission. *Mutawatir* hadith are akin to verses in the Qur'an in terms of their authority; there are less than 500 such hadith. The hadith that are categorized as *mashhur* are those narratives that have many transmitters but do not reach a number that ensures infallibility. Finally, the solitary reports are hadith that have either one or at most a few transmitters in any given generation.

In the early stages of his mission, the Prophet initially prohibited people from writing down his sayings out of concern that the Qur'an would be confused with his own words. In the later part of his mission, however, once the Qur'an was firmly rooted in the hearts of his followers, he did permit his Companions to record his words. While Hadith scholars have differed over the authenticity of numerous hadith and have agreed that many hadith accounts were fabricated for political or other purposes, Muslims do not question the authenticity of Hadith as a reliable source of Islamic knowledge in general. Recently, however, some Muslim scholars have raised the question of hadith's authenticity. In the last hundred years, largely because of Orientalist critiques of Hadith literature, certain views have developed that challenge the validity of much of the Hadith literature that was formerly considered beyond reproach. As a result, a minority of Muslims, especially in South Asia, rejected most hadith accounts altogether and demanded that the practice of Islam be based solely on the Qur'an. These "People of the Qur'an" (*Ahl al-Qur'an*) were countered by "People of the Hadith" (*Ahl al-Hadith*), who revered Hadith almost as much as they revered the Qur'an. A main responsibility of the juridical schools of Islam is to refute such extreme positions through a critical yet balanced approach to Hadith study.

THE HADITH COLLECTIONS

Hadith scholars spent over 300 years collecting, authenticating, and systematizing the corpus of Hadith. A rigorous science developed from this painstaking endeavor and provided the heuristic tools for categorizing and further subcategorizing the Hadith. Many great scholars emerged from this discipline, and some achieved great prominence as their collections gained widespread acceptance among the majority of Muslims. Certain Hadith collections known as *sunan* constitute the injunctions and prohibitions of the Prophet and focus on the legal aspects of his sayings. Others include stories of his life, such as his childhood experiences, and the sayings of his Companions and their students. Some collections include the opinions of the scholars who collected the Hadith.

In the Sunni tradition, which currently represents more than 80 percent of the Muslim world, six Hadith collections achieved a preeminent status. A seventh collection, the *Muwatta'* of Imam Malik, is usually added to this group. The *Muwatta'* is an account of the Sunna in Medina, the city of the Prophet, and is considered an important source of early Muslim practice. Of the 1,720 traditions in this collection, only 822 are attributed to the Prophet himself. The rest are from his Companions and their students. Malik attempted to discern the normative practice of the entire community of the Prophet. He understood that the Sunna could include practices performed by the Prophet's companions in his presence and of which he did not disapprove.

Of the six major collections of Hadith, the two most important are the *Sahih* of Bukhari (d. 870 CE) and the *Sahih* of Muslim (d. 875 CE). These two leaders of Hadith study employed such rigor that most Sunni scholars believe their collections to be sound in their entirety, with a miniscule probability of error in some of the solitary hadith narratives. Bukhari was known to have memorized over 600,000 different chains of transmission, which involved tens of thousands of hadith accounts. The more chains of transmission a hadith has, the more sound it is, and the more times the text is replicated, especially with exact wording, the more reliable the hadith.

The other four compilations include many traditions not found in the collections of Bukhari and Muslim. Tirmidhi (d. 883 CE), Ibn Maja (d. 886 CE), Abu Dawud (d. 888 CE), and Nasa'i (d. 915 CE) all amassed important collections, though they have a lesser stature than those of Bukhari and Muslim, since their compilations include weak (*da'if*) hadith, while the two *Sahih* collections do not.

While these seven collections are the most important in Sunni Islam, many other collections augment the scholars' knowledge of the hadith and ultimately of the Sunna. For example, Muhammad ibu 'Abdallah al-Hakim's (d. 1014 CE) collection is extremely important, as he attempted to identify hadith accounts that are not in Bukhari and Muslim but nonetheless are authentic, using the same rigorous criteria of authentication that Bukhari and Muslim used. Ahmad ibn Hanbal's *Musnad* is another such collection, comprising over 30,000 hadith, many of which can be found in other collections. Many other Hadith collections exist, most with chapters that cover a broad range of topics. These topics include creed, laws and rulings (*sunan*, including rulings on ritual purity, prayer, marriage, inheritance, and so on), *raqa'iq* (matters that deal with piety and giving up worldly possessions for

Table 10.1: The Hadith Collections

Hadith collector	Number of Hadiths
Bukhari	7,658
Muslim	7,748
Abu Dawud	5,276
Tirmidhi	4,415
Nasa'i	5,776
Ibn Maja	4,485
Malik	1,720
Total	37,078

nobler pursuits), manners (of eating, drinking, traveling, studying, and so on), Qur'anic exegesis, historical and biographical information, seditions, and signs of the end of time.[12]

Of all of the hadith collections, none has achieved the prestige of *Sahih al-Bukhari*. Muslims throughout the world revere this collection as the most important book of religious teachings after the Qur'an, primarily because of the scrupulous rigor of the criteria that Bukhari used to authenticate hadith. His personal piety also contributed to the prestige of this work. In his early childhood, Bukhari was blind for a period; when his sight returned, his mother informed him that the trial he had experienced was due to the will of God and that his sight was restored because God intended for him to serve the Sunna of the Prophet.

Soon after, Bukhari set out to master the hadith of his homeland in Central Asia and spent over four decades traveling throughout the Muslim lands collecting hadith. On many occasions, his prodigious memory was tested by other Hadith scholars who wanted to verify that he was indeed a genius of his reputation. On one occasion in Baghdad, 10 Hadith scholars intentionally introduced some slight alterations in the chains of transmission of hundred traditions in order to test the young man. In a mosque, in the presence of the public, these scholars recited the traditions along with their corresponding chains, which they had changed. Then they began to ask Bukhari questions about them. He confessed his ignorance of the traditions recited and explained that he knew them through other chains. To the astonishment of all who were present, Bukhari then proceeded to recite all hundred chains with their corresponding texts correctly.[13]

The noted Orientalist, H. A. R. Gibb, said about Bukhari's work:

> Viewed as a whole, the *Sahih* is a work of immense interest and scrupulous scholarship. Variants are carefully noted, doubtful or difficult points in the *sanads* (chains of narration) and texts are glossed. On any careful student, the book

produces a remarkable impression of honesty combined with piety. It may be true, as has been suggested, that the popular appreciation of Bukhari's collection was due largely to the fact that he brought together the traditions already accepted in religious circles as a result of the long preceding process of critical examination, but this does not exclude the element of personal worthiness which set, as it were, the seal of authentication upon them.[14]

Without a doubt, the collection and authentication of the Hadith literature is one of the most fascinating and sophisticated works of premodern scholarship. While the authenticity of hadith accounts has been under severe attack for more than a century, its defenders continue to fight back from both within the tradition and without.

THE SUNNA AND JURISPRUDENCE

Among the first community of Companions who lived and studied directly with the Prophet, a small group emerged that was recognized as more learned than the others. People referred to these Companions concerning legal matters that had no precedent during the lifetime of the Prophet. The jurists among the Companions issued *fatwas,* nonbinding legal opinions. A *fatwa* is nonbinding because another scholar may come to a different conclusion about a subject, as there is often more than one possible interpretation of the source texts.

The source texts for a fatwa are first the Qur'an, since it is the highest authority, and then the Sunna. If an issue is not clearly addressed in the Qur'an or the Sunna, the jurist then looks to see if there is any consensus among the scholars concerning the matter. If no clear proof is found in any of these three sources, the jurist exerts all of his intellectual and spiritual efforts to arrive at a sound position that is consistent with the aims and ends of the Sacred Law, through analogy or one of several other legal considerations. These considerations include analogical reasoning based on already existing texts, equity, public good, permissibility, precedents from previous Muslim scholars, and other legal considerations. This process is based on the following hadith, which is categorized as well known (*mashhur*):

> Before sending Mu'adh [ibn Jabal] to Yemen to act as a judge, the Prophet asked him on what basis he would judge. Mu'adh replied, "I will judge by the Book of God."
>
> The Prophet then asked, "And if you do not find the answer in the Book of God?"
>
> Mu'adh replied, "Then I will judge in accordance with the Sunna of the Messenger of God."
>
> The Prophet then asked, "And if you do not find it in the Sunna of the Messenger of God?"

Mu'adh replied, "Then I will exert my efforts to the utmost in order to arrive at a sound opinion, and I will spare no effort."[15]

Much of current Islamic Sacred Law is based on *ijtihad,* the exertion of intellectual effort by scholars who attempt to discern the most likely ruling of God in circumstances that are not covered by definitive texts. The jurists use sound hadith as a means to derive legal rulings about various aspects of daily life as well as of events that raise legal issues.

DISCERNING THE SUNNA FROM THE HADITH

There were many independent jurists in the formative period of the Muslim legal tradition, and they differed, sometimes radically, regarding what constituted the Sunna. However, as time passed, seven discernable legal schools formed, which are still a source of guidance for most Muslims today: the Hanafi, Maliki, Shafi'i, Hanbali, Ja'fari, Ibadi, and Zaydi. Each of these schools developed a juristic methodology that enabled it to analyze the vast Hadith literature and to discern the Sunna or the normative practice of the Messenger of God.

Because of different interpretations of texts, these schools developed various methodologies for determining legislation. The Qur'an and the Hadith contain some legal rulings. These rulings form the basis of a large body of legal precedent, from which jurists attempt to ascertain new legal rulings on the basis of common axioms and principles. The outcome of this process, which is the technical definition of the term *ijtihad,* will vary on the basis of theoretical approaches employed.

In rare cases, such as that of Malik ibn Anas, the Hadith scholars were also jurists. Such scholars not only developed legal opinions but also transmitted their own collections of hadith. Malik considered the Sunna to encompass more than the practice of the Prophet, as revealed through his authentic sayings and the sound narrations of his deeds and approvals. Thus, he included in his *Muwatta'* the normative practice of the people of Medina during the lifetime of the Prophet.

Shafi'i believed that the Sunna could be derived from solitary (*ahad*) transmissions of hadith. In other words, if a single Companion of the Prophet related a hadith and the chain of transmission was sound, that hadith could be used to derive a sound ruling, even if no other Companion corroborated the hadith with independent narrations. Abu Hanifa (d. 767 CE) and Malik disagreed with Shafi'i about this. According to Malik, determining legislation by means of solitary narrations would lead to confusion in discerning the Sunna.

An example of different approaches to determining the Sunna can be seen in the case of fasting on Friday, the day of the communal *jumu'a* prayer. Shafi'i accepted a solitary hadith transmitted with a sound chain back to the

Prophet, in which the Prophet prohibited fasting on Fridays except in Ramadan. However, Malik set aside this hadith, preferring the practice of the students of the Prophet's Companions, who were known to fast on Fridays. He reasoned that Medina was the Prophet's city and the place where he spent the last 10 years of his life. Therefore, any practice that was widespread among the scholars of Medina could only have been with the approval of the Prophet's Companions and hence with the approval of the Prophet himself.

While Abu Hanifa agreed with Malik regarding the problem of solitary hadith, he relied on the Qur'an rather than on the precedent of the people of Medina as his primary source. In the absence of a clear ruling from the Qur'an, he referred to the Sunna, but he had rigorous caveats about which hadith he used to determine the Sunna. As supplements to rulings from the Qur'an, he accepted only multiply supported (*mutawatir*) and well-known (*mashhur*) hadith accounts with several narrators in each generation. In addition, he accepted those hadith accounts only if their rulings were actually put into practice by scholars. In the case of solitary hadith, Abu Hanifa would accept only those that a Companion of the Prophet related to a group of other Companions, and so long as no one in the group disagreed with the narration. Abu Hanifa also rejected hadith accounts whose logic he deemed to be contradicting Qur'anic principles.

The fourth Sunni Imam, Ahmad ibn Hanbal, followed a methodology similar to that of Shafi'i. However, like Abu Hanifa and Malik, he accepted traditions that were related by a trustworthy follower of the Prophet's Companions without being traced back to the Prophet himself, while Shafi'i rejected such traditions.

THE SHI'A AND THE SUNNA

The Shi'a community comprises approximately 15 percent of the Muslim world, with the majority of its adherents in Iran and large numbers in Iraq, Lebanon, Kuwait, Bahrain, Afghanistan, India, Yemen, and eastern Saudi Arabia. Like the Sunnis, Shi'as have different schools of thought in their tradition. Most Shi'as belong to the school known as the *Imami* and adhere to the Twelve Imams. Following the Prophet is central to their tradition, but Shi'as give great consideration to the Prophet's direct descendants through his daughter Fatima and cousin 'Ali and ascribe to them a special place of authority within the tradition. The Shi'as also believe in Hadith but usually refer to them as *akhbar* ("news" or "reports"). Moreover, they believe that the rulings of the Twelve Imams are as important in matters of faith and law as the Prophet's are. To the Shi'a, the Twelve Imams are considered infallible in religious matters; their authority is akin to that of the Pope in modern Catholicism.

While the Shi'as accept Hadith as a primary source of legislation after the Qur'an, they reject several of the Sunni sources among the Prophet's Companions because of their political positions vis-à-vis the early dispute over 'Ali's authority after the death of the Prophet. While both groups classify hadith almost identically and deem multiple transmission narratives to be authoritative and binding, the Sunnis tend not to accept the methodology of authentication that the Shi'as employ.

For the Shi'as, the Hadith constitutes the Sunna of the Prophet and the Twelve Imams. The Shi'as have four early collections that are considered canonical and akin to the six collections of the Sunnis. Many of the traditions found in the Shi'a collections are similar or identical in meaning to those found in the Sunni sources, and many of the Sunni Hadith scholars narrate hadith on the authority of early Shi'a scholars, with certain qualifications. Shi'a transmitters can even be found in the chains of the illustrious Sunni Hadith scholar Bukhari.[16]

WOMEN AND THE SUNNA

One intriguing aspect of the sciences involving the collection and authentication of Prophetic sayings is the important role that women played in its development and transmission. In no other Islamic disciplines have there been so many notable and illustrious female scholars. Among the Prophet's Companions, only four related over 2,000 traditions; one of them was the Prophet's wife 'A'isha, who holds a preeminent position not only as a great transmitter of hadith but also in her knowledge of their application. Only one other early Hadith scholar bears such a distinction.[17] Perhaps because of 'A'isha's prestigious position among the transmitters, other women were encouraged to pursue knowledge in this area. A student of Hadith will often encounter the names of Hafsa, Umm Habiba, Umm Salama, Maymuna, and 'A'isha; all of these women transmitted hadith directly from the Prophet.

Women represent 12 percent of the Prophet's Companions who are noted for relating more than 20 hadith accounts. Among the second generation of scholars, women also held prominent places. For example, 'Abida al-Madaniyya (d. early eighth century CE) was a slave from Medina who excelled in memorizing traditions from the great Hadith scholars of Medina. The eminent Spanish Hadith scholar Habib Dahhun freed 'Abida and then married her. She returned with him to Spain, and it is reported that she related over 10,000 traditions on the authority of her teachers in Medina.[18]

The most notable scholar of *Sahih al-Bukhari* in the eleventh century CE was Karima al-Marwaziyya (d. 1070 CE) from Merv in modern Turkmenistan, whose name recurs in the most authoritative chains of the *Sahih*. The Hadith scholar Abu Dharr of Herat (d. 1042 CE) held her in such high esteem that he counseled his students to study Bukhari with her and no one else.

The greatest of the later Hadith scholars, Ibn Hajar al-'Askalani (d. 1449 CE), wrote a work of biographical notices titled *al-Durar al-kamina* (The Hidden Pearls), in which he listed over 170 prominent female Hadith scholars. Ibn Hajar studied directly with some of them and acknowledged others as the best Hadith scholars of their age. Noteworthy among the women Hadith scholars mentioned by Ibn Hajar was Umm Hani Maryam of Cairo (d. 1466 CE), who mastered several Islamic sciences, including theology, law, history, and grammar. During her life, she traveled extensively to study Hadith with the masters of her age. She was a celebrated lecturer in the Islamic colleges of Cairo. The Egyptian biographer Sakhawi (d. 1497 CE) says about her:

> She taught hadith for a long time, and many eminent scholars heard them from her; personally, everything I have learned from her teachers, I learned through her. However, I believe that she knew much more than I was able to learn. Her grandfather presumably taught her the rest of the Six Books and taught her Nashawiri's [d. 1388 CE] version of *Sahih al-Bukhari*. She was a good woman who used to weep profusely when the names of God and the Prophet were mentioned; she was consistent in her fasting and night prayers and firm in her religion.... She performed the pilgrimage thirteen times, often staying for months to study and teach in Mecca and Medina.[19]

The great Hadith scholar Jalal al-Din al-Suyuti (d. 1505 CE) states that although there have been countless forgers of hadith among men, no woman in the history of the science was ever known to have been a forger of hadith. Unfortunately, the number of female scholars of Hadith declined radically after the fifteenth century CE. Following Sakhawi's biographical collection, women are almost entirely absent from literature enumerating the scholars of the centuries that followed. Perhaps, the last noteworthy female Hadith scholar in Sunni Islam was Fatima al-Fudayliyya (d. 1831), who acquired an excellent reputation in the early nineteenth century. She taught in Mecca, where many eminent Hadith scholars were known to attend her lectures.[20] Today, one of the most active scholastic communities in the Arab world that is teaching and preserving the great canonical collections of Hadith literature is the Qubaysiyyat of Syria. This organization is made up entirely from the ranks of Syrian women and their female students from around the world.

THE SUFIS AND THE SUNNA

Sufism is the spiritual tradition within Islam, and almost all of the legal and theological schools of both the Sunni and the Shi'a traditions incorporate aspects of Sufism in their teachings. For the Sufis, the Sunna represents more than simply the actions of the Prophet and his normative practices.

While Sufis traditionally were staunch adherents of the outward manifestation of the Sunna, they placed greater emphasis on the spiritual states of the
Prophet and his practice of being mindful of God. In Bukhari's collection,
'A'isha relates that the Prophet mentioned God in all of his states. Sufis take
this tradition very seriously and attempt to fill their days with remembrance
of God, even while doing such mundane tasks as sweeping a room or working at a computer. Ahmad ibn 'Ajiba (d. 1809 CE), the noted North African
Sufi and scholar of the early nineteenth century, writes:

> The scholar has inherited [the Prophet's] sayings, may Allah bless him and give
> him peace, with the condition that he should be sincere and truthful .... The
> worshipper has inherited [the Prophet's] actions .... The Sufi has inherited
> everything [from the Prophet]. In the beginning [the Sufi] takes what is neces-
> sary for him from the outward knowledge [of the Prophet]. He plunges to its
> depth and then moves to action in the most perfect states. He has also inherited
> the behavior that the Prophet (may Allah bless him and give him peace) used to
> apply to his inward self: doing without, scrupulousness, fear and hope, patience,
> forbearance, generosity, courage, contentment, humility, reliance upon Allah,
> love, gnosis, and so on.[21]

While most Sufis are traditional Muslims in that they adhere to the normative practice of the dominant community of believers, their focus is less on
the formalism of exoteric religion than it is on the purpose of that formalism,
which is to attain direct knowledge of God. Thus, Sufis consider the spiritual
retreats of the Prophet as Sunna. The Night Journey, in which the Prophet is
described as having had direct experience of his Lord, is also Sunna for the
Sufis. In addition, the Sunna of invocation at night is very important in the
Sufi tradition.

Many Hadith scholars were Sufis. In fact, the doctrines of early Sufis, such
as Junayd (d. 910 CE), were probably diffused throughout the Muslim world
by way of Hadith scholars who were sought after for their knowledge of traditions and who passed on their Sufism along with Hadith. Abu Sa'id ibn al-
'A'rabi (d. 952 CE), the famous Hadith scholar and disciple of Junayd, studied
with Abu Dawud, the author of one the canonical Six Books. Later, scholars
in Islamic Spain taught the *Sunan* of Abu Dawud using Ibn al-'A'rabi's narration. Abu Muhammad Ja'far al-Khuldi (d. 958 CE) is another such example.
A distinguished Hadith scholar in his early career, he later became a well-
known Sufi who applied the rigors of his Hadith training to the teachings of
the Sufis. Abu Nu'aym al-Isfahani (d. 1038 CE) was also a great Hadith
scholar and Sufi; his renowned work *Hilyat al-awliya'* (The Adornment of
the Saints) is a major sourcebook for early Sufi traditions.[22] Finally, Abu
Hamid al-Ghazali (d. 1111 CE), perhaps the most prominent jurist, theologian, and Sufi in Sunni Islam, placed great emphasis on strictly adhering to
the Sunna of the Prophet as a way of achieving spiritual illumination. In his

religious classic *Bidayat al-hidaya* (The Beginning of Guidance), he states: "The commands of God Most High prescribe obligatory works and supererogatory works. The obligatory work is the capital on which the trading activities are based and through which a man comes to safety. The supererogatory [Sunna] work is the profit, which gives a man a higher degree of success."[23] In this work, Ghazali exhorts those setting out on a spiritual path to adhere strictly to the Sunna of the Prophet in order to illuminate their hearts and draw closer to God.

CHALLENGES TO THE SUNNA

While historically the Sunna of the Prophet and the traditions it is based on were not challenged as an epistemological premise in Islam, there have been several recent attempts to challenge the validity of the Hadith. Initially, these attempts came from Orientalist scholars who called into question the entire tradition of Hadith and its methodology for authenticating accounts. Some of these Western scholars went so far as to allege that most hadith accounts were in fact inauthentic and represented an attempt by scholars in the second, third, and fourth centuries of Islam to legitimize legal opinions and cultural attitudes by attributing them to the Prophet Muhammad. According to this view, this process led to the fabrication of chains of narration. One of the most influential exponents of this tradition of Western Hadith criticism was the late nineteenth-century scholar Ignaz Goldziher, a Hungarian specialist in Jewish law who applied his criticisms of the Jewish legal tradition to Islam.

Goldziher's main allegations against the Hadith tradition were as follows: Because hadith accounts were based mainly on oral traditions, they were apt to be remembered incorrectly or misunderstood. The fact that later Hadith collections had larger numbers of accounts than earlier compilations meant that the authenticity of accounts in the later collections was suspect. The system of verifying traditions by means of their chains of transmission was a later development in the field of Hadith study and could not prove the authenticity of a particular hadith account. Many hadith accounts were contradictory and followed inconsistent logic.[24]

The early twentieth-century scholar Joseph Schacht agreed with Goldziher's main criticisms about Hadith and further alleged that most written traditions came into existence only after Shafi'i's time. He asserted that the Prophet Muhammad was not primarily interested in legislation and that legislative hadith emerged during the Umayyad dynasty (661–750 CE), when the need arose to legitimize state policies. According to Schacht, the Sunna did not originally refer to the Prophet's practices but rather to the practice of the Muslim community as a whole and only received its eventual meaning because of the influence of Shafi'i.[25]

These views continue to have a great deal of influence in the field of Islamic Studies, despite sound challenges to Goldziher's and Schacht's contentions. Schacht's thesis was refuted by the Muslim scholar Muhammad Azami in the book, *On Schacht's Origins of Muhammadan Jurisprudence*.[26] A European Muslim scholar, Yasin Dutton, has written an intriguing work titled *The Origins of Islamic Law: The Qur'an, the Muwatta' and Madinan 'Amal*. In this work, Dutton argues that the concept of the Sunna, as understood by the Maliki jurists of Medina, refutes the opinions of those who doubt the authenticity of Hadith. Dutton believes that the accuracy of most hadith accounts transmitted by the Maliki school is undeniable and that the Maliki school's reliance on communally applied actions taught and practiced by its scholars, rather than on written texts of largely solitary narrations, is central to its strength. For Dutton, the Sunna is a transmitted practice rooted in action. The majority of solitary hadith do not support this view because their teachings have not been confirmed in actual practice. Malik himself did not rely on solitary hadith accounts, and his *Muwatta'* contains less than 2,000 hadith accounts out of tens of thousands of accounts that were at his disposal. Malik discarded many accounts because they were not practiced by the scholars of his time in Medina. Dutton's research demonstrates that Orientalist criticism of the Sunna based on the supposed weakness of Hadith literature is largely irrelevant to the Maliki position, which clearly distinguishes between Hadith and Sunna.[27]

Other challenges to the Sunna have arisen from within the Muslim community itself. The Egyptian engineer Rashad Khalifah rejected the Hadith tradition in its entirety and demanded that Muslims return solely to the Qur'an. Even more recently, Dr. Muhammad Shahrur, a Syrian engineer, published a critique of the Sunna as understood by classical scholars for over a thousand years. In this work, he claims that the Sunna was the Prophet's personal attempt to apply the Qur'an to his time and his environment. Thus, the meaning of the Sunna should differ according to the time and place in which it is applied. According to Shahrur, Muslims should not follow the practices of the Prophet literally but should instead implement the methodology he used to arrive at his practices. This, says Shahrur, is the Prophet's *ijtihad*.[28]

Finally, an emerging movement of American Muslims, which is largely drawn from the children of Muslim immigrants, is abandoning what they perceive as the stifling effect that Hadith has had on Islam. The followers of this movement feel that Islam should be reformed from within and that many of the centuries-old traditions of Islam must be abandoned for a faith more compatible with modern sensibilities. In his *Risala*, Shafi'i relates a tradition that appears to foreshadow such views. In this hadith the Prophet says, "Let me find no one of you reclining on his couch when confronted with an order of permission or prohibition from me, saying, 'I do not know it; we will only follow what we find in the Book of God.'"[29]

THE SUNNA AND MODERN MUSLIMS IN THE WEST

The Sunna of the Prophet has been on Western shores for many centuries. In Europe, first in Spain and later in other regions, the Sunna was brought by travelers and merchants from the Muslim East. In the Americas, Muslims were brought in slave ships as well as in trading vessels, and some of them courageously attempted to preserve whatever they could of the Prophet's way. However, never before have such large numbers of Muslims resided in the West. Documentaries about the Prophet have been shown on public television, and English dictionaries now contain the word, "Sunna." Increasingly, Western people are coming to accept the presence of Muslims and their practice of the Sunna.

Muslims in the West are also studying the books of the Sunna, and indigenous Westerners are becoming qualified to teach them. The Hadith collections of Bukhari, Muslim, and Malik are studied daily in schools and Islamic centers in Birmingham and Bradford in the United Kingdom, and in New York City and Hayward, California, in the United States. The Sunna is practiced by engineers in Silicon Valley, gas station attendants in Chicago, and taxi drivers in Philadelphia. Turbaned street merchants can be found trying to follow the Sunna in Brooklyn, and the Acacia wood tooth-cleaning stick so beloved to the Prophet is sold in Manhattan and Los Angeles, where it is called a "Sunna-Stick."

The Prophet Muhammad's prayers have opened sessions of the U.S. Senate, and two U.S. presidents started Ramadan meals in the White House with dates in emulation of the Prophet's Sunna in breaking the fast. Motivated by the example of the Prophet, large numbers of Muslims have collected charity from their communities for the victims of natural disasters and have volunteered to help refugees in the United States and elsewhere.

The American historian Michael Hart considered the Prophet Muhammad the single most influential human being ever to have lived, a claim that seems justified when one considers that a fifth of the world's population is Muslim and that most Muslims attempt to emulate the Prophet's behavior in some aspects of their lives.[30] Every morning, millions of Muslims around the world wake up reciting a prayer that the Prophet Muhammad recited: "Glory be to the One who has given me life again after taking my conscious life from me in sleep, and to God we return."[31] Muslims say this prayer because of their desire to follow the Sunna. For the same reason, Muslims say the *Basmalla* before eating a meal and the *Hamdalla* (*al-hamdulillah*, "Praise be to God") when they have finished eating. They do this to follow the Sunna. Muslims say the *Basmalla* when they start their cars, emulating the Prophet's actions when he rode his camel or his horse. They greet their fellow Muslims with the words, *As-Salamu ʿAlaykum* ("Peace be upon you"), in emulation of the Prophet. Many Muslim men grow beards as the Prophet did, and women cover their heads in reverence for the Prophet's teachings. Muslims visit the sick because they recall the virtue the Prophet described for doing so. They inculcate the modesty he exemplified and show great deference to their mothers and fathers because the Prophet enjoined it.

Muslims practice the Sunna in many aspects of their daily lives, desiring to be raised up in the Hereafter in the company of the one they try so hard to emulate in their earthly lives. By this means, they hope to receive, from the Prophet's noble hands, the promised drink from his basin of eternal life, after which, the Prophet promised, "They will never thirst again."[32]

NOTES

1. Muhammad Hashim Kamali, *Principles of Islamic Jurisprudence* (Cambridge: Islamic Texts Society, 1991), 37.

2. Malik ibn Anas, *Muwatta' al-Imam Malik,* edited and annotated by Ahmad Ratib 'Armush (Beirut: Dar al-Nafa'is li al-tiba'ah wa al-nashr wa al-tawzi', 1971), hadith numbers 1619 and 648.

3. Kamali, *Principles of Islamic Jurisprudence,* 37.

4. Majid Khadduri, ed. and trans., *Al-Shafi'i's Risala: Treatise on the Foundations of Islamic Jurisprudence,* (Cambridge: Islamic Texts Society, 1987), 109–110.

5. Ali Hasabullah, *Usul al-tashri' al-Islami* (Egypt: Dar al-Ma'arif, 1971), 35.

6. Yahya ibn Sharaf al-Nawawi, *An-Nawawi's Forty Hadith: An Anthology of the Sayings of the Prophet Muhammad,* trans. Ezzeddin Ibrahim and Denys Johnson-Davies, 10th ed. (Beirut: The Holy Koran Publishing House, 1982), 107.

7. Abu Dawud Sulayman b. al-Ash'ath al-Sijistani, *Sunan Abi Dawud,* edited and annotated by Muhammad Muhyi al-Din 'Abd al-Hamid (Cairo: al-Maktaba al-Tijariyya al-Kubra, 1935), hadith numbers 83 and 21.

8. Sidi 'Abd Allah Ould Hajj Ibrahim, *Maraq al-su'ud* (Beirut: al-Maktaba al-'Asriyya, 2004), 240.

9. Muhammad Zubayr Siddiqi, *Hadith Literature: Its Origin, Development, and Special Features* (Cambridge: Islamic Texts Society, 1993), 2.

10. Kamali, *Principles of Islamic Jurisprudence,* 47.

11. Ibid., 180.

12. Siddiqi, *Hadith Literature,* 10.

13. Ibid., 54–55.

14. H.A.R. Gibb, *Mohammedanism: An Historical Survey* (New York: Oxford University Press, 1953), 79–80.

15. Kamali, *Principles of Islamic Jurisprudence,* 45.

16. Moojan Momen, *An Introduction to Shi'i Islam* (New Haven, Connecticut: Yale University Press, 1985), 173–174.

17. Siddiqi, *Hadith Literature,* 18.

18. Ibid., 118.

19. *Cambridge Illustrated History of the Islamic World,* ed. Francis Robinson (Cambridge: Cambridge University Press, 1996), 190.

20. Siddiqi, *Hadith Literature,* 123.

21. Shaykh Ahmad ibn 'Ajiba, *The Basic Research,* trans. Abdalkhabir al-Munawwarah and Haj Abdassabur al-Ustadh, ed. Shaykh Abdalqadir as-Sufi (Cape-town: Madina Press, 1998), 53–54.

22. See *The Life, Personality and Writings of Al-Junayd,* ed. and trans. E.J.W. Abdel Kader, H.A.R. Gibb Memorial Series (London: Luzac and Co., 1962), xii–xiv.

23. William Montgomery Watt, *The Faith and Practice of al-Ghazali* (Oxford: One World Publications, 1994), 100.

24. See, for example, Ignaz Goldziher, *Introduction to Islamic Theology and Law,* translated by Andras and Ruth Hamori (Princeton, New Jersey: Princeton University Press, 1981), 38–39.

25. See, for example, Joseph Schacht, *The Origins of Muhammadan Jurisprudence* (Oxford: Clarendon Press, 1975), 4–5.

26. See M. M. Azami, *On Schacht's Origins of Muhammadan Jurisprudence* (Cambridge: The Islamic Texts Society, 1996).

27. Yasin Dutton, *The Origins of Islamic Law: The Qur'an, the Muwatta' and Madinan 'Amal* (Surrey, U.K.: Curzon Press, 1999), xiv.

28. Muhammad Shahrur, *al-Kitab wa al-Qur'an* (Damascus: al-Ahali li'l-Tiba'a, 1997), 549.

29. Khadduri, *Al-Shafi'i's Risala,* 119.

30. Michael M. Hart, *The 100, A Ranking of the Most Influential Persons in History* (New York: Hart Publishing Company, Inc., 1978), 33.

31. Muhammad ibn Isma'il al-Bukhari, *al-Adab al-mufrad,* edited and annotated by Kamal Yusuf al-Hut (Beirut: 'Alam al-Kutub, 1984), 400.

32. Muhammad ibn Isma'il al-Bukhari, *Sahih al-Bukhari* (Beirut: Dar al-Arqam, n.d.), hadith no. 6579, 1035–1036.

11

Vision of the Shariat

Daniel Abdal-Hayy Moore

At the Prophet's Mosque in Medina I had a vision of the *Shariat* (sacred law) of Islam as a giant, spectacular many-faceted chandelier of hundreds of prisms or lenses, a kind of glittering dome of raw starlight that fits down perfectly over the *Haqiqat* (sacred truth), so that its light shines out from each lens, perfectly focused, a lens or cluster of lenses beaming the light for every aspect of our lives.

One can approach the *Haqiqat* without it, and in some cases get it right, but with the Prophet's *Shariat* from Allah, peace and blessings of Allah be upon him, both the light of the *Haqiqat* can shine out clearly and one can approach the *Haqiqat* from outside with clear precision.

The lenses are such things as how to do the prayer, the proper way to contract a marriage, the laws of inheritance, etc., all the details of our lives down to things as mundane as cleaning our teeth, as well as preparing us for the rapturous experience of face-to-face meeting with Allah with correct spiritual courtesy at the highest station, thus making us well-guided human devotees of The Divine Reality.

NOTE

This poem first appeared in Daniel Abdal-Hayy Moore, *Mecca/Medina Timewarp*. Reprinted here from a Zilzal Press chapbook, by permission from the author.

12

THE *SHARI'A:* LAW AS THE WAY OF GOD

·

Mohammad Hashim Kamali

SHARI'A AND *FIQH*

Islamic law originates in two major sources: divine revelation (*wahy*) and human reason (*'aql*). This dual identity of Islamic law is reflected in the expressions, *Shari'a* and *fiqh*. The former bears a strong affinity with the revelation, whereas the latter is mainly the product of human reason. *Shari'a* literally means, "the path to the watering place," the road that the believer has to tread in order to obtain guidance. *Fiqh* means human understanding and knowledge. The Shari'a provides general directives, whereas detailed solutions to particular and unprecedented issues are explored by *fiqh*. Since the Shari'a is contained in the Qur'an, the revelation of God, and the Sunna, the teachings of the Prophet Muhammad, it has a close affinity with the dogma of Islam. *Fiqh*, however, is a rational endeavor and is largely a product of speculative reasoning, which does not command the same authority as the Shari'a.

To say, as some Muslim fundamentalists do, that the Shari'a is "contained" in the Qur'an and the Sunna would preclude the scholastic legacy of *fiqh* and its vast literature from the purview of the Shari'a, especially the parts that do not have a clear origin in the Qur'an. From a legal point of view, the core of the Shari'a is contained in the relatively small number of clear injunctions of the Qur'an and the Sunna, known as *nusus* (pl. of *nass*). Some parts of the Qur'an that consist of historical data and parables, for instance, are not included in the Shari'a. Shari'a is a wider concept than *fiqh*, since it comprises the totality of guidance that God has revealed to the Prophet Muhammad. This guidance pertains to the dogma of Islam, its moral values, and its practical legal rules. Shari'a thus comprises in its scope not only law but also theology and moral teachings. *Fiqh* is a form of positive law that does not include morality and dogma per se. Yet the *ulama*, the scholars of Islam, have agreed on the primacy of morality and dogma in the determination of basic values. By comparison with the Shari'a, *fiqh* can thus be considered the superstructure of the law and a practical manifestation of commitment to the basic values of Islam.

The Shari'a provides clear rulings on the fundamentals of Islam, its moral values, and its practical duties such as prayers, fasting, legal alms (*Zakat*), the Hajj pilgrimage, and other devotional matters. Its injunctions on the subject of what is lawful (*halal*) or unlawful (*haram*) are on the whole definitive, as are its rulings on certain aspects of civil transactions. However, the Shari'a is generally flexible with regard to most civil transactions, criminal law (with the exception of the prescribed punishments, or *hudud*), government policy and constitution, fiscal policy, taxation, and economic and international affairs. On many of these issues, the Shari'a provides only general guidelines, whereas *fiqh* elaborates Shari'a's guidelines in detail.

Fiqh is defined as knowledge of the practical rules of the Shari'a, which are derived from detailed evidence in the sources. The rules of *fiqh* are thus concerned with the manifest aspects of individual conduct. The practicalities of conduct are evaluated according to a scale of five values: (1) obligatory, (2) recommended, (3) permissible, (4) reprehensible, and (5) forbidden. The definition of *fiqh* also implies that the derivation of rulings from the Qur'an and the Sunna is through direct contact with these sources. The need to utilize the source materials of the Qur'an and the Sunna necessitates knowledge of Arabic and a certain degree of insight and erudition that would preclude the work of a nonspecialist. A jurist (*faqih*) who fulfills these requirements and has the ability to derive the rules of the Shari'a from their sources is a *mujtahid*, one who is qualified to exercise independent reasoning (*ijtihad*).

The rules of *fiqh* occur in two varieties. The first variety consists of rules that are conveyed in a clear text from the Qur'an or the Sunna, such as the essentials of worship, the validity of marriage outside the prohibited degrees of relationships, the rules of inheritance, and so forth. These rules are self-evident and independent of interpretation and *ijtihad*. This part of *fiqh* is simultaneously a part of the Shari'a. The second variety of *fiqh* consists of rules that are formulated through the exercise of *ijtihad* on parts of the Qur'an and the Sunna that are not self-evident. Because of the possibility of error in this exercise, the rules that are derived in this way do not command finality. They are not necessarily part of the Shari'a, and the jurist who has reason to disagree with them may do so without committing a transgression. Only when juristic opinion and *ijtihad* are supported by a widespread consensus (*ijma'*) does such a finding acquire the binding force of a ruling, or *hukm*, of the Shari'a.

The subject matter of *fiqh* is divided into the two main categories of devotional matters (*'ibadat*) and civil transactions (*mu'amalat*). The former are usually studied under six main headings: (1) cleanliness, (2) ritual prayer, (3) fasting, (4) the Hajj, (5) Alms Tax (*Zakat*), and (6) *jihad* (holy struggle).

These headings conform to the Five Pillars of Islam, with the addition of jihad. The schools of law do not vary a great deal in their treatment of these subjects. Juristic differences among the schools mostly occur over the category of *mu'amalat*. These are usually studied under seven headings: (1) transactions involving the exchange of values, which include contracts; (2) matrimonial law; (3) equity; (4) trusts; (5) civil litigation; (6) rules pertaining to dispute settlement in courts; and (7) administration of estates. This body of law is generally subsumed under what is known in modern legal parlance as "civil law." Laws pertaining to crimes and penalties, which in the West would be considered "criminal law," are studied under the separate heading of *'uqubat*. Rules concerning state and governmental affairs are studied under the rubric of *al-ahkam al-sultaniyya*, literally, "Sultanic rulings" (also referred to as *siyasa shar'iyya*, "Shari'a-compliant policy"). This is similar to what is known in the West as constitutional law or administrative law. Finally, laws pertaining to international relations, such as war and peace, fall under the category of *'ilm al-siyar*, literally, "the knowledge of procedure." The most detailed exposition of the entire range of classical *fiqh*, including the above categories, is Shams al-Din al-Sarakhsi's (d. 1087 CE) *Kitab al-Mabsut* (The Extensive Book), which contains 30 volumes. A twentieth-century equivalent of this work is Wahba al-Zuhayli, *al-Fiqh al-Islami wa Adillatuhu* (Islamic Jurisprudence and Its Proofs) in eight volumes and over 6,000 pages.

SOURCES OF THE SHARI'A

The sources of the Shari'a are of two types: revealed and nonrevealed. The revealed sources are two: the Qur'an, and the teachings and exemplary conduct (*Sunna*) of the Prophet Muhammad. The content of the Sunna includes the Prophet's sayings, acts, and tacit approval of the conduct of his Companions. The nonrevealed sources of the Shari'a are numerous and comprise the products of juristic reasoning (*ijtihad*). This reasoning may take a variety of forms, such as analogical reasoning (*qiyas*), juristic preference (*istihsan*), consideration of public interest (*istislah*), and consensus (*ijma'*).

Qur'an and Sunna

The Qur'an consists, by its own affirmation, of the revealed Word of God recited in Arabic to the Prophet Muhammad through the Angel Gabriel (Qur'an 26:193). Much of the Qur'an was revealed in relation to actual events and questions that were encountered by the Prophet. The Prophet also used the Qur'an as the basis of his own teaching and adjudication. Legal rulings occupy only a small portion of the Qur'an. By far the greater part of its 6,235 verses is devoted to religious and moral themes. Such themes

include belief in God, the prophethood of Muhammad, angels and the Hereafter, the human being and the universe, the history of bygone nations, their
prophets and scriptures, and even parables. Less than three percent of the text
deals with legal matters.

The legal contents of the Qur'an were mainly revealed after the Prophet's
migration from Mecca to Medina, where he established a government.
Hence, there was a need for legislation on social and governmental issues.
The contents of the Qur'an are not classified according to subject. Its pronouncements on various topics appear in unexpected places and no particular
thematic order can be ascertained. This has led many to conclude that the
Qur'an is an indivisible whole and that its legal parts should not be read in
isolation from its religious and moral teachings. The text is divided into
114 *suras* (chapters) of unequal length, 85 of which were revealed during
the twelve and a half years of the Prophet's residence in Mecca and the
remainder after his migration to Medina, where he lived for just under 10
years.

Of about 350 legal verses of the Qur'an (*ayat al-ahkam*), 140 relate to
dogma and devotional matters, including practical religious duties such as
prayer, alms, fasting, the Hajj, and so forth. Seventy verses deal with marriage, divorce, paternity, custody of children, inheritance, and bequests.
Rules concerning commercial transactions such as sale, lease, loan, usury,
and mortgage constitute the subject of another 70 verses. There are about
30 verses on crimes and penalties, another 30 on justice, equality, rights
and duties, and consultation in government affairs, and about 10 on economic matters. Some of the earlier rulings of the Qur'an were abrogated
and replaced because of change of circumstances, although the scope of these
abrogations and their precise import is a matter of disagreement among
scholars.

Muslim scholars are unanimous that the Sunna of the Prophet is a source
of the Shari'a and that his rulings on the lawful and unlawful (*halal wa
haram*) stand on the same footing as the Qur'an. The words of the Prophet,
as the Qur'an declares, are divinely inspired (Qur'an 53:3), and obedience to
him is a duty of every Muslim (Qur'an 4:80; 59:7). Thus, the words of the
Prophet were normative for those who actually heard them. Subsequent generations of Muslims, who received the words of the Prophet through verbal
and written records of narrators (*hadith*), however, needed to ascertain their
authenticity before accepting the reports as normative. The claim of authenticity may be definitive (*mutawatir*), relying on numerous sources, recurrent
and continuous testimony, or it may consist of solitary reports of odd individuals (*ahad*), which may not be free of doubt. The most definitive type of
hadith is verbal *mutawatir*, consisting of the word-for-word transmission of
what the Prophet said. These are very rare, comprising no more than 10
hadiths. Another kind of definitive hadith is the conceptual *mutawatir*. In
this kind of hadith, the concept is taken from the Prophet but the words are

supplied by the narrator. When the reports of a large number of transmitters of hadith concur in their meaning but differ in wording, this hadith is considered as *mutawatir* in meaning. This latter type of hadith is quite frequent and is found in reference to the acts and sayings of the Prophet that explain the essentials of the faith, rituals of worship, rules that regulate the application of certain punishments, and so forth. Many traditions on the subject of prohibitions, as well as hadith that explain and supplement the injunctions of the Qur'an, are classified under this type of *mutawatir.*

The Sunna of the Prophet relates to the Qur'an in various capacities. It may consist of rules that merely corroborate the Qur'an, it may clarify the ambiguous parts of the Qur'an, or it may qualify and specify general rulings in the Qur'an. These three capacities comprise between them the largest bulk of the Sunna, and Muslim scholars are in agreement that they are supplementary yet integral to the Qur'an. The Sunna may also consist of rulings on which the Qur'an is silent, in which case the Sunna represents an independent source of the Shari'a. This type of Sunna, known as "Founding Sunna" (*sunna mu'assisa*), is the focus of the argument that the Sunna is not only an explanation and supplement to the Qur'an but also an independent source of the Shari'a in its own right.

The Qur'an and the Sunna consist of two types of rulings, definitive (*qat'i*) and speculative (*zanni*). Definitive rulings are injunctions that are self-evident and need no interpretation. There are also instances where the Qur'an lays down a basic rule, which, although definitive, needs to be supplemented by additional information. In such a case, the necessary details are often supplied by the Sunna. Definitive injunctions (that is, the *nusus*) constitute the basis of unity among the various schools of Islamic law and among Muslims generally. This is why the Shari'a is often described as a diversity within a unity; it comprises a unity in essentials but differs in details; it is a unity on matters of belief and on permitted (*halal*) and forbidden (*haram*) actions but is a diversity in matters that fall outside of these categories.

A legal text is speculative (*zanni*) when it is conveyed in a language that leaves room for interpretation. Instances can also be found of a legal text that is definitive in some respects but speculative in others. For example, the Qur'an provides the following injunction: "Forbidden to you (in marriage) are your mothers and your daughters" (Qur'an 4:23). This text is definitive in the basic prohibition that it contains. However, questions may arise as to whether the term "daughters" includes illegitimate daughters and adopted daughters and if so, whether they are entitled to inheritance or not. The scope of interpretation is not just confined to words but also extends to sentences and includes the meaning they may convey in a particular context. Most of the legal content of the Qur'an is speculative with respect to meaning, although the whole of the Qur'an is definitive with respect to its authenticity. Most of the Sunna that has been transmitted down to the present by means of solitary (*ahad*) reports by single individuals is speculative with respect to authenticity, even if it conveys a clear meaning.

Muslim scholars differ in their approach to interpretation. Most allow allegorical interpretation (*ta'wil*) in addition to more straightforward interpretations of normative texts (*tafsir*) and have validated interpretations based on personal opinion in addition to interpretation founded on valid precedent in their understanding of the Qur'an and the Sunna. The scope of interpretation is enhanced further by the fact that the majority of the Qur'an is devoted to the exposition of general principles. As noted above, of a total of some 350 legal verses in the Qur'an, only a small portion is conveyed in the form of specific provisions, whereas the rest are concerned with basic principles. Many of the general rulings of the Qur'an are made specific by other verses of the Qur'an, by the Sunna, or through the independent reasoning of jurists (*ijtihad*). Since the Qur'an mainly sets forth broad guidelines, its language is often versatile. The noted jurist Abu Ishaq Ibrahim al-Shatibi (d. 1391 CE) stated: "Every scholar who has resorted to the Qur'an in search of solution to a problem has found in the Qur'an a principle that has provided him with some guidance on the issue."[1]

Shatibi also observed that the specific rulings of the Qur'an are often related to a better understanding of its general principles. For example, the Qur'an proclaims: "God permitted sale and prohibited usury" (Qur'an 2:275). It also proclaims: "God does not intend to impose hardship upon people" (Qur'an 5:6) and counsels the believers to "cooperate in pursuit of good works and piety and cooperate not in hostility and sin" (Qur'an 5:2). Another verse tells the believers to "obey God and obey the Messenger and those who are in charge of affairs" (Qur'an 4:59) and "render trusts to whom that they are due and when you judge among people, judge with justice" (Qur'an 4:58). Such commandments lay down basic values rather than specific rules and procedures. The same is true for the well-known commands to "consult them (the community) in their affairs" (Qur'an 3:159), to not "devour not each other's property in vain, unless it be through lawful trade by your mutual consent" (Qur'an 4:29), "no soul shall be burdened with the burden of another" (Qur'an 6:164), or "God commands justice and the doing of good" (Qur'an 16:90). Each of these verses is concerned with providing basic norms and general principles, which may be related to new developments and be given fresh interpretations in new and unprecedented contexts.

Independent Reasoning and Juristic Opinion

The terms for independent reasoning (*ijtihad*) and juristic opinion (*fatwa*) are often used interchangeably. The main difference between the two terms is that *ijtihad* has a greater juridical substance and often requires an explanation of its reasoning and evidential basis, whereas a *fatwa* most often consists of a verdict or opinion that is given in response to a particular question. It is not necessary for a *fatwa* to provide an explanation of its evidential basis; thus, the text of a *fatwa* may either be very brief or include greater depth and detail. Juristic opinions are often sought by individuals who seek legal advice in the context of litigation. In such cases, the *fatwa* may be cursory and brief. When a *fatwa* addresses complex issues the jurist often feels the need to probe into the source evidence, in which case his finding may be equivalent to *ijtihad.* Neither the result of *ijtihad* nor the finding of a *fatwa* binds the person to whom it is addressed, unless it is issued by a formally constituted court, in which case the decision would carry a binding force. *Ijtihad* may only be carried out by a highly qualified legal scholar (*mujtahid*), whereas a *fatwa* may be issued by a *mujtahid* or by a scholar of lesser knowledge.

Ijtihad literally means "striving" or "exertion." It is defined as the total expenditure of effort by a *mujtahid,* in order to infer, with a high degree of probability, the rules of Shari'a from the detailed evidence that is found in the sources. Two important points are to be noted in this definition: (1) *ijtihad* is to be conducted only by a qualified jurist and scholar in Shari'a, namely, the *mujtahid* and (2) *ijtihad* is envisaged as an individual effort wherein the *mujtahid* exerts himself to the best of his ability. In the following pages, we propose a modified definition of *ijtihad* that expands upon the classical notion of the term. What prompts us into proposing a new definition for this term is that the conventional theory of *ijtihad* poses some problems if one were to make *ijtihad* an integral part of the legislative processes in modern times. We thus define *ijtihad* in the modern context as "a creative and comprehensive intellectual effort by qualified individuals and groups to derive juridical rulings of given issues from the sources of Shari'a in the context of the prevailing circumstances of Muslim society."[2]

The definition thus proposed incorporates the conventional definition of *ijtihad* but adds emphasis on two points: creative thinking and the prevailing conditions of society. *Ijtihad* is designed to address new and unprecedented issues in the light of available guidelines in the sources. Creative intellectual exertion also means that existing ideas and teachings should not be taken at face value or imitated uncritically. Instead, they are to be scrutinized and their relevance to new issues independently ascertained. Our proposed definition also departs from the view that made *ijtihad* the prerogative only of a classically trained Shari'a scholar. Nowadays, *ijtihad* may be attempted collectively by scholars in Shari'a and other disciplines of vital importance to the community, hence the proviso that *ijtihad* must be comprehensive and inclusive of other viewpoints. Our proposed definition also envisages *ijtihad* as a collective endeavor and thus departs from the individualist and subjective bias of the conventional definition.

Ijtihad is the most important source of the Shari'a next to the Qur'an and the Sunna. The main difference between *ijtihad* and the revealed sources is that *ijtihad* connotes a continuous process of development, whereas the revelation of the Qur'an and the development of the Sunna discontinued with the death of the Prophet Muhammad, peace be on him. *Ijtihad* is thus the main instrument for relating the Qur'an and the Sunna to the changing conditions of society.

As a vehicle of renewal and reform, *ijtihad* has always been dominated by its dual concern for continuity and change. *Ijtihad* seeks to maintain the continuity of the fundamentals of Islam while also keeping pace with the realities of social change. These two concerns for continuity and change thus characterize the history of *ijtihad* and the role it has played in the development of Islamic law.

One who undertakes *ijtihad* must be knowledgeable in the fundamentals of jurisprudence, of Hadith and narrators of traditions, of the hermeneutics of the Qur'an (*tafsir*), and of the customs and conditions of society. Knowledge of Arabic is also a requirement for *ijtihad,* and so is the intellectual capacity that enables one to formulate independent judgments. To this we may add knowledge of logic, philosophy, economics, and sociology. A *mujtahid* should also be a person of moral integrity and piety. One who has attained this degree of competence can dissociate himself from the pressure of conformity to the views and wishes of others and be guided by a sense of conviction and dedication to truth.

The first recourse in the quest to find solutions to new issues should be to the Qur'an and then to the Sunna, failing which one should exercise one's own judgment in accordance with one's understanding of the basic principles of Shari'a. This sound approach has received the blessing of the Prophet in the renowned hadith of Mu'adh ibn Jabal. Upon his departure to the Yemen to take up a judicial post, the Prophet asked Mu'adh about the sources on which he would rely in making decisions. In reply, Mu'adh referred first to the Qur'an, then to the Sunna of the Prophet, and finally to his own *ijtihad*.[3]

Until about 1500 CE, Muslim scholars were able to adapt in the face of changing conditions and new advances in knowledge. Unfortunately, as Islamic civilization began to weaken politically and economically in the face of Western advances, Muslims began to adopt a more conservative attitude toward the law to preserve traditional values and institutions. As a result, many scholars became inclined to view innovation and adaptation to change negatively. The scholars (*ulama*) occupied themselves mainly with commentaries, compendia, and marginal notes on the books already written by eminent jurists. They added little new to the knowledge of their ancestors and even served the negative purpose of giving an aura of sanctity to the earlier works.

This was different from what prevailed during the first three centuries of Islam, when open enquiry and direct recourse to the sources of the Shari'a constituted the norm of scholarship. The four schools of Sunni law (sing. *madhhab*) that eventually formed were designed to curb excessive diversity and conflict in juridical opinions. Eventually, the scholars of these schools saw themselves as instruments of unquestioning imitation (*taqlid*). This view was prompted by the demand of conformity that the legal practitioners of the schools made of their followers.

Colonial domination of Muslim lands also lowered the self-image of Muslims and further encouraged imitation and conservative thinking. *Ijtihad* suffered yet another setback when Western-style statutory legislation became dominant and the *ulama* were left with little visible role to play. After the Second World War, an era of constitutionalism in newly independent Muslim countries marked, in effect, a renewed phase of imitation characterized by the wholesale importation of Western laws and doctrines, a trend that was encouraged both by local elites and their foreign mentors. This was the scenario that eventually gave rise to the Islamic revivalist movement of the post-1960s. Westernization and modernity had clearly not borne the same fruits in the Muslim world as they had in their original homelands in the West.

At the dawn of the twentieth century, Jamal al-Din al-Afghani (d. 1898) and his disciples Muhammad ʿAbduh (d. 1905) and Muhammad Rashid Rida (d. 1935) called for a return to original *ijtihad,* which was well received and won wide support in the succeeding decades. *Ijtihad* in modern times tends to differ from what it was in medieval times. Scholars in earlier times were preoccupied with issues such as marriage and divorce, property, inheritance, the Alms Tax, and usury. Society was not prone to rapid change and *ijtihad* could be attempted incrementally, with a high degree of predictability. This is no longer the case. The much accelerated pace of social change and its attendant complexities suggest the need for a multidisciplinary approach to *ijtihad.* It would seem difficult for a jurist now to address matters pertaining to new banking products and international financial transactions without knowledge of modern economics and finance. Technical issues in medicine and science, in labor relations, and so on also generate new demands on the skills of a modern *mujtahid.*[4]

In modern times, *ijtihad* has tended to occur in the following three forms: (1) through the modality of statutory legislation, (2) in the form of *fatwa* by scholars and judges, and (3) through scholarly writings. Examples of legislative *ijtihad* can be found in the modern reforms of family law in many Muslim countries, particularly with reference to polygamy and divorce, which have been made contingent upon a court order and are no longer the unilateral privilege of the husband. The reformist legislation on these subjects is also based on novel interpretations of the relevant portions of the Qurʾan. One also notes numerous instances of *ijtihad* in the views and legal opinions (*fatwas*) of prominent scholars and jurists, including Rashid Rida, Abu Zahra (d. 1974), Mahmud Shaltut (d. 1970), and the contemporary jurist of the *al-Jazeera* television network, Yusuf al-Qaradawi.

Whereas the conventional theory of *ijtihad* looks in the direction of legal doctrines such as analogy (*qiyas*), juristic preference (*istihsan*), presumption of continuity (*istishab*), and so forth, there is now the need to pay more attention to the goals and objectives of the Shari'a (*maqasid al-Shari'a*).[5] Muhammad 'Abduh emphasized the importance of custom and actual societal conditions in the conduct of *ijtihad*. The general welfare of the people also demanded a greater role for considerations of public interest (*maslaha*) in contemporary *ijtihad*.[6] 'Abduh's disciple, Rashid Rida, emphasized the need to inform legislation and *ijtihad* of the spirit of the Shari'a and its goals and purposes: "Many people know what is lawful and unlawful but they do not always know why a particular act was declared lawful and another unlawful. If a legal decision and the goal of the Shari'a that it seeks to maintain go hand in hand, it will enhance the prospects of enforcement."[7]

In light of these new developments, the theory of *ijtihad* needs to be revised and reformed along the following lines:

1. To recognize the validity of collective *ijtihad* side by side with that of *ijtihad* by individual scholars.

2. To allow experts in other fields such as science, economics, and medicine to carry out *ijtihad* in their respective fields if they are equipped with adequate knowledge of the source evidence of the Shari'a. They may alternatively sit together with or seek advice from the scholars.

3. *Ijtihad* has often been used as an instrument of difference and disagreement. Although these must remain valid in principle, there is a greater need for unity and consensus. Scholars and learned bodies should not encourage excessive diversity and try to find ways to encourage unity.

4. In the past, *ijtihad* was conceived mainly as a legal concept and methodology. Our contemporary understanding of the source evidence does not specify such a framework for *ijtihad*. Rather, we should think of the original conception of *ijtihad* as a problem-solving formula of wider concern for Muslims. This would confirm our view to broaden the scope of *ijtihad* to other disciplines beyond the framework of *fiqh*.

5. According to a maxim of Islamic jurisprudence, there is no need for *ijtihad* in the presence of a clear text of the Qur'an or Hadith. This maxim should also be revised because of the possibility that the text in question may be given a fresh interpretation in a different context. This by itself may involve *ijtihad*. Hence, *ijtihad* should not be precluded if it can advance a fresh understanding of the text in question.

SCHOOLS OF LAW AND MAJOR CONTRIBUTORS

A large number of schools and methodologies of Islamic jurisprudence emerged within the first three centuries of Islamic history, but only five have survived: these are the Hanafi, Maliki, Shafi'i, and Hanbali schools of Sunni Islam, to which may be added the Shiite schools of Islamic jurisprudence.

The Hanafi school of Islamic jurisprudence was named after the jurist and teacher Abu Hanifa Nu'man ibn Thabit (d. 767 CE). This school of jurisprudence has the largest following of all the surviving schools, owing partly to its official adoption by the Ottoman Empire in the early sixteenth century. It is currently followed in Afghanistan, Iraq, Jordan, Turkey, Pakistan, India, Bangladesh, Tajikistan, Kirghizstan, Turkmenistan, and in parts of Yemen, Egypt, and Iran.

Hanafi jurisprudence is distinguished by its rationalistic tendency and to some extent by its theoretical leanings in that it deals not only with actual issues but also with problems that are based on supposition. Abu Hanifa emphasized personal liberty and maintained that neither the community nor the government is entitled to interfere with the liberty of the individual so long as the latter has not violated the law. The Hanafi school thus entitles an adult woman to conclude her own marriage contract even without the consent of her guardian, whereas the other schools require the consent of the guardian to validate her marriage. Abu Hanifa also refused to validate the incarceration of the mentally handicapped or the insolvent debtor on the premise that restricting their freedom is a greater harm than the loss or disadvantage that might otherwise occur. He also held that no one, including a judge, should impose restrictions on an owner's right to the use of personal property, even if it inflicted harm on another person, provided that the harm is not exorbitant.

One of the famous statements of Abu Hanifa, and which represents a major principle of his school, is the following: "When the authenticity of a hadith is established, this establishes my procedure (*madhhab*)." Abu Hanifa also said, "When you are faced with evidence, then speak for it and apply it." Consequently, after Abu Hanifa's death, when his students differed with some of his rulings because of new evidence, they argued that Abu Hanifa himself would have come to the same conclusion, had he known of the new evidence. A ruling of a student of Abu Hanifa that differs from the ruling of the Imam is thus still regarded as a ruling of the Hanafi school. Another important statement of Abu Hanifa is as follows: "No one may issue a verdict on the basis of what we have said unless he establishes the logic of our statement." Although these guidelines were eminently practical, Hanafi scholars of subsequent generations changed them. The early Hanafi interest in original reasoning gave way to a deeply rooted traditionalism. The Hanafi jurist Ibn 'Abidin (d. 1820) stated the new position of the school as follows: "A jurist of a later period may not abandon the rulings of the leading imams and scholars of the school, even if he is able to carry out *ijtihad,* and even if he thinks that he has found stronger evidence. For it would appear that the predecessors have considered [all of] the relevant evidence and have declared their preference."[8] The only exception made was for situations of necessity, in which the jurist may give a different ruling than that of the "predecessors" of the school.

The Maliki school was founded by Malik ibn Anas (d. 795 CE), who led the Traditionist (*Ahl al-Hadith*) movement in Mecca and Medina and advocated the notion of the "Medina consensus" (*ijma' ahl al-Madina*) as the only authoritative form of consensus. His renowned work *al-Muwatta* (The Straight Path) is the earliest complete work of *fiqh* on record. It relies heavily on Hadith—so much so in fact that many have considered it a work of Hadith rather than a work of *fiqh*. Notwithstanding his leading position in the Traditionist camp, Imam Malik relied extensively on personal opinion (*ra'y*). Two of his important doctrines, public interest (*istislah* or *maslaha*) and blocking the means to mischief (*sadd al-dhara'i*), are rationalistic in their logic and rely mainly on the exercise of personal judgment. Maliki jurisprudence also attempted to forge a closer link with the practicalities of life in Medina and attached a greater weight to social custom. This is borne out by its recognition of the Medina consensus as a source of law and validation. On this basis, for example, Malik allowed the testimony of children in cases of injury between themselves, provided they had not left the scene of the incident. He also held that the wife of a missing person can seek a judicial separation after a waiting period of four years.

Maliki law also recognized judicial divorce on the ground of injurious treatment of the wife by her husband. The majority ruling on this entitles the wife to judicial recompense, whereby the court may punish the offending husband. Maliki law ruled that if the treatment in question amounted to injury, the wife may request the court for a dissolution of the marriage on that basis. Another Maliki contribution in this area is in respect of *khul'*, a type of divorce in which the wife proposes dissolution of her marriage against a financial consideration, usually by returning the dower she received from her husband. Because this type of divorce is recognized by the Qur'an (2:229), it is allowed by all the schools, but in most cases, it can be finalized only with the husband's consent. Maliki law took the matter a step further in favor of the wife by ruling that in the event of irreconcilable differences, the court may finalize a *khul'* divorce, even without the consent of the husband. For this and other reasons, the Maliki law of divorce has been adopted in the reformist legislation of many Muslim countries in the latter part of the twentieth century. Maliki law is currently predominant in Morocco, Algeria, Tunisia, Upper Egypt, Sudan, Bahrain, and Kuwait.

Muhammad ibn Idris al-Shafi'i (d. 820 CE), the founder of the Shafi'i school of Islamic jurisprudence, was a student of Malik ibn Anas and a leading figure in the Traditionist camp, but later he tried to strike a middle course between the Traditionists and the Rationalists. Shafi'i's impact on the development of the Shari'a is most noticeable in the area of methodology of the sources of law, which is outlined in his pioneering work, the *Risala*. Shafi'i's role in articulating the methodology of jurisprudence has often been compared to that of Aristotle in logic. He maintained that the Sunna was a logical extension of the Qur'an and vindicated the exclusive authority of the Prophetic Sunna as a source of Shari'a next to the Qur'an. He came close to saying that rejecting the Sunna also amounted to rejecting the Qur'an and that accepting one and rejecting the other was untenable. He took his teacher, Imam Malik, to task for placing undue emphasis on the Medina consensus and the precedent of the Companions at the expense of the Sunna of the Prophet.

Shafi'i takes an intermediate position between the Traditionist stance of the Maliki school and the pragmatism of the Hanafis. He was critical of Imam Malik's validation of public interest and of Abu Hanifa's frequent concession to details at the expense of general principles. Shafi'i's approach to the validity of contracts was almost entirely based on the form rather than the intent of a transaction. He thus overruled enquiry into the motives of parties to a contract or a sale, even in circumstances that might arouse suspicion. Under Shafi'i law, a man is within his rights to buy a sword even if he intends to kill an innocent person with it. A man may likewise buy a sword from someone he saw using it as a murder weapon. Transactions are to be judged by their conformity to the formal rules of law, not by the suspicion that the intent of a transaction is to violate the law. This reliance on the manifest form of contracts and other transactions is not peculiar to Shafi'i, as the Hanafis have also shown the same tendency, but Shafi'i exhibited it more frequently than most.

Shafi'i maintained that a *mujtahid* should not hesitate to change a previous ruling (*fatwa*) if this would make a better contribution to the quest for truth. Thus, he frequently changed his own previous verdicts, and sometimes recorded different rulings on the same issue. For example, if a man deceives a woman he marries by claiming a false family pedigree, he is liable to punishment. Shafi'i has two separate views on this subject, but neither is given preference over the other. The first view entitles the wife to choose to either continue the marriage or separate. The second view rules that the marriage is void. The Shafi'i school is now prevalent in Indonesia, Malaysia, Brunei, Lower Egypt, Southern Arabia, and East Africa, and has many followers in Palestine, Jordan, and Syria. Muslim minorities in Thailand, the Philippines, and Singapore also follow Shafi'i jurisprudence.

The Hanbali school was created by the followers of Ahmad Ibn Hanbal (d. 859 CE), who led the Traditionist movement in Baghdad. This school of jurisprudence marked a reassertion of the high profile of Hadith as source of the Shari'a. Despite the common perception of the Hanbali school as the most restrictive of all the schools, Hanbali jurisprudence is in some respects more liberal than most. This is indicated by its extensive reliance on considerations of public interest (*istislah*). Ibn Hanbal issued a ruling, for example, that permitted compelling the owner of a large house to give shelter to the homeless. He also validated compelling workers and craftsmen who go on strike in consideration of fair wages so as to avoid inflicting hardship on the public.

Hanbali jurisprudence also takes a more open view of the basic freedom of contract compared to the other schools. The legal schools differ as to whether the norm in contract law is permissibility (to allow certain behaviors) or prohibition (to restrict certain behaviors), or an intermediate position between the two. Most schools of Islamic jurisprudence tend to be restrictive, maintaining that the agreement of two parties creates a contract but that the requirements and consequences of the contract are independently determined by the Shari'a, not by the parties that drew up the contract. In this view, the parties to a contract do not create law but only a specific contract; their stipulations and terms of agreement should therefore be in conformity with the Shari'a. The parties are not at liberty to interpret the terms of a contract in a way that would violate the purpose of contracts under the Shari'a. The Hanbalis maintain, however, that the normative position regarding contracts is permissibility (*ibaha*), which prevails in the absence of a clear prohibition in the Shari'a. They reason that the Qur'an has only laid down the general principles that contracts must be fulfilled (Qur'an 5:1) and be based on mutual consent (Qur'an 4:19). Since God, as Lawgiver, has not specified any requirements other than consent, consent alone is the validating factor that creates binding rights and obligations.

The principle of permissibility under Hanbali law can also form the basis of a unilateral stipulation (*iltizam*). This means that the individual is free to commit oneself to any lawful form of agreement in all situations in which the concept of permissibility applies. Thus, a man may stipulate in a contract of marriage that he will not marry a second woman, even though marrying up to four women is allowed in the Qur'an. Since polygyny is not required but is only permissible under the Shari'a, a man is free to make monogamy the subject of a stipulation. The other schools disagree with this view, reasoning that what is allowed by the Shari'a cannot not be circumvented or nullified through contractual stipulations. Ibn Hanbal ruled that the stipulations of a marriage contract must be strictly enforced. Consequently, when one of the spouses fails to comply with the terms of the marriage agreement, the other is entitled to seek annulment of the contract. Hanbali jurisprudence is predominant in Saudi Arabia, Qatar, and Oman, and has followers in Egypt and Syria. The public interest provisions of Hanbali jurisprudence and its stress on the precedent of the Prophet Muhammad have also made it popular among Muslim reformers, particularly in the Arab world.

In Sunni law, the head of state is elected to office, but Shiite law maintains that leadership, *imama*, descends in the household of the Prophet through hereditary succession. Of the numerous Shiite schools, only three have survived to the present day: the Ja'fari school of the Ithna 'Ashari (Twelve) Shiites, the Zaydi school, and the Ismaili school. Shiites differ mainly over the line of succession after the fourth Imam. The Twelver Shiites, the largest of the three groups, recognize 12 Imams, hence their name, as opposed to the Ismailiyya, who are also called Sab'iyya (Seveners), as they focus on the first seven Imams. According to Twelver dogma, the twelfth Imam Muhammad al-Mahdi, the Imam of the Age, who disappeared in 873 CE, will reappear to establish justice on earth.

For the Sunnis, divine revelation, manifested in the Qur'an and the Sunna, ceased with the death of the Prophet Muhammad. For the Shi'a, however, divine inspiration continued to be transmitted after the death of the Prophet, to the line of their recognized Imams. Accordingly, they maintain that in addition to the Qur'an and the Sunna, the pronouncements of their Imams, whom they believe to be infallible, constitute divine inspiration and therefore binding law. The Shi'a, moreover, accept only those traditions whose chain of authority goes back to one of their recognized Imams: they also have their own Hadith collections. Since the Imam is divinely inspired, the Shi'a do not recognize the validity of juridical consensus (*ijma'*) if the Imam is present. Shiite law, which mainly originates in the teaching of the sixth Imam, Ja'far al-Sadiq (d. 765 CE), is somewhat similar to Shafi'i law but differs from it on certain issues. Temporary marriage (*mut'a*), for example, is valid only in Shiite law. The Shiite law of inheritance is also different from the law of the Sunni schools. Twelver doctrine was officially adopted in Iran under the Safavids in 1501 CE; it still commands the largest following in Iran, and it also has followers in Iraq, Lebanon, and Syria.

According to the Ismaili doctrine, the esoteric meaning of the Qur'an and its allegorical interpretation are known only to the Imam, whose knowledge and guidance is indispensable to salvation. The Ismailis are divided into two groups, Nizari and Musta'ali. The Nizaris are centered in India, Pakistan, Central Asia, and Syria, and their leader is the present Aga Khan, 49th Imam in the line of succession. The Musta'ali Ismailis believe that the 21st Imam became hidden. This group resides in southern Arabia and India.

The Zaydi Shi'a follow Zayd ibn 'Ali, the fifth Imam in the order of the Shiite Imams. They endorse the legitimacy of the first three caliphs who preceded the Prophet's cousin and son-in-law 'Ali (d. 661 CE) on the belief that an acceptable leader has a legitimate title notwithstanding the existence of a superior claimant. Their legal doctrine is the nearest of the Shiite schools to the Sunnis, and they mainly reside in Yemen.

SALIENT FEATURES OF THE SHARI'A

This section draws attention to some of the characteristic features of the Shari'a, such as its identity as a religious law, its tendency to balance continuity and change, its support for rationality, and its gradualist approach to social reform. The Shari'a also advocates the moral autonomy of the individual and seeks to balance its individualist and communitarian orientations in the formulation of its laws.

Religious and Moral Aspects

Because Islamic law originates in divine revelation, it is an integral part of the religion. This implies that adherence to its rules is at once a legal and a religious duty for Muslims. The concepts of permissible and prohibited (*halal* and *haram*), for example, are both religious and legal categories and involve duties toward God and fellow human beings. Although the legal and religious aspects of the Shari‘a tend to reinforce one another overall, there is an equally significant but often neglected aspect to the Shari‘a, which is civil and positive in character. This is the area of command and prohibition (*ahkam*), which guides court decisions and government practices. Judges do not issue judgments on religious considerations alone. A distinction is drawn between the religious and legal aspects of Shari‘a obligations. For example, if a debt is not paid by a debtor and then some property of the debtor comes into the creditor's possession, the moral teachings of the religion would entitle the creditor to take the equivalent of what is due to him without the debtor's permission. However, if the matter is brought before a court, the creditor will not be allowed to take anything unless he proves his claim through normal methods. Consider also a case in which the creditor has waived the debt by way of charity to the debtor without actually informing him of this, and later he changes his mind and sues the debtor for his claim. In this case, the creditor is entitled to receive payment judicially because the debt was not officially forgiven. However, on moral grounds the creditor would not be able to make such a claim, since an act of charity, even if it is done in secret, may not be revoked.

This distinction between what is and what is not enforceable in a court of justice can also be seen in the scale of Five Values: obligatory (*wajib*), recommended (*mandub*), permissible (*mubah*), reprehensible (*makruh*), and forbidden (*haram*). Of these Five Values, only the first and the last, the obligatory and the forbidden, are legal categories. The remaining three categories are moral in nature and thus are not actionable in court. A lawfully constituted government is authorized, however, to deem a reprehensible act forbidden and a recommended act obligatory if public interest dictates such.

The same distinction between moral and juridical obligations also characterizes the difference between adjudication (*qada*) and juristic opinion (*fatwa*). The judge (*qadi*) must decide his cases based on apparent evidence, whereas a jurisconsult (*mufti*) investigates both the apparent and the actual positions. Both are reflected in his verdict. In the event of a conflict between the two positions, the *mufti* can base his *fatwa* on religious considerations, whereas the judge must consider objective evidence only. Hence, a pious individual in a court case is not treated differently from a person of questionable piety or of no apparent religion.

This dual approach to rights and duties can also be seen in the different orientations of the legal schools with regard to externality and intent. As already noted, the Shafi'i and Hanafi schools tend to stress the external form of conduct without exploring the intent behind it, whereas the Maliki and Hanbali schools are inclined toward the opposite position. This can be illustrated with reference to the contract of marriage. If a man marries a woman with the sole intention of sexual gratification and then divorces her soon afterward, the marriage is invalid according to the Maliki and Hanbali schools but is lawful according to the Hanafi and Shafi'i schools. All that is necessary according to the Hanafi and Shafi'i schools is that the legal requirements of a valid contract of marriage are fulfilled. The other two schools base their judgment on the underlying intent of the act and maintain that distortions should be rectified whenever they become known.

This difference of attitude can also be seen with regard to legal stratagems (*hiyal fiqhiyya*), such as in the following case: Person A sells a piece of cloth to person B for $100 payable in one year. Then he immediately buys the same cloth for $80 paid on the spot. This is considered disguised usury (*riba*) because it amounts to charging an interest rate of 20 percent for a deferred payment of $100 over one year. This can be seen as circumventing the Shari'a prohibition against usury by violating its intent. The Malikis and Hanbalis reject such stratagems on this basis, but the Hanafis and Shafi'is allow such sales, provided they are not made fraudulently and that they realize a benefit.[9]

The Shari'a also contains provisions on expiations (*kaffara*), which are self-inflicted punishments of a religious character that the courts are not authorized to enforce. For example, when a person breaks a solemn oath, he may expiate it by giving charity sufficient to feed 10 poor persons, or alternatively he may fast for three days. Similar other expiations are provided for in the Qur'an. However, none of them are legally enforceable.

Morality and religion are closely interrelated. The Prophet declared in a hadith, "I have been sent to accomplish the virtues of morality." The moral overtones of the Shari'a are seen in its propensity toward duty and responsibility (*taklif*). This is so much the case that some Western scholars have characterized the Shari'a as a "system of duties" in comparison with statutory law, which often speaks of rights. The facts that the Shari'a proscribes usury, wine drinking, and gambling; proclaims legal alms (*Zakat*) as a duty; and encourages "lowering the gaze" between members of the opposite sex are all reflective of the moral underpinnings of the Shari'a. The moral nature of the Shari'a can also be seen in the rules pertaining to war, in which the Shari'a forbids maiming, injury to children, women, and the elderly, and damage to animals, crops, and buildings. The Prophet and the early Caliphs after him condemned cruelty to animals and took to task those who caused them hardship and abuse. Although infractions such as these are not enforceable in a court of law, in premodern times the market controller (*muhtasib*) was authorized to intervene and stop such practices.

Continuity and Change

It is often said by Muslims that Islamic law is immutable because it is divinely ordained. However, the divine law itself includes a certain amount of adaptability and change in its philosophy and outlook. Some of the basic principles of the Shari'a, such as justice, equality, public interest, consultation, and enjoining the good and forbidding evil, are inherently dynamic and cannot be accurately described as either mutable or immutable. They are immutable in principle and yet remain open to adaptation and adjustment on the level of implementation. The fundamentals of faith and the practical pillars on which it stands, the basic moral values of Islam, and its clear injunctions are on the whole permanent and unchangeable. However, in many other areas the Shari'a provides only general guidelines whose details may be adjusted and modified through the exercise of reasoning and *ijtihad*.

Broadly speaking, the Shari'a is immutable with regard to ends but mutable with regard to means. Moral ends such as promoting human dignity, justice, and equality; the realization of lawful benefits for the people; the prevention of harm; and removal of hardship are among the overriding objectives of the Shari'a. In their broad outlines, these objectives are permanent and unchangeable. However, the means of securing the recognized objectives of the Shari'a are flexible since they are not specified in the sources and thus remain open to considerations of public policy and justice. For example, vindicating the truth is an objective in its own right. Truth may be established by the testimony of upright witnesses or by other means as they become available, such as sound recording, photography, or laboratory analysis, which may be even more reliable than verbal testimony. The Shari'a specifies the objective of upholding the truth but leaves open the means by which the truth is ascertained. One *fiqh* rule that is often criticized in the West is that the testimony of two females is equal to that of one male. Muslim jurists of the medieval era apparently upheld this rule in light of the prevailing conditions of their time. There is a reference in the Qur'an that validates the testimony of men and women in that order. However, the reference does not specifically preclude the testimony of female witnesses in any specified number, with or without male witnesses. Many contemporary Muslim scholars believe that the legal interpretation of the Qur'an should be goal oriented and responsive to the realities of contemporary Muslim society. Thus, if the overriding objectives of truth and justice are better served by admitting the testimony of female witnesses on an equal basis with that of male witnesses—especially when women are the only witnesses available in a particular case—a judge should not hesitate to admit them as witnesses and adjust the rules of *fiqh* to that effect.[10]

Ratiocination (Ta'lil)

As a principle of jurisprudence, ratiocination is a step beyond interpretation (*tafsir* or *ta'wil*), in that the latter is confined to the words and sentences of the text, while ratiocination looks into the rationale and purpose of the text. The rules of the Shari'a are accordingly derived from the proper effective cause or causes (*'illa*) of a ruling in a text, which must be present if the rules are to be implemented. The practice of ratiocination in Islamic jurisprudence takes its origin from the Qur'an. Unlike statutes, textual rulings of the Qur'an often espouse an appeal to the reason and conscience of its audience. On numerous occasions the text explains the rationale, effective cause, intention, purpose, or consequences of its ruling. This aspect of the Qur'an, known as *Ta'lil,* is also supported in the frequent references the text makes to those who think, enquire into the world around them, and draw rational conclusions from their observations.

Ratiocination is also an essential component of analogical reasoning (*qiyas*), in that an analogy cannot be constructed without the identification of an effective cause that is common between the original case and the new case. Ratiocination is not valid with regard to devotional matters, but outside of this sphere the Shari'a encourages investigation and enquiry into its logic. Ratiocination in the Qur'an means that the laws of the Qur'an are not imposed for the sake of mere conformity to rules but that they aim at the realization of certain benefits and objectives. When the effective cause, rationale, and objective of an injunction are properly ascertained, these serve as basic indicators of the continued validity of the injunction. Conversely, when a ruling of the Shari'a outside of the sphere of devotional matters no longer serves its original intention and purpose, it is the proper role of the scholar (*mujtahid*) to substitute a suitable alternative for it.

An early instance of ratiocination is noted in the decision of the second Caliph, 'Umar ibn al-Khattab (d. 643), who suspended the influential former pagans' share in *Zakat* revenues. Although the Qur'an assigned a share of the Zakat Tax for them (Qur'an 9:60), the Caliph discontinued this practice on the argument that "God has exalted Islam and it is no longer in need of their support." The Caliph thus departed, on purely rational grounds, from the letter of the Qur'an in favor of its wider interpretation because of the change of circumstances.

It is also reported that the Prophet's widow 'A'isha reversed the ruling of the hadith that had allowed women to attend mosques for congregational prayers, stating that owing to the spread of moral corruption among the Muslims, the Prophet would have done the same were he alive. Once again, I must add that because of the change of conditions in our own time, the prevailing custom permits women's participation in almost all occupations. Thus, it would no longer make sense that the mosque should be the only place where women should not be present. The specific cause and argument may vary in each case, but the basic rationales behind the practice of ratiocination are the common good and caution against irrational conformity to rules. In the practice of Islamic jurisprudence, ratiocination is thus indispensable to juridical reasoning. The majority of legal scholars have upheld this practice on the belief that a mechanical reading of the text that is devoid of wisdom and driven only by considerations of conformity should be avoided whenever possible.

Gradualism and Pragmatism

The Shari'a favors a gradual approach to legislation and social reform. This is amply illustrated in the fact that the Qur'an was revealed over a period of 23 years and much of it was revealed in relationship to actual events. As noted earlier, the Meccan portion of the Qur'an was devoted to moral teaching and dogma and contained little legislation. Legislation is almost entirely a phenomenon of the Medina verses. Even in Medina, many of the laws of the Qur'an were revealed in stages. For example, the final ban on wine drinking (Qur'an 5:90) was preceded by two separate declarations, one of which merely referred to the adverse effects of intoxication (Qur'an 2:219). Another verse proscribed drinking during ritual prayer before wine drinking was finally banned altogether (Qur'an 4:43). This manner of legislation can also be seen with respect to the five daily prayers, which were initially fixed at two and were later raised to five. Also, the payment of the Zakat Alms Tax, which was an optional charity to begin with, became obligatory after the Prophet's migration to Medina. Finally, the practice of fasting was also optional at first and was later made into a religious duty. Some of the earlier rulings of the Qur'an were subsequently abrogated and replaced in light of the new circumstances that the nascent community experienced in Medina.[11]

Islamic law favors realistic reform but it is averse to abrupt revolutionary changes. This is conveyed in the advice that the Umayyad Caliph 'Umar ibn 'Abd al-'Aziz (d. 720 CE) gave to his ambitious son 'Abd al-Malik, who suggested to his father that God had granted him the power to end corruption in society. The Caliph advised against such a course, saying that Almighty God Himself denounced wine drinking twice before He banned it. "If I take sweeping action even in the right cause and inflict it on people all at once, I fear revolt and the possibility that they may reject [my reforms] all at once." Commenting on this account, the contemporary jurist Yusuf al-Qaradawi wrote, "This is a correct understanding of Islam. The kind of understanding that is implied in the very meaning of *fiqh* and would be unquestionably upheld by it."[12]

The pragmatism of the Shari'a is also manifested in the frequent concessions it makes to those, including the sick, the elderly, pregnant women,
and travelers, who face hardship regarding daily prayers and fasting. It also
makes provisions for emergencies, in which the rules of Shari'a may be tem-
porarily suspended on grounds of necessity. Thus, according to a legal
maxim, the opinion (*fatwa*) of a *mujtahid* must take into consideration
changes of time and circumstance. We note, for instance, that people were
not allowed in the early days of Islam to charge a fee for teaching the Qur'an,
as this was an act of spiritual merit. Later, however, it was noted that people
no longer volunteered to teach, and their knowledge of the Qur'an suffered
a decline. The jurists consequently issued a verdict that reversed the former
position and allowed payment of remuneration for the teaching of Qur'an.
Note also the pragmatic verdict of Imam Malik, which permitted the pledg-
ing of allegiance (*bay'a*) for the lesser qualified of two candidates for leadership, if this is deemed to be in the public interest. The normal rule requires
that allegiance only be given to the most qualified candidate. On a similar
note, normal rules require that a judge should be a learned *mujtahid*; however, a person of lesser qualification may be appointed should there be a
shortage of qualified persons for judicial posts. The same logic applies to
the uprightness of a witness. In the event, however, where the only witness
in a case is a person of lesser qualifications, the judge may admit him and
adjudicate the case if this is deemed the only reasonable alternative. Thus,
the judge, jurist, and ruler are advised not to opt for a more difficult decision
in the event where an easier option is justified.

Individualism and Communitarianism

Islamic law requires that government affairs be conducted in consultation
with the community and that the government should strive to secure the
public interest (*maslaha*). This is the subject of the following legal maxim:
"The affairs of the Imam are determined by reference to public interest."
According to another legal maxim, instances of conflict between public and
private interests must be determined in favor of the public. Public interest is
thus the criterion by which the success and failure of government is measured
from the perspective of the Shari'a.

Notwithstanding its communitarian orientation, the Shari'a is also inherently individualistic. The individualism of the Shari'a can be seen in the idea
that religion is primarily a matter of individual conscience. The individualistic
orientation of the Shari'a is manifested in a variety of other ways too, including the fact that the rules of the Shari'a are addressed directly to the *mukallaf,*
the legally competent individual. The individualism of the Shari'a was strong
enough to persuade the sectarian Kharijites (literally, "Secessionists") and
certain groups of Islamic rationalists to embrace the view that forming a

government was not a religious obligation. According to this view, since the Shari'a addressed individuals directly, if every person complied with its rulings, justice would prevail without the need for a government. These and similar other views were expressed on the assumption of a basic harmony between the interests of the individual and those of the community.

From a legal perspective, Islam pursues its social objectives through the reform of the individual. The individual is seen as a morally autonomous agent who plays a distinctive role in shaping the community's sense of direction and purpose. An individual is admittedly required to obey the government (Qur'an 4:59), but he obeys the ruler only on the condition that the ruler obeys the Shari'a. This is reflected in the renowned hadith, "There is no obedience in transgression, obedience is only in righteousness."[13] One can also quote two other traditions that substantiate the moral autonomy of the individual. In one of these traditions, the Prophet instructed believers to "tell the truth even if it be unpleasant." In the other, he declared, "The best form of *jihad* is to tell a word of truth to an oppressive ruler."[14]

The dignity and welfare of the person is of central concern to Islamic law. Scholars have agreed that the Shari'a should uphold five essential goals (*maqasid al-Shari'a*). These are religion, life, intellect, property, and lineage. Each of these goals is premised on the dignity of the person, which must be protected as a matter of priority. Although the basic interests of the community and those of the individual are thought to coincide within the structure of these goals, the main focus is nevertheless on the individual.

The Qur'anic principle of enjoining good and forbidding evil (*hisba*) is primarily addressed to the individual as well, although it is also a responsibility for the community and for government. The individualism behind this principle can be seen in a hadith that states: "If any of you sees an evil, let him change it by his hand. If he is unable to do that, let him change it by his words. If he is still unable to do that, then let him denounce it in his heart, but this is the weakest form of belief."[15] The ruling conveyed in this hadith is supportive of the moral autonomy of the individual and validates, at least in principle, a citizen's power of arrest. In dealing with this issue, Muslim jurists have concluded that the individual must act with conviction when he believes that the initiative he takes is likely to achieve the desired result. However, he is advised not to act if he is convinced that his intervention, however well intended, might cause a harm equal to or greater than the one he is trying to avert.

A related Qur'anic principle is that of sincere advice (*nasiha*). This principle entitles an individual to advise a fellow citizen, including the head of state and his officials, or rectify an error on his part. The main difference between *hisba* and *nasiha* is that the former is concerned with events that are actually witnessed at the time they occur. *Nasiha* is not confined to the actual moment of direct observation and, as such, is more flexible. The individualistic aspect of the Shari'a is also manifested in the Qur'anic advice to the believers, "Take care of your own selves. If you are righteous, the misguided will not succeed in trying to lead you astray" (Qur'an 5:105). Although Islam encourages the call to religion (*da'wa*), the Qur'an proclaims, "Let there be no compulsion in religion" (Qur'an 2:256). In the context of a mixed marriage, this means that a Muslim husband is required to respect the individuality of his non-Muslim wife; he is therefore not allowed to press her into embracing Islam.

The individualistic aspect of the Shari'a can also be seen in the history of the development of Islamic law. Islamic law is often characterized as a "jurists' law," mainly developed by private jurists who made their contributions as pious individuals rather than as government functionaries and leaders. This aspect of Islamic legal history is also seen as a factor for its stability, in that it was not particularly dependent on government participation and support. Governments came and went but Shari'a remained as the common law of Muslims. Another dimension of this picture was that relations between the government and the ulama were less than amicable since the period of the Umayyad dynasty (661–750 CE). The secularist tendencies of the Umayyad rulers marked the end of the Righteous Caliphate, and the ulama became increasingly critical of this change of direction in the system of government. The ulama also retained their independence by turning to prominent individuals among them, which led eventually to the formation of the schools of law. The ethical principles established by these schools often conflicted with the political goals of Muslim rulers. The immunities against prosecution, for example, which are enjoyed by monarchs and heads of state, state assemblies, and diplomats in other legal systems, are absent in Islamic law. No one can claim immunity for his conduct merely because of social or official status.

Two of the most important principles of Islamic law, personal reasoning (*ijtihad*) and consensus (*ijma'*), were put into practice by the jurists without the participation of the government in power. *Ijtihad* and *ijma'* were the nearest equivalent to parliamentary legislation in premodern Islam. *Ijtihad* was practiced mainly by individual jurists. *Ijma'* is broadly described as the unanimous consensus of the qualified scholars of the Muslim community on a particular issue. As such, *ijma'* can be initiated by individual jurists, who make their ruling binding on the government without the government's participation. The jurist who carries out *ijtihad* also enjoys independence from the government. He is expected to act on the merit of each case in line with the guidelines of Shari'a alone.

GOALS AND OBJECTIVES (*MAQASID*) OF THE SHARI'A

The Goals of the Shari'a (*maqasid al-Shari'a*) offer a comprehensive reading of the Shari'a that is particularly meaningful to contemporary Islamic jurisprudence. The concept of the Goals of the Shari'a emerged at a later stage in the history of Islamic jurisprudence and gained prominence only after the methodologies of the schools of jurisprudence lost the ability to stimulate *ijtihad*. The chief exponents of *maqasid al-Shari'a*, Abu Ishaq Ibrahim al-Shatibi (d. 1387 CE), and more recently, Tahir ibn 'Ashur (d. 1973), have emphasized that the jurist must have an adequate understanding of the goals and purposes of Shari'a to avoid errors in *ijtihad*.[16]

The Qur'an expresses its objectives when it characterizes itself as "a guidance and mercy for the believers" (Qur'an 10:75) and when it characterizes the Prophet Muhammad's mission as "a mercy to all of God's creatures" (Qur'an 21:107). Ibn Qayyim al-Jawziyya (d. 1351 CE) explains that the Shari'a aims to safeguard people's interests in this world and the next: "In its entirety, [the Shari'a] is justice, mercy and wisdom." In order to attain these objectives, the Shari'a focuses on educating the individual to administer justice and realize the benefit (*maslaha*) of the self as well as the community.[17]

Educating the Individual

Islam inspires the individual with faith and teaches the believer to be trustworthy and righteous. It is through reforming the individual that Islam achieves its social goals. Acts of devotion (*'ibadat*) are part of Islam's educational program. The *'ibadat* aim at purifying the mind and heart from corruption, selfishness, and indulgence in material pursuits. This is the declared purpose of the ritual prayer (*Salat*) in the Qur'an: "Surely prayer keeps one away from indecency and evil, and remembrance of God is the greatest (act of devotion)" (Qur'an 29:44). *Salat* involves both mental and physical training. While performing the prayer, the worshiper concentrates with full attention; one is not free to do what one likes or act in any way that would disrupt the continuity of the prayer. There is no turning to the side, no staring, laughing, eating, or drinking while one prays, all of which involve an exercise in self-control. The body must be calm and stable before the phrase "*Allahu akbar*" (God is great) is uttered. The first chapter of the Qur'an, which is recited from memory, reads in part, "We worship only Thee, O God, and beg only Thy help." Here one does not use the word "I" but "we" to show that prayer not only concerns the individual but also the community as a whole.

There is a definite time in which to discharge the obligation of *Salat*. According to most jurists, performing the dawn prayer even a minute after sunrise makes the prayer invalid, and one cannot offer the excuse of being sleepy. The purpose of observing such punctuality is to educate and train the individual. One is also commanded to face the Ka'ba in prayer. Why should Muslims face the Ka'ba when the Qur'an clearly says, "Whichever direction you turn, there is the face of God" (Qur'an 2:115)? Making all

Muslims face in a single direction is a form of social education. Turning to pray in any direction one may wish causes indiscipline and confusion. Imagine the scene if everyone in a mosque faced in different directions! Cleanliness of body and attire and decency in clothing are also required for the *Salat*. In addition, performing *Salat* in congregation nurtures equality and solidarity among worshipers and facilitates social encounters in a peaceful environment. Finally, *Salat* ends with the phrase, "May the peace and blessing of God be on His servants." This is a declaration of goodwill toward one's fellow human beings. These objectives are similarly present in fasting, the Hajj pilgrimage, and the Zakat Tax. All of these practices train the individual in self-discipline, sacrifice, and sensitivity for the well-being of others. The pilgrimage is particularly useful in broadening the individual's outlook beyond the confines of a particular locality and encourages a sense of awareness of the conditions of the Muslims worldwide.

There is a great deal in the Qur'an and the Hadith on the promotion of an Islamic ethic that enjoins the individual to practice God-consciousness (*taqwa*); to be honest; to fulfill promises; to practice pleasant manners, humility, sincerity, and beneficence; to cooperate in good works; to be courageous; and to act in a mature manner. Islamic sources also emphasize avoidance of oppression, lying, perfidy, degrading conduct, arrogance, and hypocrisy. Educating the individual in good values, moral excellence, and the attainment of ethical virtues may thus be characterized as among the cardinal goals and objectives of Islam.

Justice ('Adl)

Whereas the basic objectives of the Shari'a concerning the individual are purification of character and moral excellence, in the social sphere the objective is to establish justice. The Islamic conception of justice is not confined to corrective and regulatory justice alone. It also makes justice a part of the character and personality of the believer.

'Adl, the Arabic word for justice, literally means "to place things where they belong." It seeks to establish equilibrium through the fulfillment of rights and obligations by eliminating disparities and excesses of wealth and power in all areas of life. The Qur'an declares that justice is an overriding objective of religion: "We sent Our Messengers with evidence, the scripture, and the balance so as to establish justice among people" (Qur'an 5:25). The phrase "Our Messengers" is in the plural, which suggests that justice is a goal not only of Islam but also of all revealed religions. The reference to "the balance" (*al-mizan*) next to "the scripture" (*al-Kitab*) in this verse has been understood to mean a form of procedural justice that ensures proper implementation of the ruling in this text. According to another interpretation, it means wisdom and balance as opposed to dry literalism. The Qur'anic

standards of justice are not tainted by considerations of race, nationalism, or religion. The believer is urged to be just at all levels, as the Qur'an states:

> O believers! Stand firmly for justice as witnesses to God, even if it is against your-self, your parents, and relatives and whether it be against rich or poor.

> (Qur'an 4:135)

> And let not the hatred of a people divert you from the path of justice. Be just as it is closest to piety.

> (Qur'an 5:8)

> And when you speak, speak with justice.

> (Qur'an 6:152)

The demand for justice is also paired with the virtue of benevolence (*ihsan*): "Surely God enjoins justice and the practice of benevolence" (Qur'an 16:90). This juxtaposition of the concepts of justice and benevo-lence opens the field to considerations of equity and fairness, especially where the linguistic confines of a legal text might lead to rigidity and unfair results. Justice should be carried out in the spirit of *ihsan,* even when it is not demanded as such. Muslim legists devised the principle of juristic preference (*istihsan*) in order to find an equitable alternative when the literal reading of a text fails to deliver a just solution.[18] Ibn Qayyim explains that justice must be followed and upheld wherever it is found, whether inside or outside the declared provisions of the law. Because justice is the supreme goal of Islam, God has sent scriptures and Messengers in order to establish justice among people. Whenever there are indications of the proper path to justice, it is in accordance with the law of God to go toward it. Hence, says Ibn Qayyim, "Any path that leads to justice and fairness is an integral part of the religion and can never be against it."[19] Even if a specific ruling can-not be found in the Shari'a to show the direction toward justice in a particular situation, the search for justice should still be attempted, and the result of such effort, if sincerely undertaken, will always be in harmony with the Shari'a.

Muslims are also directed to be just in their relations with non-Muslims: "God forbids you not to be just and benevolent to those who have not fought you over your faith nor have evicted you from your homes. God loves those who are assiduous in doing justice" (Qur'an 60:8). The ruling of this verse extends to all nations and followers of all faiths and includes all of humanity.[20] In quoting this and other Qur'anic injunctions, the Muslim Brotherhood activist Sayyid Qutb (d. 1966) concludes that justice is an inherent right of all human beings under the Shari'a.[21]

It would thus appear that injustice is abhorrent to the letter and the spirit of the Qur'an. Some rulings of Islamic jurisprudence that were formulated at earlier times and in a different set of circumstances may now be deemed unjust. In my opinion, one's attitude toward such anomalies should be guided by Ibn Qayyim's penetrating assessment that unjust rulings should not be part of the Shari'a even though they are derived through its application. They should thus be revised through *ijtihad* in the light of the broad objectives of Shari'a and the prevailing interest of society.

Consideration of Public Interest (Maslaha)

It is generally held that the Shari'a in all of its parts aims at securing benefits for the people and protecting them against corruption and evil. In his pioneering work, *al-Muwafaqat fi usul al-Shari'a* (Accepted Doctrines on the Foundations of the Shari'a), the jurist Shatibi singled out the consideration of public interest (*maslaha*) as being the only objective of the Shari'a that is broad enough to comprise all measures that are beneficial to human beings, including the administration of justice and rules of worship. In doing this, he put a fresh emphasis on the concept of the Goals of the Shari'a, and his unique contribution to the understanding of this subject is widely acknowledged. Scholars agree that every ruling of the Shari'a serves the public interest: all commandments of the Shari'a are meant to realize *maslaha* and all of its prohibitions are designed to prevent corruption (*mafsada*) in various ways. The designation of actions as obligatory (*wajib*), recommended (*mandub*), and permissible (*mubah*) is meant to promote the public good, while the designation of actions as reprehensible (*makruh*) and forbidden (*haram*) is meant to prevent mischief and immorality. Should there arise a conflict between two injunctions because of the nature of circumstances, priority should be given to that which obtains the greater public good. The rescue of a drowning man, for example, takes priority over the obligatory performance of prayer if a man is found to be drowning at the time of prayer. Because it serves a greater interest, the necessity of saving a person's life trumps the necessity of worshipping God at the proper time.

The Shari'a protects the general interest both in this world and in the next. For example, the individual is urged to engage in beneficial work. Lawful earning, supporting one's family, and the pursuit and dissemination of knowledge are all considered acts of devotion and worship. Conversely, an act of devotion that is attempted as a means of escape from useful work and contribution to society loses much of its spiritual merit.

In order to be valid, the concept of *maslaha* must fulfill three conditions. One condition is that the act in question must be genuinely in the public interest and not just theoretically in the public interest. The Shari'a only protects genuine benefits that are related to safeguarding the essential interests (*daruriyyat*) of life, faith, intellect, property, and lineage. Any action that secures these values falls within the scope of genuine benefit, whereas anything that violates them is considered corruption.

The second condition of *maslaha* is that it must be general (*kulliyya*) rather than particular (*juz'iyya*) in its promotion of the public interest. *Maslaha* is general when it secures the greatest benefit for the largest number of people. It is particular or partisan if it secures a benefit only for certain individuals or groups. The final condition of *maslaha* is that a ruling in the public interest should not conflict with a clear text of the Qur'an or the Sunna. Because the rulings of the Qur'an and the Sunna are by definition meant for the good of all, an action in the public interest loses its credibility when it conflicts with a clear text of scripture.

Two other objectives of Shari'a that may be mentioned briefly are the removal of hardship (*raf* al-haraj*) and the prevention of harm (*daf* al-darar*). Both of these objectives are integral to the concept of public interest. The Qur'an declares, "God never intends to make religion a means of inflicting hardship" (Qur'an 22:78). It also declares in an affirmative sense, "God intends to put you at ease" (Qur'an 5:6; 4:28). The Prophet Muhammad's wife 'A'isha stated about the Prophet that he always chose the easier of two alternatives, so long as it did not amount to a sin. The prevention of harm is also a cardinal goal of Shari'a and is the subject of a renowned hadith: "Harm (*darar*) may neither be inflicted nor reciprocated."[22] This tradition is supplemented by a number of legal maxims such as, "The prevention of harm takes priority over the attraction of benefit," "Harm must be eliminated," and "A particularized harm may be tolerated if it prevents a generalized harm."

ADAPTATION AND REFORM

The First Five Phases of Fiqh

The initial phase of Islamic jurisprudence was the Prophetic period (c. 610–632 CE). In this period, the Qur'an was revealed and the Prophet Muhammad explained and reinforced it through his own teachings and Sunna. There was a general preoccupation with the Qur'an, and the emphasis was not as much on law as on dogma and morality. The legal rulings of the Qur'an, which were mainly revealed during the second decade of the Prophet's mission, were mainly issue oriented and practical. There was little need for speculative legal reasoning or *ijtihad,* since the Prophet himself provided definitive rulings on issues when they arose.

The second phase, the era of Companions of the Prophet Muhammad (c. 632–661 CE), was one of interpretation and supplementation of the textual subject matter of the Shari'a, and it is in this period that *fiqh* and *ijtihad* find their historical origins. Interpretation of the rulings of the

Qur'an and the Sunna by the Companions is generally considered authoritative, as they were the direct recipients of the Prophet's teachings and were witnesses of the Qur'anic revelation. The Companions were known for their frequent recourse to personal reasoning, and the more prominent among them, especially the first four Caliphs, have left a rich legacy of contributions to the Shari'a.

The third phase of *fiqh* was known as the era of the Successors and coincided with the Umayyad dynasty of Caliphs (r. 661–750 CE). Because of the territorial expansion of the Umayyad state, new issues arose that stimulated significant developments in *fiqh*. This period was marked by the emergence of two schools of legal thought that left a lasting impact on subsequent developments. These were the Traditionists (*Ahl al-Hadith*) and the Rationalists (*Ahl al-Ra'y*). The secession of the Shiites from the main body of Muslims was another major development of this period.

The next two centuries (c. 750–950 CE) are known as the era of independent reasoning (*ijtihad*) and mark the fourth phase in the history of *fiqh*. This period saw major developments, which were later manifested in the emergence of the leading schools of law, as discussed above.

The last of the five phases of the formative history of *fiqh* began around the mid-fourth century of Islam (c. 950 CE). It was generally a period of institutionalization of the dominant schools of jurisprudence, with emphasis not so much on new developments but on following the existing precedents and practices of these schools (*taqlid*). By far the longest phase of the history of *fiqh*, this period lasted for about nine centuries and witnessed the downfall of the Abbasid and Ottoman empires and the colonial domination of Muslim lands by European powers. The colonial powers propagated their own doctrines and legal codes in almost every area of the law in their dominions. As a result, the practice and development of *fiqh* underwent a sustained period of stagnation, particularly in Sunni Islam.

The Current Phase of Developments in Fiqh

The current phase in the history of *fiqh* began around the turn of the twentieth century. It is marked by a greater emphasis than before on original thinking and *ijtihad*. Following the Second World War and the ensuing period of nationalism and independence, Islamic revivalism in the Muslim world started with a demand by the Muslim masses to revive the Shari'a in the spheres of law and government. There were those who opposed this movement and called for the continuation of colonial ideas and institutions. This latter group argued that the Muslim world did not possess a self-contained Shari'a-based civil code or a constitution to provide a ready recourse for those who wished to revive the *fiqh* tradition.

Many newly independent Arab states introduced constitutions that were based on those in European countries. However, they also offered a partial revival of *fiqh* through the incorporation of clauses that declared Islam the state religion, the Shari'a as a source of law, and in some cases introduced *fiqh*-based statutory legislation. As the demand for a Shari'a-based civil code grew stronger, working groups of Shari'a and modern law experts were formed in Syria and Egypt. 'Abd al-Razzaq al-Sanhuri (d. 1969), the renowned Egyptian jurist and government minister, featured prominently in these early efforts. Sanhuri's work was marked by his tendency to incorporate salient aspects of Western and Islamic jurisprudence into Islamic revivalist projects.

The new trend toward the critical reexamination of *fiqh* became visible in the 1929 Egyptian Law of Personal Status, which drew not only from the juristic legacy of the four major Sunni schools of *fiqh* but also from the opinions of individual jurists when this was conducive to the public interest. The 1953 Syrian Law of Personal Status took a step further in the same direction and not only relied on the resources of the leading schools but also formulated new rules that had no precedent in existing *fiqh*. The Syrian legislation marked a new beginning for *ijtihad* through statutory legislation, as it departed from the traditional pattern of *fiqh* being the concern of private jurists and legal experts. This new approach to *ijtihad* through legislation was followed in the same decade by similar attempts in Morocco, Tunisia, Iraq, and Pakistan, where statutory reforms were introduced in the traditionally Shari'a-dominated laws of marriage, polygamy, and divorce.

The call for a Shari'a-based civil code in Muslim countries was accentuated by the growing support for collective *ijtihad*. This movement was characterized by two approaches: (1) recourse to the wider resources of *fiqh* in all of its diversity and (2) direct recourse to the sources of the Shari'a and its goals and objectives as aids to *ijtihad*. In 1976, Jordan promulgated a comprehensive civil code that replaced the Ottoman *Mejelle* of the previous century, which was based mostly on Hanafi jurisprudence. The Jordanian code is now widely seen as a model for Muslim countries, in that it combines influences from modern thought and from the four Sunni schools of law taken collectively. In the early 1980s, the United Arab Emirates created its own civil code based on the Jordanian model, as did the Republic of Sudan. One of the interesting features of the Jordanian code is that its articles are followed by explanatory notes that indicate the sources from where they were drawn. At the same time, the code reveals the influence of the principles of *fiqh*, such as analogical reasoning, the consideration of public interest, different varieties of *ijtihad*, and the Goals of the Shari'a. Efforts are now underway to formulate a unified, Shari'a-based civil code for all the Arab countries.

Notwithstanding their many advantages, the codes discussed above were confined to personal law alone, which isolated the wider legacy of *fiqh* in other areas. These codes also had a restrictive effect in that they confined judges and legal experts to specific provisions within *fiqh* law and minimized the need to maintain regular contact with the sources of *fiqh* in general. Following a call by the OIC (Organization of Islamic Conference) for the compilation of a comprehensive encyclopedia of *fiqh*, the University of Damascus began such a project in 1956. The government of Egypt had already started a similar project in 1951, and Kuwait followed Egypt and Syria in 1971. The Kuwait *Encyclopedia of Islamic Law (al-Mawsu'a al-Fiqhiyya)* is presently nearing completion after the publication of 45 volumes. Compilations such as this depart from the scholastic tendencies of traditional writings by treating all the major schools of *fiqh* strictly on the merits of their contributions to the reform effort. By their very terms of reference, the encyclopedia projects consolidate rather than reform existing *fiqh* by providing the raw materials of reform.

Collective *ijtihad* continued as the principal method of arriving at consultative decisions through the parallel establishment of international Islamic law academies, which were made up of prominent jurists from various Islamic countries. The first Islamic law academy was the Islamic Research Academy (*Majma' al-Buhuth al-Islami*), which was opened at Al-Azhar University in Egypt in 1961. The Muslim World League (*al-Rabita al-'Alam al-Islami*) subsequently inaugurated its own academy in Mecca and held its first session in 1978. Then the OIC created another academy in Jeddah, Saudi Arabia, which consisted of Islamic law experts from the OIC member countries, and convened its first session in 1984. India and Pakistan also formed Islamic law academies. In addition, a number of international research institutes undertake research on Islamic legal subjects.

The OIC and Muslim World League academies have permanent headquarters and hold periodical meetings that deliberate topical issues. Wide-ranging and important issues including artificial insemination, in vitro fertilization, organ transplants, the expropriation of private property for public purposes, issues of concern to marriage and divorce, and Islamic banking and finance have been submitted to these academies. Typically, *fatwas* are issued by the academies on such subjects through the practice of collective *ijtihad*.

Whereas the Islamic law academies mentioned above are nongovernmental organizations, Pakistan gave the process of collective *fiqh* a state mandate by forming an Islamic Ideology Council at the government's initiative. Malaysia's National Fatwa Council is a similar statutory body. The various states of Malaysia also maintain *fatwa* committees that aid the Muftis of each state in their deliberations.

The creation of self-contained Islamic universities also aided the development of new methods of teaching and scholarship. National Shari'a faculties began to address the needs of students at undergraduate and higher levels of competence. Research-oriented scholarship in doctoral programs take into consideration not only the traditional subjects but also new areas such as the

Islamic law of obligations, Islamic constitutional law (*al-fiqh al-dusturi*), Islamic economics, Islamic banking and finance, human rights studies, and so forth. Greater attention is now being paid not only to the methodologies of the traditional schools of Islamic law but also to works outside the established schools.

A more recent development along these lines is the introduction of Shariʻa advisory committees in major banks and financial institutions of the Islamic world, which are charged with the task of ensuring compliance with the Shariʻa in banking operations. In addition, new *fatwa* collections, sometimes in several volumes, by prominent twentieth-century Muslim jurists and scholars are too numerous to name. Future collections are likely to feature landmark decisions of prominent courts and judges in a number of Muslim countries. For example, in 1967 the Supreme Court of Pakistan verified and expanded the kinds of divorce that can take place at the initiative of the wife. Similarly, in 1999 the Pakistan Federal Shariʻa Court decreed the elimination of usury (*riba*) from the banks and financial institutions of Pakistan.

The twentieth century marked a milestone in the history of Islamic legal thought. During this period, the scope of *fiqh* was no longer confined to personal law but was extended to the sphere of public law and government. For the first time in Islamic history, Shariʻa and *ijtihad* became part of the agenda of modern parliaments and legislatures in Muslim countries. Given continued public support for the Shariʻa and sustained progress in innovative thought and *ijtihad,* the twenty-first century is likely to see more development of the Shariʻa not only in civil law and commercial transactions but also in civil litigation, laws of evidence, contracts, and constitutional law. As before, such changes are likely to be gradual and selective. The overall tendency of change will likely be toward the establishment of greater harmony between the Shariʻa and statutory legislation.

NOTES

1. Abu Ishaq Ibrahim al-Shatibi, *al-Muwafaqat fi usul al-ahkam,* ed. M. Hasanayn Makhluf (Cairo: al-Matbaʻa al-Salafiyya, 1341/1922-3), Vol. 3, 219.

2. See Mohammad Hashim Kamali, *Principles of Islamic Jurisprudence* (Kuala Lumpur, Malaysia: Ilmiah Publishers, 1998), 367; idem, "Issues in the Understanding of *Jihad* and *Ijtihad,*" *Islamic Studies* 41 (2002), 623f; Taha Jabir al-ʻAlwani, "Ijtihad," *Occasional Papers* (Herndon, Virginia: The International Institute of Islamic Thought, 1993), 4.

3. See for the text of this hadith, Abu Dawud, *Sunan Abi Dawud,* Kitab al-Aqdiya, Bab Ijtihad al-Ra'y fi'l-Qada' (Book of the Juridical Process, Chapter on Personal *Ijtihad* in Juridical Decisions).

4. See Jamal al-Banna, *Nahwa Fiqh Jadid* (Cairo: Dar al-Fikr al-Islami, 1996), 73.

5.   See for details on the movement toward a more goal-oriented *ijtihad*, M.H. Kamali, "Issues in the Legal Theory of *Usul* and Prospects for Reform," *Islamic Studies* 40 (2000), 5–23.

6.   Albert Hourani, *Arabic Thought in the Liberal Age* (Cambridge: Cambridge University Press, 1983), 151.

7.   Muhammad Rashid Rida, *Tafsir al-Qur'an al-Hakim* (also known as *Tafsir al-Manar*), 4th edition (Cairo: Matba'a al-Manar, 1373/1953-4), vol. 3, 30.

8.   Muhammad Amin ibn 'Abd Al-'Aziz ibn 'Abidin, *Majmu'a rasa'il Ibn 'Abidin* (Beirut: Dar Ihya' al-turath al-'Arabi, 1980), vol. I, 24.

9.   See Shatibi, *al-Muwafaqat,* vol. 2, 385; see also Ibn Qayyim al-Jawziyya, *I'lam al-Muwaqqi'in 'an Rabb al-'Alamin,* edited by Muhammad Munir al-Dimashqi (Cairo: Idara al-Tiba'a al-Muniriyya, n.d), vol. III, 92.

10.   See for details M.H. Kamali, *Freedom, Equality and Justice in Islam* (Cambridge: The Islamic Texts Society, 2002).

11.   The Qur'an (11:114) conveys the ruling on the daily prayers, and on Zakat (24:56). However, these verses only provide partial information, which is supplemented by Hadith. The same is true for the rules of fasting in Ramadan; 2:185 conveys the final ruling but the earlier practice is indicated in Hadith. To give all the relevant evidence on these issues would require more detail than is practical in this chapter.

12.   Yusuf al-Qaradawi, *Madkhal li-Dirasat al-Shari'a* (Cairo: Maktaba Wahba, 1990), 131.

13.   Muhammad Nasir al-Din al-Albani, *Mukhtasar Sahih Muslim* (Beirut: al-Maktab al-Islami, 1407/1987), 6th edition, 322, hadith no. 1226.

14.   Ibn Maja, *Sunan Ibn Maja,* edited by Muhammad Fu'ad 'Abd al-Baqi (Beirut: Dar al-Kutub al-'ilmiyya, 1407/1987), hadith 4011.

15.   Albani, *Mukhtasar Sahih Muslim,* 16, hadith 34.

16.   See Shatibi, *al-Muwafaqat,* vol. 4, 105 and Muhammad Tahir ibn 'Ashur, *Maqasid al-Shari'a al-Islamiyya* (Tunis: Matba'a al-Istiqama, 1966), 15–16.

17.   Ibn Qayyim al-Jawziyya, *I'lam al-Muwaqqi'in,* vol. 4, 1; see also Muhammad Salam Madkur, *Madkhal al-Fiqh al-Islami* (Cairo: Dar al-Qawmiyya li'l-Tiba'a wa'l-Nashr, 1384/1964), 85–86.

18.   See for details, Mohammad Hashim Kamali, *Equity and Fairness in Islam* (Cambridge: The Islamic Texts Society, 2005), 112. This book is a study of equity and *istihsan.*

19.   Ibn Qayyim, *Hukmiyya fi al-siyasa al-shar'iyya* (Cairo: Mu'assasat al-'Arabiyya, 1380/1961), 16.

20.   Muhammad ibn Jarir al-Tabari, *Tafsir al-Tabari* (Beirut: Dar al-Ma'rifa, 1400/1980), vol. 28, 43.

21.   Sayyid Qutb, *Fi Zilal al-Qur'an* (Beirut: Dar al-Shuruq, 1397/1977), 5th edition, vol. 2, 689.

22.   Ibn Maja, *Sunan Ibn Maja,* hadith 2340.

13

A MAN ON THE ROAD TO GOD

Daniel Abdal-Hayy Moore

I met a man on the road to God with the intense face of an owl—
A closeness of diamond-white feathers in the perfect space of an owl

Eyes of divine penetration burn all the way through to our souls
And ignite us in a blaze of love— the secret grace of an owl

Now, the owl is not revered universally as being spiritually wise –
In some places *"owl"* means *"stupid"*—what abject disgrace for an owl!

I was walking in the woodsy hills above Bolinas Bay years ago
And a white owl landed high and stared at me—inspected by an ace of
   an owl!

I may be thinking of that owl when I say this man was owl-like to me—
Maybe in Paradise they're the same—interconnected birthplace of the owl

All I know is my heart opened in his gaze on the road to a Beloved
   God—
Love flooded and obliterated us both as God's effect in place of an owl

Ameen—in the world-thick woods hearing the *Hu-Hu's*[1] of that voice
   so clear—
Feathers still tickle along my pulse-tingling arms—*unexpected embrace
   of an owl!*

NOTE

1. The *Hu-Hu* sound of the owl in this poem recalls the Arabic word, *huwa*,
"He." In Islam, the ultimate "He" is God.

14

WHAT IS SUNNI ISLAM?

Feisal Abdul Rauf

INTRODUCTION

This chapter is intended as an introduction to Sunni thought and practice for contemporary readers. The reader might be a modern Muslim—Sunni or Shi'a—seeking to better understand Sunni belief and theology, and specifically as it pertains to the development of political thought—what became known as *siyasa shar'iyya* and which today might more accurately be rendered "political science." The reader may be interested in knowing how her ancestors experienced their faith and contended over the issues that birthed the Sunni–Shi'a divide, and the basis on which they forged the term *Sunni* in the first few centuries of Islamic history. The reader would then want to know which of the issues that led to this schism are relevant today and which are impediments that need revisiting in the struggle of Muslims to define themselves as a global *Umma* (community of believers) within a globalized world community.

By contrast, the reader might be a non-Muslim interested in understanding "Sunni Islam" in the contemporary context, hoping that reading this chapter will help to understand what lies behind the current tensions in Iraq between Sunnis, Shi'as, and Kurds (notice the addition of a cultural or ethnic meaning here, with *Sunni* meaning in this case Sunni *Arabs*) and expecting that it will equip one to improve the situation on the ground. Or the reader might hope that in understanding the tension between the Saudis, who are Sunni, and the Iranians, who are Shi'a, one would get a better sense of what American foreign policy vis-à-vis relationships with Saudi Arabia and Iran entails.

Given the space constraints of this chapter, I shall limit myself to describing the factors that led to the rise of the *Ahl al-Sunna wa'l-Jama'a* and the formalized content of their beliefs, bearing in mind that the typical twenty-first-century Sunni Muslim may neither personally be aware of many of these issues nor find them relevant to her worldview.

We will see, in fact, that the division between Sunnis and Shi'as, as it developed in the first three Muslim centuries, was driven by political struggles, even though it is often described as a difference in theology. Over the course of the centuries, both the political and the theological views of the opposing factions continued to develop and change, so that today the divide between Sunnis and Shi'as is less a divide in theology, jurisprudence, or even political thought than one of hardened sociological identities independent of their original features. That is, today, Sunnis and Shi'as do not necessarily hold the same set of beliefs or theologies that they held in the first generations nor are they divided by them. Modern Sunnis and Shi'as overlap in their convictions on nearly every position in the spectrum of theology, political thought, and law.

The reader should bear in mind that some key terms that Muslims now use to describe their faith were unfamiliar to the Prophet's contemporaries and his immediate successors. The vast majority of modern Sunnis, in fact, are unaware that the phrase *Ahl al-Sunna wa'l-Jama'a* did not exist during the time of the Prophet Muhammad or in the era just after him (the seventh century CE). What is more, even the core term *Sunna* took almost three centuries to acquire the signification that it carries today. Most contemporary Muslims are also not aware that the term evolved out of a fierce debate common to many faith traditions, that is, how to maintain the core principles of the religion across different generations and contexts of time and culture. In the process, Muslims came to define the boundaries between what was deemed orthodox and what was heretical in the many opinions that were evolving among the new religion's adherents.

The word *Sunni* comes from the Arabic word *sunna,* meaning "way," "tradition," or "custom." In English, the term "Sunni Islam" refers to the larger of two groups of Muslims: the Sunnis, who represent approximately 85 percent of the global Muslim population, and the Shi'a, who represent most of the remaining 15 percent. However, it is important to note that in Arabic, the terms "Sunni Islam" and "Shiite Islam" do not really exist. Classical Muslim thinkers rather speak of *Ahl al-Sunna wa'l-Jama'a,* "The *People* of Tradition and the Community of Believers"—those called in English "the Sunnis"—and *Ahl al-Shi'a,* "The people of the Faction" of 'Ali ibn Abu Talib, the fourth Caliph. The word *Sunni,* for Arabic speakers, most properly refers to a community of people, not to a type of religion. This distinction is important because the term "Sunni Islam"—an English construction—suggests meanings not present in the Arabic. To English speakers, it refers to beliefs and practices of Sunnis that are both religious and nonreligious and further suggests that these practices originate in religious belief. However, for Muslims the term *Sunni,* as a term of identity, often refers to the history and politics of the Sunnis—aspects that may have little or nothing to do with religious beliefs per se but which, as we will see in this chapter, shaped the nuances of Islamic thought that became associated with the Sunnis.

BIRTH OF THE SUNNI–SHI'A DIVIDE

The first challenge that faced the nascent Muslim community after the Prophet's death in the year 632 CE was how to select a new leader, given that no one could truly and completely replace the Prophet. The Prophet's followers, during his lifetime, had experienced his leadership as an organic whole: legislative, executive, and judicial functions, along with the primary and defining Prophetic role of a spiritual teacher and instructor, gathered into the one individuated person of the Prophet Muhammad. However, after his death, the community was faced with the challenge of maintaining the quality of spiritual and moral life that people experienced with the Prophet in the absence of his physical presence.

The Sunni–Shi'a divide grew out of two distinct views of what qualifications the leader of the community should have. Those who became known as Shi'a maintained the vision of the political leader discharging the roles of religious and spiritual leader, lawgiver, and supreme judge. Those who became known as Sunnis accepted the great difficulty in finding a single human being who was qualified—let alone skilled—in all leadership areas as was the Prophet. Thus, in Sunni circles these roles became firmly separated. By the end of the first three centuries of Islamic history, Sunnis accepted the *Caliphs* (literally, "successors" of the Prophet) as those who wielded just political authority. The role and title of *Imam*, religious leader, devolved upon the greatest theologians and scholars, especially the founders of the Sunni schools of law. Those who exercised legal authority as the interpreters of divine law became jurisconsults (*muftis*) and legal scholars (*faqihs*), who issued legal judgments, or judges (*qadis*). Leaders having purely spiritual authority became known as masters (*shaykhs*) of the spiritual "way" (*tariqa*) known as *tasawwuf* (Sufism). Each specialty developed its own body of study, knowledge, and expertise, with each affecting the development of the others.

Eventually, the group consisting of those who thought the political leader of the community should be required to fulfill political functions only and not presume religious, spiritual, theological, and legal qualifications began calling themselves the "People of the Tradition and the Community," *Ahl al-Sunna wa'l-Jama'a*. This naming move was a political one, designed to fix this group's views firmly at the center of tradition or societal precedent (that is, the *Sunna* of the community). In fact, Sunnis were no more traditional or orthodox than were Shiites; the meanings of tradition and orthodoxy in the area of political thought, the development of theology and law, and spiritual practice were still being worked out. Sunnis simply sought to establish their position over that of the Shi'a and other groups as the more orthodox one.

The political struggle between those who became Sunnis and those who became Shi'as took place so early in Islamic history that it shaped the development of the entire spectrum of Islamic thought, including its political theory, theology (*kalam*), sense of tradition, and understanding of the law. Even so fundamental a matter as which Hadith[1] texts were deemed authentic was shaped by this political struggle, so that even Hadith collections came to be divided along Sunni–Shi'a lines.[2]

One of the major factors contributing to the success of the Ahl al-Sunna wa'l-Jama'a is the conflation of its political dominance with a moderating viewpoint developed by its jurists. These jurists held the public interest (*maslaha*) as the highest objective of Islamic law and therefore saw that—outside of a core set of theological beliefs and ritual practices, on which there was universal consensus (*ijma'*)—there was room for disagreement. By recognizing competing interpretations as equally valid and orthodox, they provided more leeway in the nonritual aspects of Islamic thought. Therefore, their moderating position bridged certain political differences that had hitherto divided the community.

The factors precipitating the split between those who came to be called Sunnis and those who became Shi'as may be classified roughly into three categories: (1) political struggles, (2) legal questions (especially regarding the formation of the Hadith), and (3) theological concerns.

POLITICAL STRUGGLES THAT SHAPED THE CONCEPT OF AHL AL-SUNNA WA'L-JAMA'A

The primary factor that shaped the development of the Ahl al-Sunna wa'l-Jama'a was politics, as the nascent and growing Muslim community sought to defend its unity and internal peace and support the existing leaders against threats posed by the claims of opposition political movements. Struggles over who the leader should be led to major and bloody schisms between various factions, out of which first evolved the Khariji, Shi'a, and Sunni political parties and then the lesser political divisions within the community.

In the first years after the Prophet Muhammad's death, the community asked: Should the leader be from among the Emigrants (*Muhajirun*), those who emigrated with the Prophet from Mecca, or from the Supporters of the Prophet from Medina (*Ansar*)? While this question became irrelevant within one generation, others persisted: Should the leader be from the Prophet's Arab tribe of Quraysh, and if so, should he be from the clan of Banu Hashim or Banu Umayya? Should the leader be from the Prophet's family or, even more specifically, from the line of his cousin and son-in-law, 'Ali? The Shi'a took the latter position. Should the leader be any person who ruled according to the principles of justice and who abided by the teachings of the Qur'an and its Law? This was the adamant position of the Kharijites. Was the personal morality of the ruler relevant if his rule was competent and just? Were errors of judgment a sin, and if so—whether the sin was a moral one or a political error of judgment—can the leader continue to rule? What is the role of the community in such a case? Did the Prophet himself give any guidance on this? Does the Qur'an give any guidance on this?

These issues deeply split the community. Paradoxically, while the Sunni–Shi'a divide continues today, most of the original issues that created this division neither define nor fuel the contemporary debate.[3] Passionate differences of opinion on these questions led to political divisions, which in turn influenced the rise and crystallization of different schools of theology and law.

By the second half of the reign of the third Caliph, 'Uthman b. 'Affan (r. 644–656 CE), the seeds of political conflict began to sprout. The challenges of administering a growing empire that included Egypt, Syria, Basra, and Kufa (in modern Iraq) compounded 'Uthman's difficulties. His tendency to appoint governors from among his clan opened him to the charge of nepotism, and his inability to rein in some of their excesses bred growing restlessness, especially in the provinces of Egypt and Iraq.

The Official Recension of the Qur'an

Another factor that played a larger political role than is now recognized was a by-product of what was perhaps 'Uthman's most valuable accomplishment: establishing the official recension of the Qur'an. This was prompted by a crisis caused by various factions in different regions that disputed the method of reciting various Qur'anic passages.[4] The governor of Mada'in (near modern Baghdad), Hudhayfa ibn al-Yaman, complained to 'Uthman, urging him to take steps to end the disagreement: "O Commander of the Faithful," he said. "Save this community (*Umma*) before they differ about the Book as [happened with their predecessors] the Jews and the Christians."[5] The Syrians contended with the Iraqis, the former following the recitation style of Ubayy ibn Ka'b and the latter that of 'Abd Allah ibn Mas'ud, with each party accusing the other of infidelity (*kufr*).[6] Frequently, the recitation of the Holy Book was made the subject of boasting. The people of Hims, for example, boasted that their way of reciting the Qur'an was superior to that of the people of Basra, whose compilation of the Qur'an they acclaimed as the "Heart of Hearts."[7]

Realizing that the unity of the Muslim *Umma* was at stake, 'Uthman decided to unify the community behind a single authorized text of the Qur'an. He asked the Prophet Muhammad's wife Hafsa to send him the manuscript she had in her possession, and he ordered Zayd ibn Thabit,

'Abdallah ibn al-Zubayr, Sa'id ibn al-'As, and 'Abd al-Rahman ibn Harith b. Hisham to make exact copies of the available manuscripts. 'Uthman then sent to every Islamic province one copy of the Qur'an accompanied by a reciter (*qari'*, pl. *qurra'*), ordering that all other Qur'anic materials, whether written in fragmentary manuscripts or whole copies, be burned.[8] With reference to the language of the text, he gave preference to the dialect of the Quraysh, the Prophet's tribe, over the other dialects whose use the Prophet had sanctioned. The reciters were unhappy with this, for they thought of themselves not as mere reciters of the Qur'an but as keepers of the Holy Word. By specializing in the different dialects of Arabic and forms of Qur'anic recitation, they served as key resources in the understanding and interpretation of the Qur'an. 'Uthman's decision reduced their power and influence. Their dissatisfaction was to play a critical and defining role in the subsequent conflict.

'Ali's Confrontations: "Let the Qur'an Decide between Us"

After 'Uthman's assassination in 656 CE by rebels dissatisfied with their governors in Iraq and Egypt, the fourth Caliph, 'Ali ibn Abu Talib, faced a turbulent *Umma*. A series of confrontations developed that resulted in 'Ali having to wage two internal battles. The first was against a group led by the Prophet's wife 'A'isha and two Companions of the Prophet, Talha and Zubayr, in the Battle of the Camel near Basra in 656 CE.[9] The second battle was against 'Uthman's relative Mu'awiya ibn Abi Sufyan, the governor of Syria, at the Battle of Siffin in 657. These conflicts deeply and permanently divided the community along essentially political lines.

During the confrontation between 'Ali and Mu'awiya at Siffin, Mu'awiya's side was losing when Mu'awiya's colleague 'Amr b. al-'As shrewdly advised him to have his soldiers hoist copies of the Qur'an on their lances, suggesting, "Let the Qur'an decide between us." Weary of fighting, and seeing that a cease-fire afforded them the opportunity to reestablish their influence, 'Ali's partisans, which included a number of Qur'an reciters, urged 'Ali to submit to arbitration. They agreed to abide by the Book of God (that is, the Qur'an) and "the just *Sunna* (precedent) that unites, not disperses," as the means of resolving the dispute. While *Sunna* here referred to the approved practice of Muslim leaders in political and administrative matters, we can clearly see in this expression the seeds of the future expression, *Ahl al-Sunna wa'l-Jama'a*.

While awaiting the verdict of the arbitration, certain individuals among 'Ali's supporters protested against recourse to arbitration with the cry, *la hukma illa li-llah,* literally, "No decision but God's." This phrase implied that it was improper to apply to humans for a decision about the leadership of the Muslims. This view was based on a divine ordinance in the Qur'an: "If two parties of the Believers fight with one another, make peace between them; but if one rebels against the other, then fight against the one that rebels, until they return to obedience to God" (Qur'an 49:9). In his battle against 'A'isha and her supporters, 'Ali had appealed to this verse, and now the dissidents logically maintained that it was his duty to continue to fight against Mu'awiya, as a similar situation prevailed.

Those who raised the cry of "No decision but God's" persuaded other partisans of 'Ali that arbitration was a sin against God, for it substituted a human decision for the divine command—especially the decision of people who were not known for having exemplary spiritual or religious status. In their eyes, it was unthinkable for 'Ali to submit to arbitration. 'Ali was a man of deep piety, renowned for his knowledge of the Qur'an from his lifetime association with the Prophet. To stoop to Mu'awiya's level was simply wrong.

A large group of 'Ali's followers that believed in this position stopped near Kufa and proclaimed their secession from 'Ali. 'Ali visited their camp and reconciled himself to their position. After his return to Kufa, however, he asserted his intention of not infringing the Siffin agreement to arbitrate. This angered the group outside of Kufa. When they learned that 'Ali had sent Abu Musa al-Ash'ari as his negotiator to the arbitration meeting, a group of 3,000 to 4,000 dissidents secretly left Kufa and hundreds more left Basra.[10] The rallying place chosen by these dissidents was Nahrawan, on a canal channeled from the Tigris River.

The result of the arbitration was inconclusive, and 'Ali decided to engage Mu'awiya in battle again. First, however, he felt it was necessary to deal with the insurgency of his former partisans, the Kharijites, so he went to them in Nahrawan. They demanded that he confess himself guilty of an act of impiety (*kufr*). This 'Ali could not possibly do, and he angrily refused. After promising safety to those who changed their minds and supported him—and there were a few who did—he attacked the Kharijites and killed most of them. This eroded 'Ali's base of support, forcing him to return to Kufa and to give up the campaign against Mu'awiya.

The struggle between Mu'awiya's partisans (*shi'at Mu'awiya*) and 'Ali's partisans (*shi'at 'Ali*) continued. In 658 CE Mu'awiya persuaded the Syrians to acknowledge him as Caliph. Three months later, he took Egypt and awarded its governorship to his friend 'Amr ibn al-'As, which eroded 'Ali's control over the territories of Islam. Before 'Ali could move again against Mu'awiya, he was killed in 660 CE by the Kharijite Ibn Muljam in revenge for members of his wife's family who had lost their lives at Nahrawan. 'Ali's son Hasan succeeded him for a short time but then agreed to abdicate for the sake of the community's unity. Mu'awiya entered Iraq in 661 CE. With Egypt and Iraq under his control, the power of Medina as the capital of the Islamic state was effectively broken, and Mu'awiya celebrated the year 661 CE as *sanat al-jama'a,* the "year of the (unification of the) community."[11] The elements of the concept of the Ahl al-Sunna wa'l-Jama'a were now in place, although not yet commonly in use.

*The Kharijites versus the Murji'a: Using Theology to Support
Political Power*

While 'Ali's battle with Mu'awiya was purely a matter of political and military strategy, the Kharijites became the first Muslim sect to base their movement on uncompromising moral principles. 'Ali's attack upon them led to
their reactionary insistence that the community of believers was obliged to
depose the Imam who "went off the right path"—their justification for abandoning 'Ali after he accepted arbitration. They declared every believer who
was morally and religiously irreproachable to be capable of being raised by
the vote of the community to the supreme dignity of the Imamate, "even if
he were an Ethiopian slave."[12] The result was that each of the leaders of the
Kharijites was recognized by them as *Amir al-Mu'minin* (Commander of
the Faithful). Consequently, the only other leaders besides their own that
they recognized as legitimate were Abu Bakr and 'Umar, whom they particularly venerated. As for 'Uthman, he was recognized as legitimate only during
the first six years of his reign, and 'Ali was regarded as legitimate only until
the Battle of Siffin. Legitimacy to them was therefore not a permanent feature inherent in the leader but rather subject to that leader's correct decisions, a principle that many Sunnis and Shi'as today would find acceptable.
The Kharijites therefore staked out a principled position in opposition to
both the Shi'at 'Ali and the Shi'at Mu'awiya.

Mu'awiya had been governor of Damascus since the time of 'Umar and
shrewdly leveraged his political power in Damascus, expanding it over the
entire territory ruled by Islam. By appointing his son Yazid as his successor,
he founded the Umayyad dynasty based in Damascus (661–750 CE). In doing
so, he revolutionized the concept of the Caliphate, transforming it into a
hereditary monarchy instead of its being based on a formula that sought the
most qualified person for the task, which was how the majority of the Muslim
population thought the Caliph should be nominated. This was also the basis
on which the first four Caliphs had been chosen.

Reactions against Mu'awiya's appointment of Yazid were strong. The Shi'a
advocated the notion of the *person* who should rule: namely, the Prophet's
family, and in particular the family of 'Ali and his descendants. They therefore
developed a political theory that rejected the first three Caliphs as having
usurped 'Ali's rightful claim to the Caliphate.

Arguments soon swirled around the question of what should be done with
a leader deemed to have done wrong, and rating the former Caliphs became a
nasty and contentious political debate. The *Murji'a* (literally, "deferrers")
wanted to eliminate discord in the Muslim community and thus proposed
deferring judgment on this matter to God. They recommended that Muslims
abstain from declaring either support for or opposition to the earlier Caliphs.
They held that Muslims do not lose the status of believers by committing a
single incorrect action; wrongdoers, including Caliphs, instead become

"aberrant believers" and are to be punished or forgiven by God. This doctrine of deferring judgment to God was a stepping-stone toward the later thinking of Ahl al-Sunna wa'l-Jama'a. Abu Hanifa (d. 767 CE), the founder of one of the four major legal schools of Sunni Islam, stressed the idea of the community (*jama'a*) of Muslims and of the Sunna as its unifying principle. For him, following the Sunna meant following the middle road, avoiding extremes, and basing decisions on scriptural proofs.

The Kharijites rejected the Murji'a doctrine of justification by faith without works. This was, after all, the logical extension of their political stance. They pushed their moral strictness to the point of refusing the title of believer to anyone who committed a mortal sin, regarding a wrongdoer as an apostate. While they regarded all non-Kharijite Muslims as apostates, their extreme wing, known as the Azraqis, believed that such a person became an infidel forever. Since an apostate could never reenter the faith, he should be killed along with his wives and children.[13] This branch of the Kharijites was finally eliminated by Hajjaj ibn Yusuf (d. 714 CE), the Umayyad governor of Iraq.

Either directly or by the impetus that they gave to reflecting on questions of faith and morality, the Kharijites accelerated the pace of development of Islamic thought. The Puritanism that characterized Kharijite thought, in its conception of the state and of faith, was located in ethical principles: the Kharijites demanded purity of conscience as an indispensable complement to bodily purity for acts of worship to be valid.

However, the Kharijites had their moderate elements too. Two other branches of Kharijite thought survived in the Ibadiyya and the Sufriyya movements. Both of these groups, unlike the Azraqis, believed that non-Kharijite Muslims were not to be assassinated. The Ibadiyya tried to establish themselves politically, but apart from a few isolated attempts in various parts of the eastern region of the Arabian peninsula and in North Africa, these efforts did not last. Today the Ibadiyya are the only significant group of Kharijites, living mainly in Oman and with small communities in Algeria and Tunisia. As a group, they represent a comparatively moderate school; their present views, in dogma as well as law, have been to some degree influenced by Sunni schools of thought and survive today mainly as a variant of these schools—proving that in the long run moderation outlasts militancy.

THE SUNNA IN THE UNDERSTANDING AND SYSTEMIZATION OF HADITH AND LAW

Before the Prophet Muhammad, the term *Sunna* referred to a way or manner of acting, the approved custom, or norm, what can be loosely called the common law. After the Prophet's time, *Sunna* embraced the total experience that the Prophet's followers in Medina knew and lived as an organic whole, including faith, religious practice, and inner spiritual development within the society's legal, sociological, and politico-economic contexts.

Semantically, the Arabic verb *sanna* means to establish, prescribe, or institutionalize a practice or custom, with the noun *Sunna* being an established act or practice that has the force of social custom or institutional precedent. The Qur'an uses the term *Sunna* and its derivatives 17 times, almost all speaking of God's precedent (*sunnat Allah*) in making an example of the unbelieving communities prior to the time of Muhammad. Notably, the Qur'an never uses the term *Sunna* to refer to Prophetic practice; thus, no Qur'anic basis exists for its later popular usage to refer to the Prophet's example. The closest the Qur'an gets to express the sense of Prophetic *Sunna* is when it describes the Prophet as a "fine exemplar" (*uswa hasana*, 33:21). In several instances, it commands believers to "obey God and obey the Prophet" (Qur'an 3:32 and 4:59, for example).

During the seventh century CE, when the Muslim community was ruled by the "Rightly Guided" Caliphs[14] and then the Umayyads, the term *Sunna* was used in debates on legal and ritual issues to indicate any normative precedent set by exemplars of the past, including the Prophet. During the Prophet's lifetime and thereafter, when faced with problems to solve, people reminded one another of how the Prophet and his closest Companions had acted under similar circumstances. This resulted in transmitted oral narratives (*hadith*) of remembered practices and customs. Such customs were called *Sunan* (the plural of *Sunna*), and a *hadith* was the report of a *Sunna*.

As time went on, people compared their information about normative practices with that of others. Thus, for example, person A would assert that he heard his grandfather say that he heard the Prophet say something about a given matter, while person B would have heard from his uncle a similar or different account of what the Prophet said or did regarding the same matter. These "chains of transmission" (*isnad*) were provided to authenticate the particular transmission of a *Sunna*. Not only were the reports of *Sunan* about what the Prophet did or said, but many were about what the Companions of the Prophet did as well.

Within a generation of the Prophet's death, the Arabian Peninsula, most of North Africa, and the region eastward to Persia came under Muslim rule. Gradually over the next two centuries, increasing numbers of non-Arabs such as Egyptians, Levantines, and Mesopotamians became Muslim. A growing need emerged to adapt the application of Islamic law to societies whose legal and cultural heritage was different from that of the Arab society. Several great intellects sought to develop a coherent and systematic Muslim hermeneutics to deal with legal matters in these contexts. In the process, they founded schools of jurisprudence that were hybrids of prevailing cultural, social, political, and legal environments and influences. They developed the principles and sources of Islamic law and in doing so shaped the direction of Islamic legal thought.

As companions of the Prophet Muhammad or their direct descendants, the inhabitants of Medina naturally regarded their practice as best reflecting the

Prophetic *Sunna*. The followers of Malik ibn Anas (d. 795 CE), the most important jurist in Medina, referred to themselves as *Ahl al-Hadith* (People of the Hadith), or alternately *Ahl al-Sunna* (People of the Tradition). However, at this point, *Sunna* referred only to the overall practice of the people of Medina and did not clearly distinguish between a *Sunna* of the Prophet or the opinion (*ra'y*) of a Companion. Those who rendered their own opinions and those who lived in more cosmopolitan societies like that of Iraq or Egypt and found themselves forced to exercise a greater level of independent judgment and personal opinion on a matter were labeled *Ahl al-Ra'y* (People of Opinion). When their opinion was not clearly based on a *Sunna*, they were disapprovingly called *Ahl al-Bida'* (People of Innovation), suggesting that any idea not based on a *Sunna* was heretical.

The jurist Muhammad ibn Idris al-Shafi'i (d. 820 CE), founder of the school of law that bears his name, argued that the Sunna of the Prophet Muhammad had a greater legal value than the *Sunna* of a Companion in the determination of a legal injunction. He therefore gave precedence to the Sunna of the Prophet as the second source of law in his framework of legal interpretation. In this framework, the Sunna of the Prophet stood next in importance only to the Qur'an and stood above the practices of those who came after the Prophet. Shafi'i's position was that, unlike the position taken by Imam Malik's followers, it was incorrect to presume an identity between the practices of the people of Medina and the Prophetic Sunna. He reinforced his argument that the various local traditions of Medina could not reflect completely and faithfully the practice of the Prophet with a critique of the practice of blindly conforming to an inherited tradition without understanding its basis in Prophetic precedent. This practice is called *taqlid* in Islamic legal terminology.[15] According to Shafi'i, the Prophetic Sunna should be strictly defined as the sayings, actions, and the tacit acquiescence of the Prophet Muhammad as related in authentic Hadith.[16]

It was also important to a coherent development of jurisprudence to distinguish between legal injunctions derived from specific Qur'anic and Prophetic directives and those derived from the Prophet's cultural context. The Qur'an and the Prophet made specific injunctions on matters that were purely religious (relating to beliefs and worship) as well as on societal matters. These latter issues included laws of personal status such as marriage and child custody; criminal law, laws on murder, theft, or libel; business or contract law; and obligations of believers to follow their leaders, which later developed into the law of nations and governance. Pre-Islamic common law and social practices that were neutral to Qur'anic and Prophetic injunctions, and that may have been incorporated into the practice of the people of Medina, thus were not by definition deemed to be of equal value to the Qur'anic or Prophetic injunctions—even when done by the Prophet himself.

The incorporation of such customary practices led to the recognition of custom (*'urf* or *'ada*) as a legitimate source of law. Custom is subsidiary to the primary sources (the Qur'an and the Sunna) but deemed to be legal within Islamic law when it does not contradict or conflict with the primary sources. In addition to this distinction, the jurists later distinguished between a *Sunna* that had the value of a legal precedent (*sunna tashriʿiyya*) and a *Sunna* that was not meant to set a legal precedent (*sunna ghayr tashriʿiyya*).[17]

Since the publication of his treatise on Islamic law (*al-Risala*), Shafiʿi's idea of the Sunna as referring exclusively to the practice of the Prophet Muhammad has dominated jurisprudence in Sunni Islam. Today, nearly all Sunni Muslims think of *Sunna* as referring only to the Sunna of the Prophet. Even Shiite Muslims have adopted Shafiʿi's concept of the preeminent importance of the Prophetic Sunna in their jurisprudence. The only difference is that they include in their definition of Sunna the collective teachings of the Shiite Imams. In the absence of the Imam of the Time, the contemporary jurisprudent—as stand-in for the Imam—can in fact override the legal judgments (*fatwas*) of his predecessors.

Over time, real differences narrowed between Shiʿa and non-Shiʿa schools of jurisprudence.[18] Strictly speaking, the use of the term *Sunna* is of a jurisprudential nature, separating the Sunna of the Prophet from the Sunna of the people, in the sense of the common understandings and practices of the people. This created the legal space for varying interpretations of law and normative practices (or *Sunnas*) of different communities, all following the spirit of the Qur'an and the Prophetic Sunna.[19] Were such a separation not to exist, there would be enormous pressure for all Muslims to abide by a single society's understanding of Sunna as being equal to the Prophetic Sunna. This situation is increasingly visible in contemporary times, when a regional or ethnic interpretation of Islam is often incorrectly deemed the only interpretation consistent with the Prophetic Sunna.[20]

Much of the disagreement among the founders of the schools of law was due to differences in the *sunan* they referred to in establishing their legal opinions. This was because the Hadith collections Muslims now see as authentic had not yet been compiled. Not surprisingly, considering Shafiʿi's emphasis on the Prophet's Sunna as a source of precedent, four of the six canonical Hadith collections of Sunni Islam are called *sunan*. The need for such collections was made more acute by the need for jurists to have reliable sources of information on which to base their judgments.[21]

THEOLOGICAL INFLUENCES THAT SHAPED THE CREED OF AHL AL-SUNNA WA'L-JAMAʿA

The conflict between ʿAli and Muʿawiya gave rise to political groups that evolved into the three main traditions: Kharijite, Shiite, and Sunni. As noted above, by the beginning of the eighth century CE, theological movements began to accompany these traditions, with each political group developing a theology to justify its position. At stake were the following issues: What is the status of "believer?" What is faith and how is it determined? What are the conditions for salvation and human responsibility? Parallel considerations concerned the nature of the Qur'an, whether as the Word of God it was created or uncreated, the divine content and attributes of the Word, the nature of the divine attributes and their connection with the divine essence, and the impact of theology upon the understanding of divine unity. These questions fueled the emergence of theology, known as *kalam,* among Muslims.

These theological questions were not purely theoretical. In the political context of the time, such controversial and divisive questions were targeted at judging contemporary leaders of the community and retroactively applying these judgments to the very first Caliphs, as well as to the succeeding Umayyad and Abbasid Caliphs. Discussions about the Imamate were not safe activities to engage in, with rulers considering many discussions seditious. However, the need continued to define political correctness while simultaneously defending religious orthodoxy against attacks from nonbelievers of all types.

The expansion of the Islamic state brought Muslims into closer contact with Jews, Christians, Zoroastrians, and members of other faiths. Greek philosophy and Persian, Egyptian, Indian, and Central Asian practices and beliefs percolated into Islamic thought and practice. As a result, many aspects of these previous traditions became "Islamized," which in practical terms meant bringing pre-Islamic ideas into dialogue with the Qur'an and Hadith.[22] Translations from works of Greek science and philosophy catalyzed the birth of a theological–philosophical vocabulary, the systemization of doctrinal positions, and the rise of schools of theology.

Mu'tazili Rationalism

One influential school of theology that developed was the Mu'tazila, founded in Basra by Wasil b. 'Ata' (d. 748 CE). This school of thought developed from the ninth century CE to the middle of the eleventh century. The Arabic verb *i'tazala* has the sense of "separating oneself, or standing aside," and originally referred to the position of being neither a Kharijite nor a Murji'ite (on the issue of the belief or unbelief of the sinful Muslim) and not taking sides with the Shi'a on the issue of who should be the leader of the community. As a theological movement, the Mu'tazila are most commonly associated with a belief in intellectual rationalism.

Mu'tazili theology was distinguished by the following five theological principles (*al-usul al-khamsa*):

1. *God's unity and uniqueness (tawhid):* The Mu'tazila believed in the absolute transcendence of God (*tanzih*), according to the Qur'anic formula, "nothing is of His likeness" (Qur'an 42:11). What they understood by this

was that God can have none of the characteristics of a body as such: He has
no form, color, length, breadth, or height. He cannot be said to be either
mobile or immobile and He has neither parts nor members. The Muʿtazila
rejected all anthropomorphic descriptions or resemblances of God (*tashbih*).
The Qurʾanic expressions that refer to God's "hand" or "face" are therefore
to be understood only figuratively, as referring to His power, blessing, or
essence. God the Creator was understood to be a purely spiritual being. For
the Muʿtazila, the Qurʾanic verse, "Vision captures Him not, while He com-
prehends all vision; for He is the Subtle, the Aware" (Qurʾan 6:103) meant
that God cannot be seen, either in this world or in the Hereafter.

2. *God's justice (ʿadl)*: The Muʿtazila conceived of God's justice as being
identical with the human recognition of justice. For the Muʿtazila, God is
subject to the same divine justice that applies to humans: what is just or
unjust for us—that which our reason tells us to be so—is the same for God.
Divine justice means that God only wills or does what is morally good
(*hasan*) and He is necessarily exempt from any act that is morally bad. God
acts with a purpose, and justice and compassion inhere in the Divine purpose.
Existents by their nature contain both good and evil. God can will only the
good and is obliged to accomplish that which is best (*al-aslah*). Thus, He neither wills nor commands that which is evil. Humans, as creators of their own
acts, act by a contingent power (*qudra*) that God has placed in them. Therefore, they are responsible for their own actions, and when they commit good
or evil, God is obliged to reward or punish them accordingly.

God's necessary justice excludes any notion of predestination. It would be
unjust on God's part, said the Muʿtazila, to decide in advance the fate of
every person in the world and to ordain that one will be saved and another
damned, without either having merited this fate by his or her actions. It is
for humans to decide their future lot, according to whether they choose to
believe or not to believe and to obey or disobey the Law. God would be
unjust if He were to predetermine faith or unbelief, and that some are "well
guided" and others are "astray." The Muʿtazila were adamant in their rejection of the doctrine of predestination. Instead, they affirmed human free will:
the absolute ownership by every individual of his or her actions, which could
not be attributed to God.

3. *The "promise and the threat" (al-waʿd wa'l-waʿid)*: This principle means
that on account of the "threat" uttered in the Qurʾan against a Muslim who
is guilty of a serious offense, every person who dies without repenting will
suffer the torments of Hell for eternity. This principle follows from human
free will. Thus, human beings as moral agents are fully responsible for their
actions and will be held accountable for their ethical behavior. God's decree-
ing of human destiny is embodied in human choice. The Muʿtazila elaborated a corollary principle of "the names and the decrees" (*al-asmaʾ wa'l-
ahkam*), whereby those possessing faith are bound to perform the acts prescribed by faith.

4. *The theory of an "intermediate state" (al-manzil bayn al-manzilatayn)*: This principle holds that a sinful Muslim cannot be classified either as a believer (*mu'min*) or as an unbeliever (*kafir*) but belongs to a separate category, that of the malefactor (*fasiq*). Such a person has failed to perform the "witness of the limbs," that is, the ritual obligations of Islam, but his faith (*iman*) in God keeps him within the community.

5. *Commanding the good and forbidding evil (al-amr bi-'l- ma'ruf wa annahy 'an al-munkar)*: According to the Mu'tazila, this obligation is laid upon every believer in accordance with numerous verses in the Qur'an (3:104, 3:110; 7:157; 9:71, and so on). This principle allows ethically committed believers to intervene in public affairs, uphold the law, and oppose impiety, both individually and collectively.

These five principles had profound political ramifications. The Umayyads, who—except for Caliph 'Umar ibn 'Abd al-'Aziz—were generally disliked for having forced a monarchy on the *Umma,* used the notion of predestination to justify their rule. Thus, they considered the doctrine of free will dangerous and subversive to their interests. They held power, they argued, because it was God's will, and therefore the *Umma* should accept them. In the long run, advancing the principle of free will ran against the political interests of both the Umayyad and the later Abbasid Caliphs, who generally sought to encourage a fatalistic attitude among the *Umma* and who were arguably responsible for strengthening Muslims' belief in destiny (*qada* and *qadar*). The third and fourth principles of the Mu'tazila were applied not only to believers in general but also used to judge contemporary and previous Caliphs. The fifth principle posited the need for including religious values in the public debate on how to build an Islamic society. Since the primary responsibility for society fell on the ruler, this principle raised the thorny question of what the public's duty was when the ruler fell short of his obligations.

The fifth principle of enjoining good and prohibiting evil was often interpreted to mean active intervention in public affairs to uphold the law and oppose impiety. The pro-Mu'tazila Abbasid Caliph al-Ma'mun (r. 813–833 CE) used this principle to put into motion an inquisition to enforce his belief that the Qur'an was created. Judges were dismissed from their position and even witnesses were regarded as unacceptable unless they publicly acknowledged that the Qur'an was created. Al-Ma'mun, himself a scholar who excelled in jurisprudence, argued that those who asserted the "uncreatedness" of the Qur'an were guilty of equating God with the Qur'an. By claiming that the Qur'an was eternal and primordial, they suggested that God did not create, originate, or produce it. They "were therefore like the Christians, who claim that Jesus was not created because he is the Word of God."[23] In Ma'mun's eyes, this was an Islamization of the Christian belief that Jesus Christ was coeternal with God, and he feared that Muslims might deify the Qur'an. After all, the Qur'an confirmed the Christian belief that Jesus was

God's word, yet it also asserted that God created Jesus (Qur'an 3:45; 4:171). This Qur'anic evidence supported the notion that God's speech was indeed created, and therefore the Qur'an was created too. Al-Ma'mun died only four months after instituting his inquisition, which continued for some 15 years, till the time of the Caliph al-Mutawakkil (r. 847–861CE).

The Response of Ibn Hanbal

The most famous person to stand up against al-Ma'mun was Ahmad Ibn Hanbal (d. 855 CE). An original and noted jurist and founder of the Hanbali school of law that bears his name, he was also a well-known Traditionist and Hadith scholar. He was the compiler of the *Musnad,* one of the largest and most important collections of Sunni Hadith. He was flogged and imprisoned for his rejection of al-Ma'mun's position on the created Qur'an, a stand that gained him enormous popularity among the masses.

Ibn Hanbal's later reputation was made possible by the Caliph al-Mutawakkil's decision to end the inquisition and restore the Sunni judges to their former positions. This move helped to insert Ibn Hanbal's views into the future development of Sunni thought. By this time the leading figures of the era of persecution were no longer on the scene and Ibn Hanbal's scholarship and popularity opened the way to an association between him and the Caliph, whose acceptance cemented his legacy as a celebrated Traditionist and as the most faithful defender of Sunni orthodoxy of his time.

The principal consequence of the failure of al-Ma'mun's inquisition was that it brought to a decisive end any notion of a Caliphal role in shaping Islamic thought. In addition, the restoration of the Sunni position permitted the development of what in due course would become recognizable as Sunni Islam. Although important scholars continued to belong to the Mu'tazila, their movement never again attained political hegemony. It was now the Sunni scholars (*ulama*), rather than the Caliphs, who saw themselves as the "heirs of the Prophets" (*waratha' al-anbiya'*). Henceforward, it would be these same scholars, who, armed with their newly won spiritual authority, would maintain a careful distance from the holders of political office and elaborate the system of classical Islamic thought.[24]

Ibn Hanbal's genius lay in his developing a worldview that, in the face of grave disagreements within the community, gave something to each side and put behind the Sunni community the divisive issues that had hitherto created contentions within the Muslim *Umma*. In the area of law, he accepted the decisions of the most important representatives of the generations that followed the Prophet's Companions (*al-Tabi'un*). In his doctrine, he accepted the consensus of the community when it was founded on the Qur'an and the Sunna or when it expressed a general truth on which the Qur'an and the Sunna were silent. His background as a Hadith scholar is visible in this position, which leans toward the Maliki and Shafiʻi notion of placing more emphasis on tradition rather than the Hanafi position, which relied more on the application of reason.

Politically, Ibn Hanbal incorporated the Murjiʼite aspiration of reconciling opposing radical political positions by resolving the issues that had split the community. It was now two centuries since the Prophet had died, and expressing hostility to his successors and to historical personalities who were long dead only furthered social conflict. Ibn Hanbal resolved this issue by creating a hierarchy of preference of Companions of the Prophet. Abu Bakr was at the top of the hierarchy, followed by ʻUmar, then the six electors appointed by ʻUmar (these included ʻUthman and ʻAli, along with Talha and Zubayr), then the fighters with the Prophet at the battle of Badr, and finally the Emigrants from Mecca (*Muhajirun*) and the Helpers from Medina (*Ansar*).[25] By doing this, Ibn Hanbal established the subsequent Sunni position of doctrinally acknowledging ʻAli's eminent position in Islam and the legitimacy of his Caliphate and rehabilitating those who fought against ʻAli: Talha, Zubayr, and Muʻawiya.

In many respects, Ibn Hanbal's political views sought to answer challenges posed by Kharijite and Shiite objections to Sunni Islam. Like the Shiites and Umayyads, but against the Kharijites, he affirmed the legitimacy of the Caliphate as being based on the Caliph's membership in the Prophet's tribe of Quraysh: "No person has any claim to contest this right with them, or to rebel against them, or to recognize any others until the Day of Resurrection."[26] Like the Shiites and Umayyads, he defended the Caliph's right to designate his successor.[27] However, like the Kharijites, he added the caveat that for such a designation to be effective, the Imam (leader or Caliph) had to publicly swear fidelity to the Word of God, thus establishing the principle of the rule of law above the rule of the Imam.[28] Within the framework of the prescriptions of the Qurʼan and the Sunna, he gave the Imam wide latitude to take measures deemed necessary to improve the material and moral conditions of the Muslim community for the common good and public interest. This affirmed the social justice provision that was so important to the Shiite conception of the Imamate.

In opposition to the Kharijite position, he felt that all members of the community owed obedience to a legally constituted Imam and could not refuse obedience by disputing the Imam's moral qualities. Striving in the cause of Islam (*jihad*) should be pursued under all Imams, whether good men or sinners; the injustice of the tyrant or the justice of the just mattered less. As long as the Friday prayer, the pilgrimage, and the two feasts (*ʻId al-Fitr* and *ʻId al-Adha*) are maintained by the holder of authority, Muslims have to accept his rule and pay him the Zakat and land taxes, whether he puts them to right use or not.[29]

Ibn Hanbal's position of accommodation to state power may strike the reader used to democratic government as unusual, and it is opposed by many contemporary Muslims, both Sunnis and Shiites. However, Ibn Hanbal, like many Muslim jurists, felt that the danger posed by civil unrest (*fitna*) was greater than the danger of an unjust ruler. Modern political science notion of "failed states" largely supports this view. If a ruler seeks to impose a ruling in disobedience to God's Word in the Qur'an, obedience to the ruling may be refused but without calling for an armed revolt. A revolt cannot be justified as long as the Imam maintains the regular observance of the Islamic prayer. However, within these severely limited constraints, Ibn Hanbal agreed that every member of the Muslim community had the duty, according to a person's knowledge and means, of commanding good and prohibiting evil, thereby incorporating a major principle of both Kharijite and Mu'tazilite ethics.

By establishing these guidelines, Ibn Hanbal separated the purely religious commandments of worship from worldly civil matters in Islamic law and gave the ruler wide latitude in the civil areas of the law as long as he honored the religious aspects. Judgment of the ruler's actions on civil matters now fell under the purview of the jurists (*fuqaha'*), who by their position and offices were given the role of maintaining the Sunna. While remaining within the limits of political loyalty, they were to keep public opinion vigilant and impose on the ruler respect for the prescriptions of religion. While for Ibn Hanbal's critics this served to consolidate the temporal ruling power of the Abbasid Caliphs, in his eyes it limited their power and served to keep them away from meddling in issues of theology and jurisprudence. This was a sore point for Ibn Hanbal because he had suffered torture under the pro-Mu'tazilite inquisition instituted by the Abbasid Caliphs.

Ibn Hanbal's ideas paved the way for the rise of political theory (*siyasa shar'iyya*) as a branch of Islamic jurisprudence. Sunni doctrine as shaped by Ibn Hanbal and those who succeeded him drew a sharp distinction between the "Rightly Guided" (*Rashidun*) Caliphs and the later Caliphate, which they admitted had devolved to a monarchy (*mulk*) and consisted of unjust Caliphs. Only the *Rashidun* were deemed to have fulfilled the conditions of the true Imamate; that is, only they had the proper spiritual, religious, and judicial qualifications for just rule. Therefore, only their legal decisions and rulings were binding as *Sunna* on the believers. The legal decisions and rulings of all Caliphs after them were not deemed precedent setting in the same way.

In the interest of social harmony, Ibn Hanbal and his followers developed a minimal set of definitions for the Caliph under their theory of the state. The Imam had to be a Muslim and from the Prophet's tribe of Quraysh. The Imamate of the ruler could be binding without any act of recognition by the Muslim community. Ibn Hanbal even went so far as to affirm the validity of previous Imamates by usurpation (*ghalaba*), thus retroactively affirming the legitimacy of the Umayyad and Abbasid dynasties. Muslims must not get involved in civil wars, and they must obey and actively support the established leader, whether just or oppressive, unless that leader violated the

Shari'a in a very narrowly defined sense: the Imamate could be forfeited only through apostasy or by neglecting the duty to provide for the communal prayer.

Ibn Hanbal's view of justice is encapsulated in a formula made famous by the later Hanbali jurist Ibn Taymiyya (d. 1328 CE): "Strictness with regard to religious obligations and tolerance with regard to worldly affairs."[30] This rule is characteristic of Hanbali thought. Nothing is to be regarded as imposing legal obligations but the religious practices that God has explicitly prescribed; conversely, nothing can be lawfully forbidden but the practices that have been prohibited by God in the Qur'an and the Sunna.[31]

After Ibn Hanbal, the concept of Sunni Islam combined the above political and social principles with Shafi'i's view of the Sunna as consisting of the normative practices of the Prophet Muhammad. To Sunnis, all of the above elements, taken together, suggested the parameters of correct belief and practice, and thus of Islamic orthodoxy. After Ibn Hanbal, Shafi'i's doctrine on the qualifications, investiture, and functions of the political leader of the Islamic state reached its climax in the work of Abu al-Hasan al-Mawardi (d. 1058 CE), whose work, *al-Ahkam al-Sultaniyya* (The Rules of Governance), became widely accepted as an authoritative exposition of Sunni political doctrine. This work had a profound impact on other thinkers such as Abu Ya'la al-Farra' (d. 1066 CE), who modified it to accommodate some points of the Hanbali tradition.

Later changes to the Sunni doctrine of the Imamate included the investiture of the Caliph either through appointment (*'ahd*) by his predecessor or by election (*ikhtiyar*). Views on who constituted the electors (*ahl al-ikhtiyar*, literally, "the people who choose"), also known as the "those who loosen and bind" (*ahl al-hall wa'l-'aqd*), varied from one elector being sufficient to the generality of the masses as electors. According to the theologian and political theorist Abu Bakr al-Baqillani (d. 1013 CE), "those who loosen and bind" the people to the ruler are primarily the religious and legal scholars, whose role is to uphold justice and the integrity of Islam. In later doctrine, the Imamate could be invalidated through loss of mental or physical fitness, and while the Shafi'is maintained that it could be forfeited through immorality, injustice, or heterodoxy, this doctrine was denied by others, including the Hanbalis and Hanafis. The primary duties of the leader were to guard the faith against heterodoxy, enforce the rule of law, protect peace in the land and defend it against external enemies, receive the legal alms and taxes and distribute them in accordance with the law, and appoint honest and reliable officeholders. The Caliph's duty to implement the rule of law and guarantee the personal security of his subjects trumped issues of his behavior and character.

Sunni thought on the Imamate continued to reflect political reality. Abu Hamid al-Ghazali (d. 1111 CE), a noted jurist and theologian who lived under the powerful Saljuq sultanate in Iran (ca. 1038–1137 CE), viewed the

Caliph as the head of the Islamic *Umma,* legitimized by a pledge of allegiance and necessitated by the importance of preserving the legality of the acts of governors and judges throughout the empire. After the fall of the Caliphate to the Mongols in 1258 CE, Sunni thinkers affirmed that the legality of judicial acts could no longer depend on the presence of a leader from the tribe of Quraysh. Considering the exercise of power as essential to the Imamate, they vested its functions in the actual ruler—a position maintained by Sunni thinkers until the present time. The only difference is that modern Sunni attitudes toward leadership have shifted toward focusing on national governments established by consultation (*shura*) and election (a modern interpretation of *bay'a*) as the best way to establish legitimate rule.

Ibn Hanbal was concerned with political unity and confessional solidarity. Opposed to what might encourage disunity, he put forth the concept of consensus as an expression of group cohesion, which was wrapped in an ethical doctrine founded on service to God through faith. In opposition to the Murji'ites, who distinguished between faith and works, he conflated these two aspects of belief, asserting that faith is itself an act: faith is "word, act, intention, and attachment to the Sunna."[32] No one may call himself or herself a believer without making an affirmation of faith in conditional form: "God willing, I am a Muslim." This point was targeted against the Mu'tazilite position that faith is completely determined by the human will. By granting the divine will an active role in determining human faith, Ibn Hanbal also intimated that Muslims cannot condemn another's faith without expressing displeasure with the divine will responsible for it—an unthinkable and absurd position.

Theologically, Ibn Hanbal was against the Kharijite principle of branding dissidents as unbelievers (*takfir*), and he encouraged an attitude of "strict construction" with regard to the interpretation of scriptural texts on this matter. In Ibn Hanbal's opinion, even a Muslim guilty of a grave sin may not be excluded from the community except on the authority of a hadith account, which must be interpreted with restrictive literalism.[33] He cited only three sins that might involve the accusation of unbelief: nonobservance of prayer, consumption of fermented liquors, and the spreading of heresies contrary to the dogmas of Islam, among which he mentioned the *Qadariyya.* This latter term, which refers to believers in the doctrine of free will, included both the Mu'tazilites and the Shi'a. This position remains a source of tension between Hanbali literalists, such as the Wahhabis of Saudi Arabia, and contemporary Shiites.

SPIRITUALITY IN THE PRACTICE OF THE AHL AL-SUNNA WA'L-JAMA'A

Unlike the Shi'a, who continued to invest their Imam with spiritual leadership, it was evident even before Ibn Hanbal's time that the Sunni Caliphs could not command spiritual mastery. Ibn Hanbal and the Sunni jurists who succeeded him created the ideational and institutional space to recognize spirituality as a separate field within the evolution of Sunni thought. Although the term "Sufism" (*tasawwuf*) had not yet come into being, he contributed to the rise of a spiritual current within Sunni practice by drawing its essential aspects into his worldview. He regarded faith (*iman*) not as just a simple body of rites but as a system of moral convictions. This included the following elements: an attitude of sincerity brought to the service of God (*ikhlas*), renunciation of the world (*zuhd*), a spirit of poverty (*faqr*), spiritual and moral courage (*futuwwa*), and scrupulousness, which leads one to avoid questionable matters between the well-marked limits of the licit (*halal*) and the illicit (*haram*) in Islamic law. By seeding Sunni thought with such ideas, Ibn Hanbal laid the groundwork for the future rise of Sufism as a pillar of Sunni thought and practice.

Parallel to the theologians and jurists who developed the concept of the *Ahl al-Sunna wa'l-Jama'a*, Sufi thinkers strove to articulate a coherent model of religious theory and practice stemming from the principles derived from the Qur'an and the Sunna. The discipline thus formed was called *'ilm al-batin*, "internal knowledge," referring to knowledge of the inner self, as opposed to *'ilm al-zahir*, "outer knowledge," which referred to the traditional sciences of Hadith, *kalam* (theology), and *fiqh* (jurisprudence). Sufis regarded the development of internal knowledge as analogous to the development of outer knowledge, in that both sciences were grounded in the Prophetic Sunna but whose amplification as a discipline developed in the succeeding centuries. Sufis considered internal knowledge as more spiritually fundamental than outer knowledge because it deals with the essential, inner dimension of human faith. However, they recognized the Shari'a and its affiliated disciplines as indispensable for Muslims seeking to lead God-fearing lives. This view reflected the spectrum of the Prophetic Sunna, since the performance of outer duties is part of the fulfillment of inner religious attitudes.

Rendering the internal knowledge "orthodox" and theologically coherent required the grounding of its principles in the normative practice of the Prophet Muhammad. At the same time as the theologians and the jurists developed the principles and structure of Sunni religious thought, the great Sunni scholars of inner knowledge authored treatises that developed the teachings and sayings of the masters of their own tradition.

Noteworthy among this literature is the work of al-Harith ibn Asad al-Muhasibi (d. 857CE), who worked in Basra and in Baghdad. His name al-Muhasibi, "He who Takes Himself to Task," alludes to his development of a science of scrupulous moral introspection. This early form of Sufi psychology was based on the practice of certain Companions of the Prophet, who wanted more than just to strive after the outward observance of the religious law and the Prophetic Sunna. Paying attention to what was happening within their souls through internal experiences, dreams, visions, and altered states of consciousness, they sought to relate these experiences to the "inner Sunna" of the Prophet, and adopted practices that favored this view, especially the Prophet's meditative practices and prayers.

Renunciation of the world or asceticism (*zuhd*) was one approach of some early Sufis. They saw the precedent for this in the Prophet Muhammad's practice of retreating to the cave of Hira' above Mecca for weeks at a time. These practices led to the appearance of the Angel Gabriel and the Revelation of the Qur'an. Renunciation and the performance of meditative practices were therefore analogous methods of connecting the human soul with spirit- or soul-knowledge and precipitating within the seeker's consciousness the individual experience of enlightenment. The rise of the Umayyad and Abbasid Caliphates, which brought with them a courtly luxury and materialistic emphasis contrary to the ideals of the original Islamic community, further prompted many God-fearing people to withdraw from the world into meditative retreats.[34]

Devoting themselves to the ardent service of God, these early ascetics not only renounced involvement with the contentious issues of the time but also battled against the worldly seductions emanating from their own egos (*nafs*). They experienced the self as the seat of all evil lusts and as a source of spiritual faults such as egoism, pride, envy, hatred, greed, and ostentatious display. They therefore saw it as their task to look into themselves and exercise self-control, with the aim of transforming the ego and all the self-serving impulses emanating from it. They realized that as long as "self-ness" (granting the ego greater importance than God's Self) dominates, complete submission to God's will is not possible. Obliteration of the personal ego was experienced as an absorption or dissolution of being in God (*fana'*). The road or path (*tariqa*, later a term for the Sufi orders) on which the mystic travels leads to this goal. The early Sufis regarded this road as a journey toward which all of humanity is invited; however, only a special few are able to respond.

In contrast to the egoistic panegyrics and love poetry that were recited at the courts of political power, Sufis substituted the love of God and love of the Prophet. They recognized in the *Burda*, a poem composed by the Prophet's contemporary Ka'b ibn Zubayr in praise of the Prophet, the basis for a literary genre that praises God and the Prophet.[35] Some Sufis gave their poems additional artistic expression by accompanying the lyrics with music and performing them in their gatherings of divine "listening" (*sama'*). God and the Prophet are invariably the two beloveds who are described and celebrated in these poems. The "hearing" of such poems, combined with sessions of invocation and remembrance of God (*dhikr Allah*), precipitates new states of consciousness (*wajd*) in the participant. In the course of the ninth century CE, the word *Sufi* became the term adopted to refer to the one who comes to "know" God in such a way.

An important forerunner of the Sufi tradition in Sunni Islam was Hasan al-Basri (d. 728 CE). As a young man, he took part in the campaigns of conquest in eastern Iran. Thereafter, he lived in Basra until his death. His fame was based on the sincerity and uprightness of his religious personality, which had already made a deep impression on his contemporaries. He was known above all for his sermons and sayings, in which he not only warned his coreligionists against sin but also commanded them to regulate their personal lives by focusing on eternity, as he did himself. Among his famous sayings are: "Re-polish your hearts (the seat of religious feeling), for they very quickly grow rusty." "Make this world a bridge over which you cross but on which you do not build." In his sermons, Hasan al-Basri constantly warned against worldly attitudes and attachment to earthly possessions. People are already on the way to death, and those who are already dead are only waiting for the others to follow. He regarded the worldly individual as a hypocrite, whose faith sat lightly on him and who sinned without concern.[36] The truly alive person is therefore the spiritually alive and awakened.

The classical period of Sufism was between the ninth and the eleventh centuries CE. This was the era when the great textbooks that gave Sufism its final doctrinal contours appeared. Among these works were Abu Nasr al-Sarraj's (d. 988 CE) *Kitab al-Luma'* (Book of Inspiration), Abu Talib al-Makki's (d. 996 CE) *Qut al-Qulub* (The Sustenance of Hearts), and Abu Bakr al-Kalabadhi's (d. 990 CE) *al-Ta'arruf li-madhhab ahl al-tasawwuf* (Introduction to the School of the Sufis). Abu 'Abd al-Rahman al-Sulami (d. 1021 CE), who in numerous comprehensive writings collected information about the Sufis and Sufism, was also influential, as was Abu al-Qasim al-Qushayri (d. 1074 CE), the author of the well-known book *al-Risala fi 'ilm al-tasawwuf* (The Treatise on the Discipline of Sufism).

Classical Sufi writing reached its peak in the works of Abu Hamid al-Ghazali and Muhyiddin ibn al-'Arabi (d. 1240 CE). Having originally been a theologian, Ghazali converted to Sufism after a crisis in his life. In his main work and magnum opus, *Ihya' 'ulum al-din* (Revival of the Religious Sciences), he recapitulates themes from earlier writers and accomplishes a synthesis of the outer theological sciences and the inner mystical life. His importance to Sunni Islam lay in his popularizing and making accessible to the public the endeavors of his Sufi predecessors and in firmly establishing Sufism within the normative practice of the *Ahl al-Sunna wa'l-Jama'a*.

The apogee of Sufi intellectual construction occurs in the writings of Ibn al-'Arabi. In a tripartite division of "God's people," he places Sufis above the ascetics but below those who realize true knowledge of God (*al-muhaqqiqun*). In this highest category, he includes the Prophet Muhammad and the greatest "friends" of God (*awliya' Allah*), a term we may render in English as "saints." The basic activity of God's friends is realization of the truth (*tahqiq*), which Ibn al-'Arabi understands in terms of the Prophet's command: "Give everything that has a reality (*haqiqa*) its right or claim (*haqq*)." Everything in existence has a *haqq*—a truth or reality, and therefore has a right and an appropriate claim—or else God would not have created it. The function of the realized Sufi is to discern the *haqq* in any situation and act accordingly. Ibn al-'Arabi proceeds to set out principles by which every *haqq* can be discerned and acted upon. For him, the People of God approach reality on the basis of the Qur'an and the Sunna. Thus, they give each thing its due according to the Shari'a, the Sunna, and the example of the People of God. Like most Sufis, Ibn al-'Arabi insists in his writings that the Shari'a is organically inseparable from the *haqiqa*, the Higher Reality.

TAHAWI AND THE FORMALIZATION OF THE SUNNI CREED

By the ninth century CE, the Sunni creed had become formalized. Perhaps nothing can better demonstrate the knitting together of the ideas presented in the preceding portions of this chapter better than the popular exposition of Sunni doctrine written by the tenth-century Egyptian theologian and Hanafi jurist Abu Ja'far Ahmad al-Tahawi (d. 933 CE). Tahawi was a contemporary of both Abu'l Hasan al-Ash'ari (d. 935 CE), who was the supreme authority for Sunni theologians, and Abu Mansur al-Maturidi (d. 944 CE), founder of the other Sunni school of theology, which flourished in Samarkand in the area of modern Uzbekistan. Tahawi is best known for his creed (*'aqida*) in rhymed prose, known as *Bayan al-Sunna wa'l-Jama'a* (Exposition of Sunna and the Position of the Community). By his time, the political and theological issues that had created rifts within the Muslim community had been argued by scholars and theologians for more than two centuries, and the belief set of those who became known as Sunni had crystallized. Tahawi's exposition of the Sunni creed is admired not only for its thoughtful delineating of the main principles of Sunni Islam but also for its poetic language and beautiful literary form. The following translation of portions of this creed is based on the translation of the entire work by E. E. Elder.[37] The reader acquainted with the historical disputes that raged over the first three centuries of Islamic history can detect how Tahawi stakes out the Sunni position on the political and theological issues that defined the controversies that led to the creation of a clarified Sunni theology.

SELECTIONS FROM TAHAWI'S CREED OF SUNNI ISLAM

We say concerning the unity of God, while trusting in the assistance of God—who is exalted in Himself—that Allah is one. He has no partner, and nothing resembles Him, nor does anything limit Him. There is no deity other than Him. He is eternal (*qadim*) without a beginning and ever existing (*da'im*) without an end. He is not destroyed nor does He perish. Nothing comes into being but as He wills. Imaginative thoughts (*awham*) do not apprehend Him nor do intelligences comprehend Him. Creatures are not like Him. He is the Living that does not die, the Ever Wakeful that does not sleep, the Creator without a need. Allah is Independent, a Sustainer without provision; He is the One who fearlessly causes things to die and raises [others] from the dead without fatigue....

He created all creatures through His knowledge and decreed for them their fates. He has set for them appointed times. None of their deeds was hidden from Him before He created them, and He knows what they will do before He creates them. He commanded them to obey Him and forbade them to disobey Him. Everything occurs by His Power and Will. Creatures have no will except as He wills. Whatever He wills for them comes into existence; whatever He does not will, does not.

He guides aright whomsoever He wills and preserves from error whomsoever He wills. He grants security to whomsoever He wills as an act of grace (*fadl*). He leads astray whomsoever He wills. He abstains from aiding and punishes whomsoever He wills as a matter of justice. Everything exists in His willing between His grace and His justice. No one can avert His destiny, replace His judgment, or prevail over His command.

We believe all of this and assure ourselves that everything is from God. Muhammad is His chosen creature, His particular faithful one, His favored Messenger, the Seal of the Prophets, the Imam of the God-Fearing, the chief of those who are sent, and the Beloved of the Lord of the worlds. Every claim to prophetic office after him is a delusion and a vain desire. [Muhamamd] is the one sent to all the Jinn and humanity with truth and guidance, with light and radiance.

We believe that the Qur'an is the speech of God. From Him it began as an utterance without any modality. He sent it down to His Prophet as a revelation. As such, the believers assent to the Qur'an as a Reality.

They assure themselves that it is in fact the speech of God—who is mighty and majestic—and not something created like the speech of human beings. Whoever upon hearing [the Qur'an] asserts that it is the speech of human beings is thereby an unbeliever. Allah has admonished, rebuked, and threatened him with hellfire, since God has said: "I will broil him in hellfire" (74:26). When God threatened with hellfire the one who said, "This is only the speech of humankind" (74:25), we knew and were assured that it was the saying of the Creator of humankind, for human sayings do not resemble His.

Whoever qualifies [God] with any of the notions of humanity is therefore an unbeliever. The one who perceives this takes warning and refrains from anything that is like the sayings of the unbelievers, for he knows that God in His attributes is not like humankind....

No one is secure in his religion but he who surrenders to Allah and to His Messenger—may God bless him and give him peace—and commits the knowledge of what confuses him to the One who knows. The foundation of Islam is firmly established on surrender and submission alone. Whoever seeks knowledge about what is forbidden to him, and whose understanding is not content to surrender, will be precluded in his quest from declaring the absolute unity of the Deity, from pure cognition and sound belief. Therefore, he vacillates between unbelief and belief, assertion and contradiction, confession and denial, troubled by the whisperings of Satan, perplexed, rebellious, and separated from the community of the faithful, neither an assenting believer nor a contradicting denier....

He who is saved (*sa'id,* literally, "happy") is saved through the destiny of God, and he who is damned (*shaqi,* literally, "miserable") is damned through the destiny of God. The principle of God's decree is His secret in His creation. Neither an angel near to His presence nor a Prophet entrusted with a message has gained knowledge of this. Speculating deeply about this subject brings one near to desertion by Allah and is a step toward denial and disobedience. Therefore, be on your guard against this in thought, consideration, and evil suggestion. Verily God has concealed the knowledge of His decree from His creatures and has forbidden them to search for it. As He has said: "He shall not be questioned about what He does, but they shall be questioned" (21:23). Whoever asks, "Why did God do this?" [i.e. questions God disapprovingly] has rejected the judgment of the Qur'an and becomes an unbeliever....

This is part of the covenant of belief, the fundamental knowledge and the confession of the unity and lordship of God, just as God said in His glorious Book: "He created everything and then decreed it absolutely" (25:2). He also said: "And the command of Allah was a decreed decree" (33:38). Thus, woe to him who becomes an adversary of God's decree or brings to the consideration of it a diseased heart....

We say that God took Abraham as a friend and spoke to Moses in a voice (4:162) for the sake of belief, assent, and submission. We believe in the Angels, the Prophets, and the Books that were sent down to those entrusted with a message. We bear witness that they are all manifestly true. We call the people who follow our direction of prayer Muslims and believers, as long as they continue to confess to what the Prophet brought and assent to what he said and narrated....

We do not impute unbelief to any of the people who follow our direction of prayer because of sin, so long as they do not make it lawful, nor do we say that a sin that accompanies belief will not harm the one who does it. We hope for those Muslims who do good works, yet we do not feel secure about them, nor do we bear witness that the Garden is theirs [by entitlement]. We ask God to forgive the evildoers; we fear for them and ask forgiveness for them as we do for ourselves and we do not despair for them. Either feeling independent of God or despairing of God removes one from the religion of Islam. The way of Reality lies midway between these two for those who follow our direction of prayer. The creature does not depart from belief except by the denial of that which brought him to it.

Belief is confession by the tongue and assent by the mind that all God sent down in the Qur'an and in the Law and by way of proof is authentic and true regarding the Messenger of God. Belief is one, and people are fundamentally equal. Differences among people arise through their nature and godliness, through forsaking vain desires, and holding on to that which is best ...

We do not approve the use of the sword against any person of the community of Muhammad unless it is required to use the sword against him. We do not approve of secession from our Imams and those in authority. Even if they rule tyrannically over us, we do not curse them or restrain any hand from obeying them. We consider obeying them an ordinance of God because judgment over human affairs is part of obedience to God (4:62). We pray for the welfare and security [of our leaders].

We follow the Sunna and the Community (*al-sunna wa'l-jama'a*) and we shun that which deviates, is contrary, and divisive. We love the people of justice and trustworthiness, and hate the people of tyranny and treachery. We say, "Allah knows best concerning the knowledge that confuses us.". . .

We love the Companions of the Messenger of God. We are not remiss in loving any one of them nor do we repudiate any one of them. We hate him who hates them or mentions them disrespectfully. We mention them only respectfully. Love for them is [being] religious, believing, and doing good; hatred for them is unbelief, hypocrisy, and perverseness. . . .

Whoever speaks well of the Companions of the Messenger of God, of his wives who are pure of any defilement, and of his progeny, who are far removed from every abomination, is innocent of hypocrisy. The learned among the Forerunners (*al-Salaf*), their Successors (*al-Tabi'un*), those who came after them of the people of narrative and precedent, and the people of *fiqh* and speculation are only to be mentioned favorably. Whoever mentions them badly is not on the right path. We do not prefer any one of the saints (*awliya'*) to any of the Prophets. We say, "One prophet is better than all the saints." We believe in what has been passed down of their miracles (*karamat*) and those narratives that are authentic from trustworthy people.

We consider the Community real and correct but divisiveness we consider a turning away from the right and an affliction.

CONCLUSION: SUNNI ISLAM TODAY AND THE ROAD AHEAD

The history of the *Ahl al-Sunna wa'l-Jama'a* shows that religious, ethical, and political concerns cannot be easily separated, as the stability of community and the common good are of paramount importance. Because of this, what begins as a religious issue may become a political power struggle, and vice versa. The original Sunni–Shi'a split attests to this, stemming as it does from a dispute over the best way to devise a social system in keeping with the ideals of Islam. The impulse that led to the Sunni–Shi'a split in the early centuries of Islam was driven by differences of opinion on how to create the best society possible, led by the best leader possible and displaying the character of the Prophet. The best society for Muslims is one that is in communion with God, and whose laws and means of governance are informed and bounded by ethics that are in keeping with God's preference for humankind. This is the only accurate definition of an "Islamic" community—or an "Islamic State"—and it has been the ambition of every Islamic political movement. Because this was the impulse that first divided the Islamic body politic, it is potentially the area in which achieving consensus could be vital for uniting Muslims in agreement on the terms of a universal social contract. This is where modern *ijtihad* (scholarship in the area of law) is needed—to remove from the historical legacy of Islamic theology ideas that were based on the politics of earlier times and re-craft an Islamic political theory that is suitable for modern times and fully in keeping with the ethics of the Qur'an and the Sunna.

All Muslims today belong to a global body politic. The Islamic *Umma* is a subset of this global body politic. As we move our eyes in our living rooms from reading the pages of early Islamic history to watching the evening news on television, we witness the continued intersection of religion and politics in current events. As Muslims contemplate their role in this new world, the larger question we all wonder about is this: How might Muslims craft a coherent understanding between religion and politics, and make this globally meaningful and relevant to today's world?

NOTES

1. A *hadith* is a report of a saying or action of the Prophet Muhammad. *Hadith* (with a capital h) in English is used to indicate the entire corpus of *hadiths*.

2. Note that the Sunni–Shi'a distinction is not true of the ethical content of the Hadith; there is a great overlap of many Sunni and Shiite hadiths. The difference is most pronounced in those hadith texts that refer to political controversies.

3. Although the original doctrine of the Shi'a was that rulership had to be from the descendants of the Prophet Muhammad through 'Ali, we see today in Shiite Iran the rule of nondescendants, such as Iranian President Mahmoud Ahmedinejad.

4. The first crisis occurred during the time of the Caliph Abu Bakr. At the battle of Yamama (632 CE) the heavy loss of life among the Qur'an readers, who were among the Prophet's Companions, prompted 'Umar ibn al-Khattab to approach Abu Bakr and urge him to make a complete compilation of the Qur'an. Abu Bakr and 'Umar approached Zayd ibn Thabit, one of the Prophet's scribes, and charged him with the task of putting together a complete compilation of the Qur'an, culled from the memory and written notes of all the Prophet's surviving companions. The completed copy of the Qur'an remained with Abu Bakr until he died, and then with 'Umar, who became the second Caliph, until the end of his life. Finally, it was entrusted to Hafsa, 'Umar's daughter and a former wife of the Prophet Muhammad. See Dr. Muhammad Muhsin Khan, ed. and trans., *Sahih al-Bukhari* (Pakistan: Sethi Straw Board Mills, Ltd, 1971), vol. 6, 478; Kitab Fada'il al-Qur'an, Bab Jam' al-Qur'an (Book of the Excellences of the Qur'an, Chapter on the Collection of the Qur'an).

5. Ibid.

6. Ibn Hajar al-'Asqalani, *al-Fath al-Bari'*, vol. 9, 14, quoted in Labib as-Said, *The Recited Koran, A History of the First Recorded Version*, trans. Bernard Weiss, M.A. Rauf and Morroe Berger (Princeton, NJ: The Darwin Press, 1975) 23.

7. Ibn al-Athir, Majd al-Din Abu'l–Sa'ada al-Mubarak ibn Muhammad, *Al-Nihaya fi-gharib al-hadith wa'l-athar,* Cairo, 1963-6, vol. III, 85-86, quoted in ibid., 23.

8. *Sahih al-Bukhari,* vol. 6, 479.

9. Talha and Zubayr were among a group of six members of a consultative committee who were nominated by 'Umar to be potential successors: 'Uthman, 'Ali, Zubayr, Talha, 'Abd al-Rahman ibn 'Awf, and Sa'd ibn Abi Waqqas.

10. *Kharaju,* meaning, "They left or exited." The name eventually given to this faction, *Khariji,* thus means, "one who exits," or in a wider sense, "secessionist." In Arabic, this group of Muslim dissidents is called *al-Khawarij,* the plural of *khariji.* They are called *Kharijites* in English.

11. Muhammad Ibn Jarir Al-Tabari, *Ta'rikh al-Umam wa'l-Muluk* (Leiden: E.J. Brill, 1964) vol. 2, 199.

12. This position was a powerful statement opposing both the Sunni position of the time that the leader had to be from the tribe of Quraysh and the Shi'a position that he had to be from the line of 'Ali.

13. Note the similarities between Azraqi Kharijite beliefs and those of some modern Muslim extremists, who also judge those disagreeing with them as apostates, even to the point of murdering them along with their innocent spouses and children.

14. This term, *al-Khulafa' al-Rashidun* in Arabic, refers to the first four Caliphs, who ruled in Medina: Abu Bakr, 'Umar, 'Uthman, and 'Ali. The names of these Caliphs adorn many a mosque in beautiful calligraphy, together with the names of 'Ali's two sons Hasan and Husayn. In such mosques, the names *Allah* (God) and Muhammad are also prominently displayed.

15. In Islamic jurisprudence, *taqlid* is the opposite of *ijtihad,* the effort of a scholar to arrive at a correct legal opinion. *Taqlid* thus means to follow the opinions of others without understanding or scrutiny, or in the words of Sayf al-Din al-Amidi (d. 1233 CE), "To accept the rulings of others when such rulings are not coupled with a conclusive argument" (*Al-Ihkam fi Usul al-Ahkam,* Cairo 1347 AH, vol. III, 166). Many Muslims today are under the impression that following *taqlid* is always a bad or shameful thing. *Taqlid* has often been used as a pejorative term in Islamic discourse. This is unfortunate because in almost every field of human endeavor, people follow the advice of experts. The proper practice of *taqlid* is thus nothing more than recognizing one's own professional limitations. Neither does *taqlid* necessarily mean that one is ignorant of religion. When a modern-day physics student learns Newton's formulas, he is a *muqallid* (imitator or follower) of Newton. Such usage does not lower a person's standing in the least unless it is applied where it does not belong; in that case the imitator would be justly criticized. The real issue of *taqlid* thus becomes one of knowing how far to follow the guidance of another. A great and innovative scholar like Imam Ghazali was a *muqallid* in that he followed the principles established by prior Imams like Shafi'i. However, he also disagreed with such authorities in certain instances.

16. According to Shafi'i, Prophetic precedent in Islamic law is made up of three types of Sunna: (1) verbal statements of the Prophet (*sunna qawliyya*), (2) normative actions of the Prophet (*sunna fi'liyya*), and (3) the tacit consent of the Prophet indicated by his silence with reference to an event that happened in his presence (*sunna taqririyya*).

17. For example, the Prophet made his Hajj pilgrimage only once, and began his Hajj from Medina. This, however, does not mean that a Muslim is prohibited from doing the Hajj several times or is required to start the Hajj from Medina.

18. *Al-Fiqh 'ala-l-madhahib al-khamsa,* jurisprudence according to the five major schools of law, is a common expression that embraces the notion that the four major schools of Sunni law (Maliki, Hanafi, Shafi'i, and Hanbali), plus the Shiite Ja'fari school of law, have come to be accepted as the dominant interpretations. The differences between the Ja'fari school of law and any one of the other four Sunni schools are no greater than the differences between any one of the Sunni schools and the other three. If not for the political differences that originally differentiated Shi'as from Sunnis, one could argue that all five legal schools flowed out of the same tradition, each school preferring certain interpretive or structural legal principles over others.

19. In Shafi'i usage, the former concept of the *sunna* of the Prophet's Companions was subsumed into the developing legal category of consensus (*ijma'*). In Hanbali thought, for example, the consensus of the Companions of the Prophet Muhammad, and in particular the practices, beliefs, and customs of the first rightly guided Caliphs, is of greater value than the consensus of later scholars. This led Ahmad Ibn Hanbal to speak of *Ahl al-Sunna wa'l-Jama'a wa'l-Athar,* in which the word *athar* meant "the precedents," referring to the precedents of the Prophet and his closest Companions.

20. It should not be forgotten that during the time of Shafi'i and the founders of the major Sunni schools of jurisprudence (who died between the years 767 and 855 CE), the "six classical works" of Sunni Hadith collection had not yet been compiled. Most of these works were composed in the following century. The founders of major Sunni schools of jurisprudence were:

1. Imam Hasan al-Basri, who lived in Medina and then in Basra (d. 729)
2. Imam Abu Hanifa, who lived in Kufa and Baghdad (d. 767)
3. Imam 'Abd al-Rahman al-Awza'i of Syria (d. 774)
4. Imam Sufyan al-Thawri of Kufa and Basra (d. 778)
5. Imam Layth ibn Sa'd of Egypt (d. 791)
6. Imam Malik ibn Anas of Medina (d. 795)
7. Imam Sufyan ibn 'Uyayna of Mecca (d. 814)
8. Imam Muhammad ibn Idris al-Shafi'i (d. in Egypt 820)
9. Imam Ishaq ibn Ibrahim, better known as Ibn Rahawayh, of Nishapur (d. 853)
10. Imam Ibrahim ibn Khalid, better known as Abu Thawr, of Baghdad (d. 855)
11. Imam Ahmad Ibn Hanbal (d. in Baghdad in 855)
12. Imam Dawud ibn 'Ali al-Zahiri (d. in Baghdad in 883)
13. Imam Muhammad ibn Jarir al-Tabari, (d. in Baghdad in 922)

The six classical works of Sunni Hadith are:

1. *Sahih* of al-Bukhari (d. 870)
2. *Sahih* of Muslim (d. 875)

3. *Sunan* of Ibn Maja (d. 886)
4. *Sunan* of Abu Dawud (d. 888)
5. *Sunan* of al-Tirmidhi (d. 892)
6. *Sunan* of al-Nasa'i (d. 915)

The compilers of the five most esteemed Shi'a books of Hadith lived even later,dying between 939 and 1067 CE. They are:

1. *Al-Usul al-Kafi* of al-Kulayni (d. 939)
2. *Man la Yastahdiruhu'l-Faqih* of al-Qummi (d. 991)
3. *Tahdhib al-Ahkam* by al-Tusi (d. 1067)
4. *Al-Istibsar fi-ma Akhtalafa fihi al-Akhbar,* also by al-Tusi
5. *Nahj al-Balagha* of al-Sharif al-Murtada (d. 1044)

21. The reader should note that the differences we are speaking of were not major. For the most part, they were minor differences on issues of ritual, such as whether one's feet had to be washed or wiped during the ablution or the definition of the part of the body that males and females have to cover during prayer or in the presence of the opposite sex.

22. A genre of traditions called *Isra'iliyyat* ("Tales of the Israelites") entered Muslim discourse via Jews and Christians. Many of these accounts dealt with biblical narratives of the Prophet Moses and the second coming of Jesus. In addition, deeply ingrained customs such as the African practice of clitoridectomy (popularly known as female circumcision), which were not practiced in the Arabian peninsula of the Prophet's time, were "Islamized" and thus continued to be practiced in the regions where they had originally occurred.

23. Tabari, *Ta'rikh,* vol. 3, 1113 and 1118.

24. Martin Hinds, *Mihna,* article in *Encyclopedia of Islam* (Brill Academic Publishers, CD-ROM 2004).

25. *Kitab al-Sunna,* 38; *Manaqib,* 159–161.

26. *Kitab al-Sunna,* 35.

27. This was the precedent of Abu Bakr (the first Caliph after the Prophet) who appointed 'Umar b. al-Khattab.

28. This can be seen as a nod to the Kharijite position of *la hukma illa lillah* ("There is no ruling but through God"). In addition, it gives more power to the ulama as interpreters of the Law.

29. *Kitab al-Suuna,* 35.

30. Islamic law divides jurisprudence into two broad categories: worship (*'ibadat*), concerning the laws of ritual worship, and worldly actions (*mu'amalat*). These are divided into four categories: criminal law, personal law, law of contracts (which today would include business law), and the law of governance or of nations (in modern parlance, constitutional and international law).

31. The popular view of Hanbali thought as rigorous or rigid is mainly due to their rejection of any form of worship that may be attributed to vestiges of foreign cultures or religions.

32. *Kitab al-Sunna*, 34.

33. Ibid., 35–36.

34. Other terms that refer to the worshiper working on his or her own inner self are *'abid* (worshipper) and *nasik* (scrupulous adherent to liturgical practices). As an outward sign of the asceticism, some Sufis wore rough woolen cloth (*suf*, from which some say the name Sufi originated) as a reaction against the more luxurious clothing of the courts. Not yet known by the appellation of Sufi, they tried to achieve a sensitive and loving relationship with God based on the Quranic verse: "He loves them, and they love Him" (5:54).

35. Not to be confused with another poem of the same name composed by the Egyptian Sufi al-Busiri in the thirteenth century CE.

36. The Sunnis and the Mu'tazilites both considered Hasan al-Basri as one of group. His name appears in the chains of teaching (*silsila*) of many Sufi orders, and he is cited innumerable times in moral works of exhortation. The influence of his ascetic piety persisted in Basra. In the chief work of the Sufi school of Basra, *Qut al-Qulub* (The Sustenance of Hearts) by Abu Talib al-Makki (d. 998), it is stated: "Hasan is our Imam in the doctrine we represent. We walk in his footsteps, we follow his ways, and from his lamp we have our light" (*Qut al-Qulub*, Cairo 1961, vol. I, 149).

37. The MacDonald Presentation Volume, Princeton University Press 1933, pp. 131ff.

15

WHAT IS SHIITE ISLAM?

Azim Nanji
Farhad Daftary

The historical formation of the worldwide Muslim community or *Umma,* as it is known in Arabic, has resulted in a great deal of diversity that reflects a rich intellectual, spiritual, and institutional pluralism. In seeking to express a response to the primal message of Islam, Muslims have developed distinct perspectives that have led various groups to coalesce around different inter-pretations of the core message of the Qur'an and the example of the Prophet Muhammad. One such perspective is that of Shiite Islam. Rather than per-ceive these expressions as sectarian in a narrow sense, it is more appropriate to recognize them as representing different communities of interpretation with diverse views of how the ideals of Islam might be realized in the life of the *Umma.* Unfortunately, much early scholarship on Shi'ism has repre-sented this perspective as a dissident voice or heterodoxy, and in some cases has even characterized it as a "Persian" response to "Arab" Islam. Recent scholarship has created a more balanced view of Shi'ism. Thus, it is now pos-sible to move beyond stereotypical assumptions and reject the view that there is an "orthodox" or "authentic" Islam, from which Shi'ism is a departure.

The Shi'a, like other Muslim groups, reflect their own diversity but share a common approach to the fundamentals of Islamic belief. While affirming, in common with their fellow Muslim believers, the *Shahada,* that is, belief in the unity of God and the model of divine guidance through God's Messen-ger, the Prophet Muhammad, the Shi'a maintain that for the spiritual and moral guidance of the community, God instructed the Prophet to designate a figure of authority to succeed him as leader of the Muslims. This authority was 'Ali, the Prophet's cousin and son-in-law. According to the Shi'a, this conception of the community's future leadership was made public by the Prophet in the last year of his life at Ghadir Khumm, where he designated 'Ali as his successor to lead the Muslims. While both Shiite and Sunni sources refer to this event, it is the specific interpretation of the role of 'Ali as an authentic leader or "Imam of Guidance" that distinguishes the

Shiite interpretation of authority and leadership from that of other Muslim communities.

The word *Shi'a* means "partisan" or "adherent." Specifically, it refers to those Muslims who became followers of 'Ali, with the conviction that he and his descendants were the rightful authorities of the Muslim community. For the Shi'a, this conviction is implicit in the revelation of the Qur'an and the history of Islam and is not merely the outcome of differences of a purely political nature following the death of the Prophet Muhammad. In order to understand how such an interpretation developed and created a distinctive Shiite identity in Muslim history, it is important to see how the Shi'a ground the concept of guidance within their interpretation of the Qur'an and the life of the Prophet.

One aspect of the Qur'anic revelation that scholars of the Shiite tradition often emphasize is the notion of authority linked to the families of prophetic figures. This notion is evoked in the following Qur'anic verses:

> Truly, God chose Adam, Noah, the family of Abraham and the family of 'Imran above all the worlds, as offspring one after the other. (Qur'an 3:33–34)
>
> Each of them we preferred above the worlds and their fathers, descendants and brothers. We chose them and we guided them to the straight path....They are the ones to whom we have given the Book, the authority and prophethood.

(Qur'an 6:84–89)

During his lifetime, the Prophet Muhammad was both the recipient and the expounder of divine revelation. His death in 632 CE marked the conclusion of the line of prophecy and the beginning of the debate over the nature of his legacy for future generations. This debate arose because of the absence of consensus over succession to the Prophet in the nascent Muslim community. From the beginning, there was a clear difference of views on this matter between the *Shi'at 'Ali,* the Party of 'Ali, who believed that the Prophet had designated 'Ali b. Abi Talib (d. 661 CE) as his successor, and those who followed the leadership of the Caliphs. This latter group eventually coalesced into the majoritarian, Sunni branch of Islam, known collectively as the "People of the Sunna and the Community," *Ahl al-Sunna wa al-Jama'a.*

The Shi'a of Imam 'Ali maintained that, while revelation ceased at the Prophet's death, the need for the spiritual and moral guidance of the community, through an ongoing interpretation and implementation of the Islamic message, continued. They believed that the legacy of the Prophet Muhammad was entrusted to his family, the *Ahl al-Bayt* (literally, "People of the Household"), in whom the Prophet had invested authority. The first member of the Prophet's family designated for leadership was Imam 'Ali, the Prophet's cousin and the husband of Fatima, his daughter and only surviving child. According to most traditions, 'Ali was the first male convert to Islam and had earned the Prophet's admiration by championing the cause of Islam, even at the risk of his life. The Shiite espousal of the right of 'Ali and that of his descendants, through Fatima, to the leadership of the Muslim community was rooted in their understanding of the Holy Qur'an and its concept of rightly guided leadership, as reinforced by Prophetic traditions (*Hadith*). For the Shi'a the most prominent of these traditions was the Prophet's sermon at Ghadir Khumm, following his farewell pilgrimage to Mecca, in which he designated 'Ali as his successor. During this sermon, the Prophet stated that he was leaving behind "two weighty things" (*thaqalayn*)—the Holy Qur'an and his family—for the future guidance of his community.

The importance of the *Ahl al-Bayt* for the Shi'a is also demonstrated in an event linked to the revelation of a well-known Qur'anic verse: "God only wishes to remove from you all impurities, O *Ahl al-Bayt* and purify you with a complete purification" (Qur'an 33:33). According to historical tradition, this verse concerns an event in the Prophet's life when the Christian leadership of the town of Najran in Arabia challenged him as to the veracity of his mission. The two sides agreed upon a mutual imprecation, but the Christians eventually declined. Those referred to as the *Ahl al-Bayt* in this Qur'anic passage were the Prophet Muhammad, 'Ali, Fatima, and the latter two's sons, Hasan and Husayn. Shiites also refer to the Qur'anic verse: "Say: I do not seek any reward from you, except love for those near to me" (Qur'an 42:23). The Shi'a believe that this verse also refers to the Ahl al-Bayt. While such interpretations are specific to the Shi'a, all Muslims hold the Prophet's family in great reverence and follow the admonition of the Qur'an: "Truly God and His angels bless the Prophet. O you who believe, bless him and greet him with peace" (Qur'an 33:50).

The Shi'a attest that after the Prophet Muhammad, the authority for the guidance of the Muslim community was vested in Imam 'Ali. Just as it was the prerogative of the Prophet to designate his successor, so it is the prerogative of each Imam of the time to designate his successor from among his male progeny. Hence, the office of the Imam, the *Imamate,* is passed on by heredity in the Prophet's bloodline via 'Ali and Fatima.

THE EARLY HISTORY OF SHI'ISM

The early partisans of 'Ali included the so-called Qur'an Readers, several close Companions of the Prophet, prominent residents of the city of Medina, tribal chiefs of distinction, and other Muslims who had rendered important services to early Islam. Their foremost teacher and guide was 'Ali ibn Abi Talib who, in his sermons and letters and in his admonitions to the leaders of the Quraysh tribe, reminded Muslims of the rights of his family.

Pro-'Alid sentiments persisted in 'Ali's lifetime. They were revived during the Caliphate of 'Uthman (r. 644–656 CE), which was a period of strife in the Muslim community. 'Ali succeeded to the Caliphate in turbulent circumstances following 'Uthman's murder, leading to the first civil war in Islam. Centred in Kufa, in southern Iraq, the partisans of 'Ali now became designated as *Shi'at 'Ali,* the "Party of 'Ali," or simply as the Shi'a. They also referred to themselves by terms with more precise religious connotations, such as *Shi'at Ahl al-Bayt* (Party of the Prophet's Household) or its equivalent, *Shi'at Al Muhammad* (Party of the Family of Muhammad). The Umayyad Mu'awiya ibn Abi Sufyan (d. 680 CE), the powerful governor of Syria, cousin of 'Uthman, and leader of the pro-'Uthman party, found the call for avenging 'Uthman's murder a suitable pretext for seizing the Caliphate.

The early Shi'a survived 'Ali's murder in 661 CE and the tragic events that followed. After 'Ali, the Shi'a of Kufa recognized his eldest son Hasan (d. 669 CE) as his successor to the Caliphate. However, Hasan chose not to assume this role and Mu'awiya assumed the Caliphate. After making a peace treaty with Mu'awiya, Hasan retired to Medina and abstained from political activity. However, the Shi'a continued to regard him as their Imam after 'Ali. On Hasan's death, the Kufan Shi'a revived their aspirations for restoring the Caliphate to the Prophet's family and invited Hasan's younger brother Husayn, their new Imam, to rise against the oppressive rule of the Umayyads. In the aftermath of Mu'awiya's death and the succession of his son Yazid (r. 680–683 CE), Husayn refused to acknowledge Yazid. Responding to the call of many of his followers and supporters, he set out for Kufa. On 10 Muharram 61 (10 October 680), Husayn and his small band of relatives and companions were brutally massacred at Karbala, some distance from Kufa, where they were intercepted by an Umayyad army. The martyrdom of the Prophet's grandson infused new fervour to the Shiite cause and contributed significantly to the consolidation of the Shiite ethos and identity. It also led to the formation of activist trends among the Shi'a. Later, the Shi'a would commemorate the martyrdom of Husayn on the tenth of Muharram. This holiday, which is more the commemoration of a tragedy than a festive celebration, is known as *'Ashura.*

During the period of Umayyad rule (661–750 CE), different Shiite groups, consisting of both Arab Muslims and new non-Arab converts, sought to support different candidates for the Imamate. The leadership of the Shi'a grew beyond the immediate family of the Prophet Muhammad and now included other branches of the Banu Hashim, the Prophet's extended family, including the descendants of the Prophet's uncles Abu Talib and 'Abbas. This was because the notion of the Prophet's family was then conceived broadly, in its old Arabian tribal sense. As the Muslim world continued to expand geographically and more people from the conquered territories became part of the growing *Umma,* the various Muslim groups, including the Shi'a, attracted new adherents.

A large group of the Shi'a, known as the *Imamiyya* (Imamis), adopted a quietist policy in the political field while concentrating on Islam's intellectual promotion and development. Their Imams traced authority through Imam

Husayn's sole surviving son, 'Ali Zayn al-'Abidin ("Ornament of the Wor-shippers," d. 712 CE), who was held in great esteem in the pious circles of Medina. It was after 'Ali Zayn al-'Abidin that the Imami Shi'a began to gain importance under his son and successor Muhammad al-Baqir (d. 731 CE). A small group chose to support Zayd, another son of Zayn al-'Abidin, and organized themselves to actively oppose Umayyad rule. This group and their followers later became known as the *Zaydiyya* (Zaydis).

Imam al-Baqir concentrated on being an active teacher during his Imamate of nearly 20 years. He also introduced the principle of *taqiyya,* the precau-tionary dissimulation of one's true religious belief and practice that was to protect the Imams and their followers under adverse circumstances. His Imamate coincided with the growth and development of Islamic jurispru-dence (*fiqh*). In this formative period of Islam, Imam al-Baqir's role was pri-marily as a reporter of Hadith and a teacher of law. Upon his death, his followers recognized his eldest son Abu 'Abdallah Ja'far (d. 765 CE), later called al-Sadiq (the Trustworthy), as their new Imam.

In addition to the Zaydis, other proponents of the Shiite position—notably the Abbasids, descendants of the Prophet's uncle 'Abbas—embarked on a direct challenge to Umayyad rule. The Abbasids paid particular attention to developing the political organization of their own movement, establishing secret headquarters in Kufa but concentrating their activities in eastern Iran and Central Asia. The Abbasid mission (*da'wa*) was preached in the name of an unidentified person belonging to the Prophet's family. This ideology aimed to maximize support from the Shi'a of different groups who supported the leadership of the Ahl al-Bayt. In 749 CE, the Abbasids achieved victory over the Umayyads. They proclaimed Abu'l-'Abbas al-Saffah (r. 749–754 CE) as the first Abbasid Caliph in the mosque of Kufa. The Abbasid victory proved a source of disillusionment for those Shi'a who had expected a descendant of 'Ali, rather than an Abbasid, to succeed to the Caliphate. The animosity between the Abbasids and the 'Alids increased when, soon after their accession, the Abbasids began to persecute many of their former Shiite supporters and 'Alids and subsequently promoted a Sunni interpretation of Islam. The Abbasids' breach with their Shiite roots was finally completed when the third Caliph of the dynasty, Muhammad al-Mahdi (r. 775–785 CE), declared that the Prophet had actually appointed his uncle 'Abbas, rather than 'Ali, as his successor.

Meanwhile, Imam Ja'far al-Sadiq had acquired a widespread reputation as a teacher and scholar. He was a reporter of Hadith and is cited as such in the chain of authorities (*isnad*) accepted by all Muslim schools of law. He also taught Islamic jurisprudence. He is credited with founding, along with his father, the Imami Shiite school of religious law. This school of law is now called *Ja'fari* after Ja'far al-Sadiq. Imam al-Sadiq was accepted as a leading authority not only by his own Shiite partisans but also by a wider circle that included many Sunni Muslims. In time, Imam al-Sadiq acquired a noteworthy group of scholars around himself, comprising some of the most eminent jurists, traditionists, and theologians of the time such as Hisham ibn al-Hakam (d. 795 CE), then the foremost representative of Imami scholastic theology (*kalam*). During Ja'far's Imamate, the Shi'a came to develop distinct positions on theological and legal issues and contributed to the wider debates and discussions within Muslim intellectual circles.

As a result of the activities of Imam al-Sadiq and his associates, and building on the teachings of Imam al-Baqir, the doctrine of the Imamate received its main outline, consolidating principles that were traced back to the teachings of the early Imams and the Prophet Muhammad. The first principle was that of *nass*, the transfer of the Imamate by explicit designation. On the basis of *nass*, the Imamate could be located in a specific individual, whether or not the recipient claimed the Caliphate or exercised political authority. This principle established a separation of powers in Shi'ism, detaching the necessity of political authority from the institution of the Imamate, according to historical circumstances. The second principle was that of an Imamate based on *'ilm*, special religious knowledge. In the light of this knowledge, which was divinely inspired and transmitted through the *nass* of the preceding Imam, the rightful Imam of the time became the source of knowledge and spiritual teaching for his followers.

Rooted in the teachings of the Imams, the doctrine of the Imamate emphasizes the complementarity between revelation and intellectual reflection. It recognizes that the Holy Qur'an addresses different levels of meaning: the apparent meaning of the text, the esoteric meaning of the text, the legal parameters that guide human action, and the ethical vision that Allah intends to realize for human beings in an integrated moral society. According to the Shi'a, the Qur'an thus offers believers the possibility of deriving new insights to address the needs of the time in which Muslims live.

The Shiite doctrine of the Imamate, expressed in numerous *hadiths* reported mainly from Ja'far al-Sadiq, is preserved in the earliest collection of Shiite traditions, compiled by Abu Ja'far Muhammad al-Kulayni (d. 940 CE). This doctrine was founded on the belief in the permanent need for a divinely guided Imam who, after the Prophet Muhammad, would act as an authoritative teacher and a spiritual guide for humankind. While the Imam historically was entitled to both temporal leadership and religious authority, his mandate was independent of temporal power. This doctrine also confirmed the belief that the Prophet designated Imam 'Ali as his legatee (*wasi*) and successor, by an explicit *nass* under divine command. After 'Ali, the Imamate was transmitted from father to son by *nass*, among the descendants of 'Ali and Fatima; after Husayn, it would continue in the line of Husayn's descendants until the end of time.

Imam Ja'far al-Sadiq died in 765 CE. A conflict soon arose over who should be the next Imam. This dispute over the succession to Imam al-Sadiq resulted in new divisions within the Shi'a and led to the eventual formation of the two main Shiite communities, the *Ithna'ashariyya* or "Twelvers" (also called Imamis), and the *Ismailiyya,* the Ismailis. The Ismailis, who followed Muhammad ibn Isma'il, a grandson of Ja'far al-Sadiq, are the second largest Shiite community after the Twelvers. The third branch of the Shi'a, the Zaydis, had their own separate historical development.

IMAMI OR TWELVER SHI'ISM

After Imam Ja'far al-Sadiq's death, the majority of his followers acknowledged one of his surviving sons, Musa al-Kazim (d. 799 CE), as his successor to the Imamate. Placed under the control of the Abbasid rulers, Imam Musa was constrained in his activities and, according to his followers, was poisoned while being detained by the Abbasid Caliph's representatives in Baghdad. He was succeeded by his son, 'Ali al-Rida (d. 818 CE), who faced similar tribulations. After also dying under suspicious circumstances, he was buried in a place that has come to be known as *Mashhad* (Place of Witness), one of the holiest sites in Iran. Imam 'Ali al-Rida was succeeded by his very young son, Muhammad al-Jawad (d. 835 CE), also known as al-Taqi (The God-Fearing). Muhammad al-Jawad died in Baghdad at the age of 25 and was buried next to Musa al-Kazim. The next two Imams, 'Ali al-Hadi (d. 868 CE) and Hasan al-'Askari (d. 874 CE), led very restricted lives under Abbasid detention. Both are believed to have died of poisoning and were buried in the Iraqi city of Samarra. The dome of their tomb in Samarra was destroyed by anti-Shiite insurgents in February 2006. Hasan al-'Askari's followers believed that his successor, Muhammad al-Mahdi, was five years old when his father died. It is further held that soon after, Muhammad al-Mahdi went into *ghayba,* literally a state of "absence" or occultation. Eventually, the main body of the Imami Shi'a held that Muhammad al-Mahdi had been born to Hasan al-Askari in 869 CE but that the child had remained hidden, even from his father. They further held that al-Mahdi had succeeded his father to the Imamate while remaining in concealment. Identified as the *Mahdi* (The Guided One) or *al-Qa'im* (The Restorer), Muhammad al-Mahdi is expected to reappear and rule the world with justice in the period immediately preceding the final Day of Judgment. Because he is the twelfth in the Imami line of Imams, his followers are called the Ithna'asharis, the Twelvers.

According to Imami tradition, Muhammad al-Mahdi's occultation fell into two periods. The first, "lesser occultation" (*al-ghayba al-sughra*) covered the years 874–941 CE. During this period, the Imam is believed to have remained in regular contact with four successive agents, called variously the Gate (*Bab*), Emissary (*Safir*), or Deputy (*Na'ib*), who acted as intermediaries between the Imam and his community. However, in the "greater occultation" (*al-ghayba al-kubra*), which started in 941 CE and continues to this day, the hidden Imam does not act through a specific representative. Imami Shiite scholars have written extensively on the eschatological doctrine of the occultation of the twelfth Imam and the conditions that are expected to prevail before his return. These doctrines were institutionalized at the end of the first half of the tenth century CE, after the line of 12 Imams had been identified.

In the first period of their religious history, the Imami Shiites benefited from the direct guidance and teachings of their Imams. In the second period of Imami history, from the occultation of the twelfth Imam until the Mongol invasion in the thirteenth century CE, eminent scholars emerged as influential guardians and transmitters of the teachings of the Imams, compiling Hadith collections and formulating the Ja'fari school of law. This period coincided with the rise of the Buyid, or Buwayhid Sultans (ca. 932–1055 CE). The Buyids were a military clan of Persian origin who came to power in Iran and Iraq and acted as overlords for the Sunni Abbasid Caliphs. The Buyids were originally Zaydi Shiites from Daylam in northern Iran, but once in power they supported Shi'ism without allegiance to any of its specific branches. They also supported the rationalist Mu'tazili school of Islamic theology. It was under their influence that Imami theology developed its rationalistic inclination. The earliest comprehensive collections of Imami traditions, which were first transmitted in Kufa and other parts of Iraq, were compiled in the Iranian city of Qom. By the late ninth century CE, when the development of Imami tradition was well under way, Qom had already served for more than a century as a center for Imami Shiite learning. The earliest and most authoritative of the Imami Hadith collections consist of four canonical compendia that deal with the subjects of theology and jurisprudence.

Shiite influences spread more widely to Iran and Central Asia after the Mongol conquest in the thirteenth century CE, creating a more favorable milieu in many formerly Sunni regions. A particularly broadly based Shiite tradition flowered in post-Mongol Central Asia, Iran, and Anatolia that in time would culminate in Safavid Shi'ism (ca. fifteenth century CE). Safavid Shi'ism has been characterized as "*Tariqa* Shi'ism," as it was transmitted mainly through Sufi *tariqa*s or orders that encouraged Shiite doctrines. These Sufi orders remained outwardly Sunni, following one or another of the Sunni schools of law, while being particularly devoted to 'Ali and the Ahl al-Bayt. Among the Sufi orders that played a leading role in spreading this type of popular Shi'ism, mention should be made of the Nurbakhshiyya and the Ni'matullahiyya. In the atmosphere of religious eclecticism that prevailed in Central Asia, 'Alid loyalism became more widespread, and Shiite elements began to be integrated into the broader practices of Sufi groups. It was under such circumstances that close relations developed between Twelver Shi'ism and Sufism as well as between Ismailism and Sufism in Iran. The most important Twelver Shiite mystic of the fourteenth century, who developed his own rapport between Imami Shi'ism and Sufism, was Sayyid Haydar Amuli (d. 1385 CE) who was influenced by the Sufi teachings of the Spanish Muslim mystic Ibn al-'Arabi (d. 1240 CE).

Among the Sufi orders that contributed to the spread of Shi'ism in predominantly Sunni Iran, the most important was the Safavi order, founded by Shaykh Safi al-Din (d. 1334 CE), a Sunni who practiced Shafi'i jurisprudence. The Safavi order spread rapidly throughout Azerbaijan, eastern Anatolia, and other regions, acquiring influence over a number of Turkoman tribes. Under Shaykh Safi's fourth successor, Shaykh Junayd (d. 1460 CE), the order was transformed into an active military movement. Shaykh Junayd was the first Safavid spiritual leader to espouse specifically Shiite sentiments. Junayd's son and successor, Shaykh Haydar (d. 1488 CE), was responsible for instructing his soldier-Sufi followers to adopt the scarlet headgear of 12 gores commemorating the 12 Imams, for which they became known as the *Qizilbash,* a Turkish term meaning "red-head."

The Shi'ism of the Qizilbash Turkomans became more clearly manifest when the youthful Isma'il became the leader of the Safavi order. Isma'il presented himself to his followers as the representative of the hidden twelfth Imam. With the help of his Qizilbash forces, he speedily seized Azerbaijan and entered its capital, Tabriz, in 1501. He then proclaimed himself *Shah* or king and at the same time declared Twelver Shi'ism to be the official religion of the newly founded Safavid state. Shah Isma'il brought all of Iran under his control during the ensuing decade. The Safavid dynasty ruled Iran until 1722 CE.

In order to enhance their legitimacy, Shah Isma'il and his immediate successors claimed to represent the Mahdi, or Hidden Imam. They also claimed 'Alid origins for their dynasty, tracing their ancestry to Imam Musa al-Kazim. Shi'ism became the established religion of the Safavid state gradually. Under Shah Isma'il (r. 1501–1524 CE) and his son Tahmasp (r. 1524–1576 CE), the Safavids articulated a religious policy that in partnership with Imami scholars actively propagated Twelver Shi'ism. However, as Iran did not have an established class of Shiite religious scholars at that time, the Safavids were obliged to invite scholars from the Arab centers of Imami scholarship, notably Najaf, Bahrain, and Jabal Amil, to instruct their subjects. The foremost of these Arab Shiite scholars was Shaykh 'Ali al-Karaki al-Amili (d. 1534 CE), also known as al-Muhaqqiq al-Thani (The Second Authority).

Under the influence of Amili and others, the Safavids encouraged the training of a class of Imami legal scholars to teach the established doctrines of Twelver Shi'ism. During the reign of Shah 'Abbas I (r. 1587–1629 CE), Imami rituals and popular practices were established, such as pilgrimage visits (*ziyara*) to the tombs of the Imams and their relatives in Najaf, Karbala, and other shrine cities of Iraq, as well as in Mashhad and Qom in Iran. The training of Imami scholars was further facilitated through the foundation of religious colleges in Isfahan, the Safavid capital. By the end of the seventeenth century CE, an influential class of Shiite religious scholars had developed in the Safavid state.

The Safavid period witnessed a renaissance of Muslim sciences and scholarship. Foremost among the intellectual achievements of the period were the original contributions of Shiite scholars that belonged to the so-called School of Isfahan. These scholars integrated the philosophical, theological, and mystical traditions of Shi'ism into a metaphysical synthesis known as Divine Wisdom or theosophy (Persian, *hikmat-i ilahi*). The founder of the Shiite theosophical school was Muhammad Baqir Astarabadi (d. 1630 CE), also known as Mir Damad, a Shiite theologian, philosopher, and poet, who served as the chief religious authority (*Shaykh al-Islam*) of Isfahan. The most important representative of the School of Isfahan was Mir Damad's principal student, Sadr al-Din Muhammad Shirazi (d. 1640 CE), better known as Mulla Sadra. Mulla Sadra produced his own synthesis of Muslim thought, including theology, peripatetic philosophy, philosophical mysticism, and Sufi studies, particularly the Sufism of Ibn al-'Arabi. Mulla Sadra trained eminent students, such as Mulla Muhsin Kashani (d. 1680 CE) and 'Abd al-Razzaq Lahiji (d. 1661 CE), who passed down the traditions of the School of Isfahan in later centuries in both Iran and India.

The Imami scholars, especially the jurists among them, played an increasingly prominent role in the affairs of the Safavid state. This trend reached its climax with Muhammad Baqir Majlisi (d. 1699 CE), who was the leading Twelver Shiite scholar and authority of the time. He is best known for compiling the encyclopedic collection of Shiite Hadith known as *Bihar al-anwar* (Seas of Light). Many of the Twelver scholars disagreed among themselves on theological and juristic issues and divided into two camps, generally designated as the *Akhbari* (the traditionalist school) and the *Usuli* (the rationalist school). Mulla Muhammad Amin Astarabadi (d. 1624 CE), one of the most influential Akhbari scholars, attacked the very idea of *ijtihad* in Islamic jurisprudence and branded the Usuli scholars enemies of the religion. Criticizing earlier innovations in *usul al-fiqh*, the principles of jurisprudence, Astarabadi recognized the *akhbar*, the traditions of the Imams, as the most important source of Islamic law and as the only valid resource for the correct understanding of the Qur'an and the way of the Prophet Muhammad.

The Akhbari school of Twelver Shi'ism flourished for almost two centuries in Iran and the shrine cities of Iraq. In the second half of the eighteenth century, when Twelver Shi'ism was already widespread in Iran, the Usuli doctrine found a new champion in Muhammad Baqir Bihbahani (d. 1793 CE), who defended the *ijtihad* of the jurists and successfully led the intellectual debate against the Akhbaris. Thereafter, the Akhbaris rapidly lost their position to the Usulis, who now emerged as the prevailing scholars of jurisprudence in Imami Shi'ism. The reestablishment of the Usuli school led to an unprecedented enhancement of the authority of the legal scholars under the Qajar dynasty of Iran (r. 1794–1925). This enhancement of scholarly status placed the practice of *taqlid*, the imitation of a noted jurist, at the center of Imami jurisprudence.

Meanwhile, Imami Shi'ism had also spread to southern Lebanon and certain regions of India. Twelver legal scholars, who were often of Persian origin, were particularly active in India. The Adil-Shahis of Bijapur (r. 1490–1686 CE) were the first Muslim dynasty in India to adopt Imami Shi'ism as the religious doctrine of their state. Sultan Quli (r. 1496–1543 CE), the founder of the Qutb-Shahi dynasty of Golconda, also adopted Imami Shi'ism. In India, the Imami *ulama* encountered the hostility of the Sunnis. Nur Allah Shushtari, an eminent Twelver theologian-jurist who emigrated from Iran to India and enjoyed some popularity at the Mughal court, was executed in 1610 CE at the instigation of the Sunni scholars. Despite such persecution, Shiite communities survived even in the Mughal empire, especially in the region of Hyderabad. Twelver Shi'ism also spread to northern India and was adopted in the kingdom of Awadh (1722–1856) with its capital at Lucknow.

Developments in the Modern Period

The modern period of Imami Shi'ism has been marked by two major influences. The first has been the expanding role and impact of European conquest and colonization in many parts of the Muslim world. The second has been the emergence of the modern nation–state as a means of uniting people with a common allegiance to territory and collective identity. While Iran was never directly conquered and ruled by European powers, it was deeply affected by the contested claims of territorial domination by various European states, in particular Russia, France, and Britain, all of which sought to cultivate a zone of influence in the region.

One aspect of the response to European encroachment involved the modernization of armies, the appropriation of technology and industry, and the gradual absorption of different systems of education and constitutional reforms. Changes took place unevenly in urban and rural areas, among various groups, and even within individual states. In general, traditional patterns of religious and educational life continued or even intensified in response to perceived alien influences. In places where the Twelver Shiite population was dominant, namely Iran and Iraq, different patterns of response to change emerged. In Iran, the religious scholars played an important role in helping the Qajar rulers resist Russian imperial designs and protested strongly against the granting of concessions by the state to foreign powers. A far more important debate also arose over the acceptance of constitutional ideas from Europe and their adaptation to the traditionally ruled Muslim state.

Shiite scholars, particularly Shaykh Muhammad Husayn Na'ini (d. 1936), argued strongly for the compatibility of constitutional ideas and Twelver traditions. In Iran, this led to a series of dramatic changes. Between 1905 and

1911, there took place a constitutional revolution, aimed at reframing the rules of governance and limiting the role of the absolute Qajar monarchs. However, this political experiment failed, and following short periods of British control, power in Iran was seized in 1921 by an army colonel, Reza Khan, who soon deposed the Qajar dynasty and declared himself Shah. Reza Shah Pahlavi (r. 1925–1941) instituted a series of reforms of a secular nature that greatly curtailed the role and influence of religious scholars and the Twelver establishment in Iran. His son and successor, Shah Mohammad Reza Pahlavi (r. 1941–1979), continued the general policies of his father. In the 1950s, a strong secular nationalist movement led by Dr. Mohammed Mossadegh gained strength. This movement was thwarted with the help of the American Central Intelligence Agency, and the position of the Shah came to be consolidated even further. Many leading religious scholars were moved to intensify debate on the issues of the time at the various centers of Shiite learning. Among them were Allama Muhammad Husayn Tabataba'i (d. 1981) and Murtaza Mutahhari (d. 1979). A number of religious leaders came to be regarded as successors to the great Ayatollah Burujirdi (d. 1961), to whom the title of *Marja'-i Taqlid* (Source of Imitation) had been given by his peers.

Meanwhile in Iraq, the Shiite religious leaders played an unsuccessful role in resisting British rule after World War I, although in conjunction with scholars from Iran they engaged actively in debating the issues of the day. Eventually, the Middle East was divided into several spheres of influence and Iraq came to be governed under a British mandate, which led to the appointment of King Faisal I (r. 1921–1933) as ruler of an independent Iraq. In 1958, there was a coup by army officers, leading to the execution of King Faisal II and a sustained period of instability. Subsequently, another military dictatorship was established in Iraq by Saddam Hussein, during whose long rule all religious opposition was brutally suppressed.

During the 1960s, a lesser known but politically active Iranian religious scholar named Ayatollah Ruhollah Khomeini called for the abolition of the monarchy in Iran. He was sent into exile in Iraq, where he continued his opposition to the Iranian regime. There were also other intellectuals, not directly linked to the religious authorities, who challenged the status quo in Iran. These nonclerical intellectuals helped marshal the resources that brought Twelver Shi'ism into dialogue with contemporary ideologies. The most famous of these intellectuals, 'Ali Shariati (d. 1977), catalyzed student and youth opposition through his writings and lectures. Traditionally trained scholars, such as Murtaza Mutahhari, also added their voices to the mounting opposition. However, Khomeini marshaled the forces of opposition to the Shah most successfully. Khomeini's leadership led to the Iranian Revolution of 1979, the abolition of the Pahlavi monarchy, and the inauguration of the Islamic Republic of Iran. After the revolution, a constitutional structure emerged in Iran that institutionalized the role of the Twelver scholars as representatives of the Hidden Imam and guardians of the state. An institutionalized ideology, *vilayat-i faqih* (the authority of the jurist), was written into the Iranian constitution. This ideology established a leading role for the supreme religious leader in the affairs of the state, while also allowing for an elected legislative body, the *majlis* or parliament, and an elected president. After Khomeini's death in 1989, the role of the supreme leader has been assumed by Ayatollah 'Ali Khamenei.

In Iran, Iraq, and parts of Lebanon, recent political developments continue to be influential in discussions and debates about the Twelver Shiite heritage. Imami Shiite communities, meanwhile, have continued to thrive in many other regions. In addition to Azerbaijan, Bahrain, Saudi Arabia, Pakistan, and India, there are Twelver Shiite communities in parts of Africa, Asia, Europe, and North America.

Doctrines and Practices of Twelver Shi'ism

For all Shi'a, the period up to the death of Imam Ja'far al-Sadiq constitutes a shared legacy. During this period, the Shi'a preserved the traditions of the Prophet and the early Imams, began the development of a tradition of legal thought, and laid the foundations of what in due course represented a strong tradition of philosophical and esoteric interpretation of Islam. "I am the city of knowledge and 'Ali is its gate; so whoever desires knowledge, let him enter the gate." This *hadith*, attributed to the Prophet Muhammad, highlights the complementarity of roles envisaged in Shi'ism. Reference has already been made to 'Ali's intimate engagement with the mission of the Prophet and his active role in the cause of Islam. This engagement is highlighted by Shiite sources to affirm 'Ali's key role in the history of the interpretation of the Qur'an, a commitment to the application of reason in matters of faith, an emphasis on ethical conduct and social justice, the importance of a personal search for knowledge, and the cultivation of an inner life in communion with God. Many of 'Ali's teachings were preserved in a work titled *Nahj al-Balagha* (The Way of Eloquence), which highlights his foundational role in inspiring Shiite intellectual and spiritual traditions. In this context, the Imam has a pivotal role in Shiite Islam, linking revelation to daily human life and giving expression to practical forms in society by which the ethical ideals of Shi'ism can be realized.

The ideal of social justice and its defense is evoked in Shiite sources, with particular reference to the life of Imam Husayn, the grandson of the Prophet. For resisting the tyrannical rule of the second Umayyad Caliph Yazid, Imam Husayn and his followers were massacred at Karbala, in present-day Iraq. This event, commemorated during the first 10 days of the month of Muharram in the Muslim calendar, has central significance in Imami Shiite spirituality. The martyrdom of Imam Husayn, who is called

Sayyid al-Shuhada' or "Lord of the Martyrs," not only catalyzed the opponents to Umayyad rule but also provided a focus for Shiite religious expression, strengthening loyalty around the Ahl al-Bayt and their cause of restoring a pious society among the Muslims. Both Muhammad al-Baqir and Ja'far al-Sadiq, the fifth and sixth Imams, respectively, consolidated the position of the Shi'a and elaborated the intellectual basis of the interpretation and practice of Shiite Islam outside of the existing political order. They also acted as important reference points for the ongoing development of Shiite spirituality and religious rituals.

A distinctive aspect of Shiite theological and legal traditions, compared to those of the Sunnis, was the elevation of reason and the use of Hadith transmitted through their Imams. The Imamis or Twelvers, like all Shi'a, regard independent reasoning, *ijtihad,* as a significant tool in jurisprudential thought. In theology, this principle allowed Twelver Shiites to give rational principles a wide scope in the intellectual tradition. In the absence of the Imam, *ijtihad* could only be exercised by competent and qualified religious scholars. Such individuals, called *mujtahids,* became the major source of authoritative guidance on daily issues facing believers. These scholars received their training in centers where religious learning was preserved and transmitted. Known as *madrasas,* these traditional centers of learning developed in key centers where the Imami Shiite community was strong. In addition to centers in Iraq, such as in Najaf and Karbala, there were also important institutions of religious learning in Iran—in Qom, Mashhad, and Isfahan—and subsequently in the Indian subcontinent. These centers trained scholars and jurists to educate and serve the Shiite community and created important networks for the preservation and continuity of Twelver Shiite learning.

While all Shi'a share the core practices of Islam with other Muslim communities, distinctive ceremonies and traditions have evolved in Shiite Islam, grounded in Shi'ism's particular set of experiences and interpretations. In addition to the Hajj pilgrimage to Mecca and visiting the Prophet's tomb in Medina, Imami Shiites regard it as important to visit the tombs of the Imams and their descendants, who in Persian are known as *Imamzadehs.* The most important of these tombs are in Najaf (the burial place of Imam 'Ali), Karbala (the burial place of Imam Husayn), al-Kazimayn in Baghdad (the tomb of the fifth and ninth Imams), Mashhad (Imam al-Rida), and Samarra (the tomb of the tenth and eleventh Imams), which is also where the twelfth Imam went into occultation. Another popular site of pilgrimage is Qom, where the sister of the eighth Imam 'Ali al-Rida is buried. There are also holy sites in Cairo (believed to be the place where Imam Husayn's head was kept) and Damascus (associated with Zaynab, the sister of Imam Husayn).

The commemoration of Imam Husayn's martyrdom is of particular significance and is remembered during the month of Muharram through processions in which intense grief is displayed. At *majalis*, sessions devoted to the commemoration of the martyrdom of Husayn, preachers recount the events of his death in sermons known as *rawda-khani*, and prayers are offered. Believers also reenact the tragedy of Husayn and chant poems, often through elaborate dramatic performances called *ta'ziyeh*. The events of Karbala are commemorated globally, wherever Twelver Shiite communities can be found, and are enriched by local tradition and poetry. The gathering places at which such events take place are known as *Husayniyyas* or *Imambaras*, which consist of extensive, decorated structures adorned with images that recall the tragedy.

ISMAILI SHI'ISM

After Imam Ja'far al-Sadiq's death in the eighth century CE, those of his followers who were loyal to his eldest son Isma'il and his descendants struggled to keep their hopes alive. The descendants of Isma'il, the eponym of the Ismaili Shiites, lived in very hazardous circumstances in various secret localities. By the middle of the ninth century CE, they had settled in Salamiyya in Syria. During this period, they concealed their identity from the public and sought to consolidate and organize the widely dispersed Ismaili community. The scholars and local leaders of the Ismailis, known as *da'is* or "Summoners," maintained contact with the Imams and organized themselves into a *da'wa*, a network of shared commitment to the Imam and intellectual values. When they emerged into the public limelight at the beginning of the tenth century, the Ismaili community was remarkably well organized and cohesive. This community relied on a missionary network of dedicated leaders or *da'is* (literally, "those who summon"), who conveyed the teachings of the Ismaili Imams effectively and with great intellectual competence.

The Ismaili *da'is* sought to extend their influence and forge alliances to create the foundations of a possible state under the rule of the Imam. The opportunity of laying the foundations for a state gained momentum at the beginning of the tenth century CE, when the Ismaili Imam of the time, 'Abdallah, moved from Syria to North Africa. In 910 CE, he was proclaimed *Amir al-Mu'minin* (Commander of the Believers), with the title of *al-Mahdi* ("The Guided One," equivalent to the idea of "The Saviour"). The dynasty of the Ismaili Imams, who for more than two centuries reigned over an extensive empire centered in Egypt, adopted the title of *al-Fatimiyyun* (commonly rendered as Fatimids) after Fatima, the Prophet Muhammad's daughter and wife of 'Ali, from whom the Imams were descended. The proclamation of Imam 'Abdallah al-Mahdi as the first Fatimid Caliph marked the beginning of the Ismaili attempt to give a concrete shape to their vision of Shiite Islam.

From their initial base in the present-day country of Tunisia, the Fatimids expanded their realm of influence and authority, advancing to Egypt during the reign of the fourth Fatimid Imam and Caliph al-Mu'izz. In 973 CE, al-Mu'izz transferred the Fatimid capital from North Africa to the new city of *al-Qahira* (Cairo), which was founded by the Fatimids in 969 CE. Henceforth, Cairo became the centre of a far-flung empire, which at its peak, extended westward to North Africa, Sicily, and other Mediterranean locations, and eastward to Palestine, Syria, the Yemen, and the Hijaz with its holy cities of Mecca and Medina. The Fatimid territories participated vigorously in international trade with North Africa, Nubia, the Middle East, Europe, Byzantium (Constantinople in particular), the islands of the Mediterranean, and India. Agriculture advanced to a level of general self-sufficiency; industry received active stimulus from the state and helped boost both inland and maritime trade.

It was, however, in the sphere of intellectual life that the Fatimid achievement seems most brilliant and outstanding. The Fatimid rulers were lavish patrons of learning. Their encouragement of scientific research and cultural pursuits attracted the finest minds of the age to the Caliphal court in Cairo, regardless of religious persuasion. Such luminaries included mathematicians and physicists, astronomers, physicians, historians, geographers, and poets. Al-Azhar, the chief Cairo mosque built by the Imam and Caliph al-Mu'izz and endowed by his successors, also became a great center of learning. The *Dar al-'Ilm* (House of Knowledge), which was established in Cairo in 1005 CE by the Imam and Caliph al-Hakim (r. 996–1021CE), became famous as a leading institution of learning. Its program of studies combined a range of major academic disciplines, from the study of the Qur'an and the Prophetic traditions to jurisprudence, philology and grammar, medicine, logic, mathematics, and astronomy. This institution, with its library of over 400,000 manuscripts, was open to followers of different religions. The impact of this cultural and intellectual flowering was not limited to the Muslim world. The influence of the academic institutions of Cairo and other centers of Ismaili scholarship spread into Europe, contributing significantly to the development of scientific thought and philosophy in the West.

Ismaili intellectuals of outstanding ability, such as Abu Hatim al-Razi, Abu Ya'qub al-Sijistani, al-Qadi al-Nu'man, Hamid-al-Din al-Kirmani, al-Mu'ayyad fi'l-Din al-Shirazi, and Nasir-i Khusraw, made significant contributions to the articulation of Muslim thought and to Shiite literature. They wrote extensively, employing the philosophical tools of the age, to promote a comprehensive understanding of the concepts of *tawhid* (unity of God), prophecy, and the Imamate on the basis of general Islamic and Shiite principles. Nasir-i Khusraw (d. after 1072 CE), the well-known poet-philosopher who spread Ismaili Shi'ism in Central Asia, sought to demonstrate the relationship between philosophy and prophetic wisdom, stressing the indispensability of prophetic wisdom for the development of human intellect. In the same vein, Hasan-i Sabbah (d. 1124 CE), the founder of an Ismaili state based at the fortress of Alamut in Iran, expounded afresh the early Shiite doctrine of *ta'lim* (literally, "education"), the need of humankind for revelational guidance as interpreted by each Imam of the age.

The founding of the Fatimid Caliphate also provided the first opportunity for the promulgation of Ismaili Shiite jurisprudential principles. The Ismaili exposition of these principles was based on Imam 'Ali's teachings, which had been the inspiration for the doctrinal elaborations by Imams Muhammad al-Baqir and Ja'far al-Sadiq. In light of these teachings, the Fatimid law was formulated and implemented, above all, with due deference to their universalistic philosophy of religious tolerance and respect for difference. The spirit of Fatimid state policy was succinctly inscribed in one of their edicts: "Each Muslim may try to find his own solution within his religion." In the same spirit, the Fatimids encouraged the private patronage of mosques and other pious endowments by Muslims of different legal schools, their policy reflecting the historical fact of a plurality of pious ways rather than a monolithic interpretation of religion. For appointments in the Fatimid judiciary, as in other branches of government, merit was a primary criterion. In elevating a Sunni jurist to the position of Chief *qadi* or judge, the Imam and Caliph al-Hakim, for example, praised the appointee's sense of justice and intellectual caliber as determining factors. The period of Fatimid rule is also noteworthy for the support and encouragement given to Christians and Jews within the state. Many Coptic and Armenian Christians as well as Jews attained important positions, and the two communities participated actively in the social, cultural, intellectual, and economic life of the larger society. The Fatimids founded this encouragement on the Qur'anic principle of respect for the *Ahl al-Kitab,* the People of the Book, which were the Christian and Jewish communities.

In the last decade of the eleventh century CE, the Ismaili community suffered a permanent schism over the question of succession to the Imam and Caliph al-Mustansir Bi'llah, who died in 1094 CE. One section of the community recognized his younger son al-Musta'li, who had succeeded to the Fatimid Caliphate as the next Imam. The other faction supported al-Mustansir's elder son and designated heir, Nizar, as the Imam. The Nizari Ismaili Imams of modern times, known under their hereditary title of the Aga Khan, trace their descent to Nizar. Today, the two Ismaili branches are the Musta'li and Nizari, named after al-Mustansir's sons who claimed his heritage.

The Nizari Ismailis

The seat of the Nizari Imamate moved to Iran, where the Ismailis had already succeeded, under the leadership of Hasan-i Sabbah, in establishing a state comprising a network of fortified settlements. With its headquarters at Alamut, in northern Iran, the Nizari state later extended to parts of Syria. Although there were continual wars among Muslims over issues of power and territory, this period of Muslim history does not paint a simple canvas of one camp fighting another. The military situation was further complicated by the presence of the Crusaders, who were in contact with the Nizari Ismailis of Syria. Shifting alliances among all these different groups was the normal order of the times.

It was within this context of debilitating warfare among Muslims and the rising Mongol threat to the Muslim world that the Nizari Ismaili Imam Jalal al-Din Hasan (r. 1210–1221 CE), who ruled from Alamut, embarked on a policy of rapprochement with Sunni rulers and jurists. The Sunnis reciprocated positively, and the Abbasid Caliph al-Nasir acknowledged the legitimacy of the Ismaili Imam's rule over a territorial state. Imam Jalal al-Din's policy, like that of his Fatimid forebears, was a practical affirmation that while differences in the interpretation of sacred texts exist among Muslims, what matters most are the overarching principles that unite them all. In these trying times of struggle, military encounters, and changing alliances, the Ismailis of the Alamut state did not forsake their intellectual and literary traditions. Their fortresses housed impressive libraries with collections of books on various religious subjects and included philosophical and scientific tracts as well as scientific equipment. Nor did the hostile environment force the Nizari Ismailis to abandon their liberal policy of patronage to men of learning, which benefited Muslim as well a non-Muslim scholars and scientists. Their settlements in Iran also served as sanctuaries for waves of refugees, irrespective of creed, who fled both local conflicts and the Mongol onslaught. Alamut finally fell to the Mongols in 1256 CE. Subsequently, many Nizari Ismailis found refuge in Afghanistan, Transoxania in Central Asia, China, and the Indian subcontinent, where large Ismaili settlements had existed since the ninth century CE.

The Ismailis who remained in Iran had to protect their identity to escape persecution. Given the esoteric nature of their tradition, Sufi orders often provided hospitality to the Ismailis. Though the Sufi orders then prevalent in the Iranian lands were predominantly Sunni, all of them held 'Ali ibn Abi Talib in high esteem. During this difficult phase, the institution of the Ismaili Imamate retained its resilience. In the fourteenth century, under the influence of the Nizari Imams, new centers of Nizari activity were established in the Indian subcontinent, Afghanistan, the mountainous regions of Hindukush, Central Asia, and parts of China. In South Asia, the Nizari Ismailis became known as *Khojas,* and they developed a distinctive devotional literature known as the *Ginan*s.

Developments in the Modern Period

The modern Nizari Ismaili community has a global presence. Historically, the community reflected a wide geographical and ethnographic diversity based on the various cultural regions of the world where its members originated and lived. Today, the Ismaili heritage includes the cultures of Central Asia, Persia, the Arab Middle East, and South Asia. During the nineteenth and twentieth centuries, many Ismailis from South Asia migrated to Africa and settled there. In more recent times, there has been migration from all parts of the Ismaili world to North America and Europe. The shared values that unite Ismailis are centered on their allegiance to a living Imam. At present, this is the 49th hereditary Imam and descendant of the Prophet Muhammad, Prince Karim Aga Khan. The authority and guidance of the Imam provides the enabling framework for the development of the Ismaili community and for the continuity of its Muslim heritage.

The modern phase of Nizari Ismaili history, as with other Muslims, can be dated to the nineteenth century and to the significant historical changes arising from the growth and enlargement of European presence and power in the Muslim world. Following a period of change and turmoil in Iran during the 1840s, the 46th Imam, Hasan 'Ali Shah, went to India. He was the first Nizari Imam to bear the title of Aga Khan, which was granted to him by the Persian monarch Fath 'Ali Shah Qajar. His leadership enabled the community in India to lay the foundations for institutional and social developments and also fostered more regular contacts with Ismaili communities in other parts of the world. After his death in 1881 he was succeeded by his son 'Ali Shah, Aga Khan II, who continued to build on the institutions created by his father, with a particular emphasis on providing modern education for the community. He also played an important role representing Muslims in the emerging political institutions under British rule in India. Following his early death in 1885, Aga Khan II was succeeded by his eight-year-old son, Sultan Muhammad Shah, Aga Khan III. Aga Khan III was Imam for 72 years, the longest in Ismaili history, and his life spanned dramatic political, social, and economic transformations. His long-term involvement in international affairs, his advocacy of Muslim interests in troubled times, and his commitment to the advancement of education, particularly for Muslim women, reflect his significant and generous contributions. It was his leadership as Imam, however, that transformed the modern history of the Nizari Ismailis, enabling them to adapt successfully to the challenges of the twentieth century.

In South Asia and Africa, the Nizari Ismailis established administrative structures, educational institutions, and health services and built on economic opportunities in trade and industry. In 1905, the Nizari Ismaili community in East Africa adopted a constitution, which laid the basis for an organized framework of institutions and governance at local, regional, and national levels. Similar constitutions were created for other Ismaili communities and were revised periodically, providing guidance for the conduct of personal law and its place within the context of the laws of each country in which the Ismailis resided. In 1986, the present Imam, Prince Karim Aga Khan, extended this practice to the worldwide Nizari Ismaili community. The revised Ismaili constitution, which serves the social governance needs of all Nizari Ismailis, facilitates a unified approach to internal organization and external relations, while taking account of regional diversity and local differences. As in the past, Ismailis follow a strong tradition of voluntary service, contributions, and donations of time, expertise, and personal resources to the Imam and communal institutions.

The present Nizari Imam assumed his post in 1957, at a time when much of the developing world, including the Muslim world, was going through an important period of transition, often marked by political change and upheaval. These continued throughout the twentieth century, making it particularly vital that the Ismailis were guided appropriately through periods of crises and tumultuous changes, as in East Africa and the subcontinent, and later in Tajikistan, Iran, Syria, and Afghanistan. Social and political dislocation often meant that humanitarian concerns for the rehabilitation and resettlement of refugees took priority, and a significant number of Ismailis emigrated to Britain, other European countries, Canada, and the United States.

While the internal institutional organizations of the Nizari Ismaili community continued to be strengthened and reorganized to respond to changing conditions, the Imam also created new institutions to better serve the complex development needs of the community and the societies in which his followers lived. This gave rise to the establishment of the AKDN (Aga Khan Development Network), with the goal of creating strategies for sustainable human development conducive to the fulfilment of the cultural, economic, social, and spiritual aspirations of individuals and communities. A number of institutions within the AKDN pursue a variety of programs in economic development, education, social development, culture, and the environment across the world, in both rural and urban settings, with a particular emphasis on disadvantaged populations.

Doctrines and Practices

The essence of Shi'ism lies in the search for the true meaning of revelation in order to understand the purpose of life and human destiny. By virtue of the authority (*walaya*) invested in Imam 'Ali by the Prophet, each Imam of the time is the inheritor of the Prophet's authority, the trustee of his legacy, and the guardian of the Qur'an. The role of the Imam in guiding the path to spiritual self-realization conveys the essence of the relationship between the Imam and his follower (*murid*), symbolized in the traditional pledge of allegiance (*bay'a*) that each *murid* makes to the Imam of the time. The replacement of the line of prophecy with that of Imamate, therefore, ensures the balance between the *Shari'a*, the exoteric aspect of the faith, and the *Haqiqa*, its esoteric, spiritual essence. Neither the exoteric (*zahir*) nor the esoteric (*batin*) aspect of the religion obliterates the other. The Imam is the path to the believer's inward, spiritual elevation and is the religious authority that makes the *Shari'a* relevant according to the needs of the time. This emphasis on an inner, spiritual life in harmony with the exoteric performance of the *Shari'a* is an aspect of the faith that finds acceptance among many communities in both branches of Islam, whether Shiite or Sunni.

The Imamate thus enables believers to go beyond the apparent or outward form of the revelation in their search for its inner spirituality and meaning. Under the guidance of each Nizari Imam, the meaning of the Qur'an unfolds afresh in each age. The ultimate Shiite expectation is not a new revelation but the complete understanding of the spiritual meaning of the final revelation granted to the Prophet Muhammad. This constitutes the Shiite notion of Islam's spiritual dynamism through the line of Imams, whose main role is to foster continuing submission to the Divine Command. This principle ensures the ever-continuing vitality of the *Shari'a*, the normative law, and the practices derived from it. These practices are the foundation of Ja'fari–Imami Shiite jurisprudence, as elaborated by Imam Ja'far al-Sadiq, who is accepted by both Imami and Ismaili Shiite Muslims as their Imam. Both communities, accordingly, subscribe to the fundamentals of Islam and its core practices. They accept the Holy Qur'an, correctly interpreted, as the source of guidance for all time. They respect the *Sunna* of the Prophet Muhammad as reported via the 'Alid Imams, in addition to the norms specified by the Imams themselves. They reserve the right of interpretation of the Qur'an to the Imams from the progeny of the Prophet. As a religious principle, they place obedience to the Imams immediately after obedience to God and the Prophet. This belief is derived from the command in the Qur'an that Muslims obey God and the Prophet and refer their disputes to those vested with authority. When in doubt about the correct course to follow, they are to submit to the Imam's judgment. The Imams are the People of Remembrance (*Ahl al-Dhikr*), endowed with the competent knowledge of the revealed message.

Shiites perform their congregational prayers in mosques, to which all Muslims go. In addition to the practices prescribed by the *Shari'a*, the Nizari Ismailis observe their own distinctive practices such as supplicatory and intercessionary prayers (*du'a*), meditative sessions of remembrance (*dhikr*), and the recitation of devotional poetry. Such practices usually take place in Ismaili *Jamatkhanas* (literally, "assembly-houses"). Ismaili assembly-houses are designated by the Imam of the time for the use of *murids* who have given the *bay'a,* the oath of allegiance, and whose *bay'a* the Imam has accepted. As an integral part of the religious landscape of the Muslim world, *Jamatkhanas* are part of an institutional category that serves a number of Shiite and Sunni communities in their respective contexts. For many centuries, a prominent feature of the religious landscape of Islam has been gathering spaces that coexist in harmony with the mosque. Historically serving communities of different interpretations and spiritual affiliations, these spaces range from the *ribat, tekke,* and *zawiya* of the Sufis to the *Husayniyya* and *Jamatkhana* of the Shi'a.

The practices of the Nizari Ismailis have evolved over many centuries in a multiplicity of cultural milieus, stretching from North Africa and the Middle East, through Iran, Central Asia, Afghanistan, and China, to South Asia. The resulting diversity of these practices corresponds to the multiple cultural, linguistic, and literary traditions of the Nizari Ismailis, which reflects the pluralism of the Muslim *Umma* within the fundamental unity of Islam. This unity among Muslims is evident, for example, in their common practices derived from the *Shari'a* and common festivals, such as *'Id al-Fitr* (the feast of fast-breaking at the end of Ramadan) and *Milad al-Nabi* (the celebration of the Prophet Muhammad's birthday), which are celebrated by Muslims of all persuasions. In addition, Shiite Muslims gather specifically for Shiite festivals such as *'Id al-Ghadir,* the commemoration of Ghadir al-Khumm, where the Prophet designated 'Ali as his successor. This unity among Muslims has historically coexisted with the right of each school of Islamic thought to practice its particular interpretation of the central tenets of Islam.

The Musta'li Ismailis

The Musta'li Ismailis share with the Nizari Ismailis a common Fatimid heritage, although they no longer have an Imam who is present in their community. Instead, they take guidance from the leadership of the *Da'i Mutlaq* (Supreme Authority), the representative of the concealed Imam, to maintain the intellectual and legal traditions of their daily life. The Musta'li Imams themselves have remained in concealment since 1130 CE. In their absence, supreme authorities known as Da'i Mutlaq have led their community. For all practical purposes, the *Da'i* is a substitute for the hidden Musta'li Imam. As in the case of Imams, the Musta'li *Da'is* appoint their successors. From the twelfth century onwards, the Musta'li Ismailis were based primarily in Yemen and later to an increasing extent in India, where they became known as Bohras. After 1589 CE, the community became divided into Daudi and Sulaymani branches over allegiance to different individuals as *Da'i Mutlaq*. There are no significant differences between the doctrines of the two branches of Musta'li Ismailism. The present *Da'i* of the majoritarian group, the Tayyibi Daudis, is Sayyidna Muhammad Burhan al-Din, the 52nd in the series. He lives in Mumbai (Bombay), where the leadership has moved from its earlier headquarters in Gujarat. The Daudis are found mostly in South Asia, to a lesser extend in Yemen, and in small immigrant communities in Britain, North America, and Sri Lanka. The other Musta'li group, the Sulaymanis, recognize 'Abdallah ibn Muhammad al-Makrami as the 51st *Da'i*, with his headquarters in Yemen. Following the annexation of the province of Najran from the Yemen to Saudi Arabia in 1934, a smaller community of Sulaymanis is also to be found there with a much smaller number in India.

Since 1817, the office of *Da'i Mutlaq* of the Daudis has remained in the progeny of Shaykh Jiwanji Awrangabadi. Two recent *Da'is* have played important roles in the modern Tayyibi Daudi community. Sayyidna Tahir Sayf al-Din became leader in 1915 and was succeeded in 1965 by his son, the present *Da'i* Sayyidna Muhammad Burhan al-Din (b. 1915). Sayyidna Muhammad has continued to emphasize the strong tradition of learning in the Daudi community. This is reflected in the development of two major libraries in the Indian cities Mumbai and Surat and the enlargement of their main seminary, Jami'a Sayfiyya, in Surat, an academy of learning and training for religious scholars and functionaries of the community. There are well-established *madrasas* for the religious education of all Daudi Bohras as well as schools for secular education. The tradition of retaining the heritage of learning through manuscript study has been well preserved, and scholarly and literary works, primarily in Arabic, continue to be developed within the community. The Musta'li Ismailis, both Daudi and Sulaymani, have preserved a significant portion of the Arabic literature of the Ismailis of earlier times.

The Daudi community is organized under the leadership of the *Da'i*, with its headquarters in Mumbai. A representative, known as *Shaykh* or *'Amil*, leads the local community and organizes its religious and social life, including the maintenance of places for religious worship and ritual, as well as communal buildings. Every Daudi, on attaining the age of 15, is obliged to take an oath of allegiance (*mithaq*) to the Imams and *Da'is*. The majority of Ismaili Bohras are in business and industry and have a well-deserved reputation for entrepreneurship and public service. They also run many charitable organizations for the welfare of their communities worldwide.

The Sulaymani community is of predominantly Arab origin and lives mostly in Yemen. It is found in both urban and rural areas, with strong tribal roots. The Sulaymani community of Najran in Saudi Arabia has often found it difficult to practice its faith openly and freely because of pressure from the official Wahhabi sect of Saudi Arabia. The much smaller Sulaymani community in India has produced noted public officials and scholars. There are certain differences between the traditions and the social practices of the Arabic-speaking Yemeni Sulaymanis and the Daudis of South Asia, who use a form of the Gujarati written in Arabic script. The Daudi Bohras have also incorporated many Hindu customs in their marriage and other ceremonies.

ZAYDI SHI'ISM

The influence and geographical distribution of the Zaydis, named after their fourth Imam Zayd ibn 'Ali Zayn al-'Abidin (d. 740 CE), have been more restricted than the Twelvers and the Ismailis. In fact, after some initial success in Iraq, Zaydi Shi'ism remained confined to the Caspian region, northern Iran, and most importantly in Yemen, where Zaydi communities have continued to exist to the present.

The Zaydi branch of Shi'ism developed out of Zayd ibn 'Ali's abortive revolt in Kufa in 740 CE. The movement was initially led by Zayd's son Yahya, who escaped from Kufa to Khurasan and concentrated his activities in what is now eastern Iran and Central Asia. Yahya was eventually tracked down by the Umayyads and killed in 743 CE. In the early Abbasid period, the Zaydis were led by another of Zayd's sons, 'Isa (d. 783 CE). By the middle of the ninth century CE, the Zaydis shifted their attention away from Iraq and concentrated their activities in regions far removed from the centers of Abbasid power. These regions included Daylam, in northern Iran, and Yemen, where two Zaydi states were soon founded.

The Zaydis elaborated a doctrine of the Imamate that clearly distinguished them from the Twelver Shiites and the Ismailis. The Zaydis did not recognize a hereditary line of Imams, nor did they attach any significance to the principle of designation, *nass*. Initially, they accepted any member of the Ahl al-Bayt as a potential Imam, although later the Imams were restricted to the descendants of Hasan or Husayn. According to Zaydi doctrine, if an Imam wished to be recognized he would have to assert his claims publicly in an uprising (*khuruj*), in addition to having the required religious knowledge. Many Zaydi Imams were learned scholars and authors. In contrast to the Twelvers and the Ismailis, the Zaydis excluded underage males from the Imamate. They also rejected the eschatological idea of a concealed Mahdi and his expected return. In fact, messianic tendencies were rather weak in Zaydi Shi'ism. Because of their emphasis on active policies, the observance of *taqiyya*, the dissimulation of actual beliefs, was also alien to Zaydi teachings. However, the Zaydis developed the doctrine of *hijra*, the obligation to emigrate from a land dominated by unjust, non-Zaydi rulers.

The Zaydis were less radical than were Imami Shiites in their condemnation of the early Caliphs. They held that 'Ali had been Imam by designation of the Prophet. However, this designation was unclear and obscure, so that its intended meaning could be understood only through investigation. After Husayn ibn 'Ali, the Imamate could be claimed by any qualified descendant of Imams Hasan or Husayn who was prepared to launch an armed uprising against the illegitimate rulers and to issue a formal summons (*da'wa*) for gaining the allegiance of the people. Religious knowledge, the ability to render independent rulings (*ijtihad*), and piety were emphasized as the qualifications of the Imam. In contrast to the beliefs of the Imami Shiites, the Zaydi

Imams were not considered immune from error and sin (*ma'sum*), except for the first three Imams. The list of the Zaydi Imams has never been completely fixed, although many of them were unanimously accepted by their followers. There were, in fact, periods without any Zaydi Imam, and at times, there was more than one Imam. Because of their high requirements for religious learning, the Zaydis often backed 'Alid pretenders and rulers as summoners (*Da'is*) or Imams with restricted status, in distinction from full Imams (*sabiqun*).

By the tenth century CE, the Zaydis had adopted practically all of the principal doctrines of Mu'tazili theology, including the unconditional punishment of the unrepentant sinner—a tenet rejected by the Twelvers and the Ismailis. In law, the Zaydis initially relied on the teachings of Zayd b. 'Ali himself and other 'Alid authorities. By the end of the ninth century, however, four legal schools had emerged on the basis of the teachings of different Zaydi scholars, including Imam al-Qasim ibn Ibrahim al-Rassi (d. 860 CE), who founded a school of jurisprudence that became prevalent in the Yemen and the Caspian region. In later times, Zaydi law became greatly influenced by the Shafi'i Sunni school of jurisprudence.

In 864 CE, Hasan b. Zayd, a descendant of Imam Hasan, led the Daylamis in a revolt against the region's pro-Abbasid ruler and established the first Zaydi state in Tabaristan, in northern Iran. Subsequently, the Daylami Zaydis were divided into two rival factions, the Qasimiyya and the Nasiriyya. There was much antagonism between the two Zaydi communities of northern Iran who often supported different leaders. Matters were further complicated by ethnic differences and the close ties that existed between the Qasimiyya Zaydis and the Zaydis of Yemen. In the course of the twelfth century, the Caspian Zaydis lost much of their prominence to the Nizari Ismailis who had successfully established themselves in northern Iran with their seat at Alamut. Subsequently, the Zaydis were further weakened because of incessant factional quarrels among different pretenders. However, minor 'Alid dynasties and Zaydi communities survived in northern Iran until the sixteenth century, when the Zaydis of that region converted to Twelver Shi'ism under the Safavids. Henceforth, Zaydi Shi'ism was confined to Yemen.

In Yemen, the Zaydi Imamate was founded in 897 CE by Imam Yahya b. Husayn al-Hadi Ila'l-Haqq (d. 911 CE), a descendant of Hasan and grandson of the jurist Qasim ibn Ibrahim al-Rassi. With the help of the local tribes, he established himself in northern Yemen, which remained the stronghold of Zaydi Shi'ism in South Arabia. Al-Hadi's legal teachings provided the foundation of the Hadawiyya legal school, which became authoritative in parts of the Caspian Zaydi community while serving as the only recognized legal school in the Yemen. The descendants of Imam al-Hadi eventually quarreled among themselves and failed to be acknowledged as Imams, thus undermining Zaydi rule in the Yemen. In the eleventh century, the Yemeni Zaydis experienced further problems because of schismatic movements in their community.

The Zaydi Imamate was briefly restored in the Yemen by Ahmad b. Sulayman al-Mutawakkil (1138–1171 CE), who promoted Zaydi unity. The Zaydi Imamate prevailed in the Yemen even after the occupation of South Arabia by the Sunni Ayyubids in 1174 CE, although the power of the Imams was now considerably restricted. The Yemeni Zaydis were at times obliged to develop better relations with the Sunnis against their own doctrines. For example, Imam al-Mu'ayyad Bi'llah Yahya ibn Hamza (1328–1346 CE) praised the early Caliphs among the Companions of the Prophet as deserving equal respect to 'Ali. In later centuries, as the Zaydi Imams extended their rule to the predominantly Sunni lowlands of Yemen, the Zaydis attempted to achieve a certain doctrinal rapport with their Sunni subjects. On the other hand, the Yemeni Zaydis maintained their traditional hostility toward the Sufis, even though a Zaydi school of Sufism was founded in Yemen in the fourteenth century. The Zaydis also had prolonged conflicts with the Yemeni Ismailis and wrote numerous polemical treatises in refutation of Ismaili doctrines.

The final phase of the Zaydi Imamate in Yemen started with al-Mansur Bi'llah al-Qasim ibn Muhammad (1597–1620 CE), founder of the Qasimi dynasty of Imams who ruled over much of the Yemen until modern times. The city of San'a served as the capital of an independent Zaydi state and Imamate for more than two centuries until 1872, when Yemen became an Ottoman province for a second time. The later Qasimi-Zaydi Imams ruled over Yemen on a purely dynastic basis until 1962, although they still claimed the title of Imam.

SELECTED BIBLIOGRAPHY

Akhavi, Shahrokh. *Religion and Politics in Contemporary Iran*. Albany, New York, 1980.

Algar, Hamid. *Religion and State in Iran*. Berkeley, 1969.

Amir-Moezzi, Mohammad 'Ali. *The Divine Guide in Early Shi'ism: The Sources of Esotericism in Islam,* trans. D. Streight. Albany, New York, 1994.

_____ and C. Jambet. *Qu'est-ce que le Shi'isme?* Paris, 2004.

Arendonk, C. van. *Les débuts de l'Imamate Zaidite au Yémen,* trans. J. Ryckmans. Leiden, 1960.

Arjomand, Said A., ed. *Authority and Political Culture in Shi'ism*. Albany, New York, 1988.

Ayoub, Mahmoud. *Redemptive Suffering in Islam*. The Hague, 1978.

Blank, Jonah. *Mullas on the Mainframe: Islam and Modernity among the Daudi Bohras*. Chicago, 2001.

Cole, Juan. *Sacred Space and Holy War: The Politics, Culture and History of Shiite Islam*. London, 2002.

Corbin, Henry. *En Islam Iranien*. Paris, 1971–1972.

_____. *History of Islamic Philosophy,* trans. L. Sherrard. London, 1993.

Crone, Partricia. *Medieval Islamic Political Thought*. Edinburgh, 2004.

Daftary, Farhad. *The Ismailis: Their History and Doctrines.* Cambridge, 1990.
_____. *A Short History of the Ismailis.* Edinburgh, 1998.
_____. *Ismaili Literature: A Bibliography of Sources and Studies.* London, 2004.
Fahd, Toufic, ed. *Le Shi'isme Imâmite.* Paris, 1970.
Fyzee, Asaf A.A. *Compendium of Fatimid Law.* Simla, 1969.
Halm, Heinz. *The Fatimids and their Traditions of Learning.* London, 1997.
_____. *Shi'ism,* trans. J. Watson and M. Hill. 2nd ed. Edinburgh, 2001.
Hussain, Jassim M. *The Occultation of the Twelfth Imam.* London, 1982.
Jafri, S. Husain M. *The Origins and Early Development of Shi'a Islam.* London, 1979.
Keddie, N.R., ed. *Religion and Politics in Iran: Shi'ism from Quietism to Revolution.* New Haven, 1983.
Kohlberg, Etan. *Belief and Law in Imami Shi'ism.* Aldershot, Hants, 1991.
_____, ed. *Shi'ism.* Aldershot, Hants, 2003.
Lalani, Arzina R. *Early Shiite Thought: The Teachings of Imam Muhammad al-Baqir.* London, 2000.
Madelung, Wilferd. *Religious Schools and Sects in Medieval Islam.* London, 1985.
_____. *The Succession to Muhammad: A Study of the Early Caliphate.* Cambridge, 1997.
_____. "Shi'a," *Encyclopaedia of Islam,* revised ed., vol. 9, pp. 420–424. Leiden, The Netherlands: E.J. Brill.
_____. "Zaydiyya," *Encyclopaedia of Islam,* revised ed., vol. 11. pp. 477–481. Leiden, The Netherlands: E.J. Brill.
Marquet, Yves. *La Philosophie des Ihwan al-Safa.* New ed., Paris, 1999.
Momen, Moojan. *An Introduction to Shiite Islam.* New Haven, 1985.
Mottahedeh, Roy. *The Mantle of the Prophet.* London, 1986.
al-Mufid, Muhammad b. Muhammad. *Kitab al-Irshad: The Book of Guidance into the Lives of the Twelve Imams,* trans. I.K.A. Howard. London, 1981.
Nanji, Azim. "An Ismaili Theory of *Walayah* in the *Da'a'im al-Islam* of Qadi al-Nu'man," in D.P. Little, ed., *Essays on Islamic Civilization presented to Niyazi Berkes.* Leiden, 1976, pp. 260–273.
_____. *The Nizari Ismaili Tradition in the Indo-Pakistan Subcontinent.* Delmar, New York, 1978.
_____. "Isma'ilism," in S.H. Nasr, ed., *Islamic Spirituality: Foundations.* London, 1987, pp. 179–198.
Nasr, S. Hossein. *Ideals and Realities of Islam.* Revised ed., Cambridge, 2001.
_____ et al., eds. *Shi'ism: Doctrines, Thought and Spirituality.* Albany, New York, 1988.
Newman, Andrew. *The Formative Period of Twelver Shi'ism.* Richmond, Surrey, 2000.
al-Nu'man, al-Qadi Abu Hanifa. *Da'a'im al-Islam,* trans. A.A.A. Fyzee, revised by I.K. Poonawala, as *The Pillars of Islam.* New Delhi, 2002–2004.
Sachedina, Abdulaziz. *Islamic Messianism: The Idea of the Mahdi in Twelver Shi'ism.* Albany, New York, 1981.
Serjeant, R.B. "The Zaydis," in: A.J. Arberry, ed., *Religion in the Middle East.* Cambridge, 1969, vol. 2, pp. 285–301.
al-Shahrastani, Muhammad b. Abd al-Karim. *Kitab al-milal wa'l-nihal,* partial English trans. A.K. Kazi and J.G. Flynn as *Muslim Sects and Divisions.* London, 1984.

Sobhani, Ja'far. *Doctrines of Shiite Islam*, trans. and ed. R. Shah-Kazemi. London, 2001.

Tabataba'i, S. Muhammad Husayn. *Shi'ite Islam*, ed. and trans. S. H. Nasr. London, 1975.

Walker, Paul E. *Early Philosophical Shi'ism*, Cambridge, 1993.

Watt, W. Montgomery. *The Formative Period of Islamic Thought*. Edinburgh, 1973.

Wellhausen, Julius. *The Religio-Political Factions in Early Islam*, trans. R. C. Ostle and S. M. Walzer. Amsterdam, 1975.

16

BEGINNING THE PRAYER

●

Daniel Abdal-Hayy Moore

I stand facing Mecca
the house all around me
parallel with everything
hands up to my ears
   the Prayer begins

Hands across chest
   time-space capsule surrounds me
no god but Allah
   all other forgotten
here's eternity's signature
   signed through space
     with severe strokes

Parallel lines on the prayer mat
   past actions cast behind me
     trees in linear groves
stand straight in the Prayer in
      this world
bend from the
   waist into
    the Next

There are parallel lines
   to the limits
past the
    edge of the
      earth are darknesses

the body stands straight then
prostrates
what does it bow to but
    Absence

Absence that is
    a Presence
we can't see with our bare
    eyes but Know
eyes don't see Allah physically
but are themselves
    proof by
        pure seeing

We prostrate in parallel lines
we stand straight with
    angels in the prayer line
rows of Mediterranean Cypresses
    tall silhouettes against white sky
favorites of foggy graveyards

We stand with
    arms at our sides
against the
    beating chests of our
        turmoils
eyes half-slitted
    not staring

Gaze made to
    fall on the
inside
last actions done
    cast behind me
dead while alive
standing still
    concentrated
by praying

From the
    Next world we
rise into

This one

NOTE

Reprinted by permission of the author.

17

WHAT IS SUFISM?

Ahmet T. Karamustafa

Both "Sufi" and "Sufism" are terms adopted from their Arabic originals.[1] In Arabic texts dating from the first few centuries of Islam, one can find the terms *sufi* and *mutasawwif,* which refer to devotees of a particular type of piety. This mode of pious living was most commonly referred to by the name *tasawwuf,* which is the Arabic equivalent of the modern English word "Sufism." There was controversy over the origins of the term *sufi* among the authors of these early texts, and modern scholars have reproduced this controversy at different levels in their own writings. However, there is considerable agreement among both early authors and modern scholars that the word *sufi* most probably comes from *suf,* the Arabic word for "wool," and that it was originally used to designate "wearers of woolen garments."[2]

It is likely that the word *sufi* was coined as early as the eighth century CE to refer to some renunciants and ascetics who wore wool as a sign of their renunciation of this world as opposed to other renunciants and the majority of Muslims who wore linen and cotton.[3] The practice of wearing wool as a sign of moral and political protest was bound up with social and cultural negotiations that took place around the concepts of renunciation, earning a living, and trust in God that were prevalent among Muslims during the second half of the eighth century CE. The details are hard to assemble, but some renunciants, though not all, expressed their renunciation by wearing wool, and hence the term "wool-wearer" came to carry the connotation of "renunciant" or "ascetic."

During the first century of Abbasid rule (ca. 750–850 CE), renunciation was a widespread form of piety in Muslim communities. Whether they wore wool or whether they were referred to as Sufis or not, renunciants of this period were not organized into a single homogenous movement but came in different colors and stripes. Those renunciants who were designated by the term *sufi* shared an aversion to worldly life but diverged in the way they translated their renunciation into social and spiritual terms. The collective term *sufiyya,* which first appeared in this period, designated not one distinct social group but several different social types. Most properly understood, it was the name of a particular orientation toward piety marked by the socially unconventional, and thus remarkable, habit of donning woolen garments.[4]

In this same period, a remarkable development was under way among renunciants. Whatever their approach to renunciation and to the question of how far to detach themselves from mainstream social life, some prominent renunciants and the communities that formed around them began to direct their energies increasingly to the cultivation of the inner life. This inward turn manifested itself especially in new discourses on spiritual states, stages of spiritual development, closeness to God, and love. It also led to a clear emphasis on knowledge of the inner self acquired through the examination and training of the human soul. The proponents of this inward turn explored the psychological aspects of the renunciant themes of repentance, turning toward God, and placing one's trust in God through the scrupulous observation of divine commands. They reached the conclusion that true repentance could not be achieved without a rigorous examination of the conscience and the soul. For these "interiorizing" renunciants, the preoccupation of eschewing this world in order to cultivate the other world was transformed into a search for the other world within the inner self.[5]

Interestingly, the "discovery" and cultivation of the inner dimensions of the person was concomitant with a similar inward reorientation among the same circles of renunciants in an attempt to achieve a deeper understanding of the divine revelation. The concern with attaining knowledge of the inner self was accompanied by a parallel effort to discern the inner meaning of the Qur'an and the Sunna by using a method of interpretation based on inference and allusion. Moreover, in a further intriguing twist, these interiorizing developments were bundled up with a doctrine of selection, whereby knowledge of the soul and the understanding of the inner meanings of divine speech and the example of the Prophet were thought to be "God-given" as opposed to being the fruit of human effort. According to this doctrine, only God's elect, designated most notably as "friends" and "protégés" of God (*wali*, pl. *awliya'*), could attain ultimate self-knowledge and thus have access to aspects of divine knowledge. This idea of divine selection, later expressed by the interrelated terms *walaya* and *wilaya,* was most prominent among Shiites. However, it also seems to have been in circulation among all Muslims, especially in the form of Hadith reports about various categories of God's *awliya'.*[6]

The exact origin and trajectory of these trends are obscure, but some of the pioneering figures in this process, who were not all renunciants, can be identified. These include the female renunciant Rabi'a al-'Adawiyya (d. 801 CE) in Basra, Shaqiq al-Balkhi (d. 810 CE) in northeastern Iran, Abu Sulayman al-Darani (d. 830 CE) in Syria, Dhu'l-Nun al-Misri (d. 860 CE) in Egypt, al-Harith al-Muhasibi (d. 857 CE) in Baghdad, Yahya ibn Muadh al-Razi (d. 872 CE) in central Iran, and Bayazid al-Bastami (d. 848 or 875 CE) in northeastern Iran. Since the historical record on these figures is ambiguous, it is not always possible to establish associations between particular trends and specific figures. Nevertheless, we can be more specific about the legacy of some of these "interiorizing" renunciants and early mystics. By way of illustration, let us review briefly the case of Bayazid (a contraction of "Abu Yazid").

Little is known about the biography of Bayazid, who seems to have spent his life in his native Bastam, to the east of Nishapur in northeastern Iran.[7] He was the earliest mystic to have left behind a substantial number of 'ecstatic utterances' (shath), most famously "Glory be to me! How great is my majesty!" and "I am he."[8] Bayazid explained how he thought God could talk through him in such a fashion in the following statement:

> Once [God] raised me up and caused me to stand before Him and said to me, "O Abu Yazid, My creatures desire to behold you." I answered, "Adorn me with Your unity and clothe me in Your I-ness and raise me to your oneness, so that when Your creatures behold me they may say that they behold You, and that only You may be there, not I."[9]

Bayazid evidently thought that this request was granted, since many of the sayings attributed to him evince a complete erasure of his human subjectivity and its total replacement with God, conceived as the absolute 'I,' the only true subject in existence. In an early Arabic text of uncertain attribution, Bayazid reportedly recounted his "heavenly ascent" (mi'raj, thus paralleling the celebrated night journey and ascent of Muhammad) through the seven heavens to the divine throne, where he experienced such intimacy with God that he was "nearer to him than the spirit is to the body."[10] His often shocking, even outrageous, utterances became the subject of commentary by later mystics, who considered them the verbal overflow of experiential ecstasy.[11] Departing from Qur'anic usage, where reciprocal love between God and humans is expressed by the word mahabba (Qur'an 5:59), Bayazid characterized the relationship of love between the mystic and God as 'ishq (passionate love), a term normally used for love between humans. Through his powerful expressions of love for God, Bayazid later came to symbolize the insatiable, intoxicated lover:

> Yahya ibn Muadh [al-Razi, d. 872 CE] wrote to Abu Yazid [Bayazid], "I became intoxicated by the volume that I drank from the cup of his love." Abu Yazid wrote to him in his reply, "You became intoxicated and what you drank were mere drops! [Meanwhile] someone else has drunk the oceans of the heavens and the earth and his thirst has still not been quenched; his tongue is hanging down from thirst and he is asking, "Is there more?"[12]

We possess no clues as to how Bayazid achieved his experience of proximity to God. Reportedly, he was scrupulous in his observance of regular Islamic rituals, but he apparently rejected renunciation as an option. He said, "This world is nothing; how can one renounce it?' and advocated inner detachment from everything other than God instead.[13] In spite of the obscurity that surrounds his thought and practice, Bayazid achieved lasting fame as the clearest example of the possibility of direct, mystical communication with God even after the completion of the mission of Muhammad.[14]

Although similar portraits can be drawn for each of the other interiorizing figures listed above, here it will be sufficient to point to their connection with the major themes of the inward turn that characterized early Sufism. The tradition of examining the soul seems to have been especially strong in Basra among the followers of Hasan al-Basri (d. 728 CE), and it culminated in the thought of Muhasibi in Baghdad (Muhasibi was originally from Basra). The attempt to fathom the inner meaning of the Qur'an also had deep roots in Basra among the same circles, but it was cross-fertilized by similar trends originating from the sixth Shiite Imam Ja'far al-Sadiq (d. 765 CE) in Medina and perhaps was further developed by Dhu'l-Nun. The idea of spiritual states and of a spiritual path consisting of different stages was nurtured by Darani in Syria, Shaqiq in Khurasan, and Dhu'l-Nun in Egypt. Rabi'a al-'Adawiyya and Bayazid exemplified love of God as a central preoccupation. Moving outside the boundaries of "sober" renunciation, Yahya ibn Muadh epitomized joyfulness as an outcome of reliance on God's mercy. The experience of closeness to God was, as noted above, famously verbalized in the ecstatic utterances of Bayazid. The idea that God appoints special agents from among the believers is not clearly connected with any early renunciant or mystic of this period.

While the trends of inner knowledge and divine selection of *awliya'* were certainly in the air and were cultivated by some eminent renunciants and early mystics of the first half of the ninth century CE, they did not form a coherent and unified whole but could only be found as correlated and occasionally intertwined strands of piety. In the second half of the ninth century, however, and especially in Baghdad, which had emerged as the political and cultural capital of the Abbasid domains, they coalesced with several other elements of religiosity to form a distinct type of piety that became the foundation of what would prove to be one of the most durable pietistic approaches in Islam. Furthermore, for reasons that remain obscure, the members of this Baghdad-centered movement came to be known as Sufis and the new movement was given the name *sufiyya*.

Thus, from the middle of the ninth century, the term *sufi* came to be used increasingly as a technical term to designate a group of people who belonged to a clearly identifiable social movement in Baghdad based on a distinct type of piety. The most prominent members of this movement were Abu Sa'id al-Kharraz (d. 899 CE or a few years earlier), Abu'l-Husayn al-Nuri (d. 907 CE), and Abu al-Qasim al-Junayd (d. 910 CE). In time, the Baghdad Sufis themselves adopted this name and began to use it for themselves. Henceforth, the word no longer signified "wool-wearing renunciant" but came to be applied to the members of this new group. In this way, an epithet that had signified certain trends of renunciatory piety now became the name of a distinctive form of pious living that could no longer be characterized simply as renunciation.

The early Sufis of Baghdad were most concerned with obtaining experiential knowledge (*ma'rifa*) of God, while distilling the reality of the Islamic profession of faith, "There is no god but God," into their daily lives. Human life presented itself to them as a journey toward the ever-elusive goal of achieving "God-consciousness," an ongoing attempt to draw near God. In the Sufi perspective, human beings, viewed as servants of God, experienced such proximity to their Lord before the beginning of time. Before their creation, all human beings bore witness in spirit to God's Lordship on the Day of the Covenant (Qur'an 7:172). As a reward for this act of acknowledgment, they were promised an even more intimate closeness to God at the end of time. While on earth, however, they had to strive to preserve and renew the memory of their proximity to their Creator by turning their backs on everything other than God and by living their lives in constant recognition of His presence.

In practice, this meant the training and domestication of the lower self through measures that included, for many but not all Sufis, asceticism, seclusion, and poverty as well as continuous cultivation of the heart. The heart was understood as the spiritual organ of God's presence in the person, and its chief sustenance was the remembrance or mention of God through invocation (*dhikr*) and "hearing" or witnessing God in poetry and music (*sama'*). Paradoxically, the journey (*suluk*) toward the Lord started only when the Sufi realized his own weakness as an autonomous agent and acknowledged God as the only true actor in the universe. Only when the reins of human action were turned over to God did the individual become a wayfarer (*salik*) and begin the journey toward the goal of achieving proximity to the Creator.

This journey was envisaged as a path (*tariq* or *tariqa*) marked by various stations (*manzil*), locations (*maqam*), and states (*hal*) that the wayfarer passed through. However, at this earliest stage of Sufism there was not yet any systematic thinking, let alone any agreement, on the number, nature, and order of these states and stations. Nor was there a consensus on the destination of the journey. Everyone agreed that closeness to God entailed a sharp turn from lower concerns of this world toward the realm of ultimate matters and a movement away from the lower self toward the inner locus of God's presence, but it proved difficult to characterize the final encounter with God located at the end of the journey. While some, like Kharraz and Nuri, described the highest stage of intimacy with God as the dissolution of self-consciousness, others like Junayd viewed the ultimate goal as a reconstituted self, a human identity recomposed in the image of God after being thoroughly deconstructed during the Sufi journey. All agreed, however, that the ultimate Sufi experience was to be viewed as the passing away or reabsorption of the created human being into the only true/real (*haqq*) being of

God and, most emphatically, not as a divinization of the human. More generally, the encounter between the Sufi and God was a "unidirectional merger," whereby the Sufi was thought to flow into God. However, movement in the other direction was off limits or at least extremely limited, since such a flow from the divine into the human could pave the way for the divinization of the human and lead to the suspect, even heretical, doctrines of incarnation and inherence (*hulul*).

No matter what their approach to the thorny issue of encounter with the Divine, those who shared the common aim of drawing close to God through experiential knowing enjoyed a special camaraderie with one another in the form of circles of fellowship, mutual mentoring, and relationships of master and disciple. Not all human beings became Sufi wayfarers, let alone grew close to God: that privilege was, it seems, reserved for the few "Friends of God" (*awliya' Allah*) that were conscious of their special status and viewed themselves as the spiritual elect. Many friends, much like the prophets, saw themselves as God's special agents among humans, rendered distinct by their special status as intermediaries between the divine and the human planes of being. In their view, they channeled God's mercy to humankind and served to increase God-consciousness among the otherwise heedless, self-absorbed human race through their personal example and their tireless advocacy of God's cause in human affairs.

The special status of the friends of God manifested itself in a number of practices that simultaneously underscored their distinctness from common believers and served to forge bonds of fellowship, loyalty, and mutual allegiance among the spiritual elect. They began to assemble in certain places of congregation and travel in groups, developed distinctive prayer rituals in the form of invocations and auditions to poetry and music that frequently led to rapture or ecstasy (*wajd*), and adopted special initiation practices, notably investiture with a white woolen robe (*khirqa*).[15] It seems likely, although difficult to verify, that other initiatic acts that came to be characteristic of Sufism, such as the handclasp, the bestowal of a cord with prayer beads (*tasbih*), and the entrusting of the initiate with an invocation formula, were also practiced by the first Sufis of Baghdad.[16]

While the institution of the *Sufiyya* was taking shape in Baghdad, individuals and social groups with similar views and practices could also be found among Muslim communities in other locations, even though these latter were not generally known as Sufis. Most notable among these were Sahl al-Tustari (d. 896 CE) in lower Iraq, al-Hakim al-Tirmidhi (d. probably between 905 and 910 CE) in Central Asia, and a group of mystics in northeastern Iran who were known as the "People of Blame" (*Malamatiyya*). There was a considerable overlap between the ideas and practices of Tustari, Tirmidhi, the People of Blame, and the Baghdad Sufis. They shared a number of common features: (1) the stress on the necessity of a permanent reorientation of the individual self toward God in the form of repentance (*tawba*); (2) the assumption of a fierce antagonism between the lower self and the heart; (3) the acceptance of human weakness and the recognition of God as the only true agent and savior; (4) the invocation as the sure link between God and His chosen servants; (5) the idea of a primordial covenant; (6) belief in the existence of a spiritual elect.

Nevertheless, the similarities among these different mystics and the broader communities around them were by no means comprehensive. Certain aspects of the thought and practice of Tustari, Tirmidhi, and the People of Blame, such as vegetarianism, a proclivity for having visions, and a peculiar "light" cosmology centered on the idea of "the light of Muhammad," did not have clear parallels among the Sufis of Baghdad. There were also points of disagreement. For instance, when Junayd was told that the followers of Tustari fasted during the day and ate from food saved in their baskets at night, he expressed regret that they did not forgo reliance on saved food.[17] Tustari endorsed earning a living as part of the Sunna of the Prophet Muhammad, while Junayd preferred complete reliance on God (*tawakkul*), unadulterated with the search for sustenance.[18] Although the Sufis of Baghdad were discrete about their status as God's elect, both Tustari and Tirmidhi were explicit about their own standing among the Friends of God. Tustari used to say: "I am the proof of God for created beings and I am a proof for the saints of my time." Tirmidhi, who gave one of the most systematic treatments of the concept of "friendship with God" (*walaya*) in Islamic thought, claimed the key role in this saintly hierarchy for himself.[19] The People of Blame, on the other hand, viewed all claims of spiritual rank with utmost suspicion and preferred anonymity and social conformity.[20] However, despite such real differences in approach, there was a sense of generic affinity among the various regional mystical tendencies and the term *Sufiyya* was already used by some at the beginning of the tenth century CE to express this shared commitment to the cultivation of the inner life.

Already during the days of Junayd, Nuri, and Kharraz, Baghdad Sufis taught numerous students from different regions of the Abbasid Empire. These students later spread the distinctive teachings and practices of their Sufi teachers to southwestern Iran, western Arabia, and northeastern Iran. For example, Abu 'Abdallah Ibn Khafif (d. 982 CE) of Shiraz in southwestern Iran played a major role in the establishment of Baghdad style Sufism in his home city. Ibn Khafif is better known than many of his contemporaries because one of his disciples, Abu'l-Hasan al-Daylami (fl. tenth century CE), wrote a biography of his teacher. Not counting the relatively short autobiography of Tirmidhi, this is the earliest biography we possess for any Muslim mystic. During the lifetime of Ibn Khafif, there were at least seven different Sufi centers in Shiraz, including Ibn Khafif's own lodge (*ribat*), and the total number of Sufis in that city was reportedly in the thousands. Many of these Sufis, like Ibn Khafif himself, were disciples of Baghdad Sufis, especially of Junayd. In Mecca, several students of Baghdad Sufis lived as permanent "visitors" (*mujawir*) of the Sacred Mosque (*al-Masjid al-Haram*) at the beginning of the tenth century CE.

Elsewhere in the Middle East, the picture was similar, with Sufi lodges reported in different towns in Syria, Iraq, and southwestern Iran. The mystics of these regions were all closely connected, keeping in touch with one another through travel and written correspondence. The majority, it appears, were connected to the first generation of Baghdad Sufis as well as to Tustari of Basra. They honored especially Junayd and Tustari as their most important leaders. The legacy of local figures continued to exercise considerable influence, but the impact of Baghdad and, to some extent, Basra Sufi networks was definitely on the rise. This was increasingly the case also with northeastern regions of Iran, where Baghdad-style Sufism grew firm roots during the course of the tenth century.[21]

The growth of Sufism in northeastern Iran came about as a merger between the Sufis of Iraq and the indigenous People of Blame of this region, especially in its major urban center Nishapur, a merger in which the dominant partner was increasingly Sufism, the new arrival in town.[22] During the course of the tenth century, the Sufis emerged as the more vocal and visible mystical movement in Nishapur and, it appears, also in many other locations in northeastern Iran, while the People of Blame remained faithful to their principles of anonymity and disappeared into the background. Our understanding of the merger between Sufis and the People of Blame in Nishapur is based largely on the rich literary legacy of a key figure whose many works form the principal source for the history of both Sufism and the Path of Blame, Abu 'Abd al-Rahman al-Sulami (d. 1021 CE). Sulami's extant works, in particular his biographical anthology *Tabaqat al-sufiyya* (Generations of the Sufis), his compendium of Sufi Qur'an interpretation *Haqa'iq al-tafsir* (Truths of Qur'anic Exegesis), and his treatise on the Path of Blame, along with his many other works of varying length, have a distinct place in the corpus of early Sufi literature. Indeed, in most of his treatises, Sulami's voice is that of an authoritative representative of Sufism, and the care he took in recording the biographies, sayings, and discourses of Sufis, male as well as female, is ample proof of his special standing as a most valuable informant for the early history of Islamic mysticism.[23]

The Path of Blame was originally a Nishapur-based phenomenon. Elsewhere in northeastern Iran, the spread of Mesopotamian Sufism did not necessarily take the form of a blending of this latter trend with indigenous mystical approaches; rather, it appears to have occurred through importation. It is likely that we owe one of the earliest surviving "surveys" of Sufism, *Kitab al-luma' fi'l-tasawwuf* (The Book of Light Flashes on Sufism) of Abu Nasr al-Sarraj (d. 988 CE), to this process of transplantation of a mystical school that had first taken shape in Iraq to the different cultural environment of northeastern Iran. Sarraj evidently traveled widely in Syria, Iraq, and Egypt in order to meet Sufi shaykhs and their students and to collect accurate information about their lives and teachings. In all, he managed to gather firsthand information from 39 Sufi authorities on approximately 200 Sufis.[24] Sarraj poured his findings into 157 chapters. He organized the chapters into an introduction on the place of Sufism within Islam and 13 "books" devoted to the subjects of states and stations, adherence to the Qur'an, following the model of the Prophet, Qur'an interpretation, Companions of the Prophet, Sufi conduct, differences of opinion on Sufi doctrine, Sufi writings and poetry, audition, ecstasy, miracles, Sufi terminology, ecstatic utterances, and errors associated with Sufism. The result was a comprehensive compendium as solid in substance as it was rich in detail.

The spread of Sufism to Central Asia is more difficult to trace. Nevertheless, we can be confident that Sufism was definitely introduced to the Muslim communities in the region, since one of the earliest extant Sufi manuals, *al-Ta'arruf li-madhhab ahl al-tasawwuf* (Introducing the Way of the People of Sufism), was written in Bukhara by Abu Bakr al-Kalabadhi (d. 990 CE).[25] Representatives of Baghdad Sufism were probably still rare in Central Asia, but there is no doubt that some Sufis were to be found there. Nonetheless, even if they were present, Sufis were clearly not very well known in these regions. Indeed, the organization of Kalabadhi's book, true to the somewhat prosaic and distanced ring of its title, also gives the impression that its author was engaged in an attempt to introduce his readers to a new and foreign subject.

The diffusion of Sufism to regions beyond Iraq during the course of the tenth century CE and its fusion with indigenous mystical trends went apace with the emergence of a self-conscious Sufi tradition. The situation in Syria, lower Iraq, Egypt, and North Africa is less than clear, but especially in northeastern Iran, the need to introduce Sufism to new audiences seems to have contributed to the construction of a coherent narrative about Sufism, as exemplified in the surveys of Sarraj, Kalabadhi, and the various works of Sulami. However, the foreign nature of Sufism in regions other than Iraq was not the main reason for the appearance of academic overviews of *tasawwuf* from the mid-tenth century onwards. More significant was the passage of time. Sufism, which had crystallized in Baghdad during the last quarter of the previous century, now literally had a history, and the Sufis of the late tenth century, who were already a generation or two removed from the time of Junayd and his companions, felt the need to preserve, evaluate, and analyze the complex legacy of the first masters. Their life examples, their sayings, and their behavior had to be recorded, their debates scrutinized, and their vision perpetuated. Moreover, as was the case with all modes of piety, the boundaries of "normative" Sufism needed to be ascertained in order to consolidate and fortify the tradition and simultaneously to dissociate it from similar but suspect approaches of all kinds.

The emergence of a normative Sufi tradition during the tenth century CE can be traced most clearly in the appearance of a specialized literature that was self-consciously about Sufis and Sufism. Very often, the fundamental building blocks of this body of writing were reports about individual Sufis. These were anecdotal in nature and normally transmitted a saying or a statement of the Sufi in question. Two major genres of Sufi literature grew out of these historical reports about the Sufis: the survey and the biographical compilation. These two genres were sometimes combined in the form of discrete sections into a single work. The material they conveyed was compiled and packaged in various ways to serve different but related functions: pedagogical guidance for those who aspired to become Sufis, pious commemoration of past masters, building corporate solidarity among Sufis, and confident self-presentation and self-assertion vis-à-vis other groups competing for authority within the Muslim community. The specialized Sufi literature of the tenth and eleventh centuries CE was produced by Sufis of two divergent orientations: "Traditionalists" who were averse to all scholarship that assigned a prominent role to human reason and "Academic" Sufis who, by contrast, were aligned with legal and theological scholarship.

The Traditionalist camp, which refused to recognize any sources of knowledge other than the Qur'an and the example of the Prophet Muhammad, is well represented by Abu Talib al-Makki (d. 996 CE). Makki was the author of *Qut al-qulub* (The Sustenance of Hearts). This book had a remarkable afterlife: one of the most celebrated Islamic works of all times, Abu Hamid al-Ghazali's (d. 1111 CE) *Ihya' 'ulum al-din* (Bringing the Religious Sciences to Life) was in part a reworking and expansion of Makki's often dense and at times abstruse compendium on piety.[26] Other prominent Traditionalists included Abu Nu'aym al-Isfahani (d. 1038 CE), the author of a voluminous biographical compendium titled *Hilyat al-awliya' wa tabaqat al-asfiya'* (The Ornament of God's Friends and Generations of Pure Ones). Another was Abu Mansur al-Isfahani (d. 1027 CE), a prominent contemporary of Abu Nu'aym in Isfahan, who authored several works on Sufism, including the earliest independent treatise on invocation (*dhikr*) and a short work on Sufi conduct (*adab*). Still another was 'Abdallah al-Ansari (d. 1089 CE), a well-known Qur'an commentator, Hadith scholar, and tireless polemicist and preacher on behalf of Traditionalism.[27]

Abu Mansur and Ansari in particular directed their formidable talents and energies to the dissemination and popularization of Sufi thought and practice by training disciples and preaching Sufi values to audiences in their native towns, Isfahan and Herat. Ansari dictated many works to his personal secretary and to several scribes from among his disciples, among them the first treatise on Sufism written in Persian, a spiritual itinerary in 10 sections of 10 stages titled *Sad maydan* (Hundred Fields). Ansari updated this spiritual itinerary 25 years later, this time in Arabic, with a treatise titled *Manazil al-sa'irin* (The Stages of Wayfarers). The *Stages*, partly because it was in Arabic, proved to be very popular and attracted many commentaries. Remarkably, within less than half a century, it had made its way to Islamic Iberia (al-Andalus), where it formed the basis of Ibn al-'Arif's (d. 1141 CE) *Mahasin al-majalis* (The Beauties of Spiritual Sessions). Ansari's concern for peda-gogical guidance of his disciples, so conspicuous in the works mentioned so far, gave rise to another major work in Persian. It appears that Ansari used Sulami's *Generations* as a basis for some of his lectures, and his students' notes of their master's commentary and expansion of Sulami's work were later compiled to form another *Tabaqat al-sufiyya* (Generations of Sufis). However, to this day Ansari is best known among Persian-speaking audiences for a collection of sayings that go under the name *Munajat* (Intimate Conversations).[28]

For the Traditionalists, Makki, Abu Nu'aym, Abu Mansur, and Ansari, as well as the circles of followers and students around them, Sufism was an inte-gral part, even the very core, of Islam. In their writings on Sufi subjects, they spoke "from within" with a confident and self-assured voice, and they gener-ally did not acknowledge the existence of contending views on Islam, such as semi-rationalist and rationalist legal and theological discourses, except when they denounced them. Their counterparts Sarraj, Sulami, and Kalabadhi, however, struck a different note in their surveys on Sufism. Theirs was a more distanced approach, at times almost academic in tone, and they were moti-vated by a desire to introduce their audiences, the literate cultural elites of northeastern Iran and Central Asia, to this new and largely foreign subject. Because these elites were immersed in legal and theological discourses, these latter authors adopted a more accommodating stance than the Traditionalists vis-à-vis the prevalent legal schools as well as philosophical theology and did not shirk from using legal and theological vocabulary in explaining Sufism to their readers. Theological discourses were on the rise, and the legal schools were consolidating themselves in eastern Iran and Central Asia. Thus, the temptation to develop a theologically and legally up-to-date form of Sufism was irresistible. A generation after Sulami, two Sufi authors, Qushayri and Hujviri, rose to this challenge with such skill that the surveys they produced eclipsed most earlier works of this genre and came to assume almost canoni-cal status for later Sufis and observers of Sufism alike.

Abu'l-Qasim al-Qushayri (d. 1072 CE) was a student of Sulami and a pro-lific scholar, with no less than 22 titles to his name. However, his reputation as a Sufi author rests primarily on his survey of Sufism, which was simply known as *al-Risala* (The Treatise).[29] While Qushayri's *Risala* is comparable in approach to Kalabadhi's *Ta'arruf*, in substance it can be viewed as a judi-cious combination and rewriting of Sulami's *Tabaqat* and Sarraj's *Luma'*. Throughout the *Risala*, Qushayri's voice is authoritative and scholarly. According to Qushayri, there is a complete correspondence between the goals of Islamic scholarship and Sufism, yet scholars should yield to the Sufi shaykhs and show humility toward them since these latter have reached the final destination. Conversely, Sufi shaykhs should not shirk from using rational arguments in training their disciples when necessary.[30] This happy marriage between Sufism and legal–theological scholarship is the hallmark of the *Risala,* and Qushayri's harmonious packaging of the two modes of learning and piety, as well as the astute inclusion of biographical notices in his survey of Sufism, assured enduring popularity to his work.

A similar blending of scholarly tendencies and Sufism, albeit in a different cultural milieu and a different language, can be seen in 'Ali al-Hujviri's (d. between 1073 and 1077 CE), *Kashf al-mahjub* (Uncovering the Veiled), the first major survey of Sufism in the Persian language.[31] In this work, Hujviri drew a broad portrait of Sufism and similar mystical movements and succeeded in giving his readers an inclusive and panoramic survey of the different Sufi approaches to some key theoretical issues. This ecumenical approach of Hujviri was another permutation of the fusion of Sufism and legal–theological scholarship that Qushayri had accomplished so effectively before him. Like Qushayri, Hujviri used scholarly, specifically theological, tools to describe Sufism for his readers. In doing so, he not only broadened the scope of Sufism to include indigenous mystical trends but also rendered this inclusive model of Sufism intelligible to cultural elites familiar with the approaches and idioms of the world of scholarship. Significantly, he incorporated rational argumentation into his discussion of Sufi doctrines on a regular basis. He not only evoked the authority of legal and theological scholars but also adopted their style of exposition and argumentation over and above the faithful reproduction of reports about the major Sufis of the past, which had been the method preferred by all previous surveyors of Sufism.

Qushayri and Hujviri succeeded in aligning Sufism with legal and theological scholarship. The " fully accredited" and scholastically legitimated Sufism that was forged in northeastern Iran and Central Asia in the eleventh century CE gradually assumed authoritative status across the Muslim world. Even more than the surveys of Qushayri and Hujviri, this process was facilitated by the popularity of a seminal work and true Islamic best-seller that carried the fruits of "accredited" Sufism to the farthest reaches of Islam. This was *Ihya' 'ulum al-din* (Bringing the Religious Sciences to Life) by Abu Hamid al-Ghazali. In time, the bridge thus drawn between Sufis and legal and theological scholars came to be crossed in both directions by an increasing number of Sufi–scholars and scholar–Sufis, leading to a cross-fertilization that ushered in a new phase of Islamic cultural history.

The development of a specialized Sufi literature was only the literary aspect of the emergence of the Sufi tradition as a major social and cultural phenomenon in Islam. The shaping of Sufism as a distinct tradition was also evident in the formation of local groups of disciples around major Sufi masters. Such communities had existed from the first phase of Sufi history, as exemplified by what appear to have been tightly knit groups around Junayd in Baghdad and Tustari in Basra. These groups were held together by the charisma of the master and the efficacy of his life example as perceived by his followers. Concomitantly with the formation of these first communities, similar groups came to exist in other locations, such as the one around Ibn Khafif in Shiraz, which may have numbered as many as a few hundred devotees. Under Ibn Khafif's guidance, beginning-level aspirants to Sufism were required to earn a living, dress simply, refrain from eating meat, eat and sleep little, and cultivate truthfulness (*sidq*) and sincerity (*ikhlas*).[32] A second-generation disciple of Ibn Khafif, Abu Ishaq al-Kazaruni (d. 1033 CE), created a widespread network of lodges centered on his hometown of Kazarun. Kazaruni asked his disciples to acquire and apply knowledge of the Shari'a, to avoid ostentatious dress and behavior, to keep the company of the poor, the trustworthy (*sadiqan*), and the virtuous (*salihan*), and to avoid the company of the powerful. These latter included kings, commanders, oppressors, judges and administrators, and the worldly (*ahl-i dunya*). His followers were further instructed to not sit with women and beardless youths, to be kind, mild, and modest, and to exercise nobility and generosity. They were not allowed to go to the cemetery to recite the Qur'an for a fee, to overdo charity so as to avoid becoming needy oneself, to accept gifts from commanders and high administrators, to oppress anyone, to keep night prayers, to take an hour every day for invocations, and to serve one's companions, the poor, and travelers.[33]

The local communities that formed around particular Sufi masters did not survive beyond a few generations. It was not long, however, before another kind of community came into existence that proved to have more staying power than the local circle of disciples. This was the "spiritual lineage," the idea that those who studied under a particular master shared a common spiritual heritage in the form of the master's unique "path" or "method" (*tariq* or *tariqa*). Spiritual lineages were often connected with one another across time and space, and thus united Sufis across the Muslim world into a far-flung spiritual family. From this point, it was but a short step to the idea that all those who shared the same pedigree made up a quasi-familial community. Such spiritual lineages took some time to develop, and the different stages of this development are difficult to document. It is, however, likely that the growing significance of the concept of the spiritual lineage (*silsila* or *nasab*) was bound up with an increasing emphasis, especially during the course of the eleventh century CE, on the role of the Sufi shaykh as a "master of training" (*shaykh al-tarbiyya*) as opposed to his role as "master of instruction" (*shaykh al-ta'lim*).[34]

In the first century of Sufi history, instruction (*ta'lim*) took the form of a shaykh imparting Sufi wisdom in a conversation or in a lecture to a single aspirant (*murid*) or to a circle of aspirants or other interested listeners in meetings held at the shaykh's house, or more typically, in a mosque. Such instruction, as exemplified by the teachings of Ibn Khafif and Kazaruni, was considered a necessity and was valued highly by serious aspirants, who were expected to follow the example of their shaykhs. By contrast, training (*tarbiyya*) meant spiritual direction: the shaykh took an interest in, and even assumed responsibility for, the spiritual progress of the aspirants, and he directed, supervised, and criticized their behavior. It is clear that in this first phase of Sufi history, instruction and training were inextricably intertwined: Sufi masters taught by training and trained by teaching. From the mid-tenth century CE on, however, training gradually began to gain an added significance until in the following century when it even became a subject for detailed theoretical discussion.

This new emphasis on training manifested itself in expressions on the significance of obedience to one's shaykh. In an analogy that became increasingly popular, the shaykh was compared to the physician. Hujviri declared, "The shaykhs of this path [Sufism] are the physicians of hearts." If there was any doubt about the status of the Sufi master, this was dispelled by establishing a clear correspondence between him and the Prophet Muhammad: "The shaykh in his congregation is like the Prophet in his community."[35]

The new emphasis on teaching and the corresponding elevation of the Sufi master to the position of an awe-inspiring "spiritual director" vis-à-vis his novices formed the thread with which lasting spiritual lineages were woven around particularly efficacious masters of training. Increasingly, aspirants who were accepted as novices by a shaykh were initiated not only into Sufism but also into a particular lineage held together by bonds of loyalty and devotion. Such bonds were extended from the novices and experienced disciples to the master and were reciprocated by bonds of guidance and protection running in the other direction from the master toward his novices and disciples. Aspirants to the Sufi way submitted to the authority of the master with complete trust. In return, the master pledged to guide them to their goal and to protect them from hidden dangers on the road of spiritual development. This "director–novice" relationship (often known as *suhba*) was solemnized through formal initiation and graduation ceremonies. Such ceremonies involved elements such as the oath of allegiance (*bay'a*) and the handclasp during the initial instruction of the formula of invocation, as well as the bestowal of a "certificate of graduation" (*ijaza*) accompanied by a special insignia, most notably a cloak (*khirqa*) when the novice attained his goal. The rise to prominence of the director–novice relationship led to the formation of extended spiritual lineages, some of which were powerful enough to spawn social communities held together through devotion to a particular master. Perhaps the most visible manifestation of these new spiritual families and the main social locus for the formation of communities around them was the Sufi lodge.

From its tentative beginnings in the first half of the tenth century CE, the Sufi lodge grew into a more durable institution. By the time Qushayri composed his *Risala* in 1045 CE, where, among other things, he recorded the growing emphasis on the "master of training," the lodge had emerged as a social site for the manifestation of the spiritual power of Sufi shaykhs as training masters.[36] Abu Sa'id-i Abu'l-Khayr (d. 1049 CE), a contemporary of Qushayri from eastern Iran, appears to be the first Sufi master who explicitly spelled out rules for communal living for his resident disciples. Abu Sa'id expected the inhabitants of his lodge to follow these rules: (1) to keep clean and ritually pure; (2) to reside only in a place where they can engage in pious works; (3) to perform the ritual prayers together at the beginning of the appointed times; (4) to pray during the night; (5) to pray for forgiveness at dawn; (6) to recite the Qur'an and not to talk until sunrise; (7) to engage in sessions of invocation and litanies (*wird*) between the evening and night prayers; (8) to welcome the needy, the poor, and whoever joins their company and to serve them; (9) to eat only together; (10) not to leave the company of others without their consent. In addition, the residents of Abu Sa'id's lodge were asked to spend whatever free time they had only for three purposes: to gain knowledge or to say litanies, to earn a living, or to bring benefit and comfort to others.[37] These rules bear a close resemblance to Ibn Khafif's and Kazaruni's recommendations to their aspirants, and similarly do not impose rules of celibacy or the avoidance of gainful employment. Abu Sa'id also provided two separate lists of 10 qualifications that a true master and a sincere disciple, respectively, should possess.[38] With the establishment of lodges as prominent social institutions, Sufi spiritual lineages were slowly but surely being woven into the fabric of the larger societies around them.

The ascendancy of training masters who increasingly came to preside over communities of Sufis that resided in lodges coincided with the rise to prominence of saint cults among Muslims. Originally based on the belief in the existence of a divinely appointed company of saints, Muslim saint cults began to take shape during the ninth and tenth centuries CE. There is little doubt that they were in full bloom by the eleventh century CE, when clear references to this practice began to appear in intellectual life. If, according to Sufi theorists, the *awliya' Allah* were friends and protégés of God due to their proximity to Him, for the common people the *awliya'* represented direct pathways to God because of this closeness. Having excelled in devotion and service to God, they became intermediaries as well as patrons who functioned as linchpins in the relationship between God and human beings. In practical terms, the saint cults manifested themselves as an ideological and ritual complex organized around the concept of spiritual power (*baraka*), and the ritualistic performance of visiting tombs and other holy places (*ziyara*). *Baraka* was the holy power inherent in a saintly figure that set him or her apart from everyone else; it was normally conceived as a fluid force that emanated from the saint, alive or dead, and permeated the places, persons, and objects around him, and its ultimate proof was the saintly miracle (*karama*).[39] *Ziyara* was a complex of rituals that included prayer, supplication, votive offerings, sprinkling fragrances and water, sleeping next to tombs, residing within their confines, circumambulation of them, touching and rubbing them, and taking soil and rocks from them.[40] Through the rituals of visitation, devotees became beneficiaries of the saint's power. In this sacred transaction, the *awliya'* were perceived as patrons who could intercede in the divine court on behalf of their devotees. In all regions, "the most important criterion of whether a person merited the status of sainthood was the manifestation of evidentiary miracles," followed closely by mediation and intercession.[41] Miracles were often perceived as the realization of the saint's intermediary and intercessory powers; it was through miracles that the saint functioned as a patron and intermediary for his devotees.

Significantly, Muslim saint cults were not simply the social realization of theories of sainthood formulated by mystics. Instead, they developed separately from, though in conversation with, Sufi theories of sainthood. In this regard, it is important that the *awliya'* most venerated by the people were not necessarily identical with the favorite *awliya'* of the Sufis. Popular saints were not always mystics; conversely, those considered Friends of God by the inner circle of mystics were not always accorded saintly status by the public. Popular saints included pre-Islamic prophets, the family of the Prophet Muhammad and his descendants, Companions of the Prophet and their followers, martyrs of early battles and conquests, Shiite Imams, the first four Caliphs, and Sufis, rulers, scholars, theologians, and even judges.[42] While a high proportion of popular saints of the eleventh and twelfth centuries were learned, and many were acquainted with or actively practiced Sufism, Sufis did not have a monopoly over sainthood.[43] Nevertheless, the overlap between the two spheres was significant, and Sufis, along with those learned and proficient in religious matters, made up the majority of saints.

When viewed against the backdrop of the formative history of the saint cults, the ascendancy of the training master as well as the elevation of the authority of the Sufi shaykh to new heights gain new meaning. The rise of the authoritative spiritual director who presided over a community of disciples occurred in tandem with the rise of the popular saint, who acted as a patron and an intermediary for the broad community of his devotees. In this way, many training masters came to exercise authority not only over his immediate disciples but also over a much larger community of devotees who relied on him for intercession and intermediation. Through this conjunction of Sufi and popular models of sainthood, Sufism gradually ceased to be a form of piety that appealed almost exclusively to the urban middle and upper-middle classes and began to spread through the whole social canvas of premodern Islamic societies, from political elites to wage-earners in urban centers to peasants and nomads in the countryside. Sainthood increasingly came to be defined almost exclusively in Sufi terms, and Sufi masters began to exercise considerable power in all spheres of social life.

From the twelfth century CE onwards when Sufism became mainstream, the Sufi presence in Islamic societies took the form of distinct social groupings generally known as "orders" (*tariqa*, pl. *turuq*).[44] These were institutionalized mappings of spiritual lineages onto the social fabric and appeared as networks of lodges woven around nodes of master–disciple relationships. The lodges were built and maintained primarily by the financial support of local and regional elites that was made available to the Sufis in the form of pious foundations (*waqf*). Since the Sufi masters, who often doubled as popular saints, were frequently buried in their lodges, many Sufi lodges became tomb-shrines and centers for the practice of saint cults. Since the twelfth century CE, Sufi orders of local, regional, and international scope have proliferated at an astonishing rate throughout the Muslim world. The most widespread and durable of these have been the Qadiriyya, Kubrawiyya, Shadhiliyya, Naqshbandiyya, and Khalwatiyya orders, followed by such regional orders as the Chishtiyya in South Asia and the Mevleviye in Anatolia. These orders represent an extremely wide range of Sufi activity at different levels of institutionalization, and they continue to define Sufism for Muslims in the present day.

The twelfth century CE formed a watershed for the spiritual, intellectual, and artistic landscape of Sufism. Up to this point, Sufis, concerned with cultivating their own tradition, had largely maintained an inward orientation. However, the alignment of this distinct form of piety with legal and theological scholarship at the hands of "academic" Sufis like Qushayri and Hujviri opened the floodgates through which legal, theological, and philosophical thinking could flow into Sufism. Indeed, from the end of the eleventh century, Sufis began to open up to the different intellectual discourses that were widely available in Islamic societies. These included not only legal, theological, and philosophical speculations but also an array of "occult" sciences, including interpretation of dreams and other visionary experiences as well as divination and prognostication. This influx of various intellectual currents into Sufi thought was accompanied by a concomitant fusion of different pietistic orientations during the same period, so that Sufism, which had been associated mostly with renunciation and asceticism, came to blend with other forms of piety such as messianism, apocalypticism, and esoterism. The expansion of the scope of Sufi thought and practice to all levels and aspects of social and intellectual life also resulted in an unprecedented literary and artistic florescence. Poetic and musical expression, which had been a special feature of Sufism from its very beginnings, now reached new artistic heights in all of the cultures (most notably Arabic and Persian) of the Muslim world. This confluence of Sufism with other intellectual, artistic, and spiritual trends produced a stellar array of seminal Sufi figures during this period, of whom Abu Madyan (d. 1197 CE), Najm al-Din Kubra (d. 1221 CE), Ibn al-'Arabi (d. 1240 CE), and Jalal al-Din Rumi (d. 1273 CE) are prominent examples. The almost complete blending of Sufism into all forms of Islamic social and cultural life from the twelfth century CE onwards makes it practically impossible to write the history of Sufism as if it were a self-contained tradition of mystical thought and practice. In a very real sense, nearly all of subsequent Islamic history was colored if not permeated by Sufi themes and practices. Clearly, the Sufis had succeeded in conveying the significance of their central concern, which was to obtain experiential knowledge (*ma'rifa*) of God's unity by distilling the reality of the Islamic profession of faith, "There is no god but God," into their daily lives. This was acknowledged by the great majority of their fellow Muslims in all walks of life.

NOTES

1. This chapter is a much condensed and selective version of my forthcoming study on the history of early Sufism titled *Sufism: The Formative Period* (Edinburgh: Edinburgh University Press, 2006).

2. For a synopsis of early usages of the term *sufi*, see Julian Baldick, *Mystical Islam: An Introduction to Sufism* (New York: New York University Press, 1989), 30–32.

3. The earliest use of the term, *sufi* is associated with Abu Hashim of Kufa (d. 767–768 CE) and it was definitely in circulation by the first half of the ninth century. See Louis Massignon, *Essay on the Origins of the Technical Language of Islamic Mysticism*, trans. Benjamin Clark (Notre Dame, Indiana: University of Notre Dame Press, 1997), 105.

4. For a catalog of Muslim ascetics in the eighth century CE, see Massignon, *Essay*, 113–119. For a longer treatment, see Tor Andrae, *In the Garden of Myrtles: Studies in Early Islamic Mysticism* trans. Birgitta Sharpe (Albany, New York: State University of New York Press, 1987), 33–54.

5. For a pithy discussion of the theme of repentance among early renunciants, see Gerhard Böwering, "Early Sufism Between Persecution and Heresy," in *Islamic Mysticism Contested: Thirteen Centuries of Controversies and Polemics,* ed. F. de Jong and Bernd Radtke (Leiden: Brill, 1999), 45–50.

6. The clustering of the themes of inner life, inner meaning of the Qur'an, and doctrine of selection is suggested by Bernd Radtke in "Baten," *Encyclopaedia Iranica* 2: 859–861 (quote on 860).

7. "Bestami (Bastami), Bayazid," *Encyclopaedia Iranica* 4: 183–186 (Gerhard Böwering).

8. "Shath," *The Encyclopaedia of Islam*, new edition 9: 361b (Carl Ernst); for an in-depth treatment of ecstatic utterances, see Carl W. Ernst, *Words of Ecstasy in Sufism* (Albany, New York: State University of New York Press, 1985).

9. Abu Nasr 'Abd Allah ibn 'Ali al-Sarraj, *Kitab al-luma fi'l-tasawwuf*, ed. Reynold A. Nicholson (London: Luzac & Co., 1914), 382; trans. Nicholson in the English section 102 (with minor changes).

10. Reynold A. Nicholson, "An Early Arabic Version of the Miraj of Abu Yazid al-Bistami," Islamica 2, no. 3 (1926): 403–408, trans. in Michael Anthony Sells, *Early Islamic Mysticism: Sufi, Quran, Miraj, Poetic and Theological Writings* (New York: Paulist Press, 1996), 244–250; the quote is from 249.

11. For the earliest of such commentaries, most notably by Junayd (d. 910 CE), see Sarraj, *al-Luma*, 380–395. This selection is translated in Sells, *Early Islamic Mysticism*, 214–231. Sells also translated (on pages 234–242) some sayings of Bayazid found in two later sources.

12. Ahmad ibn 'Abdallah Abu Nu'aym al-Isfahani, *Hilyat al-awliya' wa-tabaqat al-asfiya'* (Beirut: Dar al-Kitab al-'Arabi, 1967), 10: 40; translation reproduced, with

minor omissions, from Jawid A. Mojaddedi, *The Biographical Tradition in Sufism: The Tabaqat Genre from al-Sulami to Jami* (Richmond, Surrey: Curzon Press, 2001), 54.

13. "Bestami (Bastami), Bayazid," *Encyclopaedia Iranica* 4: 184 (Gerhard Böwering).

14. The evolution of Bayazid's image in the Sufi biographical tradition is traced in detail in Mojaddedi, *Biographical Tradition*.

15. Massignon, *The Passion of al-Hallaj, Mystic and Martyr of Islam*, trans. Herbert Mason (Princeton, New Jersey: Princeton University Press, 1982), 3, 226–228 contains a very useful, albeit brief, catalog of "ritual practices peculiar to" the Sufis, many of which must have been practiced by the Baghdad Sufis.

16. By contrast, the prayer-rug (*sajjada*) and its use as a form of investiture does not seem to date back to the ninth century. The earliest attestation of the use of the *sajjada* by Sufis is a passing reference in the *Kitab al-luma*ʿ of al-Sarraj who died in 988 CE. See Sarraj, *al-Lumaʿ*, 201. For a depiction of Junayd with a string of prayer beads, see ʿAbd al-Karim ibn Hawazin al-Qushayri, *al-Risala al-Qushayriyya*, ed. ʿAbd al-Halim Mahmud and Mahmud ibn al-Sharif (Cairo: Dar al-Kutub al-Haditha, 1966), 119.

17. Fritz Meier, *Abu Said-i Abu l-Hayr (357–440/967–1049): Wirklichkeit und Legende* (Tehran: Bibliothèque Pahlavi, 1976), 4.

18. For Tustari's stance on labor, see for instance Qushayri, *al-Risala*, 421, where Tustari is credited with the saying, "Earning a living is Sunna, and he who keeps to the Prophet's state does not abandon his Sunna."

19. Gerhard Böwering, *The Mystical Vision of Existence in Classical Islam: The Quranic Hermeneutics of the Sufi Sahl al-Tustari* (d. 283/896) (Berlin and New York: De Gruyter, 1980), 64, citing ʿAbd al-Wahhab al-Shaʿrani's *al-Tabaqat al-kubra*, two vols. (Cairo, 1315/1897), vol. I, 67. On Tirmidhi's views of "friendship with God," see Muhammad ibn ʿAli al-Hakim al-Tirmidhi, *The Concept of Sainthood in Early Islamic Mysticism: Two Works by al-Hakim al-Tirmidhi*, trans. Bernd Radtke and John O'Kane, Curzon Sufi Series (Richmond, Surrey, U.K.: Curzon Press, 1996), passim (for instance 207).

20. On the Malamatiyya, see Sara Sviri, "Hakim Tirmidhi and the Malamati Movement in Early Sufism," in *Classical Persian Sufism from Its Origins to Rumi*, ed. Leonard Lewisohn (London and New York: Khaniqahi Nimatullahi Publications, 1993), 583–613.

21. Detailed information on the spread of Sufism to southwestern Iran, western Arabia, and northeastern Iran can be found in Florian Sobieroj, *Ibn Hafif As-Sirazi und seine Schrift zur Novizenerziehung (Kitab al-Iqtisad)* (Beirut: Orient-Institut der Deutschen Morgenländischen Gesellschaft im Kommission bei F. Steiner Verlag Stuttgart, 1998).

22. This confluence of Sufiyya and Malamatiyya is documented in Christopher Melchert, "Sufis and Competing Movements in Nishapur," *Iran* 39 (2001): 237–247.

23. See Abu ʿAbd al-Rahman Muhammad ibn al-Husayn as-Sulami, *Early Sufi Women: Dhikr an-niswa al-mutaʿabbidat as-sufiyyat*, ed. and trans. Rkia Elaroui Cornell (Louisville, Kentucky: Fons Vitae, 1999), especially the translator's introduction, where a lost work titled *Brothers and Sisters among the Sufis* is mentioned (p. 39). Of

Sulami's works, there are about thirty titles extant in manuscript, many now published, out of a total of over one hundred attributed to him. See "al-Sulami, Abu Abd al-Rahman," *The Encyclopaedia of Islam,* new edition 9: 811b (Gerhard Böwering).

24. These figures are listed by Nicholson in Sarraj, *al-Luma',* xiii–xxii.

25. For a concise but up-to-date account on Kalabadhi, see "Abu Bakr Kalabadi," *Encyclopaedia Iranica* 1: 262–263 (W. Madelung). An English translation is available: Abu Bakr Muhammad ibn Ibrahim Kalabadhi, *The Doctrine of the Sufis,* trans. A.J. Arberry (Cambridge: Cambridge University Press, 1989).

26. Abu Talib Muhammad ibn 'Ali al-Makki, *Qut al-qulub fi mu'amalat al-mahbub wa wasf tariq al-murid ila maqam al-tawhid,* ed. Sa'id Nasib Makarim (Beirut: Dar Sadir, 1995), two vols. On Makki, see John Renard, *Knowledge of God in Classical Sufism: Foundations of Islamic Mystical Theology,* The Classics of Western Spirituality (New York: Paulist Press, 2004), 33–38, and 112–263 (selections from the *Sustenance* in translation).

27. "Abu Noaym el-Esfahani," *Encyclopaedia Iranica* 1: 354–355 (W. Madelung); "Abdallah al-Ansari," *Encyclopaedia Iranica* 1: 187–190 (S.L. de Beaureceuil); Abu Mansur is examined by Nasrollah Purjavadi in a number of articles in Persian (too many to list here) published in the journal *Maarif* during the 1990s.

28. Ansari's works are introduced with excerpts and further references in A.G. Ravan Farhadi, *'Abdullah Ansari of Herat (1006–1089 C.E.): An Early Sufi Master* (Richmond, Surrey, U.K.: Curzon Press, 1996). However, the best synopsis of what we know on the Arabic and Persian works associated with Ansari is Bo Utas, "The *Munajat* or *Ilahi-Namah* of 'Abdullah Ansari," *Manuscripts of the Middle East* 3 (1988): 83–87. The relationship between Ansari's *The Stages of Wayfarers* and Ibn al-'Arif's *The Beauties of Spiritual Sessions* is discussed in B. Halff, 'Le *Mahasin al-majalis* d'Ibn al-'Arif et l'oeuvre du soufi hanbalite al-Ansari,' *Révue des Études Islamiques* 39 (1971): 321–333. The work of Ibn al-'Arif is available in a bilingual edition: Ahmad ibn Muhammad Ibn al-'Arif, *Mahasin al-Majalis, The Attractions of Mystical Sessions,* trans. William Elliot and Adnan K. Abdulla (Amersham, U.K.: Avebury, 1980).

29. A section of this work is available in English translation, with an up-to-date introduction on Qushayri by Hamid Algar: 'Abd al-Karim ibn Hawazin Qushayri, *Principles of Sufism,* trans. B.R. Von Schlegell (Berkeley: Mizan Press, 1992).

30. Qushayri, *Risala,* 738.

31. For an English translation of this work, see Ali ibn Usman Hujviri, *Revelation of the Mystery (Kashf al-Mahjub),* trans. Reynold Alleyne Nicholson (Accord, New York: Pir Press, 1999); for an up-to-date account, see "Hojviri," *The Encyclopaedia of Islam,* new edition 12: 429–430 (Gerhard Böwering).

32. Florian Sobieroj, "Ibn Khafif's *Kitab al-Iqtisad* and Abu al-Najib al-Suhrawardi's *Adab al-Muridin*: A Comparison between Two Works on the Training of Novices," *Journal of Semitic Studies* 43 (1998): 327–345.

33. Mahmud ibn 'Uthman, *Firdaws al-murshidiyya fi asrar al-samadiyya. Die Vita des Scheich Abu Ishaq al-Kazaruni,* ed. Fritz Meier (Leipzig: Bibliotheca Islamica, 1948), 369–390 (chapter 30).

34. These points are noted and discussed in Fritz Meier, "Qushayri's *Tartib al-suluk*," in: *Essays on Islamic Piety and Mysticism*, John O'Kane (Leiden: E.J. Brill, 1999), 94–95 (first published in 1963); see also Fritz Meier, "Khurasan and the End of Classical Sufism," in: *Essays on Islamic Piety and Mysticism*, 190–192. These earlier works should now be read in conjunction with Laury Silvers-Alario, "The Teaching Relationship in Early Sufism: A Reassessment of Fritz Meier's Definition of the *Shaykh al-Tarbiya* and the *Shaykh al-Ta'lim*," *Muslim World* 93 (2003): 69–97.

35. Both quotes are from 'Ali ibn Usman Hujviri, *Kashf al-mahjub*, ed. Valentin Zhukovsky (Tehran: Kitabkhana-i Tahuri, 1999), 62; see also Hujviri, *Revelation*, 55.

36. For this early phase in the development of the Sufi lodge, see the evidence assembled in the following three entries in *The Encyclopaedia of Islam*, new edition: "Khankah," 4: 1025a–1027a (J. Chabbi); "Ribat," 8: 493b–506b (J. Chabbi); and "Zawiya," 11: 466b–470a (S. Blair, J. Katz, C. Hamès).

37. Muhammad ibn al-Munawwar, *Asrar al-tawhid fi maqamat al-Shaykh Abi Sa'id*, ed. Muhammad Riza Shafi'i Kadkani (Tehran: Muassasa-i Intisharat-i Agah, 1987), 316–317; English translation: Muhammad ibn al-Munavvar, *The Secrets of God's Mystical Oneness*, trans. John O'Kane (Costa Mesa, California: Mazda Publishers, 1992), 493–495.

38. Ibn al-Munavvar, *Asrar*, 1: 315–316; idem., *Secrets*, 491–493.

39. On *baraka*, see Josef W. Meri, *The Cult of Saints Among Muslims and Jews in Medieval Syria* (Oxford and New York: Oxford University Press, 2002), esp. 101–118.

40. For a detailed discussion of the different aspects of *ziyara*, see Christopher Schurman Taylor, *In the Vicinity of the Righteous: Ziyara and the Veneration of Muslim Saints in Late Medieval Egypt* (Leiden, The Netherlands; Boston: Brill, 1999), and Niels Henrik Olesen, *Culte des saints et pèlerinages chez Ibn Taymiyya (661/1263–728/1328)* (Paris: P. Geuthner, 1991).

41. Vincent J. Cornell, *Realm of the Saint: Power and Authority in Moroccan Sufism* (Austin: University of Texas Press, 1998), 112.

42. Meri, *Cult*, 80–81; cf. Taylor, *Ziyara*, 87.

43. Meri, *Cult*, 117; Taylor, *Ziyara*, 83–84.

44. For detailed coverage of this subject, see the multi-authored entries in *The Encyclopaedia of Islam*, new edition on "Tariqa," 10: 243b–257b and "Tasawwuf," 10: 313a–340b.

INDEX

'Abbas, 221

Abbasid dynasty, 199, 202, 224; Shi'a Islam and, 221–22, 223; Sufism under, 206, 249–50, 255

'Abd al-Malik (imam), 168

'Abduh, Muhammad, 157, 158

Ablutions (wudu'), 12, 131

Abraham, 28, 36, 105, 109–11, 112, 113; God's promise to, 121 n.10; and the Hajj, 111–13; and Ishmael, 27, 28, 32, 111, 112; and the Ka'ba, 16, 25, 27–28, 30, 112–113; Muhammad and, 109–10, 113, 119, 150 n.26; as submitter to God, 103, 119

Abrahamic traditions: non-Islamic, beliefs regarding, 10–11, 36, 120; prophets shared by, 10–11, 103–4, 119–120. See also Christianity; Judaism

Abu Bakr (caliph), 51, 192, 201, 212 n.4, 213 n.14

Abu Dawud, 133, 140

Abu Hanifa Nu'man ibn Thabit, 136, 137, 159, 193, 214 n.20. See also Hanafi school of law

Abu Mansur al-Isfahani, 258, 259

Abu Muhammad Ja'far al-Khuldi, 140

Abu Nu'aym al-Isfahani, 140, 258, 259

Abu Sa'id-i Abu'l-Khayr, 262–63

Abu Yazid. See Bayazid al-Bastami

Accepted Doctrines on the Foundations of Shari'a (Shatibi), 175

Action(s): and faith, 192–93, 198, 204;

of Muhammad, as Sunna, 129–30; "right" ('amal), 79–80, 83

'Ada (custom), 195–96. See also Custom

Adab, 88

Adam, 53, 90, 102, 108–9; fall of, 108; and the Ka'ba, 16, 25

Adaptability, of Shari'a, 166

'Adl (justice), 173–75, 198

Administrative law, 151

The Adornment of the Saints (Abu Nu'aym), 140

Al-Afghani, Jamal al-Din. See Jamal al-Din al-Afghani

Afterlife, 39, 54, 198

Aga Khan, 163, 235

Aga Khan Development Network (AKDN), 236

Ahad ("solitary hadith"), 132, 136, 137, 142, 152–53

Ahkam (command and prohibition), 164

Al-Ahkam al-Sultaniyya (The Rules of Governance) (al-Mawardi), 203

Ahl al-Bayt, 218–19

Ahl al-Bida', 195

Ahl al-Hadith ("People of the Hadith"; Traditionists), 160, 161, 177, 195

Ahl al-hall wa'l-'aqd, 203

Ahl al-Ikhtiyar, 203

Ahl al-Kitab ("People of the Book"), 36, 233

Ahl al-Qur'an, 132

About the Editor and Contributors

————————————— • —————————————

VINCENT J. CORNELL is Asa Griggs Candler Professor of Middle East and Islamic Studies at Emory University. From 2000 to 2006, he was Professor of History and Director of the King Fahd Center for Middle East and Islamic Studies at the University of Arkansas. From 1991 to 2000, he taught at Duke University. Dr. Cornell has published two major books, *The Way of Abu Madyan* (Cambridge, U.K.: The Islamic Texts Society, 1996) and *Realm of the Saint: Power and Authority in Moroccan Sufism* (Austin, Texas: University of Texas Press, 1998), and over 30 articles. His interests cover the entire spectrum of Islamic thought from Sufism to theology and Islamic law. He has lived and worked in Morocco for nearly six years and has spent considerable time both teaching and doing research in Egypt, Tunisia, Malaysia, and Indonesia. He is currently working on projects on Islamic ethics and moral theology in conjunction with the Shalom Hartmann Institute and the Elijah Interfaith Institute in Jerusalem. For the past five years (2002–2006), he has been a key participant in the Building Bridges Seminars hosted by the Archbishop of Canterbury.

KARIMA DIANE ALAVI is Director of Education at the Dar al-Islam educational center in Abiquiu, New Mexico. She presents workshops on Islam both at Dar al-Islam and at national conferences. She has been interviewed on Spirituality TV and on National Public Radio. In the 1970s, she taught at the University of Isfahan, Iran. Upon her return to the United States, she taught Islamic Studies at the Sidwell Friends School in Washington, D.C. With Susan Douglass, she authored the curriculum unit *Emergence of Renaissance: Cultural Interactions Between Europeans and Muslims.* Alavi has also published articles for social studies publications and for Muslim and Christian magazines.

FARHAD DAFTARY is Associate Director and Head of the Department of Academic Research and Publications at the Institute of Ismaili Studies, London. He is Consulting Editor of *Encyclopaedia Iranica* and a member of the Advisory Board of the *Encyclopaedia of Islam* (third edition). Dr. Daftary has written extensively on Ismaili Shi'ism. He is the author of *The Ismailis: Their History and Doctrines* (1990), *The Assassin Legends* (1994), *A Short History of the Ismailis* (1998), and *Ismaili Literature: A Bibliography of Sources and Studies* (2004).

HAMZA YUSUF HANSON embraced Islam in 1977 and studied in the Middle East, North and West Africa, and the United States. He received teaching licenses in various Islamic disciplines including the science of Hadith and has chains of transmission back to the Prophet Muhammad. In 1996, he founded the Zaytuna Institute, an Islamic seminary in Northern California. He currently lectures in the United States and other countries and is the editor of *Seasons,* the journal of the Zaytuna Institute. He is the author of *Purification of the Heart* and has translated several Islamic classical texts from the Arabic language.

MOHAMMAD HASHIM KAMALI is Professor of Islamic Law and Jurisprudence and Dean of ISTAC (International Institute of Islamic Thought and Civilization), International Islamic University of Malaysia, Kuala Lumpur. He studied law at Kabul University and was Public Prosecutor with the Ministry of Justice in Afghanistan. He was a Fellow of the Institute for Advanced Studies, Berlin, Germany, from 2000 to 2001. He served on the Constitutional Review Commission of Afghanistan, May–September 2003, during which period he was appointed as its Interim Chairman. He has published 15 books and over 100 articles on Islamic law and related fields. He is on the advisory boards of 10 academic journals in Malaysia, the United States, Canada, Kuwait, India, and Pakistan. Since May 2005, he has been a member of the UN-sponsored Constitutional Law Experts Working Group on the constitution of Iraq.

AHMET T. KARAMUSTAFA is Associate Professor of Islamic Studies at Washington University in St. Louis. He is the author of *God's Unruly Friends* (1994), a book on ascetic movements in medieval Islam, and *Sufism: The Formative Period* (2006), a comprehensive historical overview of early Sufism. He has also written several articles for *Cartography in the Traditional Islamic and South Asian Societies* (1992). Currently, he is working on a book project titled *Islamic Perspectives on Religion.*

JOSEPH LUMBARD is Assistant Professor of Islamic Studies at Brandeis University, Massachusetts. Formerly an Advisor on Interfaith Affairs to King Abdullah II of Jordan, he has published articles on Sufism and Islamic philosophy and has lectured around the world. In 2004, he published the edited volume *Islam, Fundamentalism, and the Betrayal of Tradition* (Bloomington, Indiana: World Wisdom Books).

BARRY C. McDONALD edited *Seeing God Everywhere: Essays on Nature and the Sacred* (Bloomington, Indiana: World Wisdom Books, 2003). He also coedited, with Patrick Laude, *Music of the Sky: An Anthology of Spiritual Poetry* (Bloomington, Indiana: World Wisdom Books, 2004). His poetry has appeared in numerous journals, including *Sacred Web, Crosscurrents, Sophia, The American Muslim,* and *Sufi.*

MUSTANSIR MIR is University Professor of Islamic Studies at Youngstown State University in Ohio. His research interests include Qur'anic studies, Islamic intellectual history, and studies of the South Asian Muslim reformer, Muhammad Iqbal. Mir is the author of *Verbal Idioms of the Qur'an* (1989), *Tulip in the Desert: A Selection of the Poetry of Muhammad Iqbal* (2000), and *Understanding the Islamic Scripture: Selected Passages from the Qur'an,* translated and with commentary (forthcoming).

DANIEL ABDAL-HAYY MOORE is a widely regarded American Muslim poet. His first book of poems, *Dawn Visions,* was published by Lawrence Ferlinghetti of City Lights Books in San Francisco (1964). He became a Sufi Muslim in 1970, performed the Hajj in 1972, and lived and traveled in Morocco, Spain, Algeria, and Nigeria. Upon his return to California, he published *The Desert is the Only Way Out* in 1985 and *Chronicles of Akhira* in 1986. A resident of Philadelphia since 1990, he has published *The Ramadan Sonnets* (1996) and *The Blind Beekeeper* (2002). He has also been the major editor for a number of works, including *The Burda of Shaykh Busiri* (2003), translated by Hamza Yusuf, and *State of Siege* (2004), the poetry of the Palestinian poet, Mahmoud Darwish, translated by Munir Akash.

JAMES WINSTON MORRIS is Sharjah Chair of Islamic Studies at the University of Exeter. He has previously taught Islamic and comparative religious studies at Princeton University, Oberlin College, the Sorbonne (EPHE) in Paris, and the Institute of Ismaili Studies in London. His field research and studies of living spiritual traditions have taken him to Iran, Afghanistan, Morocco, Egypt, Turkey, and Southeast Asia. He has published widely on many areas of religious thought and practice, including the Islamic humanities, Islamic philosophy, Sufism, the Qur'an, and Shiite thought. His most recent books are *Orientations: Islamic Thought in a World Civilisation* (2004), *The Reflective Heart: Discovering Spiritual Intelligence in Ibn 'Arabi's 'Meccan Illuminations'* (2005), *Knowing the Spirit* (2006), and *Openings: From the Qur'an to the Islamic Humanities* (forthcoming).

AZIM NANJI is Director of the Institute of Ismaili Studies, London. Previously, he held academic and administrative appointments at the University of Florida and other American and Canadian universities. He has published widely and is the recipient of several academic awards. Professor Nanji's publications include *The Nizari Ismaili Tradition in the Indo-Pakistan Subcontinent* (1976), *The Muslim Almanac* (1996), and *Mapping Islamic Studies* (1997).

FEISAL ABDUL RAUF is the Founder and Chairman of the Cordoba Initiative, a multi-faith organization whose objective is to heal the relationship between the Muslim World and the West. He is also the Founder of ASMA Society, serves as the Imam of Masjid Al-Farah in New York City, and is an active member of the World Economic Forum's C-100, which works to promote understanding and dialogue between the Western and the Islamic worlds. He was recently awarded the Peacebuilder Award by the Alliance for International Conflict Prevention and Resolution. Imam Feisal frequently interviews with various media and has appeared on CNN, CBS, NBC, ABC, PBS, and BBC. His published writings include *Islam: A Search for Meaning* and *Islam: A Sacred Law*. His latest book, *What's Right With Islam: A New Vision for Muslims and the West,* was chosen by the *Christian Science Monitor* as one of the top four nonfiction books of 2004.